THE DIVINIZATION OF THE CHRISTIAN

Jules Gross

THE
DIVINIZATION
OF THE CHRISTIAN
CHRISTIAN
ACCORDING TO THE GREEK FATHERS

TRANSLATED BY PAUL A. ONICA

INTRODUCED BY KERRY S. ROBICHAUX
& PAUL A. ONICA

A&C PRESS

ANAHEIM, CALIFORNIA

Originally published as *La divinisation du chrétien d'après
les pères grecs: Contribution historique à la doctrine de la grâce*
© 1938 Editions J. Gabalda

First Edition 2002

Library of Congress Control Number: 2002103924

ISBN (cloth): 0-7363-1600-0

A & C Press, P.O. Box 2032, Anaheim, CA 92814-0032
A & C Press, an imprint of Living Stream Ministry

Printed in the United States of America

02 03 04 05 06 07 08 09 10   5 4 3 2 1

TABLE OF CONTENTS

PART THREE
THE PERIOD OF CONSOLIDATION

INTRODUCTION TO THE ENGLISH EDITION

By Kerry S. Robichaux and Paul A. Onica

I

Jules Gross's *La divinisation du chrétien d'après les pères grecs: Contribution historique à la doctrine de la grâce* is a seminal work, and to researchers in patristic studies, particularly to those concerned with the doctrine of divinization, or deification (Gk. *theosis*), an introduction to it is hardly necessary. Yet for many researchers who are unfamiliar with this aspect of patristic theology a recommendation of Gross's work may be in order. The 1938 work traces the notion of divinization in the writings of the ancient Greek world and especially focuses on the doctrine of divinization that was universally held by the Greek fathers of the early church. It may come as a bit of a surprise to some that deification was so universally accepted in the early church, and because of this, Gross's work finds a necessary place in the survey of research on this period. The eminent modern scholar of historical theology Jaroslav Pelikan also attests to the fundamental nature of this doctrine in the patristic period, even equating salvation itself with deification in his own work on the period: "For the Greek patristic tradition, especially in its mystical forms, the final goal and result of this saving knowledge, this forgiveness, and this rescue from death was 'deification'" (155). Elsewhere, regarding the relationship between salvation and the Holy Spirit as discussed in the fourth and fifth centuries, Pelikan comments simply: "Yet salvation was not merely vivification but deification" (216). It is also interesting to note that in his index to the same volume, under the heading "Deification," Pelikan directs: "*See* Salvation" (384). For many modern scholars, particularly those working in a Protestant context, deification as salvation is one of the "hard sayings" of the early church, and one which has generally been either ignored or reinterpreted in a more palatable way. It is not uncommon for biblical scholars to summarily discount the notion of human beings becoming God as unscriptural. G. W. Butterworth, for example, writing on deification in the writings of Clement of Alexandria, remarks: "There is nothing in either the Old or the New Testament which by itself could even faintly suggest that man might practice being a god in this world and actually become one in the next" (163). Gross's work, in fact, may seem to be an attempt to reinterpret the ancient doctrine in a less than Christian light. Following some 50 years after Adolf von Harnack's well-known critique of the doctrine in his *History of Dogma* (III:121-304), Gross's *La divinisation du chrétien* may seem to flesh out Harnack's characterizations of deification as pagan and Hellenic, especially by setting a treatment of the patristic doctrine alongside an extensive treatment of the pagan notion in the Hellenic world.

But a careful reading of Gross's research can yield an effectively opposite conclusion, and this is perhaps where the greater value in the work is to be sought. It cannot be denied that ancient Greek religion held to a variety of deificatory doctrines, and Gross's work substantially details this variety. Indeed, *La divinisation du chrétien* is probably the unique place to look for a thorough treatment of the non-Christian notions of divinization in the Hellenic world. Leaving a more thoughtful evaluation of Hellenic divinization to Gross's reader, we may simply say here that the pagan concept was, like so many religious notions of the ancient world, eclectic and far from well-defined. It bore one quality in this work and another, sometimes even opposite, quality in that work, and thus took on a highly mythical and superstitious character that little deserved universal acceptance even among the pagans. On the other hand, Gross's presentation of "Christian divinization," if we may so term it, shows a striking degree of agreement among the various models, so much so that we constantly feel as if we are reading about one unified thought on the matter, held universally by a number of writers across a period of some 500 years. The effect of Gross's Book One, "The Preparation," on the Hellenic background of deification, is a façade, a dreamy and lofty apprehension for a concept that has no inner workings and thus no actual mechanism for its accomplishment. The effect of Gross's Book Two, "The Doctrine of the Greek Fathers," is a cogent belief system, a full-blown understanding of how humans may become God and, more importantly, how they may not. Contrary to Harnack's sweeping critique, Gross shows in detail how the early Greek-speaking church could hold to a notion which seemed so dangerously pagan but was, to their mind, thoroughly Christian. Far from being under the influence of Hellenic superstitions, the Greek fathers, as Gross depicts them, were deliberate and studied in their advancing of the doctrine, giving to it a viability in Christian thought that has long outlived any theoretical pagan roots. Thus, while not denying a Hellenic precursor, Gross goes far to show that divinization in the thought and teaching of the Greek fathers is thoroughly Christian and highly defensible for Christian faith. While submitting to the constraint of showing fully the pagan and Hellenic context for the doctrine, Gross just as ably demonstrates how non-pagan and non-Hellenic Christian divinization was in the early church.

Further, Gross attempts to show that there is indeed a biblical basis for the doctrine in his few chapters relating to the Old and New Testaments. Here again one may possibly see in his treatment an attempt to show that even Scripture had been Hellenized, something Harnack attempts to alarm us with, but Gross's obvious respect for the individuality of the biblical writers argues against this. Rather, he tries to show that on a deeper level the biblical authors are referring to something more than an ethical Christian life, to something more mystical than moral, and that by their various modes of expression they are indeed referring to divinization. Certainly there is room for argument in this matter, but Gross finds a refreshing set of meanings for the more mystical expressions in the Bible, particularly in the New Testament, and sees in them hints at divinization. If nothing more, he gives us cause to reflect on what may be time-worn concepts and introduces us to the possibility of viewing biblical truth in a new way. If Butterworth is correct and there is indeed nothing in the Scriptures which "could even faintly suggest" that human beings may become God, then Gross has merely ventured upon a study in possibilities. But if his contentions hold, and well they may, he has provided us with yet another unique catalog of deification texts from ancient sources, sources of considerably more weight than his others. In any event, the value of Gross's work as a repository of materials with even the slightest hint of divinization in them cannot be disputed.

The doctrine of divinization did not maintain its prominence throughout the Christian church beyond the first five centuries, but that is not to say that it has lost its place altogether. Certainly in the East, in Orthodoxy, the doctrine has survived and holds a key position in the general notion of salvation for that tradition. After the first five centuries of the church, divinization theology took on a sophisticated and elaborate structure in the Eastern churches. In the fourteenth century, particularly through the labors of Gregory Palamas (d. 1359), the doctrine obtained its current Orthodox form, which is now highly intertwined with the theology of the sacraments. Yet even in the West the doctrine can hardly be seen as having been sidelined. A number of Catholic writers, particularly those of the mystical tradition, mention or even emphasize deification. (In the second part of this essay we will refer the reader to other studies that detail the post-patristic development of the doctrine in the Western church.) And even recently the doctrine has gained at least a nominal standing once again in Catholic theology, as exhibited in the recent *Catechism of the Catholic Church*, where we are told that the Word became flesh that we might become God (§460), repeating Athanasius's famous aphorism of the fourth century. Even in Protestantism the doctrine has lately received more than merely negative attention, as a small number of scholars, like F. W. Norris and Robert V. Rakestraw, have attempted to examine it for a Protestant relevance.

These more modern indications of interest hopefully portend a "renaissance" for the ancient doctrine. And for such a renaissance a translation of Gross's work is most opportune, especially when the doctrine is more often misunderstood than properly understood. There is indeed a certain amount of "shock value," as Rakestraw (266) terms it, in the notion of human beings becoming God, but the Greek fathers can hardly be accused of sensationalism when one understands not only their times but also their handling of the notion. Gross is excellent in his ability to draw out the nuances of the Greek fathers, who came to the doctrine of an assimilation to God with much the same concern that we moderns have, that is, the integrity of the otherness of God. Contrary to the natural suspicions which arise when one first considers deification (and which, unfortunately, Harnack seems to have fallen prey to), the Greek fathers steered ably between this theological Scylla and Charybdis to present a notion of human deification which properly respects God's transcendence while acknowledging the mystical character of His incarnation. One should not dismiss, or for that matter approach, the topic of deification without a careful reading of the Greek fathers, and Gross provides the complete and authoritative catalog of their opinions.

But in addition to the theological perils of the doctrine, there is the stigma of hellenization, which we also suspect a translation of Gross's work into English will help to dispel. Unfortunately, much earlier scholarship on the patristic period fails to credit the writers then with the sophistication that they actually possessed. Contrary to modern natural expectations, the Greek fathers were not completely oblivious to their Hellenic background. Further, they can hardly be accused of being so thoroughly influenced by the world of ideas that surrounded them that they could not transcend those influences, any more than a nineteenth-century Harnack (or a twenty-first-century critic of Harnack) could be accused of being unable to transcend his own world of surrounding ideas. Unlike some modern analysts, the fathers easily identified the influences that bore upon them and met them squarely in their extensive writings. We suspect that they would take great umbrage at the modern criticism of a pervasive Hellenic influence and would strenuously counter that indeed they were advancing something that transcends their human and social background, particularly in the matter of human beings being made God. It is easy to confuse Christian theosis with some of the very pagan notions that preceded it, such as apotheosis, and to therefore dismiss the former because of the undesirable nature of the latter. But the fathers of the early church were not so easily confused, probably because they were so close to the sources of confusion and were therefore forced to clearly enunciate the differences. Only a careful reading of how they approached this subject will reveal how thoroughly unconfused they really were, and here again the value of Gross's work suggests itself. Our earnest hope is that the reader will read for these differences and at least try to hear how the fathers saw in deification a decidedly Christian doctrine. Perhaps the bugaboo of hellenization can finally be dispelled from the notion of deification as held by the Christian church.

Yet for all their theological richness, the Greek fathers should not be considered as having the final word on the matter, and our intention in presenting Gross's work to English scholarship is not to suggest a wholesale return to patristic theology in this or any other matter. Indeed, there are basic differences between the thought of the ancient Christian church and that of the modern which rightly motivated the Reformers to turn away from much of the patristic tradition. The fundamental complaints regarding the patristic period which have been raised over the past five centuries cannot easily be overlooked. Here we are not referring to what is probably the leading objection to the doctrine of deification, at least by modern Protestant theologians, that is, the seeming confusion of the Creator and the creature that the doctrine, viewed superficially, may invite; this complaint, we feel, is ably met by the fathers in their own presentation of the doctrine, for, as we have said, they too shared the concern. Rather, we are referring to other characteristics of the patristic church, which colored not only the doctrine of deification but much of what they believed and taught. Chief among these is the pervasive mysticism that developed in the early church. Jules Gross details the similar development of a mysticism related to the doctrine of deification, and this will at once repel many modern Protestants. But as Gross notes, the mystic embellishments are not uniform among the proponents of deification in the patristic period, and a mysticism of deification is more incidental than defining. Because of this, we need not dismiss the core doctrine altogether on account of mysticism.

A second complaint regards the relationship of the sacraments to deification. Many of the patristic advocates of deification tie the efficacy of the doctrine to the sacraments, particularly the Eucharist. Eastern Orthodoxy has gone far to develop this notion, and to this day the sacraments are understood to provide the major practical mechanism for divinization for Orthodox Christians. This, of course, runs counter to the attitude of many Protestants and touches a fundamental difference that to this day divides the Christian church. Yet the same theological solutions that reformation and post-reformation theologians have advanced to account for the sanctifying actions of the Spirit without recourse to sacraments would obtain for deification as well. Hence, the sacramental quality of patristic deification also appears to be highly extrinsic, and because of this it appears that the doctrine of deification need not be sacramental to survive theologically. This gives us hope that deification could become more universally Christian than it is mainly Eastern Orthodox now.

But beyond the classic complaints against the fathers, we may identify particular shortages in the patristic view of deification, which, to our knowledge, have yet to be voiced by modern analysts, and which further thought may remedy. First, while the fathers are emphatic regarding the fact of deification, they are weak and nebulous regarding the actual practice of deification, even when they propose the sacraments as a practicality. It is unfortunately true that patristic deification is a tremendously lofty theological construct with few stairways into it, and we suspect that this is one reason the notion eventually lost its appeal in the West. There did not seem to be much for the common (and Latin-speaking) Christian in all these theological structures. It would take the intellect of the Christian East to make the doctrine palatable in practice, and this was done both by developing more fully the sacramental aspects of the patristic concept, as we have noted, and by providing a fresh mechanism through hesychasm, advanced in the fourteenth century. Yet even so, the doctrine of deification in modern Orthodoxy is more theological than experiential. Hopefully, a fresh examination of deification would overcome the historical weakness of the Christian church to simply theologize and not provide practical guidance into the experience.

Second, the very individual nature of patristic deification requires reconsideration. The fathers are not without numerous references to Christian love among the believers, and this no doubt demonstrates their understanding of a corporate dimension of the Christian life. But these references never attain to the exceptional descriptions of the life of the Body of Christ expressed by Paul. In the particular discussions on deification in the fathers there are similar references, here and there, to Christian love, but these are far outweighed by the more pervasive descriptions of individual deification, by the more common attitudes regarding deification as a journey of the individual mystic. Somehow the corporate nature of the Christian life, the life of the believers as members of the Body of Christ, needs to overarch any identity they have as human beings who have been made God. In fact, there should be a single view that holds the believers at the same moment both as corporate persons and as deified persons, and this we would expect to see in a modern apprehension of deification.

II

We expect that Gross's work will enlighten the modern reader concerning this very central ancient doctrine, and our hope is that in reading Gross many will come to treasure the notion of deification and no longer view it as a bygone curiosity. We also hope that his work will serve as an introduction to other equally able studies on the doctrine. Like Gross's *La divinisation du chrétien,* most of these works were done in French, the principal language of patristic studies, and our hope is to provide some of these as well in translation to English scholarship in the future. In the sixth chapter of René Laurentin's *L'Esprit Saint, cet inconnu,* published in 1997, under the section entitled "Divinisation," is a footnote which lists four works which are recognized as more or less authoritative on the subject of deification. Gross's book is listed first followed by *La doctrine de la déification dans l'Église grecque,* by Myrrha Lot-Borodine (to which we will return momentarily), then by a 1935 article by Y. Congar, "La déification dans la tradition spirituelle de l'Orient" (*VSpir* 43), and finally by the 1957 article, "Divinisation," by various contributors in *Dictionnaire de spiritualité*. In his own brief section, Laurentin traces the teaching of deification and its implications in the New Testament, in the Greek fathers through Dionysius the Pseudo-Areopagite (*c*. 500), and in Thomas Aquinas (d. 1274), Pope Leo XIII (d. 1903), and Pope John Paul II. Laurentin deals with the apparent conflict between our real experience of divinization, as indicated in the Bible and in the church fathers, and God's transcendence and our own consciousness of humility.

Lot-Borodine's book, mentioned second by Laurentin, was subsequently and posthumously enlarged under the title, *La déification de l'homme selon la doctrine des Pères grecs,* being composed in its final form of three major articles, published over the period of 1932-1950. The first two articles were thus contemporary with the work of Gross, whom Lot-Borodine appreciates for his vast documentation but criticizes for restricting the range and significance of the Greek doctrinal synthesis, especially in relation to the originality of the physical theory of redemption as the basis for theosis (212-213). Unlike Gross, Lot-Borodine's approach to the overall subject is experiential as well as scholarly. Reflecting her own (Russian) orthodox roots, she views deification as the transfiguration of the human nature by the uncreated divine energies through the deifying action of the Holy Spirit. This has been realized in the transfigured humanity of Christ. Such an accomplished divinization, according to her view, is continued in the believers in the sacramental life. The spiritual energies contained in the glorified humanity of Christ are communicated in the rites of Christian initiation. And, finally, it is the mystical life that is the top expression of the process of divinization. Lot-Borodine goes farther chronologically than Gross in her treatment of the subject, extending her investigation to Gregory Palamas and Nicolas Cabisilas (b. *c*. 1322). And unlike Gross she also touches on the writings of some Latin fathers—Ambrose, Augustine, and John Cassian. In addition, in his brief Angelus prayer message of August 11, 1996 entitled, "Eastern theology has enriched the whole Church," Pope John Paul II, in speaking of the past defense of hesychasm in the East, noted its emphasis on "the concrete possibility that man is given to unite himself with the Triune God in the intimacy of his heart, in that deep union of grace which Eastern theology likes to describe with the particularly powerful term of 'theosis,' 'divinization'". Shortly thereafter the Pope notes as "worthy of mention" the "study of the doctrine of 'divinization' by the Orthodox scholar, Loth Borovine."[1]

A third major authoritative source noted by Laurentin is the article "Divinisation" in *Dictionnaire de spiritualité*. This article by seven different contributors is composed of five major, chronologically arranged sections—ranging from antiquity to the late seventeenth century. Herein lies its virtue. The first section deals with the concept of divinization in the religious thought of the ancients.

---

[1] Undoubtedly a transcriptional error for "Lot-Borodine."

The next section deals with the teaching in the Greek fathers, although mention is also made of Gregory Palamas and Simeon, the New Theologian (d. 1022). Thus far, the scope of the material covered is more or less equal with that of Gross. The final three sections, however, which amount to almost eighty percent of this book-length article, go far beyond the bounds of Gross's study. Indeed, the third section deals with the teaching of divinization in the writings of the Latin fathers, from Tertullian (d. *c.* 225) to Gregory the Great (d. *c.* 604). The fourth section, the lengthiest of all and comprising well over one-half of the article, is on the period of the Middle Ages. There are three sub-sections, which cover the monastic writers of the twelfth century, the theologians of the thirteenth century, and the Rhenish-Flemish school of the fourteenth century and beyond. Over thirty, mostly Latin-writing authors are surveyed. The fifth and final section scans the writings on divinization in the western tradition to the latter part of the seventeenth century, through the French missionary-scholar, Louis Laneau (d. 1696). Primary and secondary sources are referred to and quoted throughout, albeit the latter obviously only up to the early 1950s.

In addition to Laurentin's work and the seminal studies to which he refers, two recently published dictionaries of Christianity in the English language reflect the increased interest and attention being given to the matter of deification by scholars today. First, the third edition of *The Oxford Dictionary of the Christian Church*, published in 1997, now features an article on "deification," with Gross's book being the initial entry of some otherwise recent and pertinent bibliographical sources, whereas in the second edition such an article was completely lacking—there being only a brief paragraph on "apotheosis." And this short piece dealt mainly with the pagan roots of the concept, and, of course, there was no reference to Gross's work. The current article on deification very briefly traces the doctrine's development in the Eastern tradition, but does make the interesting point of how, in the West, through the patristic revival in the Oxford Movement (1833-45), the concept of deification was recovered. A second and even more recent English work that reflects the same tendency toward the renewed study of deification is the second edition of the *Encyclopedia of Early Christianity*, published in 1999. In the first edition there was no article at all on deification, divinization, or any related concept. But in the newer edition there are now nearly three pages on "Divinization," with a very ample bibliography of both primary and secondary sources, the latter group being headed by Gross's book. This article suggests that the real sources of the doctrine are found in the Bible—both Old and New Testaments—before briefly tracing its development among the Greek fathers up to Maximus the Confessor (d. 662), with a notation on the eventual and crucial contribution of Gregory Palamas. A short survey of the western development of terminology and doctrine is also presented, ranging only from Tertullian to Leo the Great (d. 461).

Finally, mention should be made of at least two very recently published monographs, both in 1999 and in English, on the subject of deification, and both of which owe much to Gross's pioneering work while venturing beyond his chronological boundaries. The first is A. N. Williams's *The Ground of Union: Deification in Aquinas and Palamas*. In the first chapter, devoted to the history of the doctrine, the author calls theosis, from the third century onward, "the dominant model of the concept of salvation" (27). In the survey of the doctrine's development that follows, Gross's book, primarily, and Lot-Borodine's, to a lesser degree, are drawn upon. As the title might indicate, this book is presented in the hope of resolving, by highlighting common ground, long-standing differences between the Eastern and Western churches concerning the doctrine of God and the nature of salvation—tied together in the doctrine of deification. This then is to be the author's vehicle for producing an increased receptiveness, by readers from either tradition, to ecumenical rapprochement. Williams points out that this doctrine, while remaining in the forefront in the East, was thought to have all but disappeared from Western theology by the Middle Ages. But by a careful examination of the *Summa Theoligica* of Thomas Aquinas she endeavors to show that this was not the case, and by a comparison of the *Summa* with the *Triads in Defense of the Holy Hesychasts* and *Capita Physica* of Gregory Palamas, she further endeavors to show "the consonance of their doctrines of deification" (33). The second 1999 monograph on deification that should be briefly noted is Emil Bartos's *Deification in Eastern Orthodox Theology: An Evaluation and Critique of the Theology of Dumitru Stăniloae*. Focusing on the doctrine of deification, which affords the theoretical basis for how Eastern Orthodox theologians in general, and the Romanian theologian Stăniloae in particular, understand the major doctrines of the Christian faith, the author examines the major doctrines of anthropology, christology, soteriology, and ecclesiology as they relate to deification in Stăniloae's scheme. In doing so Bartos, of necessity, traces the history and development of the doctrine, and is thus at least somewhat indebted to Gross's seminal study. As with A. N. Williams's book, Bartos's work also embraces the goal of contributing to ecumenical dialogue between Eastern and Western theologians by using the doctrine of deification—long neglected but now being studied again in the West—as a useful and mutually acceptable vehicle.

Works Cited

Balás, David L., O. Cist. "Divinization." Pages 338-340 in *Encyclopedia of Early Christianity*. 2d ed. Edited by Everett Ferguson. New York & London: Garland Publishing, Inc., 1997, 1999.

Bartos, Emil. *Deification in Eastern Orthodox Theology: An Evaluation and Critique of the Theology of Dumitru Stăniloae*. Carlisle: Paternoster Press, 1999.

Butterworth, G. W. "The Deification of Man in Clement of Alexandria." *The Journal of Theological Studies* 17 (1916): 157-169.

Catholic Church. *Catechism of the Catholic Church.* New York & Toronto: Image Books (Doubleday), 1995, c1994.

Congar, M.-J. "La déification dans la tradition spirituelle de l'Orient." *Vie Spirituelle* 43 (1935): 91-107.

Cross, F. L. and E. A. Livingstone, eds. "Deification." Page 465 in *The Oxford Dictionary of the Christian Church.* 3d ed. Oxford & New York: Oxford University Press, 1997.

Des Places, Édouard, et al. "Divinisation." Columns 1370-1459 in vol. 3 of *Dictionnaire de spiritualité.* Paris: G. Beauchesne et ses fils, 1957.

Gross, Jules. *La divinisation du chrétien d'après les pères grecs: Contribution historique à la doctrine de la grâce.* Paris: J. Gabalda, 1938.

Harnack, Adolf von. *History of Dogma.* Vol. 3. Translated by J. Millar. 7 vols. London: Williams & Norgate, 1896-99.

John Paul II, Pope. "Eastern theology has enriched the whole Church." Angelus, August 11, 1996. No pages. Cited Nov. 7, 2000. Online: http://www.cin.org/jp960811.html. 1996 Catholic Information Network (CIN), August 27, 1996.

Laurentin, René. *L'Esprit Saint, cet inconnu: découvrir son expérience et sa Personne.* Paris: Librairie Arthème Fayard, 1997.

Lot-Borodine, Myrrha. *La déification de l'homme selon la doctrine des Pères grecs.* Paris: Éditions du Cerf, 1970.

Norris, F. W. "Deification: Consensual and Cogent." *Scottish Journal of Theology* 49.4 (December 1996): 411-428.

Pelikan, Jaroslav. *The Emergence of the Catholic Tradition (100-600).* Vol. 1. of *The Christian Tradition: A History of the Development of Doctrine.* Chicago: University of Chicago Press, 1971.

Rakestraw, Robert V. "Becoming like God: An Evangelical Doctrine of Theosis." *Journal of Evangelical Theology* 40.2 (June 1997): 257-269.

Williams, A. N. *The Ground of Union: Deification in Aquinas and Palamas.* New York & Oxford: Oxford University Press, 1999.

TRANSLATOR'S PREFACE

A few notations should be made regarding issues of translation and presentation in this rendering into English of *La divinisation du chrétien d'apres les pères grecs: Contribution historique à la doctrine de la grâce* by Jules Gross. On the strictly translational side, Gross's distinctive academic style has been retained as much as possible. Furthermore, since Gross translated all his primary sources into French, in the interests of a smooth and accurate transmission of his thought and logic the decision was made to translate these sources from the French, rather than going back to the Greek or other original languages each time. Wherever possible, these French-to-English renderings have then been compared to existing English translations. And in the overall process of the translation and citation of original sources, additional errata, such as those involving volume or page numbers, were occasionally noticed and have been corrected. In places changes have been made to the citations in Greek, where it seemed that there was an error, adjusting them to the texts in Thesaurus Linguae Graecae, *CD ROM E* (Irvine, CA: University of California, 1999). As to scriptural quotations, the *New Revised Standard Version* has been employed in the main. In the chapters that dealt specifically with the Old and New Testaments, where occasionally the author made his own scriptural translations into French— from the original languages, as it seems—these have been translated directly into English.

Some issues on the presentational side should also be addressed. First, the corresponding page numbers of the original French edition have been printed in the margin of this translation for convenience of reference. In the overall interests of conformity to more modern practice, new indices have been fashioned out of some of Gross's original tables. His original and somewhat bulky table of contents has been modified and slimmed down in the hopes of making it more serviceable to the present-day reader. A new subject index, incorporating material from Gross's table of contents as well as from his name table, has been created. His original name table has been worked into an authors' index. Newly added as research aids are a scripture index and a table of abbreviations, the latter dealing in large part with Latin titles referred to in the translation. Of course, the method of citation employed in footnotes has been updated, with a more modern style being utilized in this translation. Occasionally, French titles to primary source materials were cited by Gross. If no accepted English equivalent exists for these citations, the standard Latin titles have been cited in the translation.

A special word of thanks is due to the French publisher, J. Gabalda and company, for the kind permission to publish Gross's valuable work in the English language. Jim Batten is also to be acknowledged and thanked for his many hours of reading through the English text with the translator, and for offering numerous, useful suggestions from the standpoint of the readability of the finished product. Jim also produced the subject index and the other newly-added features. Thanks are also due to Kerry Robichaux and Roger Good for their careful reading of the translated text and constructive comments. Any errors still remaining in the text and notes are the responsibility of the translator.

Paul A. Onica

TABLE OF ABBREVIATIONS

Authors and Works

Alex. Aphr. *De an.*	Alexander of Aphrodisias. *De anima* [On the Soul]
Anast. S. *Hod.*	Anastasius of Sinai. *Hodegus* or *Viae dux* [Guide for the Way]
Apul. *Metam.*	Apuleius. *Metamorphoses* [Golden Ass][1]
Ar. *Ran.*	Aristophanes. *Ranae* [Frogs]
Arat. *Phaen.*	Aratus. *Phaenomena* [Phenomena]
Aris.	Aristotle
Eth. nic.	*Ethica nichomachea* [Nichomachean Ethics]
Metaph.	*Metaphysica* [Metaphysics]
Phys.	*Physica* [Physics]
Asclep. lat.	*Asclepius* [Latin Asclepius]
Ath.	Athanasius of Alexandria
C. Ar.	*Orationes contra Arianos* [Orations against the Arians]
Ep. Adelph.	*Epistula ad Adelphium* [Letter to Adelphius]
Ep. Aeg. Lib.	*Epistula ad episcopos Aegypti et Libyae* [Letter to the Bishops of
Ep. Aeg. Lib.	Egypt and Libya]
Ep. Epict.	*Epistula ad Epictetum* [Letter to Epictetus]
Ep. fest.	*Epistulae festales* [Festal Letters]
Ep. Serap.	*Epistulae ad Serapionem* [Letters to Serapion concerning the Holy Spirit]
C. Gent.	*Contra gentes* [Against the Pagans]
Inc.	*De incarnatione* [On the Incarnation]
Syn.	*De synodis* [On the Councils of Ariminum and Seleucia]
Vit. Ant.	*Vita Antonii* [Life of Anthony]
Athenag.	Athenagoras of Athens
Leg.	*Legatio pro Christianis* [Supplication for the Christians]
Res.	*De resurrectione mortuorum* [On the Resurrection of the Dead]
Barn.	Barnabas [Letter of Barnabas]
Bas.	Basil of Caesarea
Ascet.	*Sermones ascetici* [Ascetical Discourses]
Eun.	*Adversus Eunomium* [Against Eunomius]
Ep.	*Epistulae* [Letters]
Hom.	*Homilia, In illud: Quod Deus non est auctor malorum* [Homily: That God Is Not the Author of Evil]
Hom. Ps.	*Homiliae in Pss.* [Homilies on the Psalms]
Reg. fus.	*Regulae fusius tractatae* [Standards Treated More Fully]
Spir.	*Liber de Spiritu sancto* [On the Holy Spirit]

---

[1] If a common English title exists, that is the one given for the work.

Boeth. *Consol. Philos.*	Boethius. *De consolatione philosophiae* [*Consolation of Philosophy*]
Chrys.	John Chrysostom
Catech. illum.	*Catechesis ad illuminandos* [*Instructions to Those About To Be Illuminated*]
Comm. Gal.	*Commentarium in Gal.* [*Commentary on Galatians*]
Diab.	*De diabolo tentatore* [*On the Devil the Tempter*]
Exp. Ps.	*Expositiones in Psalmos quosdam* [*Expositions on Certain Psalms*]
Fr. cont.	*Fragmenta de continentia* [*On Abstinence, fragments*]
Hom. Col.	*Homiliae in epistulam ad Colossenses* [*Homilies on the Letter to the Colossians*]
Hom. 1 Cor.	*Homiliae in epistulam i ad Corinthios* [*Homilies on the First Letter to the Corinthians*]
Hom. Eph.	*Homiliae in epistulam ad Ephesios* [*Homilies on the Letter to the Ephesians*]
Hom. Gen.	*Homiliae in Genesim* [*Homilies on Genesis*]
Hom. Heb.	*Homiliae in epistulam ad Hebraeos* [*Homilies on the Letter to the Hebrews*]
Hom. Jo.	*Homiliae in Joannen* [*Homilies on John*]
Hom. Matt.	*Homiliae in Matthaeum* [*Homilies on Matthew*]
Hom. Rom.	*Homiliae in epistulam ad Romanos* [*Homilies on the Letter to the Romans*]
Hom. 1 Tim.	*Homiliae in epistulam i ad Timotheum* [*Homilies on the First Letter to Timothy*]
Hom. 2 Tim. *Hom. 2 Tim*	*Homiliae in epistulam ii ad Timotheum* [*Homilies on the Second Letter to Timothy*]
Hom. Tit.	*Homiliae in epistulam ad Titum* [*Homilies on the Letter to Titus*]
Laud. Paul.	*De laudibus sancti Pauli apostoli* [*On the Praises of the Apostle Paul*]
Paenit.	*De paenitentia* [*On Repentance*]
Praes. imp.	*Homilia dicta praesente imperatore* [*Homily Given in the Emperor's Presence*]
Stat.	*Ad populum Antiochenum de statuis* [*To the People of Antioch on the Statues*]
Cleanth.	Cleanthes [*Hymn to Zeus*]
Clem. A.	Clement of Alexandria
Exc.	*Excerpta Theodoti* [*Excerpts from Theodotus*]
Paed.	*Paedagogus* [*Christ the Educator*]
Prot.	*Protrepticus* [*Exhortation to the Greeks*]
Quis div.	*Quis dives saluetur* [*What Rich Man Can be Saved?*]
Strom.	*Stromata* [*Miscellanies*]
Clem. R. *1 Clem*	Clement of Rome. *1 Clement* [*Letter of Clement to the Corinthians*]
2 Clem.	*2 Clement* [*Ancient Christian Sermon*]
Corp. herm.	*Corpus hermeticum* [*Corpus Hermeticum*]
Cyr.	Cyril of Alexandria
Ador.	*De adoratione in spiritu et veritate* [*On Adoration in Spirit and Truth*]
Apol. orient.	*Duodecim capitum defensio adversus orientales episcopos* [*Defense of the Twelve Chapters against the Oriental Bishops*]

Comm. Is.	*Commentarius in Is.* [*Commentary on Isaiah*]
Comm. Jo.	*Commentarius in Jo.* [*Commentary on John*]
Comm. Joel	*Commentarius in Joel* [*Commentary on Joel*]
Comm. Mal.	*Commentarius in Mal.* [*Commentary on Malachi*]
Dial. Trin.	*De Trinitate dialogi* [*Dialogues on the Trinity*]
Ep.	*Epistulae* [*Letters*]
Ep. Calos.	*Epistula ad Calosyrium* [*Letter to Calosyrius*]
Expl. I Cor.	*Explanatio in I Cor.* [*Explanation on First Corinthians*]
Expl. Rom.	*Explanatio in Rom.* [*Explanation on Romans*]
Fr. Heb.	*Fragmenta explanationis in Heb.* [*Explanation on Hebrews, fragments*]
Fr. Lc.	*Fragmenta commentarii in Lc.* [*Commentary on Luke, fragments*]
Fr. Mt.	*Fragmenta in Mt.* [*On Matthew, fragments*]
Glaph. Gen.-Dt.	*Glaphyra in Pentateuchum* [*Polished Comments on the Pentateuch*]
Hom. pasch.	*Homiliae paschales* [*Paschal Homilies*]
Inc. unigen.	*De incarnatione unigeniti dialogus* [*Dialogue on the Incarnation of the Only-begotten*]
C. Juln.	*Contra Julianum* [*Against Julian*]
C. Nest.	*Contra Nestorium* [*Against Nestorius*]
Regin.	*De recta fide ad regin.* [*On the True Faith to the Royal Ladies*]
C. Thdr. Mops.	*Fragmenta contra Theodorum Mopsuestentum* [*Against Theodore of Mopsuestia, fragments*]
Thes. Trin.	*Thesaurus de Trinitate* [*Treasury on the Trinity*]
Cyr. H.	Cyril of Jerusalem
Catech.	*Catecheses illumindorum* [*ad illuminandos*] [*Instructions to Those About To Be Illuminated*]
Procatech.	*Procatechesis* [*Prologue to the Catechetical Lectures*]
Did.	*Didache* [*Teaching of the Twelve Apostles*]
Didym.	Didymus of Alexandria
Exp. Ps.	*Expositio in Pss.* [*Exposition on the Psalms*]
Fr. 2 Cor.	*Fragmenta in 2 Cor.* [*On Second Corinthians, fragments*]
Fr. Judae	*Fragmenta in Judae* [*On Jude, fragments*]
Fr. Pr.	*Fragmenta in Pr.* [*On Proverbs, fragments*]
Fr. Ps.	*Fragmenta in Pss.* [*On the Psalms, fragments*]
Trin.	*De Trinitate* [*On the Trinity*]
Diog. Laert.	Diogenes Laertius [*Lives of Eminent Philosophers*]
Diogn.	*Diognetus* [*Letter to Diognetus*]
Dion. Ar.	Pseudo-Dionysius the Areopagite
Cael. hier.	*De caelesti hierarchia* [*On the Celestial Hierarchy*]
Div. nom.	*De divinis nominibus* [*On the Divine Names*]
Eccl. hier.	*De ecclesiatica hierarchia* [*On the Ecclesiastical Hierarchy*]
Ep.	*Epistulae* [*Letters*]
Myst.	*De mystica theologia* [*On the Mystical Theology*]
Epict. Diatr.	Epictetus. *Diatribai (Dissertationes)* [*Discourses*]
Epicur.	Epicurus
Ad Menoec.	*Epistula ad Menoeceum* [*Letter to Menoeceus*]
Rat. Sent.	*Ratae Sententiae* [*Principal Doctrines*]

Eus.	Eusebius of Caesarea
Comm. Ps.	*Commentaria in Psalmos* [*Commentary on the Psalms*]
Marc.	*Contra Marcellum* [*Against Marcellus, Bishop of Ancyra*]
Praep. ev.	*Praeparatio evangelica* [*Preparation for the Gospel*]
Firm. *Err. prof. rel.*	Firmicus Maternus. *De errore profanarum religionum* [*On the Error of the Pagan Religions*]
Gr. Naz.	Gregory of Nazianzus
Carm.	*Carminum libri duo* [*Two Books of Poems*]
Ep.	*Epistulae* [*Letters*]
Or.	*Orationes* [*Orations*]
Gr. Nyss.	Gregory of Nyssa
Anim. et res.	*De anima et resurrectione* [*On the Soul and the Resurrection*]
Apoll.	*Adversus Apollinaris* [*Against Apollinaris*]
Beat.	*Orationes de beatitudinibus* [*Orations on the Beatitudes*]
Comm. not.	*Ad Graecos ex communibus notionibus* [*To the Greeks, from Universal Ideas*]
C. Eun.	*Contra Eunomium* [*Against Eunomius*]
Hom. Cant.	*Homiliae in Canticum* [*Homilies on the Song of Songs*]
Hom. Opif.	*De opificio hominis* [*On the Creation of Man*]
Infant.	*De infantibus praemature abreptis* [*On Infants' Early Deaths*]
Instit.	*De instituto Christiano* [*On the Christian Way of Life*]
Mort.	*De mortuis* [*On the Dead*]
Or. Catech.	*Oratio catechetica* [*Catechetical Oration*]
Ordin.	*In suam ordinationem* [*On His Ordination*]
Ps. 6	*Homiliae in Ps. 6* [*Homilies on Psalm 6*]
Tres dii	*Quia non sint tres dii* [*That There Are Not Three Gods*]
Virg.	*De virginitate* [*On Virginity*]
Vit. Mos	*De vita Mosis* [*On the Life of Moses*]
Hdt. *Hist.*	Herodotus. *Historiae* [*Histories*]
Herm.	[*Shepherd of Hermas*]
Mand.	*Mandata pastoris* [*Commandments*]
Sim.	*Similitudines pastoris* [*Similitudes*]
Hes. *Op.*	Hesiod. *Opera et dies* [*Works and Days*]
Hipp.	Hippolytus of Rome
Antichr.	*De antichristo* [*On the Antichrist*]
Cant. Mos.	*In canticum Mosis* [*On the Song of Moses*]
Comm. Dan.	*Commentarium in Danielem* [*Commentary on Daniel*]
Fr. Gen.	*Fragmenta in Genesim* [*On Genesis, fragments*]
Haer.	*Refutatio omnium haeresium* [*Refutation of All Heresies*]
Hom.	Homer
Il.	*Ilias* [*Iliad*]
Od.	*Odyssea* [*Odyssey*]
Iambl. *Myster.*	Iamblichus. *Liber de mysteriis* [*Book on the Mysteries*]
Ign.	Ignatius of Antioch
Eph.	*Epistula ad Ephesios* [*Letter to the Ephesians*]
Magn.	*Epistula ad Magnesios* [*Letter to the Magnesians*]
Phld.	*Epistula ad Philadelphios* [*Letter to the Philadelphians*]

Pol.	*Epistula ad Polycarpum* [*Letter to Polycarp*]
Rom.	*Epistula ad Romanos* [*Letter to the Romans*]
Smyrn.	*Epistula ad Smyrnaeos* [*Letter to the Smyrnaeans*]
Trall.	*Epistula ad Trallianos* [*Letter to the Trallians*]
Iren.	Irenaeus of Lyons
Epid.	*Epideixis* [*Demonstration of the Apostolic Preaching*]
Haer.	*Adversus haereses* [*Against Heresies*]
Jo. D.	John of Damascus
Dialect.	*Dialectica* [*Dialectic*]
Fid. orth.	*De fide orthodoxa* [*On the Orthodox Faith*]
Imag.	*De sacris imaginibus orationes* [*Orations On the Sacred Images*]
C. Man.	*Contra Manichaeos* [*Against the Manichees*]
Rect. sent.	*De recta sententia* [*On the Correct Thought*]
Spir. neq.	*De octo spiritibus nequitiae* [*On the Eight Spirits of Evil*]
Volunt.	*De duabas in Christo voluntatibus* [*On Two Wills in Christ*]
Just.	Justin Martyr
1 Apol.	*Apologia i* [*First Apology*]
2 Apol.	*Apologia ii* [*Second Apology*]
Dial.	*Dialogus cum Tryphone* [*Dialogue with Trypho*]
Fr. res.	*De Resurrectione, fragmenta* [*On the Resurrection, fragments*]
Justn. Orig.	Justinian I. *Epistula ad Menam* or *Liber adversus Origenem* [*Letter to Menas Against Origen*]
Max.	Maximus Confessor
Ambig.	*Ambiguorum liber* [*Book of Ambigua*]
Ascet.	*Liber asceticus* [*Ascetic Book*]
Cap.	*Capitum quinque centuriae* [*Five Hundred Various Chapters*]
Carit.	*Capita de caritate* [*Four Hundred Chapters on Love*]
Myst.	*Mystagogia* [*Church's Mystagogy*]
Opusc. theol.	*Opuscula theologica et polemica* [*Theological and Polemical Opuscula*]
Or. dom	*Expositio orationis dominicae* [*Exposition of the Lord's Prayer*]
Prol. Dion.	*Prologus in opera pseudo-Dionysii Areopagitici* [*Prologue on the Works of Dionysius the Pseudo-Areopagite*]
Qu. dub.	*Questiones et dubia* [*Questions and Doubts*]
Qu. Thal.	*Questiones ad Thalassium de scriptura* [*Questions to Thalassius on the Scripture*]
Schol. div. nom.	*Scholia in Dion. Ar. div. nom.* [*Scholia on "On the Divine Names" of Dionysius*]
Schol. eccl. hier.	*Scholia in Dion. Ar. eccl. hier.* [*Scholia on "On the Ecclesiastical Hierarchy" of Dionysius*]
Schol. myst.	*Scholia in Dion. Ar. myst.* [*Scholia on "On the Mystical Theology" of Dionysius*]
Meth.	Methodius of Olympus
De Autex.	*De Autexousio* [*On Free Will*]
Lepr.	*De lepra* [*On Leprosy*]
Res.	*De resurrectione* [*On the Resurrection*]
Symp.	*Symposium* [*Banquet of the Ten Virgins*]

Or.	Origen of Alexandria
Adnot. Lev.	*Adnotationes in Leviticum* [*Comments on Leviticus*]
Cels.	*Contra Celsum* [*Against Celsus*]
Comm. Cant.	*Commentarium in Canticum* [*Commentary on the Song of Solomon*]
Comm. Jo.	*Commentarii in evangelium Joannis* [*Commentaries on the Gospel of John*]
Comm. Matt.	*Commentarium in evangelium Matthaei* [*Commentary on the Gospel of Matthew*]
Comm. Rom.	*Commentarii in Romanos* [*Commentaries on Romans*]
Hom. Ezech.	*Homilae in Ezechielem* [*Homilies on Ezekiel*]
Hom. Gen.	*Homilae in Genesim* [*Homilies on Genesis*]
Hom. Jer.	*Homilae in Jeremiam* [*Homilies on Jeremiah*]
Hom. Luc.	*Homilae in Lucam* [*Homilies on Luke*]
Hom. Num.	*Homilae in Numeros* [*Homilies on Numbers*]
Princ.	*De principiis* [*On First Principles*]
Res.	*De resurrectione* [*On the Resurrection*]
Phil.	Philo of Alexandria
Abr.	*De Abrahamo* [*On the Life of Abraham*]
Agr.	*De agricultura* [*On Agriculture*]
Cher.	*De cherubim* [*On the Cherubim*]
Conf.	*De confusione linguarum* [*On the Confusion of Tongues*]
Decal.	*De decalogo* [*On the Decalogue*]
Det.	*Quod deterius potiori insidari soleat* [*The Worse Attacks the Better*]
Deus	*Quod Deus immutabilis sit* [*That God is Unchangeable*]
Fug.	*De fuga et inventione* [*On Flight and Finding*]
Her.	*Quis rerum divinarum heres sit* [*Who is the Heir of Divine Things?*]
Leg.	*Legum allegoriae* [*Allegorical Interpretation*]
Mut.	*De mutatione nominum* [*On the Change of Names*]
Opif.	*De opificio mundi* [*On the Creation of the World*]
Plant.	*De plantatione* [*On the Planting of Noah*]
Post.	*De posteritate Caini* [*On the Posterity of Cain*]
QE	*Quaestiones et solutiones in Exodum* [*Questions and Answers in Exodus*]
Sacr.	*De sacrificiis Abelis et Caini* [*On the Sacrifices of Abel and Cain*]
Somn.	*De somniis* [*On Dreams*]
Spec.	*De specialibus legibus* [*On the Special Laws*]
Philostr. *Vit. Apoll.*	Philostratus. *Vita Apollonii* [*Life of Apollonius*]
Pi. *Nem.*	Pindar. *Nemeonikai* [*Nemean Odes*]
Pl.	Plato
Apol.	*Apologia* [*Apology of Socrates*]
Gorg.	*Gorgias* [*Gorgias*]
Leg.	*Leges* [*Laws*]
Phaed.	*Phaedo* [*Phaedo*]
Phaedr.	*Phaedrus* [*Phaedrus*]
Phileb.	*Philebus* [*Philebus*]
Resp.	*Respublica* [*Republic*]
Theaet.	*Theaetetus* [*Theaetetus*]

Tim.	Timaeus [Timaeus]
Plot. Enn.	Plotinus. Enneades [Enneads]
Porph. Marc.	Porphyry. Ad Marcellam [To Marcella]
Ptol. Flora.	Ptolemy. Epistula ad Floram [Letter to Flora]
Tat. Or.	Tatian. Oratio ad Graecos [Oration to the Greeks]
Thdr. Mops.	Theodore of Mopsuestia
Comm. Col.	Commentarii in Col. [Commentaries on Colossians]
Comm. Eph.	Commentarii in Eph. [Commentaries on Ephesians]
Comm. Gal.	Commentarii in Gal. [Commentaries on Galatians]
Comm. Phil.	Commentarii in Phil. [Commentaries on Philippians]
Comm. Rom.	Commentarii in Ro. [Commentaries on Romans]
Comm. 1 Tim.	Commentarii in 1 Tim. [Commentaries on 1 Timothy]
Fr. Gen.	Fragmenta in Gen. [On Genesis, fragments]
Fr. inc	Fragmenta de incarnatione filii dei [On the Incarnation of the Son of God, fragments]
Fr. Jo.	Fragmenta in Jo. [On John, fragments]
Fr. mir.	Fragmentum ex sermone de miraculis [Discourse on Miracles, fragment]
Thdt.	Theodoret of Cyrrhus
Comm. Ps.	Commentarii in Ps. [Commentaries on Psalms]
Ep.	Epistulae [Letters]
Eran.	Eranistes [Dialogues]
Inc.	De incarnatione domini [On the Incarnation of the Lord]
Qu. in Ex.	Quaestiones in Ex. [Questions on Exodus]
Qu. in Gen.	Quaestiones in Gen. [Questions on Genesis]
Theoph. Autol.	Theophilus of Antioch. Ad Autolycum [To Autolycus]
Theophr. Sens.	Theophrastus. De sensu [On sense-perception]

Journals, Reference Works, and Series

Bib	Biblica
DAFC	Dictionnaire apologétique de la foi catholique
DB	Dictionnaire de la Bible. Edited by F. Vigouroux. 5 vols. 1895-1912
DBSup	Dictionnaire de la Bible: Supplement. Edited by L. Pirot and A. Robert. Paris 1928–
DTC	Dictionnaire de théologie catholique. Edited by A. Vacant et al. 15 vols. Paris 1903–1950
EO	Échos d'Orient
GCS	Die griechischen christlichen Schriftsteller der ersten [drei] Jahrhunderte. Edited by the Academy of Berlin. Leipzig, 1897–
Greg	Gregorianum
LTK	Lexikon für Theologie und Kirche
PG	Patrologia graeca. Edited by J.-P. Migne. 162 vols. Paris, 1857-1886
PL	Patrologia latina. Edited by J.-P. Migne. 217 vols. Paris, 1844-1864
RAM	Revue d'ascétique et de mystique
RAp	Revue Apologétique
RB	Revue biblique

RevScRel	*Revue des sciences religieuses*
RGG	*Die Religion in Geschichte und Gegenwart.* 2d ed. Tübingen, 1928
RHE	*Revue d'histoire ecclésiastique*
RHR	*Revue de l'histoire des religions*
RSPT	*Revue des sciences philosophiques et théologiques*
RSR	*Recherches de science religieuse*
S	Swete, H.B. *Theodori episc. Mopsuesteni in epistolas B. Pauli commentarii*, 2 vol., Cambridge, 1880 and 1882.
Schol	*Scholastik*
TQ	*Theologische Quartalschrift*
TU	Texte und Untersuchungen zur Geschichte der altchristlichen Literatur. Leipzig, 1882–
TWNT	*Theologisches Wörterbuch zum Neuen Testament.* Edited by G. Kittel and G. Friedrich. Stuttgart, 1932-1979
VSpir	*Vie spirituelle*
ZAM	*Zeitschrift für Aszese und Mystik*
ZKT	*Zeitschrift für katholische Theologie*

INTRODUCTION

Is it not a paradox to envisage the divinization of humankind? As if there v were not an insurmountable distance between God and us!

Yet such seems to be the heart of the most intimate aspirations of humanity. Under disparate forms, a vague but powerful desire is expressed just about everywhere for a life like that of God or of the gods, which is considered as the ideal of perfection and happiness.

Already those of the primitives who believe in a reward in the hereafter imagine it as an existence with the supreme Being "freed from death, disease, from suffering, and full of all kinds of delights."[1] In its way, the biblical account of the temptation testifies of a similar desire from the time of this life onward. In Hellenism also, deification was regarded as the highest purpose of our destiny.

The same ideal, although conceived of differently, would also be the soul of all philosophy—especially unbelieving philosophy, in fact—from the time of the Renaissance. "What is the dominant doctrine," Fonsegrive wrote forty years ago, "of modern times, from Bacon and Descartes to Condorcet, Auguste Comte, and Berthelot? It is that, by the progress of science, humankind will succeed in mastering the formidable forces of nature, will overcome adversity and death itself, find paradise on earth, and finally arrive at apotheosis. Humankind, by their own strength and the raw forces of the universe, will succeed in divinizing themselves."[2]

Is not the analogy between this ambition and the purpose proposed for vi humankind by Christianity striking, as the same author has remarked?[3] Indeed, the highest goal of the Christian religion, he writes elsewhere, "is to make us partake of the very nature of God—*divinae consortes naturae*, says Saint Peter— to divinize us and thus, by the grace of God, to make us gods."[4]

It is analogy, let us say, and not identity. For in modern philosophy the idea of divinization risks being hardly "anything but a vague piece of poetry,"[5] unless it is a pure illusion born of an immoderate pride.

---

[1] W. Schmidt, *Origene et évolution de la religion* (trans. Lemonnyer; Paris, 1931), 339.

[2] George L.-Fonsegrive, *Le catholicisme et la vie de l'esprit* (2d ed.; Paris, 1906), 18.

[3] Fonsegrive, *Le catholicisme et la vie de l'esprit*, 8: "There is divinization, after all, on both sides."

[4] George L.-Fonsegrive, *Le catholicisme et la religion de l'esprit* (Paris, 1913), 21.

[5] Jean Rivière, *Le dogme de la rédemption: étude théologique* (3d ed.; Paris, 1931), 89.

In the spiritual Christian, on the contrary, this ideal becomes reality. Is not all our theology of sanctifying grace, nearly to the word, a doctrine of deification?

Following the New Testament, the fathers indeed saw the new life imparted to the Christian as a participation in the divine life itself. But this shared concept is already expressed in the Scripture with some important nuances. Saint Paul mainly considers the "conversion," the "healing" of the sinner, while "Saint John is absorbed in the contemplation of the divine life imparted to people by Jesus Christ," and of the "elevation" and "adoption" of humankind by God.

The Pauline conception has been developed especially by Saint Augustine and the Latins, whereas the Johannine conception "has been exploited with an enthusiastic partiality by the Greek fathers."[6] Consequently, there is nothing surprising in the fact that, among the latter, the idea of divinization is "absolutely central."[7] It was of service to them in expressing, in a concrete and living way, the mysterious reality which the Latins designated under the more restrained term of *grace*.[8]

vii   For the understanding of the doctrine of our supernatural elevation, it is thus of the utmost importance to know the origin and development of the theme of divinization. It is in the tradition of the Greek fathers especially that we must seek out this history, from whence comes the object and limits of the present work.

Assuredly, the subject is not entirely new. For a long time Protestant historians of dogma have given it prominence, not however without minimizing its religious value.[9] Among us, Rivière has traced its main lines in dealing with the dogma of the redemption.[10] But only a few rare studies have been specifically devoted to deification as such, some of which are but simple monographs;[11] others, of a general scope, amount to sketches[12] or remain unfinished.[13]

One might as well say that a comprehensive exposition of the doctrine of the Greek fathers on the divinization of the Christian still does not exist. It is precisely this deficiency that we have proposed to make up.

---

[6] Pierre Rousselot, "La grâce d'après saint Jean et d'après saint Paul," *RSR* 18 (1928): 87-90.

[7] Rousselot, "La grâce," 92.

[8] Cf. H. Lange, *De gratia* (Freiburg im Breisgau, 1929), 166, 186.

[9] Cf. Adolf Harnack, *Lehrbuch der Dogmengeschichte* (3 vols.; 4th ed.; Tübingen, 1909), 2:44, 65-66, etc.; *Das Wesen des Christentums* (2d ed.; Leipzig, 1900), 144-147; R. Seeberg, *Lehrbuch der Dogmengeschichte* (4 vols.; 2d ed.; Leipzig, 1910), 2:74-78, 317-319; F. Loofs, *Leitfaden zum Studium der Dogmengeschichte* (4th ed.; Halle, 1906), 200, 232-233, 320.

[10] J. Rivière, *Le dogme de la rédemption: essai d'étude historique* (Paris, 1905), esp. 142-159. Cf. L. Richard, *Le dogme de la rédemption* (Paris, 1932), 87-92.

[11] For example, Karl Bornhaeuser, *Die Vergottungslehre des Athanasius und Johannes Damascenus* (Gütersloh, 1903).

[12] V. Ermoni, "La déification de l'homme chez les pères de l'église," *Revue du clergé français*, Yr 3 (1897), 11:509-519; O. Faller, "Griechische Vergottung und christliche Vergöttlichung," *Greg* 6 (1925): 405-435; M. Lot-Borodine, "La doctrine de la 'déification' dans l'église grecque jusqu'au XIe siècle," *RHR* 105 (1932): 1-43; 106 (1932): 525-574; 107 (1933): 8-55.

[13] So, Louis Baur, "Untersuchungen über die Vergöttlichungslehre in der Theologie der griechischen Väter," *TQ* 98 (1916)—101 (1920).

Since the idea of deification has served as a link between Hellenism and Christianity, it was essential to start out by following the analogous movements which have become clear in the Greek world. On the opposite side, the biblical and Judaic facts had to take their place. The originality of the Greek fathers was to make use of the Judeo-Christian revelation with the resources that the environment supplied to them.

In view of the vastness of the subject, it would be presumptuous to pretend to have exhausted it. We dare hope, at least, to have omitted nothing essential and, especially, to have not misrepresented the thought of our doctors. Brought back to its initial sources, our doctrine of sanctifying grace will perhaps gain here an increased interest and vitality.

BOOK ONE

THE PREPARATION

Part I: HELLENIC ANALOGS

Part II: BIBLICAL AND JUDAIC PARTICULARS

BOOK TWO

THE DOCTRINE OF THE GREEK FATHERS

Part I: THE PERIOD OF FORMATION
Part II: THE PERIOD OF APOGEE
Part III: THE PERIOD OF CONSOLIDATION

There is no doubt that the Greek fathers, like all the others, and following the example of the church itself, see the Holy Books—the Old Testament as much as the New—as the divinely inspired source of all truth from which they sustain their faith, the infallible standard on which their thought has to be fixed in an absolute manner. That being the case, it is in the Bible especially that we must seek out the roots of their teaching.

But though they may be fervent Christians, they are inevitably also children of their time and environment. Indeed, all grew up and were formed in the institutions, customs, and surroundings of their age. Also, they all profited, although to very different degrees, from the immense heritage which ancient Greece had handed down to the Greco-Roman world.

Prior to their conversion, several of them had even been adherents of philosophy and, having become Christians, they retained the mantle of the philosopher. Others, and not the least of them, although born of fundamentally Christian families, frequented before their late baptism[1] the schools of Athens, Constantinople, and Caesarea,[2] where under the direction of the most celebrated pagan rhetors of the time, such as Themistius and Libanius, they drank "in large draughts from the cup of secular culture."[3] Moreover, before they withdrew from the world, did not Saint Basil and Saint Gregory of Nyssa themselves teach rhetoric?

Among all these, some of whom we reckon as geniuses, Christian preaching did not therefore come into empty minds. When the time came for them to assimilate it, to fathom it and express its contents, they very naturally utilized, along with the Greek language, numerous other elements of Hellenic culture.[4]

In order to better understand their thought, and to measure in particular the influence that their pagan training was able to exert on the expression of their faith, it is thus essential to be acquainted with the atmosphere in which they lived, thought, and struggled.

---

[1] We know that Saint Basil, Saint Gregory of Nazianzus, and Saint John Chrysostom, when they received baptism, had passed at least twenty years of age.

[2] Cf. Gustave Bardy, "L'église et l'enseignement au IVe siècle," RevScRel 14 (1934): 525-549; 15 (1935): 1-27.

[3] Bardy, "L'Église et l'enseignement," 539. Cf. André Bremond, "Rationalisme et religion," Archives de Philosophie 11 (1935): 4:16-17: "Basil, the two Gregories, and John Chrysostom were true Hellenes, with a tinge of orientalism! They received Hellenism from the flagging hands of the last rhetors."

[4] Furthermore, an analogous observation can be made with the last authors of the Old Testament, as well as with the writers of the New.

One could expect here a priori—and our investigation is about to confirm it—that this general rule also applies to the doctrine of the Greek fathers on the divinization of the Christian. Assuredly this doctrine thrusts its vital roots into the inspired Books. But it also contains so many elements of Hellenic origin that several critics have wanted to see here the most manifest evidence of a hellenization of Christianity, which would be carried out to the detriment of the religious moralism preached by Jesus.

This is why before starting on the exposition of the patristic doctrine, it is essential to point out similar currents of thought which appear in the Hellenic world, even if they would only be indirect analogs, in order to make known the environment in which the biblical seed was going to develop.

BOOK ONE

THE PREPARATION

BOOK TWO

THE DOCTRINE OF THE GREEK FATHERS

CHAPTER ONE

LITERATURE

Throughout all of Hellenism one encounters, under the most diverse forms,   5
the idea that the supreme human happiness consists in a certain assimilation to
divinity. Before blossoming in the mysteries, philosophy, and Hermetism, this
ideal already becomes apparent in literature, in the strict sense of the word.

After the invasion of the Dorians at the beginning of the twelfth century
B.C., Greek civilization, enriched by the still more extensive blending of the
tribes and the increasingly frequent contact with their eastern neighbors,
greatly develops to the point of becoming capable of producing, around the
eighth century,[1] the oldest masterpiece of Hellenic literature, the epics of
Homer, in which for the first time a culture common to the Greek tribes is
affirmed, one that rises above the limits of time and space.   6

In poetic scenes of a beauty that still delights us after so many centuries, the
Iliad and the *Odyssey* depict not only the moral standards—the social and
political organization of the time—but also the general state of knowledge, and
of religious beliefs in particular. Only the latter interest us here, or more
precisely, a small part of them, namely, the ideas which appear, in what has
been called the "Hellenic Bible"[2] concerning divinity and the possibilities for
humankind to rise to it.

I

What especially characterizes divinity in the eyes of Homer is immortality,
to such a degree that for him the terms θεός and ἀθάνατος are synonyms.[3] The
immortality of the gods implies an eternal youth[4] as well as a happy life[5] in the
unchanging abode of Olympus, well above human miseries.[6]

---

[1] Cf. Helmut Berve, "Von den Anfängen bis Perikles," *Griechische Geschichte* (Geschichte der
führenden Völker 4; Freiburg im Breisgau, 1931), Part 1, 88. See also Louis Gernet and André
Boulanger, *Le génie grec dans la religion* (L'évolution de l'humanité 11; Paris, 1932), 22-26. According to
these latter authors, the poems called Homeric would only have been "composed in their more or less
definitive state, at a rather late date which could not be much earlier than the time of Solon or the
Pisistratides," i.e. at the beginning of the sixth century. They acknowledge nevertheless that these
poems "have been composed with various elements, transmitted by a tradition more or less ancient"
(23-24).

[2] Édouard Kammer, *Ein ästhetischer Kommentar zu Homers Ilias* (Paderborn, 1906), 102.

[3] See *Il.* 1.503; *Od.* 1.31, and many other passages.

[4] Cf. *Od.* 5.218, where Odysseus says to the goddess Calypso on the subject of Penelope: "She is
only a mortal, whereas you are immortal and prepared for an eternal youth [ἀγήρως]."

[5] *Il.* 20.54: μάκαρες θεοί. *Od.* 5.122: θεοὶ ῥεῖα ζώοντες.

[6] *Od.* 6.41-47.

Although the father of Western poetry attributes to his gods the human customs of thinking, feeling, and behaving, along with a bodily form, thus making
them, according to a judicious remark of Aristotle, "eternal human beings"
[ἀνθρώπους ἀιδίους],[7] and although he presents them as constantly involved in
the affairs of mortals, he sometimes declares strongly that "the race of immortal
gods is very different from that of human beings, who crawl on the earth."[8]
Countless are the lines, it is true, in which the leaders or even the simple war-
riors are described as θεῖοι, ἀντίθεοι, ἰσόθεοι, etc.; but it is evident that in the
mouth of our poet these qualifiers are only *epitheta ornantia*, which leave intact
the difference in nature between human beings and gods. Also, the greatest
transgression that a person can commit consists in the presumptuousness of
"wanting to be equal to the gods,"[9] as the history of the arrogant Niobe proves,
who was so harshly chastised "for having dared to compare herself to Latona."[10]

Nevertheless, the blessed eternity of the gods does not seem to be absolutely
inaccessible to mortals. Indeed, Homer knows of several cases in which simple
mortals have been received into the great Olympic family. So it is that Clitus,
with whom Aurora fell in love, was carried away by that goddess and placed
among the immortals.[11] The handsome Ganymede, abducted by Zeus,[12] became
his cupbearer.[13]

A similar privilege is proposed to Odysseus by Calypso who wants to make
him "immortal and always young [ἀθάνατον καὶ ἀγήραον]."[14] "This signifies
that she will make him a god, just as she is a goddess. The immortality of the
gods has as a condition the use of miraculous food—of ambrosia and of nectar;
if people feed on these divine foods in a continuous way, they also become
immortal gods."[15]

Finally, according to the famous myth of the "Elysian Fields," to which the
fourth canto of the *Odyssey* alludes,[16] a destiny comparable to the existence of
the gods is reserved for certain privileged people. There the valiant Proteus,
"servant of Neptune, who knows the depths of the ocean completely," predicts
to King Menelaus that he will not suffer the common lot of death. On the contrary, he will be sent "by the immortals to the Elysian Fields, to the borders of
the earth, where the blond Rhadamanthus is found. There a very easy life is
granted to humans: there is never any snow, nor long winters, nor rain; but

---

[7] Arist. *Metaph.* 3(b).2; (997b:11).
[8] *Il.* 5.441-442.
[9] *Il.* 5.440-441.
[10] *Il.* 24.602. Cf. *Od.* 5.212-213.
[11] *Od.* 15.249-251.
[12] *Il.* 5.265-266.
[13] *Il.* 20.232-235. On the other carryings away, see Erwin Rohde, *Psyché: Le culte de l'âme chez les Grecs et leur croyance à l'immortalité* (French ed.; Paris: Auguste Reymond, 1928), 60-61.
[14] *Od.* 5.135-136, 208-209.
[15] Rohde, *Psyché*, 60-61.
[16] *Od.* 4.560-569. This fourth canto is attributed by critics to a later poet. Cf. Rohde, *Psyché*, 57-58.

Oceanus always sends the gentle breaths of the zephyr which refreshes people." This happiness will come to him from the fact that he is the husband of Helen and the son-in-law of Zeus.

In that case it is a matter of an exceptional lot, granted to mortals because of family ties which unite them with the gods. Furthermore, it is in no way a question of the destiny of the soul separated from the body. The miraculous carrying away, with which Menelaus will be honored, has the whole person as its object. As a special privilege his soul will remain forever united with his body and never descend into Hades.

In the "Elysian Fields," or "land to come,"[17] the privileged enjoy a happiness without alloy or end, just as the gods. However, the latter do not share with them either the Olympian dwelling place[18] or the government of the world. Thus, on the subject of persons being sent to the Elysian Fields we can speak of a kind of accidental divinization. Moreover, deification is entirely extrinsic, without relation to morality, and in this it conforms to the Homeric concept of divinity, which essentially means blessed immortality.

But the great mass of human beings do not escape death. After the incineration of the body, the *psyche*—an ephemeral shade or vapor, which, though devoid of strength, is nevertheless "like the perfect image of the person and of that one's bodily configuration"[19]—descends into Hades, which never releases its prey. There it flutters about, restless and aimless, leading an existence which wrings from the soul of Achilles this bitter complaint: "I would prefer to be the most destitute slave of laborers on earth than to reign over the entire nation of the shades."[20]

Is not the legend, then, of the Elysian Fields, this enticing vision of a place of endless delights, like a dream of divinization, born of the horror which the human heart must have instinctively felt when confronted with this gloomy prospect of the Homeric Hades, born also and especially of its longings for an afterlife unlimited in light and happiness? There is nothing surprising about the fact that this myth exerted such a great influence among the Greeks on the development of faith in a life beyond the grave.

9

---

[17] Such would be the true etymology of the Greek expression 'Ηλύσιον πεδίον. Cf. Rohde, *Psyché,* 63.

[18] The fact of dwelling in Olympus is not an essential condition of divinity, as the example of Calypso shows. Cf. Rohde, *Psyché,* 105.

[19] Walter F. Otto, *Die Manen oder von den Urformen des Totenglaubens* (Berlin, 1923), 11-13. With this author, we part with Rohde concerning the meaning of the word *psyche* in Homer. Under the influence of the animism of Tylor, Rohde saw in the *psyche* a two-fold substantial self, a second self of the human being, which would become free at the moment of death. Cf. Rohde, *Psyché,* 3-7.

[20] *Od.* 11.489-491.

II

This influence is already perceptible in Hesiod before the last third of the seventh century.[21]

Indeed, the Boeotian poet also makes use of the legend of the Elysian Fields in his poem *Works and Days* when he draws a portrait of the human races who, in the five ages of the world, would have populated the "nourishing land."[22] He mentions there other cases too in which a kind of deification would have been granted by the gods to entire generations of mortals. Here, in brief, is this myth of the five races of the world:

The just and peaceable people of the first age, called the "golden age," have experienced death, although for them it was gentle like sleep. But once the ground has covered them, "according to the will of powerful Zeus, they are good spirits who walk around on the earth as guardians of mortals, dispensers of blessing; such is the royal honor which was accorded to them."[23]

10   In this way, therefore, after death the foremost human beings are transformed into "spirits" elevated to a nearly divine existence. Indeed, having been constituted as people's guardians, they carry on a superhuman activity, comparable to that of the gods; furthermore, they are honored in the manner of the gods.[24] However, on one point their condition remains clearly inferior: the new spirits are not admitted into the Olympian dwellings; they are "of the earth" [ἐπιχθόνιοι], that is to say, bound to the earth as their place of abode. This qualification having been made, one can say that the people of the golden race were divinized, but—and this detail is important—only after their death.

The second race, "certainly inferior" and for this reason called "silver," became blameworthy, because it engaged in a "wild immoderateness" and did not render "homage to the blessed gods who possess Olympus." "So the wrathful Zeus, son of Cronos, buried them. And when the ground had covered them in their turn, they became those whom the mortals call the blessed subterraneans [ὑποχθόνιοι μάκαρες], second in rank; but nevertheless, some honor still accompanies them."[25]

The fate that has befallen the souls of the second generation, while being inferior to that of the souls of the golden age, is still quite outstanding, too outstanding in our opinion, if their faults are taken into account. The poet calls

---

[21]   Cf. Paul Mazon, introduction to *Hésiode* (Collection des Universités de France; Paris, 1928), 14. We quote from this edition.

[22]   *Op.* 106-202.

[23]   *Op.* 121-126. Cf. 254-255, where the poet speaks of "thirty thousand immortals, guardians of mortals, clothed in mist, scattered everywhere on the earth, who watch over the sentences and the crimes." The passage above shows that the noun *spirit*, with Hesiod "just as with Homer, refers to the immortal gods" (Rohde, *Psyché,* 79).

[24]   Cf. *Op.* 142.

[25]   *Op.* 127-142. The reading τοὶ μὲν ὑποχθόνιοι μάκαρες θνητοῖς καλέονται, adopted by Muzon, seems preferable to that other, τοὶ μὲν...μάκαρες θνητοί, upheld and explained with much ingenuity in Rohde, *Psyché,* 83-84.

them μάκαρες, like the gods themselves, but blessed "subterraneans" to indicate that by sojourning in the interior of the earth, they are "second in rank" in comparison with the ἐπιχθόνιοι spirits of the golden race. But just as the latter, they are an object of veneration. This shows that a certain influence on human destinies is attributed to them, an influence which is not specified; however, nothing requires us to conceive of it as harmful. Although to a lesser degree, the people of the silver race have thus been divinized as well.

The people of the third race or "bronze race" were terrible. "They died by their own hands and set out for the musty dwelling of shuddering Hades, without making a name for themselves. Dark death took them, as fearsome as they were, and they left the shining light of the sun."[26]

Up to now the sequence of the different human races has been marked by a progressive decline. This "gradual course toward the worst" seems interrupted in the fourth generation by "the divine race of heroes, called demigods, whose generation has preceded us on the boundless earth. Of these, some perished in harsh war and in the grievous fray" whether in front of Thebes or in front of Troy. "Thus, there the finishing of death takes hold of some, whereas to others, Zeus, son of Cronos and father of gods, has granted a life and a dwelling place far from men by settling them in the outermost confines of the earth. And there they live, their heart free from worries, in the isles of the blessed [ἐν μακάρων νήσοισι], by the ocean with swirling depths, these fortunate heroes for whom the fertile soil bears a fresh and flourishing crop three times a year."[27]

In Hesiod, the Elysian Fields of the *Odyssey* has given way to the "isles of the blessed," but the rest has not changed. The heroes, having settled in these isles, have not known death; they have been transferred there entirely, body and soul. "Blessed," they enjoy there a pleasant and eternal life just like the gods. But no influence is granted to them on the course of the world.

The "iron race" is the fifth and last, that to which Hesiod himself belongs. It is a harsh and perverse generation which "Zeus will wipe out in its turn."[28]

In Hesiod's account of the five ages of the world, it is not difficult to recognize the idea of a divinization, or more precisely of a "spiritualization," of the dead, a strong ancient belief which is at the root of the worship of ancestors. But at the time of Hesiod this worship was languishing. One considers that "the phalanges of these spirits no longer receive any increase in the present. For a long time the souls of the dead are destined for Hades....Worship...is now only directed at those who are dead for a long time; the number of objects of its veneration no longer increases. This is due to the fact that the belief has been modified; the dominant idea is that which is expressed in the Homeric

---

[26] *Op.* 152-155.
[27] *Op.* 156-173.
[28] *Op.* 174-201.

poems....Only at the farthest horizon the isles of the blessed are gleaming; but the circle of those who have been transported there alive, according to the fantastic vision of the poets, is now closed, just as the cycle of Homeric poetry is closed. The present no longer sees such marvels."[29]

III

One will have noticed that the term hero [ἥρως], which is a purely honorary title with Homer[30] as was also "demigod,"[31] takes on a new, more restricted meaning in the poem of Hesiod. The heroes of Hesiod are exclusively the kings and the champions of the legendary age. They are not the object of worship; only the souls of the first two human races are honored by humankind.

From the end of the the seventh century, some documents—notably the *Odes* of Pindar and the history of Herodotus—attest that some regular sacrifices are offered not only to the gods but also to the heroes.[32] Yet the heroes thus honored next to the immortals are no more human beings, like those of Hesiod; they are, with one or two odd exceptions,[33] spirits of dead people, human souls separated from their bodies, to whom the gods have granted an existence and activity superior to those which they enjoyed before their separation. At the very most one could compare these heroes of a later age with the transfigured souls of the gold and silver races, described by Hesiod as "terrestrial spirits" and as "blessed subterraneans."

"Heroization" is not an ordinary fate. Quite to the contrary, it is a privilege rarely granted to an elite, to the souls of renowned persons. The object of this transfiguration was especially the great leaders of the epic, the descendants of the gods, the more or less legendary ancestors of the royal or noble families, the founders of cities; in brief, people who had lived in a distant past. Furthermore, a certain number of indications leads us to believe that the worship of the heroes came from that of the ancestors.

Later, in historical times, the circle of souls raised to the dignity of heroes grows more and more. Thus, there are "heroized" generals who, notably in the Median wars, saved the homeland; lawmakers; and indeed even certain victors of the Panhellenic games. It is not rare that such "canonization" is carried out at the instigation of the oracle of Delphi.[34]

---

[29] Rohde, *Psyché*, 89-90.
[30] Cf. *Od*. 1.100-101, etc.
[31] Cf. *Il*. 12.23.
[32] For the references, see Rohde, *Psyché*, 121-164. In that which concerns Pindar, see *ibid.*, 431-446.
[33] The legend makes known a few cases of human beings "carried away" and then promoted to the rank of "heroes," such as Amphiaraus, Trophonius, and especially Cleomedes. See Rohde, *Psyché*, 94-96, 131-132, 147-148.
[34] Cf. Gernet and Boulanger, *Le génie grec*, 178.

Perhaps the distinction between gods and heroes was not always very clear.[35] In the age which concerns us, it is affirmed with clarity. Though immortal like the gods, the heroes are inferior to them in everything else. Nonetheless, they have at their disposal considerable power, either to protect their worshipers or to avenge themselves on those who despise them or just neglect them. It is especially the gift of healing and divination that is acknowledged as belonging to them. But whereas the celestial gods are freed from every local tie and are able to take action wherever it pleases them, the presence and activity of the heroes are limited to a specific place, either to their tomb, or to their shrines or effigies.

Despite this unquestionable inferiority of the heroes in comparison to the gods, heroization appears as a kind of divinization of human souls. It is important to show that while remaining something extrinsic to the soul, deification is increasingly understood as a reward granted for exceptional merits. And that is how it tends to take on a moral character.[36]

14

IV

Concerning what we have just said, the adoration of heroes is basically only the remnant of an ancestor worship and of the dead in general. On the existence of the latter in the pre-Homeric period of the Creto-Mycenaean civilization, the archeological discoveries of the last fifty years hardly leave any doubt at all.[37] If the Greeks at that time—with Homer we can call them Achaeans—honored the shades of ancestors by numerous offerings, it is because they attributed to their dead a certain afterlife, including consciousness and activity. Subsequently, this belief must have gotten weaker, at least in aristocratic circles, to the point of leaving scarcely any traces in the Homeric poems. In fact, the Greek individuals of the epic seem to find their full satisfaction here below in the delights of earthly life. For them, existence vanishes in death; whatever, if anything, remains of it can only be a shadow without substance, incapable of acting and enjoying, something that can neither protect nor terrify anyone and consequently does not deserve any consideration.

But in the seventh and sixth centuries, at the same time as that of the chthonian gods and heroes, the worship of the dead is revived. This rebirth is expressed in the powerful development that funeral rites, feasts of the departed, and sacrifices offered to the latter undergo. This is an evolution which, on more than one point, prompted restrictive measures on the part of lawmakers.[38]

---

[35] Cf. Gernet and Boulanger, *Le génie grec,* 103: "Between gods and heroes there was firstly indistinction." Such particularly famous dead were honored sometimes as heroes, sometimes as gods. This was the case for Hercules and Achilles. See also Rohde, *Psyché,* 151.

[36] On the striking analogies which exist between the pagan worship of heroes and the Christian veneration of saints, see Karl Pruemm, *Der christliche Glaube und die altheidnische Welt* (2 vols.; Leipzig, 1935), 2:198-206.

[37] See Rohde, *Psyché,* 29 ff.; Berve, *Griechische Geschichte,* 19.

[38] Cf. Gernet and Boulanger, *Le génie grec,* 160-164.

A worship of this kind must have depended "on the assumption, sometimes even expressed, that the soul of the dead is capable of enjoying through the senses gifts that are offered to it and of which it has need."[39] This does not prevent popular imagination from continuing to see Hades as the customary dwelling place of parted souls, but it grants them the possibility of escaping Hades in order to go back to the earth. That is how it was believed, from the testimony of Plato, that the souls of the deceased "fluttered around the funereal monuments and tombs, close to which apparitions of souls were seen in the form of shadows."[40] Even more, on the days of their feasts, one senses that the shades are present in their ancient dwelling places, but this presence is met with as an embarrassment, so much so that one dismisses them quite brusquely at the close of the feast.[41]

However contradictory these notions may be on certain points, one idea clearly emerges from them: "The *psyche* of the dead enters into the crowd of invisible beings, who are better and loftier,"[42] and it becomes a kind of hero or spirit.

From what precedes, a few general ideas stand out, which deserve to be emphasized.

In non-philosophical Greek literature, God appears not as of another nature but as a being of the same nature as we.[43] The difference which separates gods and human beings, in fact, consists essentially in immortality. It is this apparently contradictory conception of the relationships between the two groups that Pindar has formulated in an admirable verse: "Human beings and gods are from a single race; from a single mother, indeed, we both have the breath of life.[44] Yet all the power, as assigned, separates us; we are nothing, whereas the sky of bronze remains forever an unshakeable dwelling. Nevertheless, by our lofty intelligence and our body, we are somewhat approaching, although we may be unaware, the very night[45] of the immortals, drawing toward whatever

---

[39]   Rohde, *Psyché*, 200.

[40]   Pl. *Phaed.* 81d.

[41]   Thus in Athens on the evening of the feast of the Anthesteria one cries to the souls: "Get out [θύραζε], Ceres, the Anthesteria have passed!" See Rohde, *Psyché*, 196-197; Otto, *Die Manen*, 50-52.

[42]   Rohde, *Psyché*, 188. The expression βελτίονες καὶ κρείττονες is from Aristotle.

[43]   Cf. H. Schwarz, *Der Gottgedanke in der Geschichte der Philosophie*, Synthesis 4, 27, cited by Hermann Kleinknecht, "θεός," *TWNT* 3:70.

[44]   The common mother, of whom gods and men are born, according to the common belief of the Greeks, is Earth.

[45]   Fr. A.-J. Festugière, *L'idéal religieux des Grecs et l'Évangile* (Paris, 1932), 24, sees in μετὰ νύκτας of the text an "allusion to the dreams that have come from the gods and which enlighten us."

fleeting course destiny wrote that we must pass through."[46] Both gods and human beings are therefore joined by the ties of a common origin, of a primeval parent, and separated by a chasm. But however deep the latter may appear, it is not absolutely impassable. As a matter of fact, by a special favor numerous mortals have crossed it.

This shows that the belief in a divinization of simple people is genuinely Hellenic since it thrusts its roots deep into the worship of heroes and of the dead.[47]

The blossoming of this worship in the seventh and sixth centuries should have had the effect of popularizing the idea of a conscious immortality of the soul and of stimulating the Greek genius to go deeply into this idea, which is what actually happened.

17

---

[46] Pi. *Nem.* 6.1-7. Here are these celebrated verses, according to the edition of Aimé Puesch, in *Collection des Universités de France, Pindar*, (Paris, 1923), 3:80:

῟Εν ἀνδρῶν,
  ἓν θεῶν γένος· ἐκ μιᾶς δὲ πνέομεν
ματρὸς ἀμφότεροι· διείρ-
  γει δὲ πᾶσα κεκριμένα
δύναμις, ὡς τὸ μὲν οὐδέν, ὁ δὲ
  χάλκεος ἀσφαλὲς αἰὲν ἕδος
μένει οὐρανός. Ἀλλά τι προσ-
  φέρομεν ἔμπαν ἢ μέγαν
νόον ἤτοι φύσιν ἀθανάτοις,
καίπερ ἐφαμερίαν οὐκ
  εἰδότες οὐδὲ μετὰ νύκτας
ἄμμε πότμος
  οἵαν τιν᾽ ἔγραψε δραμεῖν ποτὶ στάθμαν

[47] There seems no doubt that the veneration of heroes and shades prepared the Greeks for the acceptance of the eastern worship of the sovereign powers. But the difference between the two kinds of worship could not escape them. Accustomed to venerating people miraculously taken away from this visible world or the spirits of the dead, they were not at all accustomed to the worship of living mortals, who were inhabitants of this earth that is common to all. At the very most, in a quite exceptional case, honors reserved until then for heroes had been acknowledged for someone who was living (see Gernet and Boulanger, *Le génie grec*, 471-472, where the example of Lysander, the conqueror of Aigos-Potamos, is put forward). The deification of Alexander did not come off without difficulty either. Later, princes of Macedonian kingdoms of the East were rendered divine honors under the titles of θεοὶ σωτῆρες and θεοὶ ἐπιφανεῖς. In the Hellenistic period, the term θεός became the official appellation of kings and, in particular, of Roman emperors. See Kleinknecht, "θεός,"68. A brief historical survey, as substantial as it is balanced, on the Greco-Roman worship of sovereign powers is found in Pruemm, *Der christliche Glaube*, 176-194. Cf. Gernet and Boulanger, *Le génie grec*, 470-481.

CHAPTER TWO

THE MYSTERIES

18   The household worship of ancestors, practiced by the Greeks from earliest times, implied the idea of a certain immortality. But the latter offered to the Greeks of the seventh and sixth centuries a character that was so vague and impersonal that the diminished condition of shades could hardly have seemed like an enviable destiny. This was even less so because the desire for a happy afterlife, which had found its poetic expression in the myths of the Elysian Fields and the isles of the blessed, was revived and became widespread at this time. This thirst for a fully conscious and blessed immortality, not finding the means to be quenched in the traditional belief in the shades, led the elite to turn to the institutions which always come to mind when the hopes among the Greeks for things beyond the grave are spoken of—the mysteries.

The mysteries,[1] being secret cults reserved for the initiated who were obligated to the strictest silence, and not being well known, show certain common features in spite of a great divergence of details. Indeed, all claim to give to their followers the assurance of salvation [σωτηρία], namely, the guarantee of being delivered from the tyranny of destiny and consequently from every

19   misfortune, and of obtaining a happy lot in this world and in the other to come. "In the course of time, the notion of blessed immortality comes to predominate. And we can say, in a general way, that the mystery religions are religions of immortality."[2]

Corresponding to this uniform goal are means that are actually more or less identical. They are less doctrinal teachings than representations [τὰ δεικνύμενα] and symbolic practices [τὰ δρώμενα], renewing, so to speak, the "passion"[3] of agricultural divinities, in order to represent the revival of vegetation in springtime, as well as being mysterious formulas. In short, they are proceedings which appeal more to the senses than to the intelligence, as Aristotle had already observed.[4]

These rites of initiation generally involve, beyond the preparatory practices of purification, an initial stage [μύησις], which makes the candidates "mystae" [μύσται], followed by one or more other stages. The last, the highest and final

---

[1] The term μυστήρια, in the sense of secret cults, is encountered for the first time in Hdt. *Hist.* 2.51, alongside of ὄργια, employed in the same sense. The etymology of μυστήρια is much debated. Still, one finds with Herodotus the term τελετή for referring to the mysteries (*Hist.* 2.171, 4.79).

[2] Festugière, *L'idéal religieux*, 134.

[3] Cf. Athenagoras, *Leg.* 32 (PG 6:964a): τὰ πάθη, αὐτῶν [sc. θεῶν] δεικνύουσι μυστήρια.

[4] Cf. Festugière, *L'idéal religieux*, 140.

stage, is the "vision" [ἐποπτεία], and those who have received it are called "seers" [ἐπόπται].[5]

In the majority of the mysteries, the ceremonies of consecration are supposed to produce their effects independently of the moral tendencies of the subject. The hope of salvation is solely based on the fact of the initiation, to which a magical efficacy seems to be attributed.[6]

But if the expected result of all the mysteries is salvation, the nature and conditions of salvation are not understood everywhere in the same way. In this respect, the principal Hellenic mysteries display varieties which constitute a distinctive appearance.

I

The Eleusinian mysteries, very ancient and the most Greek of all the mysteries,[7] originally had as their object two agricultural goddesses, Demeter and her daughter Kore or Persephone. In the course of the ages, other divinities were associated with them, in particular, Iacchus son of Zeus and Persephone, who is later identified with Dionysius. Originally strictly local and reserved for a select group, the Eleusinian mysteries extended beyond their original scope very early to become Panhellenic.[8] From the fifth century until their suppression in the fourth century after Jesus Christ, they enjoyed great prestige, particularly under the Empire.

By its impressive ceremonies the cult of Eleusis, which has been called "the flower of Hellenic religion," aroused in the initiates the firm conviction that a pleasant life in this world and, above all, a blessed immortality in the hereafter were assured to them. On this point, the Homeric hymn to Demeter, which recounts the Eleusinian legend, is explicit: "Happy among the people who live on the earth are those who have seen these [sacred rites]; but they who have not been initiated into the holy things [ὃς δ' ἀτελὴς ἱερῶν] and do not participate therein will never have the same destiny when they arrive at the gloomy darkness."[9]

What is promised is not at all survival after death, which is presupposed, but—and here is "the great novelty of the Eleusinian rites"[10]—a better existence in Hades. However no preciseness is given to the nature either of the initiate's future happiness or of the "changeable" destiny reserved for the profane. In any case, it is not a question of a deification, an idea foreign to the religion of

20

---

[5] Usually one particularly distinguishes two degrees of initiation, which are sometimes called the "small" and the "great" mysteries. Cf. Rohde, *Psyché*, 234.

[6] Magic scoffed at by Plato in *Phaed.* 69c; *Resp.* 364b-365a.

[7] See Gernet and Boulanger, *Le génie grec*, 130.

[8] Cf. Gernet and Boulanger, *Le génie grec*, 130.

[9] Text cited by M.-J. Lagrange, "Les mystères d'Éleusis et le christianisme," *RB* 16 (1919): 161.

[10] Lagrange, "Les mystères d'Éleusis," 163.

21   Eleusis.[11] Yet it will not be long before this idea makes its appearance in other mysteries, notably those of Dionysius and of Orpheus.

II

Hardly less ancient and celebrated than the Eleusinian mysteries, those of Dionysius, a god of obscure origins[12] who ranks among the leading ones of Greek religion, are marked by a psychological feature which, although absent from the religion of Eleusis, is, quite the opposite, characteristic of the mysteries of eastern origin,[13] that is, the "holy frenzy." The followers who devote themselves to the practices of the Dionysian religion "are outside of themselves, having plunged either into dreamy ecstasy, or rather into a wild intoxication."[14]

Dances and orgiastic excursions, performed by groups of initiates called *thiasoi*, seem to have given to the mystae the sensation of being collectively united with the god, of being "in god" [ἔνθεοι], of living in god, and of enjoying a boundless life.[15] The omophagia, that is to say, the manducation of raw flesh, sometimes practiced in these states of "enthusiasm," would have been, according to some, a means of uniting with the deity, who was believed to be present in the consumed flesh; thus, it was "a sacrifice of communion."[16] According to others, it was an expression of a union already realized.[17]

Even if one disputes the idea of a personal union with the god as well as the concept of a blessed immortality as being original elements of the Dionysian 22   religion,[18] it is nevertheless a fact that the subsequent belief whereby the soul would, so to speak, go out of itself in the orgiastic ecstasy to be united to the god and live with him, implied, at least vaguely and in seed-form, the conviction that the soul is related to the divine and capable of divine life.

These ideas underlying the cult of Dionysius seem to have been extracted from it, probably under the influence of Thracian and Cretan conceptions, by a strange mystical movement commonly called Orphism.[19]

Herodotus (fifth century) is the first writer to mention the Ὀρφικά. He makes them a species of the Βακχικά genre and also describes them as "orgies"

---

[11]   Cf. M.-J. Lagrange, "La génération et la filiation divine dans les mystères d'Éleusis," *RB* 38 (1929): 63-81, 201-214; Festugière, *L'idéal religieux*, 23, 38-41; Rohde, *Psyché*, 241; Gernet and Boulanger, *Le génie grec*, 367.

[12]   See Rohde, *Psyché*, 268-270; Gernet and Boulanger, *Le génie grec*, 114-117. Fr. A.-J. Festugière, "Les mystères de Dionysos," *RB* 44 (1935): 192-193, maintains that Dionysius is "of Thraco-Phrygian origin." The same for M.-J. Lagrange, *L'orphisme* (Paris, 1937), 50.

[13]   Cf. Pruemm, *Der christliche Glaube*, 1:352.

[14]   Pierre Lavedan, *Dictionnaire illustré de la mythologie et des antiquités greques et romaines* (Paris, 1931), 338.

[15]   Cf. Rohde, *Psyché*, 279.

[16]   Lagrange, *L'orphisme*, 57; cf. 182-186.

[17]   Cf. Festugière, "Les mystères de Dionysos," 196. On the controversial question of the Dionysian omophagia, its existence, and its significance, see Pruemm, *Der christliche Glaube*, 2:390-395.

[18]   The fact is denied in Gernet and Boulanger, *Le génie grec*, 126, and Festugière, "Les mystères de Dionysos," 211.

[19]   Cf. Lagrange, *L'orphisme*, 79-95.

[ὄργια], or mysteries.[20] In *The Frogs*, Aristophanes speaks of Orpheus as of the one who "taught us the initiations [τελετάς], and to abstain from murders,"[21] that is to say, from the meat of killed animals. So from the fifth century at the latest, therefore, Orphism appears as a group of associations and secret doctrines of which Orpheus, the famous poet-musician of legend, would have been the founder. In reality, the origins of the Orphic sects, which developed on the fringe of the official religion, are very obscure.[22]

The organization of these associations is less known than their doctrine. The Orphic initiation particularly comprised a "threefold purification by air, fire, and water."[23] The worship seems to have consisted mainly in a sacred banquet, in which the raw flesh of a bull was consumed in remembrance of Dionysius. Later this ritual must have been reduced "to libations and to the incensing of various substances, with vegetable oblations."[24] Moreover, the mystae observed certain ascetic precepts, such as abstinence from everything which has life, as well as from eggs, etc.[25] And so they were called the pure or the holy.[26]

But what especially characterizes Orphism, and what distinguishes it at the same time from the official Dionysian religion and all the other mysteries, is that it combines, in a "sacred discourse" [ἱερὸς λόγος],[27] religion with a "semi-philosophical speculation."[28] This is a combination which allows it to depart from a passive and flimsy sentimentalism and develop a popular wisdom focusing especially "on the twofold nature of the individual, and on the greatness of the soul by virtue of which it is immortal and divine."[29]

Made for living with the gods, the soul, in punishment for a previous offence—the nature of which is not specified—is imprisoned in a body and condemned to an earthly life. That being the case, its most profound aspiration, its most sacred obligation, is to free itself from the bodily ties which weigh it

[20] Hdt. *Hist.* 2.81. For the exegesis of this passage, see Rohde, *Psyché*, 351-352.

[21] Ar. *Ran.* 1032. *The Frogs* was performed in 405 B.C. See other testimonies as well in favor of the antiquity of Orphism in Rohde, *Psyché*, 348-358; Lagrange, *L'orphisme*, 77-95.

[22] Fr. Pruemm, *Der christliche Glaube*, 1:355, opts for the opinion which has the Orphic movement go back to the seventh century. Fr. Festugière, on the contrary, only sees in Orphism a collection of literary traditions that are not very old, as well as purificatory and magical practices. He questions, moreover, the fact that Orphism had ever been inserted into the Dionysian mysteries. For his part, while approving "the discrimination of Fr. Festugière" between the latter and Orphism, Fr. Lagrange "resolutely takes a stand" for the ancient origins of the latter as well as for "its Dionysian connections" (*L'orphisme*, 7, 77-95, 97).

[23] Lagrange, *L'orphisme*, 100-102.

[24] Lagrange, *L'orphisme*, 113.

[25] Cf. Euripid. *Hipp.* 952. See also the verse of Aristophanes cited earlier and Pl. *Leg.* 6.782: Ὀρφικοί τινες λεγόμενοι βίοι ἐγίγνοντο ἡμῶν τοῖς τότε, ἀψύχων μὲν ἐχόμενοι πάντων, ἐμψύχων δὲ τοὐναντίον πάντων ἀπεχόμενοι.

[26] Cf. Rohde, *Psyché*, 367, 237; Lagrange, *L'orphisme*, 96-118.

[27] Hdt. *Hist.* 2.81.

[28] Rohde, *Psyché*, 358. See also Auguste Diès, *Le cycle mystique* (Paris, 1909), 47-53.

[29] Pruemm, *Der christliche Glaube*, 1:355. Cf. Lagrange, *L'orphisme*, 87.

down, certainly not by violence, but by the mysteries and an "Orphic life" of purification and asceticism.[30]

24   Upon death, a person's soul descends into Hades, where it will be judged. "Some terrible things" [δεινά][31] await the uninitiated there [ἀμύητος καὶ ἀτέλεστος], who will have a place in the quagmire [ἐν βορβόρῳ]. "They, on the contrary, who have been purified and initiated [ὁ δὲ κεκαθαρμένος τε καὶ τετελεσμένος], once they have arrived there, will dwell in the company of the gods [μετὰ θεῶν]."[32] "Upon the beautiful field, which stretches out to the edge of the deep Acheron,"[33] they will take part in the "banquet of the holy ones" [συμπόσιον τῶν ὁσίων] and will enjoy an "intoxication without end" [μέθη αἰώνιος].[34]

Perhaps, according to the Orphic theologians, the final reward was obtained only after complete purification by a series of reincarnations, whereas, for the profane, there was no possibility of getting out of the terrible "cycle of births."[35]

Thus, in Orphism there appeared for the first time the distinct idea that every soul is of divine origin and nature and consequently immortal by essence, *god* being a synonym of *immortal* for the Greek. The myth of the child Dionysius-Zagreus, devoured by the Titans, was used to illustrate this truth and explain the psychological dualism of the human person in the first century of our era. Having come out of the ashes of the Titans, after they were struck down by Zeus, human beings are composed of a Titanic element, violent and antidivine, and of a Dionysian or divine element.[36]

But the divinity of the soul has undergone an obscuring as a result of imprisonment in a body. By an Orphic life, it can nevertheless be recovered and regain its place with the gods. Consequently, the final end put forward by Orphism is divinization, or more precisely, the re-divinization of the soul. However, we must recognize that the images by which this deification is presented are still quite unrefined.

III

25   Very early, the cult of Isis and Osiris-Serapis of Egyptian origin was associated with that of Dionysius.[37] This is because between these two religions there were real affinities.

---

[30] See especially Pl. *Crat.* 400C; *Phaed.* 62b-c; *Leg.* 6.782c, quoted in note 25. Other references, in Rohde, *Psyché*, 365-367.

[31] Pl. *Resp.* 2.365a.

[32] Pl. *Phaed.* 69c.

[33] Orphic fragment 154, cited in Rohde, *Psyché*, 368.

[34] Pl. *Resp.* 2.363c-d. Cf. *Phaed.* 69c; Rohde, *Psyché*, 367-369. Even if it would be proved that the Orphism of the classical age was not a Dionysian cult of mysteries, the texts of Plato by themselves would compel one to admit the existence of mysteries, which cultivated the hopes beyond the tomb of which we are speaking. For us, this is the essential point.

[35] Cf. Rohde, *Psyché*, 369-370; Diès, *Le cycle mystique*, 49-50.

[36] Cf. Festugière, "Les mystères de Dionysos," 377.

[37] Cf. Hdt. *Hist.* 2.42: "All Egyptians do not honor the same gods in the same way, with the exception of Isis and of Osiris, whom they say is Bacchus; these all honor the same."

"In each, the followers commemorated the story of a god who both presided over vegetation and governed the underground world, a god put to death by an enemy and torn to shreds, and a god whose scattered limbs a goddess gathered together and miraculously brought back to life. The Greeks therefore must have been inclined to receive a cult in which they recognized their own divinities and myths along with something more poignant and magnificent. It is a very remarkable fact that, among the multitude of deities honored in the provinces of the Ptolemies' kingdom, those of the circle, or if one likes, of the cycle of Osiris, his spouse Isis, their son Harpocrates, and their faithful servant Anubis, are the only ones who were really adopted by the Hellenic populations."[38]

Due to the profound Hellenization which it had sustained under the Ptolemies in the third century before Jesus Christ, and due also to its extraordinary plasticity, with its ritual appeal and especially its eschatological promises, the religion of Isis exercised a great attraction on the Greco-Roman world. At the beginning of the third century of the Christian era it reached its peak. "Only Isis and Serapis remained, in all the pantheons of the East, up to the end of paganism, having been put among the number of the great divinities which the Hellenic world venerated."[39]

From antiquity there seems to have been in Egypt, beside the official religion of Isis, "a secret cult to which one was admitted only after a progressive initiation."[40] The regulations of the Ptolemies gave to this cult "the form of mysteries prevalent in the Hellenic world," bringing it closer in particular to those of Eleusis.[41]

Of all the ancient mysteries, the secret rites celebrated in honor of the Isis-Osiris group are the best known, thanks to the writings of Apuleius (second century) and of Plutarch. The following is how the hero Lucius, of the *Metamorphoses* of Apuleius, describes his own initiation:

Resolved to enter into the "sacred militia"[42] of Isis, he first plays the part of a kind of novitiate in the enclosure of the temple, in the course of which he observes abstinence and continence, and is present at the service.[43] Each night in a dream he sees the goddess. Despite his burning desire to be admitted to the initiation, he must wait for the call from on high. At last the awaited sign is given by Isis both to the postulant and the initiating priest. After the "opening"

---

[38] Franz Cumont, *Les religions orientales dans le paganisme romain* (3d ed.; Paris, 1929), 121-122. See also Philippe Virey, *La religion de l'ancienne Égypte* (Paris, 1910), 310-313.

[39] Cumont, *Les religions orientales*, 126.

[40] Cumont, *Les religions orientales*, 154.

[41] Cumont, *Les religions orientales*, 155.

[42] Apul. *Metam.* 11.15. We quote according to the edition of J. van der Vliet (Leipzig, 1897).

[43] The preparatory exercises at the initiation, sometimes very hard—originally purely ritualistic practices—became, in the second century of our era, the means of moral purification. See Cumont, *Les religions orientales,* 144-145.

(*apertio*) of the sanctuary, the morning service and sacrifice having been finished, the ceremonies begin.[44]

The candidate is solemnly baptized and receives from the high priest "instructions that the human voice cannot convey." Having practiced ten more days of abstinence from meat and wine, the neophyte, clothed in a linen robe, is led to the heart of the sanctuary. There, in a holy evening gathering, this one sees and hears things, the sworn secrecy of which allows the speaking of them only in a very veiled way. "I approached," he says, "the boundaries of death and, after having tread upon the threshhold of Proserpina, I returned from it by passing through all the elements. In the middle of the night, I saw the sun shining with a dazzling light. I saw face to face the gods of the underworld and the gods of heaven, and I adored them very close by."[45]

In the morning, the mystes is raised on a platform before the image of the goddess, arrayed in "the twelve sacred tunics," wrapped in a sumptuous mantle embellished with symbolic figures and called the "Olympic stole," with a torch in the right hand, and the forehead encircled with a wreath of palm leaves, the points of which project like rays. Thus, having become in a way an image of the sun god, the initiate is shown to the crowd. A joyful banquet concludes the day of the sacred rebirth (*natalem sacrorum*).[46]

Henceforth, the whole life of the mystes belongs to "Queen Isis." Under her powerful protection, this one will live happily, even "beyond the time limit fixed by destiny." And when descending to the underworld, the mystes will see, in the subterranean semicircle, the goddess shining through the darkness of Acheron and reigning in the dwelling places of the Styx. "Now an inhabitant of the Elysian Fields," the mystes will often adore the benefactress.[47]

Even if it is difficult to conjecture what could have taken place in the course of the mysterious evening gathering,[48] the general significance of this central part of the initiation is not difficult to find out. Indeed, everything leads us to believe "that they imposed on the neophyte a simulation of the trials of Osiris,"[49] of his death and of his return to life. We understand consequently how the consecration is called a kind of "voluntary death" and a rebirth to a

---

[44]   *Metam.* 11.21-22.
[45]   *Metam.* 11.23.
[46]   *Metam.* 11.24. Rohde, *Psyché*, 620, emends: *natalem sacrum*; this reading seems preferable.
[47]   *Metam.* 11.6. On the entirety of the initiation see E. Reitzenstein, *Die hellenistischen Mysterienreligionen* (Leipzig, 1910), 7-9, 66-85.
[48]   See some attempts at explanation in B. Heigl, *Antike Mysterienreligionen und Urchristentum* (Münster in Westphalia, 1932), 43-44.
[49]   Lavedan, *Dictionnaire*, 550-551. Cf. Albrecht Dieterich, *Eine Mithrasliturgie* (Leipzig, 1910), 162.

new salvation.[50] In brief, "by the initiation the mystes is reborn to a super-human life and becomes the equal of the immortals."[51]

IV

Among the mystery religions of eastern origin, that of Cybele-Attis was the most widespread in the first century of our era.

The Phrygian cult of the Great Mother of Anatolia was originally celebrated by wild orgies, in the course of which castrations and other bloody mutilations were not uncommon.[52] "This mixture of barbarianism, sensuality, and mysticism had put off the Greeks, who, except in a few ports with a cosmopolitan population, remained hostile and contemptuous toward Cybele."[53] But in the imperial era, or a little before, when Attis, the lover of the goddess according to the myth, was associated with the cult of the Great Mother, and when this cult had become more humane and had been transformed into a mystery religion along the lines of that of Eleusis, it made its way also into the Hellenized lands at the time of the emperor Claudius (A.D. 41-54).[54]

The rites of initiation, not particularly well-known, seem to have included ceremonial washings with water and, at least from the Christian second century, a kind of baptism in the blood of a bull (*taurobole*) or of a ram (*eriobole*).[55] After a sacred meal, the rites came to an end with the promotion of the candidate to the rank of "eunuch *a cubiculo*" or "chambermaster" of Cybele.[56] This is what seems to be the result of a formula of initiation reproduced by Clement of Alexandria: "I have eaten to the tambourine, I have drunk to the cymbal; I have carried the *kernos* [sacred earthen vase]; I have entered beneath the curtain of the nuptial bed."[57] The same formula, but slightly modi-

---

[50] Apul. *Metam.* 11.21: "Traditionem ad instar voluntariae mortis...celebrari, quippe cum transactis vitae temporibus iam in ipso finitae lucis limine constitutos...numen deae soleat elicere et sua providentia quodam modo renatos ad novae reponere rursus salutis curricula." [To engage in [such] instruction was like a voluntary death..., and indeed for those who, having passed through their time of life, were now at the very threshold of death...the divine power of the goddess usually, by providence itself, would bring it about that they were, in a certain manner, reborn and would bring them back again once more to the course of fresh health.] Cf. *Metam.* 11.16: "renatus quodam modo" [reborn in a certain manner].

[51] Cumont, *Les religions orientales,* 156.

[52] Cumont, *Les religions orientales,* 80.

[53] Lavedan, *Dictionnaire,* 639.

[54] See M.-J. Lagrange, "Attis et le christianisme," *RB* 16 (1919): 419-480, notably 473-479. The author acknowledges that some Christian influences could have played a part in the transformation undergone by the religion of Cybele from the second century of our era.

[55] Cf. Heigl, *Antike Mysterienreligionen,* 48.

[56] According to Lagrange, "Attis et le christianisme," 454. This learned exegete absolutely excludes the idea of a mystical marriage with the divinity.

[57] Clem. *Protr.* 2 (PG 8:76b).

fied, is found again in Firmicus Maternus (fourth century): "I have eaten to the tambourine, I have drunk to the cymbal; I have become a mystes of Attis."[58]

29   "A syncretism of doubtful reputation"[59] has made Attis a god by resurrection and the standard type of the divinization of his mystae. Or so it seems, at least judging from a curious piece of writing which is reproduced by Saint Hippolytus[60] containing an account of the mysteries of Attis according to a Naassene gnostic. According to this piece of writing—from which Reitzenstein believed it possible to extract a pagan opuscule[61]—the Phrygians would have spoken of Attis sometimes as a "dead man buried in the body as in a tomb and sepulchre," and sometimes as a resuscitated man, having become "god through change" [ἐκ μεταβολῆς θεόν].[62] By mystically imitating the death and resurrection of their god, the devotees of Attis would be equal to him, that is, divinized.[63]

V

A similar hope was the strength of the most virile and noble of mystery religions: the Persian cult of the god of light, Mithras. Here, more than anywhere else, courage, truthfulness, self-control, and the struggle against evil, not only outside but also inside the person, were preached. However, these qualities were not sufficient to overcome the aversion which the Greeks felt toward everything that came from the Persians, their hereditary enemies, and "we can say in a general way that Mithras always remained an outcast of the Hellenic world."[64]

For this last reason, it will suffice here to say that the Mithraic initiation of seven stages seems to have symbolized the ascension of the soul, separated from its body, through the seven planetary spheres, all the way into the region of the sun-god and before the throne of Jupiter-Ormuzd, with whom it will one day find blessed immortality.[65] "The Mithraists did not believe, like the

---

[58]   Firm. *Err. prof. rel.* 19.1 (PL 12:1022). In the edition of Migne, who reproduces that of Flacius Illyricus (Strasbourg, 1562), the last member of the formula only contains these two words: γέγονα μυστικός. The more recent critical editions, e.g. that of Conrad Ziegler (GCS; Leipzig, 1907), where the text appears in chapter 18, has: γέγονα μύστης Ἄττεως.

[59]   Lagrange, "Attis et le christianisme," 447.

[60]   Hipp. *Haer.* 5.6 (GCS 3:79-99).

[61]   R. Reitzenstein, *Poimandres*, (Leipzig, 1904), 81-101.

[62]   Hipp. *Haer.* (GCS 3:93, 12-14, 20-23); Reizenstein, *Poimandres*, 83.

[63]   Firmicus Maternus calls the candidate at the initiation a person "about-to-die" [moriturus]: "In quodam templo, ut in interiores partes homo moriturus possit admitti, dicit: De tympano manducavi, de cymbale bibi, et religionis secreta perdidici." [In a certain temple, a person who is 'about to die,' in order that he can be admitted into the more secret parts, says, "I have eaten from the tambourine, I have drunk from the cymbal, and I have thoroughly learned the secrets of religion."] Cf. Dieterich, *Eine Mithrasliturgie*, 162-163.

[64]   Franz Cumont, *Textes et monuments figurés relatifs aux mystères de Mithra* (Brussells, 1899), 1:241. Cf. Idem, *Les religions orientales*, 232-233. It is only in the third century after Christ, the period of its peak, that the cult of Mithras seems to have made its way into the peripheral regions of the Greek world.

[65]   Cf. Or. *Cels.* 6.22; (PG 11:1324-1325).

followers of Serapis, that the abode of the blessed was situated in the depths of   30
the earth; for them, this dark kingdom was the domain of perverse beings.
The souls of the just go and live in the infinite light that stretches out above
the stars, and casting off all sensuousness and covetousness by passing
through the planetary spheres, they will become as pure as the gods, whose
companions they henceforth will be."[66]

The mysteries, in which the religious feeling of the Greeks found its most
intimate and lofty satisfaction, present themselves as a strange mixture of elements foreign to religion and ideas of genuine religious worth. Of the latter,
the main ones are the idea of the superiority of the spiritual part of the human
being over its material part, as well as the hope, not for some sort of immortality, but for a happy afterlife for that spiritual part, similar to the existence of
the gods and in their company.

Whereas previously such a destiny appeared to be reserved for an elite, in the
mysteries it is, as it were, brought within the reach of all. In order to obtain it, one
must secure the protection, the good graces, of a savior-god by the imitation of
his "passion." However, from the second century of our era at least, we observe
a progressive moralization of the means of salvation and of salvation itself.

Since, upon death, all are supposed to descend into Hades, it is into the in-
fernal realm, from the confines of the world, that the theology of the mysteries
transports the paradise of the deceased, the famous Elysian Fields.[67]

To be received one day into this blessed abode and escape from the commu-
nal quagmire—this is what the mystae seek above all. Their immediate goal is
not therefore "to become gods, or children of a god, or like god." But inasmuch as the immortality to which they aspire "involves a happiness equal to
that of the gods, that is to say, unchanging and without end,"[68] they therefore,
indirectly and implicitly, await a genuine divinization.

---

[66]   Cumont, *Les religions orientales*, 248-249.
[67]   On this point, the non-Hellenized mysteries of Mithras are an exception.
[68]   Festugière, *L'idéal religieux*, 138.

CHAPTER THREE

HERMETISM

31   In the second and third centuries of our era, a period of great syncretism, a reconciliation took place, no doubt under the threat of rising Christianity, between the mystery religions which had been rivals in the past, a reconciliation to such an extent that we can speak of "a common doctrine."[1]

At the same time there appears as the fruit of the mysteries that strange mixture of Egyptian doctrines and Hellenic speculations known by the name of Hermetism. This, "a literary expression rather than a determining factor of syncretism, attempted, by a skillful balance of Greek and eastern elements, to construct a theology acceptable to all minds; however, it appears to have never been generally adopted into the Alexandrian mysteries which were earlier than it, and was, moreover, unable to get away from the contradictions of Egyptian thought."[2]

Hermetism draws its name from a group of writings which are presented as a revelation given by the Egyptian god-enlightener Hermes Trismegistus (three times great) particularly to his son Tat, who was like a dividing-in-two of his own person.[3] Only the Greek and Latin treatises which contain religious and philosophical doctrines are of interest to us.[4] We will distinguish here three groups of writings: the actual *Corpus hermeticum*, consisting of eighteen treatises in the edition of W. Scott; the *Latin Asclepius*, wrongly attributed to Apuleius; and finally, some extracts of the *Anthologium* of Stobaeus, known as *Fragments of Stobaeus*.[5]

---

[1]   Gernet and Boulanger, *Le génie grec*, 415. Cf. Cumont, *Les religions orientales*, 319-328.
[2]   Cumant, *Les religions orientales*, 138-139.
[3]   Cf. M.-J. Lagrange, "L'hermétisme," *RB* 33 (1924): 493.
[4]   Others concern astrology, magic, alchemy, etc. What has reached us of the Hermetic writings is doubtless only a small remainder of a very extensive literature. Cf. Reitzenstein, *Poimandres*, 1-7.
[5]   We quote the edition of Walter Scott, *Hermetica* (4 Vols.; Oxford, 1924-1936). Vol. 1, which appeared in 1924, gives the text with an English translation [In the portions quoted here, however, the author supplies his own translation—Transl.]; vols. 2 and 3, which appeared in 1925 and 1926, contain a detailed commentary; vol. 4, entitled *Testimonia*, which appeared in 1936, contains the "testimonies" relating to the *Corpus hermeticum* that we find in the ancient writers, from Athenagoras to Cosmas Melodus (eighth century). In his article cited earlier, "L'hermétisme," 33:481-497; 34:82-104, 368-396, 547-574; 35:240-264, Fr. Lagrange gives an analysis of the principal Hermetic writings and a translation of *Corpus herm.* 1 (*Poimandres*) and 13.

It is generally supposed that certain of these documents date back perhaps to the end of the second century of our era, but that the majority would not be prior to the third.[6] However, there is no doubt that the subjects dealt with here are not any more ancient. Everything leads us to believe that the unknown authors were Hellenized Egyptian priests.

The substance of the doctrine contained in the *Corpus hermeticum* is supplied by Greek philosophy, particularly by Platonism and Stoicism. But throughout, the influence of eastern speculation has made itself strongly felt. This influence, as well as the Egyptian temperament of the writers, accounts for the religious fervor that distinguishes these writings from all other works of Hellenic speculation.

Out of the disconcerting chaos of disparate and often contradictory concepts which the *Hermetica* contain, a few general ideas emerge which are of major interest to us. Indeed, salvation [σωτηρία], presented as the deliverance from the tyranny of fate [εἱμαρμένη] by virtue of a divinization by gnosis, is like a leitmotiv to them.[7]

I

The following is how salvation and the means to reach it are understood in the first document of the *Corpus hermeticum*, the famous *Poimandres*, or "shepherd of men"[8]:

"Νοῦς, the First, which is life and light [ζωὴ καὶ φῶς], being bisexual, gave birth to another νοῦς; this one, the Second, created from fire and from spirit seven administrators, who encompass in scope the perceptible world; and their administration is called Fate [εἱμαρμένη]. Nature had the animals without reason brought forth with inferior elements....Now the Father of all things, who is life and light, gave birth to a Human Being like himself, with whom he became enamored as though with his own child; for this one was very fine-looking, having the image [εἰκόνα] of the father...and to whom he handed

[6] Cf. Scott, *Hermetica*, 1:10; Lagrange, "L'hermétisme," 35:262. These two writers reject the hypothesis of Reitzenstein (*Poimandres*, 1-36), whereby the *Shepherd of Hermas* is dependent upon *Poimandres* in its primitive form, which consequently would be prior to the second century. See as well A. Puech, *Histoire de la littérature greque chrétienne* (3 vols.; Paris, 1928), 2:655: "Whatever the period to which it may be necessary to have the first seeds of this [Hermetic] literature go back—and this period can be very ancient—it is not before the end of the second century, and it is in the course of the third, particularly, that they took the form in which we possess them."

[7] Cf. L. Cerfaux, "Gnose préchrétienne et biblique," *DBSup* 3:678.

[8] A well-chosen title since the treatise is presented as a revelation of "Poimandres, the understanding of absolute power [ὁ τῆς αὐθεντίας νοῦς]" (*Corp. herm.* 1.2 [Scott 1:114]).

over all creations."[9] The Human Being, a child of the supreme god and brother of the demiurge, was, by virtue of essence, above Fate.[10]

But this Human Being from above, the archetype of humanity, turning his attention toward inferior Nature, "was mirrored in the water and, like Narcissus, fell in love with his own image; but believing that he embraces the image, he is joined to Nature."[11] Indeed, "having received that which she loved, Nature [φύσις] grasps him entirely; and they are blended, smitten with love as they were."[12] But in crossing the spheres of the planets, humankind received all the evil passions from them. For these reasons, "among all the animals which are on the earth, only humankind is two-fold, mortal because of the body, immortal because of the essential Human Being. For although immortal and masters of all things, they endure the lot of mortals, being subject to Fate. Being above the Harmony [of the spheres] [ὑπεράνω γὰρ ὢν τῆς ἁρμονίας], they have become enslaved to Fate. Although bisexual, having issued from a bisexual father, and exempt from sleep, having issued from a [father] exempt from sleep, they are overcome by love and forgetfulness."[13]

However, only the human body is subject to εἱμαρμένη. After the dissolution of the body, the human being, who has received the νοῦς, "soars on high across the Harmony" [ὁρμᾷ ἄνω διὰ τῆς ἁρμονίας] and on the way casts aside the vices acquired in the descent. Finally, the human being enters into the "eighth nature," the ὀγδοάς, the intermediary realm between the planetary spheres and that of the supreme god,[14] rises up even to the father, and, having become a power [δυνάμεις γενόμενοι], enters into God [ἐν θεῷ γίνονται]. "Such is the benefit, such is the end, for those who have had gnosis: deification" [τοῦτό ἐστι τὸ ἀγαθόν, τοῦτο τὸ τέλος τοῖς γνῶσιν ἐσχηκόσι θεωθῆναι].[15]

So therefore, according to the *Poimandres*, the salvation of humankind, that is, the liberation from the authority of destiny achieved by means of gnosis, is a

[9] *Corp. herm.* 1.9-12 (Scott 1:118-120). — "We know how very widespread at that time [in the second century] the conviction was that the stars determine events here below, that is, the character and the actions of men" (Pierre de Labriolle, *La réaction païenne* [Paris, 1934], 158). From time immemorial the notions concerning the origin and the destinies of man are linked to the idea that we are made from the universe. In the mythological cosmology of the *Poimandres*, Fr. Lagrange sees reminiscences of the biblical cosmology ("L'hermétisme," 35:250).

[10] *Corp. herm.* 1.12; (120).

[11] Lagrange, "L'hermétisme," 35:244.

[12] *Corp. herm.* 1.14 (122).

[13] *Corp. herm.* 1.13-15 (120-122). See *Commentary*, 2:36-46. We find some analogous notions in *Asclep. lat.* 1.7b, 10-11 (Scott 1:296-298, 304-306). We recognize the traditional theme of the duality in humankind. Cf. Reitzenstein, *Poimandres*, 69. Also note at which point Hermetism is dependent on the idea that developed at that time concerning the organization of the universe.

[14] See Reitzenstein, *Poimandres*, 53-55.

[15] *Corp. herm.* 1.24-26 (126-128). Even if the word θεωθῆναι was a later gloss, as Scott thinks, the idea of a deification is clearly expressed in ἐν θεῷ γενέσθαι of the preceeding phrase. See *Commentary* 2:67. Reitzenstein, *Poimandres*, 336, l. 25, gives θεωθῆναι as authentic. Besides, this term is certainly employed in *Corp. herm.* 10.6 (190) (see following note); 13.10 (246). See below, 34, n. 24.

genuine divinization, or better stated, a return to the original divine state. But this return only takes place, and the supreme σωτηρία is only attained, after "the dissolution of the material body."[16]

II

Elsewhere, in the same *Corpus hermeticum*, divinization is presented as being realized from this life onwards. This is the case in *Libellus 13*, which is devoted to a "secret discourse of Hermes Trismegistus with his son Tat on regeneration [παλιγγενεσία]."[17]

Here Tat asks his father to enlighten him on the subject of regeneration, which in his "common discourses" [λόγοι γενικοί]—which are very obscure— he had declared necessary for "being saved." Reminding Hermes of his promise to convey to him his secret doctrine "when he would be freed from the world," Tat affirms himself ready.

What he desires to know above all is "from which womb and from which seed a person can be regenerated." And Trismegistus explains to him that "the womb is wisdom [σοφία], which conceives in silence, and the seed is the genuine good," while that which makes them productive is "the will of God."[18]

In the course of the dialogue, little by little, rising above himself and entering into ecstasy, Tat is deified. Although by his remarks he himself testifies of the mysterious transformation which takes place in him, he is not immediately aware of it, and Hermes finds himself obliged to inform him of it. "Are you unaware," he says to his son and disciple, "that you have become god and son of the One, like me? [ἀγνοεῖς ὅτι θεὸς πέφυκας καὶ τοῦ ἑνὸς παῖς, ὃ κἀγώ]"[19] This is a mystical anticipation of divinization after death, of which the *Poimandres* speaks.

III

Nevertheless, in each case the conditions and means of deification are analogous. Above all, it is essential to withdraw from the sensory world.[20] Then the "ten" virtues have to drive out the "twelve" vices.[21] Finally, departing as it were

[16] The same idea is in *Corp. herm.* 10.6 (190): "It is impossible, my son, that the soul should be deified [ἀποθεωθῆναι] as long a time as it remains in the human body; but it is necessary that it be changed and then divinized by the contemplation of the splendor of the Beautiful." See also *Asclep. lat.* 1.10-11; 3.37 (Scott 1:304-308; 3 [*Commentary*]: 56, 225). An ascension of the soul to heaven after the death of the human being is spoken of here as well.

[17] Scott 1:238-254. French translation by Lagrange, "L'hermétisme," 35:252-259.

[18] *Corp. herm.* 13.1-2 (238).

[19] *Corp. herm.* 13:14 (248).

[20] *Corp. herm.* 1.22; 13.1, 7a, 10 (126, 238, 242, 246).

[21] *Corp. herm.* 13.7b-10 (242-246). The twelve vices, due to the harmful influence of the stars, correspond to the twelve signs of the Zodiac, which, according to Egyptian tradition, govern fate. The decade was already considered by the Pythagoreans as a sacred number, generator of the soul or of life in humankind. See Scott 2 (*Commentary*): 392-393; Reizenstein, *Poimandres*, 70-78.

from themselves, the individuals who have received mercy from God[22] pass through a mystical death and ascension. These set them free from the "tent" of the body [τὸ σκῆνος τοῦτο][23] and thereby from fate and, by virtue of an "intellectual birth" [νοερὰ γένεσις], divinize them.[24]

Therefore, in Hermetism salvation, that deliverance from the dark εἱμαρμένη, is obtained—the merciful help of God being presupposed[25]—by a regeneration of purely intellectual nature; by means of gnosis, of ecstatic contemplation, the "real" human being, of divine origin but humbled by incorporation, rises again to God and is joined to Him. The salvation is to such an extent that in a hymn of thanksgiving the mystes is able to exclaim: "Am I other than you? For you are that which I am; you are that which I do; you are that which I say."[26]

In this exclamation how can we fail to recognize the typical formula of the mysticism of the magic papyri: "I am you and you are me"? In our case, the union of the mystae with their God even seems to be an absorption of the "higher" human being by "the One and the All." This fits in perfectly with the quite pronounced pantheistic tendency which characterizes Hermetic literature.[27]

Assuredly, formulas of this kind are hardly of Greek inspiration; by contrast, they are not uncommon in Egyptian documents of every period.[28]

⌘

A comparison of the Hermetic mysteries with the mystery cults, which was the question above, in the first place reveals fundamental similarities. Both start from the body-soul duality in humankind and recognize an unquestionable superiority in the spiritual element. The goal that is pursued is the same: σωτηρία, namely, deliverance from the εἱμαρμένη.

---

[22] Cf. *Corp. herm.* 13.7b (244), where there is mention of a person "on whom God has had mercy" [τοῦ ἐλεηθέντος ὑπὸ τοῦ θεοῦ]. In *Corp. herm.* 1.32 (130), gnosis is called a "grace" [χάρις] of God.

[23] *Corp. herm.* 13.12 (246).

[24] *Corp. herm.* 13.10 (246). Here the use of the term θεωθῆναι is not questionable. Cf. Reitzenstein, *Poimandres*, 343.

[25] *Corp. herm.* 1.22; 13.2, 10 (126, 238, 246).

[26] *Corp. herm.* 5.11 (164): διὰ τί δὲ καὶ ὑμνήσω σέ; ὡς ἐμαυτοῦ ὤν, ὡς ἔχων τι ἴδιον; ὡς ἄλλος ὤν; σὺ γὰρ εἶ ὃ ἂν ὦ, σὺ εἶ ὃ ἂν ποιῶ, σὺ εἶ ὃ ἂν λέγω.

[27] See, among other passages: *Corp. herm.* 5.11; 13.17-19 (164, 250-252). But especially see *Asclep. lat.* 2a (288): "Non enim hoc dixi, omnia unum esse et unum omnia, utpote quae in creatore fuerint omnia, antequam creasset omnia? Nec inmerito ipse dictus est omnia, cuius membra sunt omnia. Huius itaque, qui est unus omnia, vel ipse est creator omnium, in tota hac disputatione curato meminisse." [Have I not indeed said this, namely, that all things are the One and the One is all things, in view of the fact that all things were in the creator before He created all things? Not undeservedly has it been said of Him that He is all things, of whom all things are the parts. And so in this entire discussion of ours, be careful to remember this One who, as the One, is all things, even the creator of all things.] Cf. Kleinknecht, "θεός," 78.

[28] See Scott, 2 (*Commentary*): 167-168, where we find some references, among others, to the magic *papyri*. Some examples taken from the latter are given in Reitzenstein, *Poimandres*, 20-21, where the formula cited above is also encountered: σὺ γὰρ ἐγὼ καὶ ἐγὼ σύ.

But concerning the means employed by either religion for realizing this goal, profound differences prevail. In the mystery religions, that which saves is less a doctrinal teaching than a δρώμενον, a liturgical act which has an effect on the emotional part of the human being. By a particularly ritualistic assimilation of the initiate to the Divinity, the initiation assures to the first the protection of the second.

The Hermetic mysteries, on the contrary, knowing neither cult nor liturgy, are based entirely on a λόγος, a virtually inspired and infallible scripture. Being "literary mysteries," they are directed straight to the νοῦς and lead to a superior wisdom, γνῶσις,[29] and by it to the vision [θέα] of God. They thus appear as a mystico-philosophical transposition of "worship" mysteries, as "the philosophical religion of the Νοῦς or intelligence."[30]

Finally, we find that the connection between salvation and divinization is infinitely closer in Hermetism than in the mystery cults. The latter indeed establish between the initiate and the Divinity only a moral union, a relationship of membership and protection. The mysteries of *gnosis*, on the contrary, establish between the mystae and their God a direct and immediate contact, going as far as identification. When all is said and done, the way of salvation advocated by Hermetic theosophy is the divinization of humankind as a result of resorption into the divine One, out of whom they came.[31]

38

---

[29]   On this point, a fine passage of the *Poimandres* is particularly revealing: Μαθεῖν θέλω τὰ ὄντα καὶ νοῆσαι τὴν τούτων φύσιν, καὶ γνῶναι τὸν θεόν (*Corp. herm.* 1.3 [114]). We could place these words as a motto at the heading of the *Corpus hermeticum*.

[30]   Lagrange, "L'hermétisme," 35:263. Cf. Festugière, *L'idéal religieux*, 127-132.

[31]   We have not thought it necessary to bring up—because it does not seem to arise concerning the precise question of divinization—the difficult problem of the influence that the writings of the Old and New Testaments were able to exert on Hermetic literature.

CHAPTER FOUR

THE PHILOSOPHY OF THE CLASSICAL ERA

39   It is a long way from the σωτηρία of the worship mysteries, conceived of as a rather unrefined bliss, to the salvation of the literary mysteries, which consists in the union of the soul with God by means of gnosis. This refinement, this spiritualization, assumes an effort of reflection which itself became possible only because of the birth and progress of philosophical speculation. But if it is true that the mysteries were under the guidance of philosophy rather than the latter being under the guidance of the mysteries,[1] it is no less certain that the first philosophers were preferably inspired by the sayings "of ancient theologians and seers," by cosmogonies and the myths of the poets, Homer and Hesiod especially, as well as by religious practices.

On two points in particular religion seems to have influenced philosophy and vice versa: the notion of divinity and the immortality of the soul.[2] From the progress made in these matters, the ideal of divinization which was anticipated by the poets and the followers of the mystery religions derived great benefit for itself.

I

However, the first philosophical systems developed by the Greek genius proved to be rather hostile to the ancient beliefs and resistant to all religious mysticism.

At the start of the sixth century, we see philosophical reflection coming to life in the Hellenic world, at first in the Ionian towns, which at that time were 40   in the vanguard of Greek civilization. In an initial period which extends from 600 to about 450 B.C., the attention of thinkers is turned to the outside, to the cosmos. Hence it is called the "cosmological" period of Greek philosophy.

The human soul seems to have preoccupied the mind of these early pioneers of philosophy very little. It must have seemed to them like a detail of secondary importance. This is because, for the Ionian physiologists, the psyche is really the vital energy of a person, the principle of the thoughts and desires; but this psychic strength they "understood as absolutely inherent to matter and to the things which are formed of it," as something that participates in "the unique force which builds up and governs the universe."[3] This is

---

[1]   See Édouard Zeller, *Die Philosophie der Griechen* (6 vols.; 6th ed.; Leipzig, 1919), 1:1:62.
[2]   Cf. *ibid.* 68-88. See also M. Louis, *Doctrines religieuses des philosophes grecs* (Paris, 1909), 3-50.
[3]   Rohde, *Psyché*, 381. Cf. Zeller, *Die Philosophie der Griechen*, 1:1:253-270.

what is called the theory of hylozoism. As a manifestation of the universal soul, which the All-Divine enlivens, the human soul can be described as divine and immortal. But there is no question of an individual and conscious immortality for it.

Although Pythagoras himself seems to have believed in the immortality of the soul and metempsychosis,[4] some of his disciples, such as Philolaos, conceived of the soul in terms of their mathematico-musical theory as "the harmony of opposing elements, whose coming together forms the body."[5]

For Empedocles, the famous philosopher, poet, physician, purifier, and miracle-worker, the author of the theory of the four elements, what is called psyche is only the sum total of the human body's vital energies, which perish with it.[6]

Applying his atomic theory to the soul, Democrites sees it as a combination of round and smooth atoms, thus particularly mobile and penetrating. Imperishable like the others, the atoms which form the soul disperse upon a person's death, exactly like those which make up the body. This means that the human personality purely and simply disappears.[7]

The same conclusion results from the very obscure psychology of Anaxagoras, the first Greek thinker who, in order to explain the universe, had recourse to a spiritual principle. For him, the souls of plants and of animals, as much as those of people, seemed to be only graduated manifestations of that intelligence [νοῦς], of that thinking principle, which he probably conceived of as immaterial. And he believed that the first organized movement of the inert mass of "material" seeds began from this intelligence.[8]

The surprising thing here is that, beside this rational psychology, in several philosophers of the cosmological period, such as Heraclitus,[9] Parmenides, the Pythagoraeans, and Empedocles especially, we find the Orphic conceptions of the divine origin of the soul, its offense, and its exile into an earthly body; of the purifying metempsychosis; and of a final deliverance with a return to that blessed life which the soul had enjoyed before its fall.[10] This shows what a strong attraction the religious psychology of the time must have exerted upon the elite Greeks, so strong that it could assert itself in this way on philosophers whose cosmological systems were in uncompromising opposition to this kind of belief. This standpoint is all the more significant since the official religion, which did not possess a professional priesthood and did not have inviolable

41

---

[4]   Cf. Rohde, *Psyché*, 395-397.

[5]   Rohde, *Psyché*, 402.

[6]   Rohde, *Psyché*, 404-409.

[7]   Rohde, *Psyché*, 418-421.

[8]   Rohde, *Psyché*, 421-424.

[9]   Rohde, *Psyché*, 383-390. See also Hans Eibl, *Die Grundlegung der abendländischen Philosophie* (Bonn, 1934), 10-12.

[10]   Rohde, *Psyché*, 391-425. On that which concerns Empedocles, see also A. Dies, *Le cycle mystique*, 83-99.

dogmas to defend, hardly seems to have reacted against philosophical systems which, nevertheless, were basically causing its ruin.[11]

II

42   After the Median wars civilization in general and intellectual activity in particular had an admirable expansion in Greece. An increasingly broader thrust toward learning led philosophical studies to come out of the shadow of their more or less exclusive schools and be mingled with public life. Since practical knowledge especially was being asked of them—in the first place, an introduction to the art of speaking, so important in a democracy—their consideration concentrated on humankind.

This new orientation, occurring at the same time as the individualism favored by political and social evolution, prompted a crisis in traditional beliefs in the second half of the fifth century, which led some, along with the Sophists, to skepticism, and others to the mysteries, Orphism in particular.[12]

These different tendencies appeared to be incarnate in the powerful personality who was to inaugurate the period of the blossoming of Greek philosophy—Socrates, that extraordinary man "with a burning heart and a cool head."[13]

One has written that "Socrates will always be an enigma."[14] But if it has still not been possible to establish with certainty his authentic thought, there is nevertheless no doubt that it had humankind as its center, and more precisely "the care and the salvation of the human soul."[15] It also seems that in his *Apology* Plato has faithfully reported the conceptions of his master concerning the immortality of the soul. There the philosopher, condemned to death, confesses not to know anything for certain on the latter subject.[16] However, he envisages two possibilities: either a deep and dreamless sleep, or else a crossing of the soul from this world into another place, namely Hades, which he conceives of somewhat in the way that Homer does. In any case, death does not seem like an evil to him. This was sufficient enough for Socrates to look death straight in the face with that calm and that serenity which were to fill posterity with admiration.[17]

---

[11] Such reactions are known only for Athens. Several of these proceedings for "impiety" seem to have been above all else of political inspiration. See Zeller, *Die Philosophie der Griechen*, 1:1:60; F. Ueberweg and F. Heinze, *Grundriss der Geschichte der Philosophie* (4 vols.; Berlin, 1903-1916), 1:215-218; Berve, *Griechische Geschichte*, 2:4; Gernet and Boulanger, *Le génie grec*, 345-354.

[12] See Berve, *Griechische Geschichte*, 2:31.

[13] Th. Gomperz, *Griechische Denker* (2d ed. Leipzig, 1903), 36.

[14] Gernet and Boulanger, *Le génie grec*, 384. On the open controversy revolving around Socrates, see Zeller, *Die Philosophie der Griechen* (4th ed. Leipzig, 1889), 2:1:91-100.

[15] Bremond, "Rationalisme et religion," 3. See especially Pl. *Apol.* 29d-30b, where Socrates points out to the Athenians that their first concern ought to consist in making the soul as virtuous as possible, virtue being the source of all other positive things.

[16] Pl. *Apol.* 29a-b, 37b.

[17] *Apol.* 40c-41d.

However, his uncertainty did not prevent our philosopher either from placing genuine human happiness in the practice of virtue, that is, in a life in accordance with divine reason, or from thinking himself to be invested "by God" with the task of bringing his fellow citizens back, by means of knowledge, to virtue and thereby to happiness.[18]   43

III

Along with the method of his master, Plato continued his ideal of perfection. But by incorporating the latter into his own system, which is a powerful synthesis of the religious, moral, and philosophical traditions of classical Greece, and by clarifying it and founding it upon a metaphysical base, he was to assure its vitality and influence.

The entire philosophical thought of Plato is dominated by the mind-matter and being-becoming dualisms. The disciple of Socrates seems to have been deeply impressed, on the one hand, by the doctrine of Heraclitus concerning the imperceptible unreality "of the world of sensory phenomena, which oscillate in the ebb and flow of becoming,"[19] and on the other hand, by the conviction of Socrates concerning the existence of the universal.[20] This last item, the true reality, "the reality in itself" [ὃ ἔστι],[21] is nothing other than "the world of the immutable Being, who has not had any beginning and will not have an end, a world from which all the phenomena of this inferior world draw that which they contain of reality. The reality itself, the totality of Ideas, does not mingle with that which becomes and perishes, but constitutes, in a way, a supreme goal toward which all who aspire to the unconditional fullness of the Being aim."[22]

"Being the immutable reality [τὸ κατὰ ταὐτὰ εἶδος ἔχον], unbegotten and imperishable [ἀγέννητον καὶ ἀνώλεθρον],"[23] the Idea is necessarily eternal.[24] One might as well say that it is divine.[25] "This is that which, first and foremost, deserves the name of God. And if a hierarchy exists among Ideas, if there is an Idea which can be esteemed the first, supreme Idea and the Aim of all, by virtue of the fact that it subordinates all the others which take it as their aim, this Idea—the Idea of the Good—because it is the Being above all else, is at the same time, the divine and the most divine. Thus climbing the ladder of being,   44

---

[18]   *Apol.* 23, 28-29. On the "task" of Socrates, see Louis, *Doctrines religieuses*, 59-95.

[19]   Rohde, *Psyché*, 482-483.

[20]   Cf. *Phaed.* 65d-e.

[21]   *Phaed.* 75d.

[22]   Rohde, *Psyché*, 483. Cf. Zeller, *Die Philosophie der Griechen,* 2:1:699-765; Gomperz, *Griechische Denker,* 320-321. See *Phaed.* 74d and 75. See also *Symp.* 210-212b, where this conception on the subject of the beautiful is developed in an admirable way.

[23]   *Tim.* 52a.

[24]   *Phaed.* 79c-e. The world of Ideas is here called τὸ καθαρόν τε καὶ ἀεὶ ὂν καὶ ἀθάνατον καὶ ὡσαύτως ἔχον.

[25]   Cf. *Phaed.* 80a-b, where τὸ θεῖον is clearly opposed to τῷ θνητῷ.

from visible appearances to invisible Ideas, and from Idea to Idea, to that which governs them as their highest reason and that which gives them their completion, the mind finally grasps the highest Being; it sees God."[26]

But according to the principle as old as Greek philosophy itself, that the like is only known by the like,[27] the νοῦς, the superior part of the soul, would not be able to see the Ideas if the soul were not "related to the divine, to the immortal, to the intelligence, to the simple, to the indissoluble, and to the immutable"[28]—in short, to the Ideas, especially to those of life.[29]

"By some misfortune met with by forgetfulness and inability," in other words, following an intellectual degeneration, the soul, a "celestial offspring,"[30] "falls to the earth,"[31] where it takes residence in an earthly body, which it moves by its strength and with which it forms what is called an animal [ζῷον].[32] Nevertheless, in its "pure" essence and according to its "real nature," it remains immaterial or spiritual[33] and "unbegotten,"[34] just like the Ideas and the soul of the world from which it is "derived."[35] If the soul is not immutable like the Ideas, it is at least "simple,"[36] "absolutely indissoluble, or practically so,"[37] "imperishable," and "immortal."[38] By virtue of its own nature, the soul is νοῦς, a pure faculty of thinking and willing;[39] instincts and passions only come to it from the body and will disappear with it.[40]

Having come from the realm of the true Being, of the Good and the Beautiful, the soul is called to return into its divine homeland, to live there "absolutely without body for all the rest of its life,"[41] joined "with beings similar" to itself, and to come to know "all that is without mixture."[42] However, only the

---

[26]   Festugière, *L'idéal religieux*, 43-44.

[27]   By the testimony of Theophrastus, Empedocles already taught: τὸ μὲν γὰρ φρονεῖν εἶναι τοῖς ὁμοίοις, τὸ δ'ἀγνοεῖν τοῖς ἀνομοίοις (*Sens.* 10:1-2). Cf. Zeller, *Die Philosophie der Griechen*, 1:2:997.

[28]   *Phaed.* 80a-b; *Resp.* 611e.

[29]   *Phaed.* 106d.

[30]   *Tim.* 90a. The essence of the soul is here called δαίμων and φυτὸν οὐκ ἔγγειον ἀλλ' οὐράνιον.

[31]   *Phaedr.* 248c; cf. 246c.

[32]   *Phaedr.* 246c.

[33]   *Resp.* 10.611c, 612a. In the first books of the *Republic* (bks. 2-5, especially 4.435c-441c) and in *Phaedr.* 246, a trichotomist conception of the soul stands out quite clearly, which would be composed of a concupiscible part [ἐπιθυμητικόν], an irascible part [θυμοειδές] and a reasonable part [λογιστικόν or νοῦς]. But in the tenth book of the *Republic*, 611b-612a, Plato seems to abandon this tripartition of the soul as incompatible with its immortality and its relationship "with the divine, the immortal, and the eternal" (611e).

[34]   *Phaedr.* 245d.

[35]   *Phileb.* 30a.

[36]   *Resp.* 10.612a: μονοειδής. Cf. *Phaed.* 80b.

[37]   *Phaed.* 80b.

[38]   *Phaedr.* 245c-d. Cf. *Phaed.* 80a-b.

[39]   *Phaedr.* 247c.

[40]   *Resp.* 10.611b-612a.

[41]   *Phaed.* 114c, 115d.

[42]   *Phaed.* 67a.

person whose soul is completely pure will achieve this supreme happiness, for "not to be pure and yet seize on that which is pure...is not permitted."[43]

But how does one achieve this purity? The soul is in the body just as in a "jail."[44] For as long a time as it is molded with the body, "that bad thing,"[45] it is troubled by it and prevented "from gaining truth and clear thought."[46] The "ancient tradition"—that of Orphism[47]—has therefore good reason to require purification [κάθαρσις]. This consists in "keeping the soul as separate as possible from the body, in getting it accustomed to being reduced to itself, to concentrating itself on itself by withdrawing from every contact with the body, to living, as much as it can both in the actual circumstances as well as in those which will follow, isolated and by itself, entirely detached from the body, as if it were out of its bonds."[48]

Then soaring upwards to its homeland, the world of Ideas, to the neighborhood of the true and the immutable, the soul "ceases to wander...and also always maintains its identity because it is in contact [ἐφαπτομένη] with things of this kind."[49] Therefore, the "flight" from here below to the height "likens one to God as far as possible."[50] It renders the soul like and thereby "dear" to God.[51] In brief, it divinizes the soul in the sense that it releases it from any obscuring and restores to its original state the divine element which is in it.

Unfortunately, few men fulfill this supreme exercise of purification. Consequently, a selecting of souls by a judgment becomes necessary in Hades, following which two categories are revealed: one, the category of souls whose "life was of a distinguished sanctity;" and the other, the category whose life was not such. The first ones are liberated from the inner regions of the earth and established "on the heights of the pure abode, on the top of the earth." Dwelling places more beautiful still are reserved for the elite of these souls, for the philosophers "purified as much as is necessary." Forever removed from corporality, they enjoy, with their equals and near the gods, a bliss without end.[52]

---

[43] *Phaed.* 67b.

[44] *Phaed.* 62b. Cf. *Phaed.* 67d; *Phaedr.* 250d; *Crat.* 400c, where Plato makes allusion to the Orphic play on words: σῶμα-σῆμα (see above, 23); *Gorg.* 493a.

[45] *Phaed.* 66b: ἕως ἄν...συμπεφυρμένη ᾖ ἡ ψυχὴ μετὰ τοιούτου κακοῦ.

[46] *Phaed.* 66a.

[47] On that which concerns the influence of Orphism on Plato, see Lagrange, *L'orphisme*, 165-175.

[48] *Phaed.* 67c-d.

[49] *Phaed.* 79c-d. Cf. A. J. Festugière, *Contemplation et vie contemplative selon Platon* (Paris, 1936), where the author points out that the Platonic θεωρία is "a kind of spiritual contact which immediately unites the knowing one with the known" (43).

[50] *Theaet.* 176b: Φυγὴ δὲ ὁμοίωσις θεῷ κατὰ τὸ δυνατόν. Cf. *Resp.* 10.613, where it is proposed as an ideal as well: ὁμοιοῦσθαι θεῷ.

[51] *Leg.* 4.716: Ὁ μὲν σώφρων ἡμῶν θεῷ φίλος, ὅμοιος γάρ. Cf. André Bremond, *La piété grecque* (Paris, 1914), 186-193.

[52] *Phaed.* 108c, 113d-114c. The "more beautiful dwelling places" seem to be the stars. Cf. *Tim.* 41d. According to *Phaedr.* 248e-249a, the perfect reward could only be attained after three incarnations separated by an interval of a thousand years.

The second class of souls includes three subdivisions. First, those who "have led an average life," in which the bad and the good are mixed; then, the souls whose faults are curable"; and finally, the group of souls "incurably" criminal.[53]
The first ones—this is "the great mass of the deceased"[54]—atone for their offenses in the Acherousian lake and because of their good acts obtain rewards proportional to the merit of each."[55] The souls of the second subdivision are "thrown down into Tartarus." They have, nonetheless, the possibility of getting out of there and purifying themselves in the lake. After expiation, which lasts at least a thousand years,[56] they are "sent forth again," like the souls of the first group, "to the animal generations."[57] The criminal souls, whose state is without remedy, "are hurled into Tartarus, from which they never again depart."[58]

What is especially striking in the Platonic synthesis is the fact that it combines, in a sufficiently homogeneous whole, mythical, religious, mystical, and rational elements. And what is more, the philosopher is quite open about it; the principle features of his doctrine on the soul are derived from the "ancient tradition," on conceptions that became widespread through the mysteries, and Orphism in particular.[59] The difference between the body and the soul, the origin of the latter, its imprisonment in the body following a fall, its immortality, the obligation for "catharsis," the judgment of the parted souls, and the metempsychosis—all these ideas, characteristic of Orphism and of the mysteries, are found again in Plato. However, they are no more in the state of beliefs and vague aspirations; rather, they are organized into a philosophical system.

Plato even goes so far as to make use of the terminology of the mysteries. But this, it seems, is a simple literary and educational stratagem. Indeed, deep down in his heart the philosopher despises the secret cults for their practices and unrefined expectations.[60] If he nevertheless speaks their language, it is to embellish his discourse and make it better understood,[61] and especially to cause more surely the ruin of them and of their conceptions from the inside by a total transposition of their essential notions.

[53]   *Phaed.* 113d-e. Cf. *Gorg.* 525c.
[54]   *Phaed.* 113a.
[55]   *Phaed.* 113d-e.
[56]   *Phaedr.* 249a-b. Cf. *Resp.* 10.615a.
[57]   *Phaed.* 113a.
[58]   *Phaed.* 113a. Cf. *Gorg.* 525c; *Resp.* 10.615c-616a. According to *Phaedr.* 249b, on the contrary, all the guilty souls can, after expiation, "choose a second life." On the eschatology of Plato, see Jean Ithurriague, *La croyance de Platon a l'immortalité et la survie de l'âme humaine* (Paris, 1931), 77-99.
[59]   Cf. Gernet and Boulanger, *Le génie grec,* 387-388.
[60]   Plato bans the mysteries from his ideal republic as the sources of disorder and of superstition. Cf. *Leg.* 9.909d-910.
[61]   According to Auguste Diès, *Autour de Platon* (Paris, 1927), 545, Plato "wishes...to make the most possible descend from intelligence and reason in this mythology, which alone can represent to the child which is in us, to the imagination enamored with symbols and idols, the abstract and suprasensitive truth." See also Ithurriague, *La croyance de Platon,* 11-18.

Thus, just like the mysteries, Plato speaks of "initiates"; but for him the true mystae, or "bacchants," are those who are devoted to philosophy.[62] Likewise, "catharsis," a completely ritualistic and magical purification, changes with the philosopher into liberation of the soul, into emancipation of the mind from the domination of the senses, in brief, into intellectual and moral purification.[63] The mystical journey of initiation which ends in sight is transformed into the dialectical ascension of the νοῦς toward God. Finally, deification, which in the secret cults "never really risked signifying much more than the 'banquet of the saints' and 'the eternal exhiliration' scoffed at in the Republic,"[64] this outward divinization by assumption, becomes in Plato an inner assimilation of the soul to God, owing to the vision of the divine Reality.[65]

By thus clarifying and spiritualizing the still vague and mythical traditional elements, and by integrating them into his system, Plato, of incomparable genius, succeeded in summarizing the most profound intuitions and lofty aspirations of the Greek soul. The divinization that he proposes as the aim of human activity is unquestionably the most sublime ideal ever to have been conceived of outside of Christianity. 49

In spite of its undeniable grandeur, the Platonic conception of θεοποίησις involves some grave deficiencies. Intellectualistic to excess, it does not sufficiently take account of the entire human being, of the fundamental unity of a human being's nature,[66] and in actual practice excludes the mass of the humble from deification. Based on a much too abstract idea of divinity and on an exaggerated optimism concerning the strengths of the νοῦς, which too often appears as the unique agent of salvation, Platonic deification reserves only a rather diminished role for divine assistance.[67]

Despite these deficiencies, the Platonic ideal will exercise a powerful influence on the subsequent conceptions of salvation, including those of the fathers. In particular, the connection which Plato "established between the ideas of being, of the divine, and of immortality," just as the synonymy that he

---

[62] *Phaed.* 69c-d.

[63] Moral purification is expressly mentioned in the *Symposium,* 210-212c. It appears there as a quasi-necessary consequence of intellectual purification: whoever has succeeded in seeing the divine and simple Beauty [τὸ θεῖον καλὸν...μονοειδές] can no longer lead a bad life, but "brings forth true virtue."

[64] Diès, *Autour de Platon,* 448.

[65] On all these points, Hermetism is manifestly dependent on Platonic thought, although the influence of the latter was perhaps not direct. Cf. Reitzenstein, *Poimandres,* 304-308; Festugière, *L'idéal religieux,* 129.

[66] Platonic anthropology is very wrong in breaking up the unity of the human being. On this error and its grave consequences, see Marcel de Corte, "Anthropologie platonicienne et aristotélicienne," *Études carmélitaines,* fascicle entitled, "L'Esprit et la vie," 23rd Year (April 1938), 59-73.

[67] Cf. Festugière, *Contemplation,* 52-53; Bremond, "Rationalisme et religion," 38-43. This author writes here, concerning the exposition of Fr. Festugière, "some compensatory reservations."

saw between divine assimilation or deification, on the one hand, and salvation or bliss, on the other, will be henceforth vital for theological speculation.[68]

Finally, Platonic contemplation, which ascends toward the Beautiful, which is identical to the Good, in a surge of benevolent love increasing all the way to ecstasy, will supply to Christian mysticism, through Plotinus, its terminology and intellectual framework.

IV

Nonetheless, the immediate impression produced by the philosophy of Plato does not seem to have been very deep nor very lasting. From the second half of the fourth century, in fact, the Greek mind turns increasingly toward a moderate rationalism not very favorable to mysticism. The Platonic school itself was unable to escape this new orientation, which is manifested in a particularly striking fashion in the philosophical evolution of the greatest of Plato's disciples.

In the dialogues of his youth, unfortunately lost, notably in his "Eudemus" or "On the Soul," Aristotle still appears to be inspired by the doctrine of his master.[69] Early on he must have abandoned it in order to work out an anthropology in harmony with his own sense of mystery.

Already the point of view which the two thinkers take is very different. Whereas Plato sets himself in the superterrestrial world of ideas, whence he considers things of earth and where he places true human happiness, more precisely, that of the human νοῦς, Aristotle starts from the real world and assigns to the whole human being an end which must be achieved in this very life. "Among the Greek thinkers who are heirs of Socratic wisdom," the Stagirite is "the least Socratic in the sense that he is the least preoccupied with the salvation of the soul. The problem of happiness, which is that of all the Schoolmen after him, is not primary and predominating in his doctrine."[70]

However, this profound divergence did not prevent the disciple from retaining the ethical idealism of the master as a precious inheritance. In fact, Aristotle also sees happiness [εὐδαιμονία] in perfection. But far from conceiving perfection as the acquisition of a good thing superior to man, the philosopher places it within "an activity in accordance with the supreme virtue," that is to say, in accordance with the virtue "of the best part [τοῦ ἀρίστου] of ourselves," namely, the νοῦς, "the most divine in us."[71] This is the "contemplative" activity [θεωρητική] which focuses on "the good and divine things," and which can be done with the maximum of continuity and finds in itself its end as well as its

---

[68]   Festugière, *Contemplation*, 39. Cf. Bremond, "Rationalisme et religion," 38; Festugière, *Contemplation*, in particular the "Conclusion," 449-457.

[69]   Cf. W. D. Ross, *Aristotle* (Paris, 1930), 18; Rohde, *Psyché*, 506.

[70]   Bremond, "Rationalisme et religion," 43.

[71]   *Eth. nic.* 10.7 (1177a:12-17).

most pure and most stable enjoyment.[72] A life sufficiently long in contempla- 51
tion, this is "the perfect human happiness."[73]

But "such a life exceeds the human nature [κρείττων ἢ κατ' ἄνθρωπον]; individuals will not be able to live it as such, but they will insofar as they have in themselves a divine element [θεῖόν τι]....If then, compared to the human being, the νοῦς is something divine, the life according to the latter is also divine compared with the human life. And it is not necessary to follow those who say that being human beings and mortal we ought to think only about human and mortal things; we ought, on the contrary, to gain immortality as much as is possible and to do everything to live in conformity with what is better in us."[74]

Insofar as it involves contemplation, human happiness is actually "a certain assimilation" [ὁμοίωμά τι] to the divine bliss itself, which can consist only in a "contemplative activity."[75] This means that God, as "the unchanging Prime Mover,"[76] who "moves as an object of love,"[77] as "the unbegotten First Princi-ple"[78] and pure Action,[79] is first both pure intelligence and purely intelligible, which comes down to saying that He is "the subsisting intellection of the sub-sisting sovereign good,"[80] "the thought from His own thought."[81] Also, "pro-vided that the gods take some care of human affairs, which seems to be the case," the wise person who lives a life of the νοῦς will be "the person most loved by the gods" [θεοφιλέστατος].[82]

However, the beatifying contemplation which divinity enjoys eternally 52
is only realizable for the elite of the wise "from time to time" [ποτέ][83] and for "a short duration."[84] Moreover, the combination of a whole series of favorable circumstances is necessary, in particular, health, fortune, and inner peace.[85]

---

[72] *Eth. nic.* 10.7 (1177a:12-1177b:6).

[73] *Eth. nic.* 10.7 (1177b:24-25).

[74] *Eth. nic.* 10.7 (1177b:26-34).

[75] *Eth. nic.* 10.8 (1178b:20-32). On the Aristotelian conception of happiness, see Ross, *Aristotle*, 266-269, 323-325; M. Wittmann, *Die Ethik des Aristoteles* (Ratisbonne, 1920), 7-42, 308-322.

[76] *Phys.* 8.6 (258b:11-12): τὸ πρώτως κινοῦν ἀκίνητον.

[77] *Metaph.* 12.a.7 (1072b:3): κινεῖ ὡς ἐρώμενον.

[78] *Metaph.* 3.b.4 (999b:7-8): τὸ ἔσχατον ἀγέννητον.

[79] *Metaph.* 12.a.6 (1071b:19-20): δεῖ ἄρα εἶναι ἀρχὴν τοιαύτην ἧς ἡ οὐσία ἐνέργεια. Cf. 1072b:8: ἐνεργείᾳ ὄν.

[80] *Metaph.* 12.a.7 (1072b:18-19): ἡ δὲ νόησις ἡ καθ' αὑτὴν τοῦ καθ' αὑτὸ ἀρίστου.

[81] *Metaph.* 12.a.9 (1074b:33-35). On the Aristotelian conception of the divine essence, see Alfred Boehm, *Die Gottesidee bei Aristoteles auf ihren religiösen Charakter untersucht* (Strasbourg, 1914), 88-103.

[82] *Eth. Nic.* 10.9 (1179a:22-32).

[83] *Metaph.* 12.a.7 (1072b:25).

[84] *Metaph.* 12.a.7 (1072b:15): μικρὸν χρόνον.

[85] *Eth. Nic.* 1:8 (1099b:2-8); 10.9 (1178b:33-1179a:9).

Being hardly accessible during this existence, will the happiness proposed by Aristotle at least be reached in an afterlife? Some have definitely, but wrongly, maintained that such would have been the thought of the philosopher.[86]

Assuredly, according to the Stagirite, something of the person survives; but this is the active principle of intellection that Alexander of Aphrodisias will call the active intellect [νοῦς ποιητικός],[87] in contrast to the passive intellect [νοῦς παθητικός]. Whereas the latter is "perishable" [φθαρτός], the active intellect is "immortal and eternal."[88] Now "this impersonal νοῦς, this νοῦς shared by all the νόοι παθητικοί, this νοῦς as a ray of light which allows our mirror to capture the intelligible that the sensory conceals, this νοῦς which—whatever it may be to the just—can very well last forever, is not ours indefinitely."[89] In brief, Aristotle denies the personal immortality of the soul. At death, the soul "as the seat of destiny" disappears.[90] The best evidence of this is the fact that the Aristotelian ethic lacks perspective on a superterrestrial and eternal life; the supreme ideal that it proposes for human activity, however elevated it may be, is of this world.[91]

All in all, Aristotle has taken up again the thought of Plato, whereby true happiness for humankind consists in their assimilation to God, in their divinization. What has changed are only the conditions of this assimilation. But in the system of Aristotle, with his negation of personal immortality, this supreme happiness is inaccessible to humankind in actual practice.

Consequently, it is no surprise that subsequent thinkers turned away from so difficult and cold an ideal in order to try to find easier and more appealing formulas for happiness.

[86]   This is the opinion of Saint Thomas and nearly of his entire school. Quite recently, the Thomist interpretation has found an ardent defender in the person of Marcel de Corte, *La doctrine d'intelligence chez Aristote* (Paris, 1934). Yet it does not seem that the exegesis of this author has seriously weakened the conception of Zeller and of Jaeger, which we have adopted. Cf. G. Fritz, in *RevScRel* 17(1937): 336-343.

[87]   Cf. Rohde, *Psyché*, 518, note.

[88]   *De an.* 3.6 (430a:17-25).

[89]   Festugière, *L'idéal religieux*, 57.

[90]   É. Bréhier, *Histoire de la philosophie* (Paris, 1927), 1:458.

[91]   Cf. Festugière, *L'idéal religieux*, 56-57.

CHAPTER FIVE

THE PHILOSOPHY OF THE HELLENISTIC ERA

With Alexander, the pupil of Aristotle, a new period of Greek history begins. From the philosophical viewpoint, this era, called Hellenistic, which witnesses the decline of the Greek city and with it so many traditional values, is initially dominated by skepticism. Assuredly, philosophy increasingly becomes the "religion of the elite." But it is a philosophy which turns away from speculation and the mystical in order to move toward scientific research, which above all means a wisdom from life. And so, without overtly renouncing the Platonic ideal of assimilation to divinity, Epicureanism and Stoicism transform it into a more or less trivial eudemonism. Nevertheless, with Neopythagorism, the mysticism of divinization begins to get even, reaching its culmination in Plotinism.

I

Epicureanism claims to be a rational method of happiness. Varying the Platonic theme in his way, Epicurus proclaims that happiness consists in "living as a god among human beings."[1]

In the Epicurean system, which is based on the atomism of Democritus, the gods, as "immortal and blessed beings,"[2] though made of atoms like us, but of finer ones,[3] find their bliss in ataraxia, or the exemption from trouble. In fact, they look after neither the world nor men.[4]

In order to become happy like them, individuals must thus aim, in everything they do, "at removing suffering and trouble."[5] With this goal in view, the wise must apply themselves above all to eliminate from their lives empty hopes and fears. In the first place, they will free themselves from the fear of death, which, as "loss of all sensitivity, is nothing for us."[6] And "the knowledge of this truth will render us capable of enjoying this mortal life by suppressing the prospect of an infinite duration and removing from us the desire for immortality."[7] To attain to "the achievement of the happy life," philosophers have only to gain

---

[1] Epicur. *Ad. Menoec.* (in H. Usener, *Epicuren* [Leipzig, 1887], 68, lines 7-8): ζήσεις ὡς θεὸς ἐν ἀνθρώποις.

[2] *Ad. Menoec.* (59, ll. 16-17). Cf. *Ad. Herod* (29:3-4); *Rat. sent.* 1 (71).

[3] Cf. Usener, *Epicuren*, 238-240.

[4] *Rat. sent.* 1 (71).

[5] *Ad. Menoec.* (62, ll. 16-17).

[6] *Ad. Menoec.* (60, ll. 15-17). Cf. *Rat. sent.* 2 (71).

[7] *Ad. Menoec.* (60, ll. 17-20).

"an exact knowledge [ἀπλανὴς θεωρία] of desires, since they are capable of relating every preference and dislike to the health of the body and the ataraxia of the soul."[8]

To us this is very far from that ὁμοίωσις τῷ θεῷ that Plato and Aristotle advocated. But while reducing it to the level of a vulgar hedonism, Epicurus bears witness to the persistence of that ideal which places the happiness of humankind in their assimilation to God.

II

The same principle is at the root of the Stoic moral ethic. This is because Stoicism, the philosophy par excellence of the Hellenistic world, also wants to be a school of wisdom and true happiness.

As a materialistic pantheism which stemmed from the physics of Heraclitus, the doctrine of the Stoa sees the principle of the universe in "primordial matter, the ethereal fire, the blowing of fire which keeps or changes and, under a thousand figures, constitutes the world." Being given a spiritual dimension increasingly in Stoic speculation, this primordial fire becomes "the reason, the law…, the divinity" of the cosmos, the logos which "acts as 'relationship' [σχέσις] in inorganic matter, as 'nature' [φύσις] in plants, as 'soul devoid of reason' [ἄλογος ψυχή] in the other living beings, as reasoning and thinking soul [ψυχὴ λόγον ἔχουσα καὶ διάνοιαν] in the human being."[9]

The human soul is thus a fragment, an emanation of divinity; it is "divine like all that is in the world, but more purely than the rest."[10] This is what the poet Aratus wants to express in the line quoted by Saint Paul (Acts 17:28): τοῦ γὰρ καὶ γένος ἐσμέν.[11] "To become aware of our relationship with the divine λόγος, to remain attentive to the Spirit who dwells in us is simply, for the philosopher, to understand the unity of the system and how every fragment of matter, as well as every psychological movement, desire, volition, and thought, are linked to the primordial matter."[12]

The result of this relationship between the individual and divinity is that human duty and happiness consist in the absolute submission to universal reason; to follow the dictates of the divine order, "to live according to nature,"[13] "to follow the gods,"[14]—"this is to be wise, this is to be happy."[15] To succeed in it

---

[8] *Ad. Menoec.* (62, ll. 12-15).

[9] Rohde, *Psyché*, 518-519. Heraclitus is the father of the idea of the logos appointed to destiny as we know it.

[10] Rohde, *Psyché*, 519. Cf. Zeller, *Die Philosophie der Griechen* (4th ed.), 3:1:203-204.

[11] Arat. *Phaen.* 5.5. Cf. Cleanthes, *Hymn to Zeus*, in H. von Arnim, *Stoicorum veterum fragmenta* (Leipzig, 1903-1905), 1:537:121, line 37: ἐκ σοῦ [i.e., Διὸς] γὰρ γένος εἶσ' ἤχου μίμημα λαχόντες.

[12] Festugière, *Contemplation*, 71.

[13] Diog. Laert. 8.88: τὸ ἀκολούθως τῇ φύσει ζῆν. Quoted in Zeller, *Die Philosophie der Griechen*, 3:1:214.

[14] Epictetus, *Diatr.*, 1.12.5: ἔπεσθαι θεοῖς. Quoted in Rohde, *Psyché*, 521.

[15] Cleanth. *Hymn to Zeus* (Arnim, *Stoicorum veterum fragmenta*, 1: 537:122, lines 19-20).

to the point of rising above all the activities of the body and the soul, of settling in an imperturbable self-control, the ἀπάθεια, constitutes the height of virtue and of happiness.[16] Having reached this summit, the philosophers [σπουδαῖοι] "are truly divine, having, as it were, a god in them."[17]

In sound logic, the Stoic doctors would have to admit that upon the death of the individual the soul returns into the divine fire of which it is only an emanation. But a good number among them dream of an afterlife for the separated soul, with appropriate recompense, which would last until the moment of the universal conflagration.[18] The numerous supporters of the Portico, who endeavored to give to their system a shade of religious mysticism, were scarcely more consistent with themselves.[19]

Though just as earthly and utilitarian as that of Epicurus, the Stoic ideal is more virile and lofty. It appears, indeed, as the crowning of a great effort, the goal of which is the establishment, by an exact knowledge of the laws of the universe, of the reign of virtue, of the divine. Consequently, one realizes that many fathers reserved a choice place for the Stoic ἀπάθεια in their moral doctrines.

III

The Stoic moralists finished off their model of the wise individual by themselves uncovering a major flaw: that of being unrealizable in actual practice.[20] Also, toward the beginning of the first century before Jesus Christ, as the disappointment caused by the current moral standards became increasingly accentuated, many minds felt led to acknowledge that help from on high was indispensable for realizing the ethical ideal. This very pronounced change of mind in favor of the religion which characterizes the final period of Greek philosophy was to such a degree that one could call it "the period of religious metaphysics."[21] However great the influence of the eastern religions on this new religious philosophy, Platonism nevertheless remains the root of it.

Thus Neopythagorism is in substance only a transposition of Platonic metaphysics complicated by a fantastic arithmology.[22]

By emphasizing the opposition between the world of the divine and the sphere of that which changes, this evolution of ideas returns to dualism, and thus well conveys the inner confusion of minds disgusted with sensory pleasures and thirsting for purification, for salvation, for divinization by personal union with God.

---

[16] Cf. Arnim, *Stoicorum veterum fragmenta*, 3:449; Zeller, *Die Philosophie der Griechen*, 3:1:239-240.

[17] Diog. Laert. 7:119 (Arnim, *Stoicorum veterum fragmenta*, 3:606).

[18] Cf. Gernet and Boulanger, *Le génie grec*, 495-496; Zeller, *Die Philosophie der Griechen*, 3:1:205-206; G. Krafta and H. Eibl, *Der Ausklang der antiken Philosophie* (Munich, 1928), 103-107.

[19] Cf. Bremond, *La piété grecque*, 49-53.

[20] Cf. Festugière, *Contemplation*, 69.

[21] W. Windelband and E. Rothacker, *Lehrbuch der Geschichte der Philosophie* (Tübingen, 1921), 177.

[22] Cf. É. Bréhier, *Histoire de la philosophie*, 1:440-441.

But how to attain to God, unless by the traditional means of asceticism, which alone is capable of purifying the soul, the prisoner of the body, from the stains of matter? It is due to the soul, indeed, that "there is a certain relationship [ξυγγένεια] of humankind with God, because of which they alone among living things are acquainted with the gods and think about [φιλοσοφεῖ] their own nature, as well as about the means of participating in the divine....Their very form [εἶδος] resembles God....Virtues come to them from God [θεόθεν], and those who receive them are like God and even divine [ἀγχιθέους τε εἶναι καὶ θείους]."[23]

This is what would have happened to the famous prophet and preacher of the Neopythagorean sect, Apollonius of Tyana; in order to be entirely purified, he would have obtained divinization and would have assured himself of blessed immortality.[24]

Immortality, in general, is not proven; it is necessary to believe in it. Besides, Neopythagorism as a whole "is less reasoning than faith." It is a religious mysticism with a very vague doctrinal foundation. It is so vague that it is difficult to say if the supreme God, distinct from the world but unknowable, is for the Neopythagoreans a personal being or simply "the highest region of the universe, whether the sun or the thin air." We have the same impression concerning the immortality of the soul: we do not know if our mystics conceived of it as a personal afterlife or as the return of the soul to the divine element, of which it is an emanation.[25]

All these points will be made clear in the last great system which the Greek genius produced and for which Neopythagorism prepared the way.

IV

"The most logical and the most accomplished"[26] of the philosophical systems of antiquity, Neoplatonism appears as a synthesis, which is realized in the superior unity of religious principle, of the main elements of Greek and Hellenistic philosophy as well as of mystical aspirations of eastern origin. The One, the supreme God, being both the first principle and the final goal of all things, comprises the heart of the Neoplatonic vision of the world. The return, or the ascension, of the soul to the One is the main theme of Neoplatonism.[27] It is thus with good reason that Neoplatonism has been described as religious philosophy.

[23]   Philostr. *Vit. Apoll.* 8.7; in F. C. Conybeare, *Philostratus* (London, 1912), 2:312.

[24]   On "the actual facial appearance of this Apollonius," see de Labriolle, *La réaction païenne*, 175-177. Cf. Zeller, *Die Philosophie der Griechen* (4th ed.), 3:2:165-175; Mario Meunier, *Apollonius de Tyane ou le séjour d'un dieu parmi les hommes* (Paris, 1936).

[25]   Cf. Festugière, *Contemplation*, 73-85. The quotations which precede are borrowed from this author.

[26]   Windelband and Rothacker, *Lehrbuch*, 179.

[27]   É. Bréhier, *La philosophie de Plotin* (Paris, 1928), 23, has well emphasized the close connection of these two themes in the thought of Plotinus: "To discover the principle of things, which is the goal of philosophical research, is at the same time, for Plotinus, the 'end of the journey,' that is to say, the fulfillment of destiny." According to a long-standing idea, "all things come out of the One and return back into him." See H. Diels, *Doxographi Graeci* (Berlin, 1879), 179.

The *Enneads* of Plotinus are the charter of Neoplatonism. The true founder and greatest representative of that school, "Plotinus was called to a high mission; in him the spirit of Hellenism was to show to the world, for the final time, all its beauty, profoundness, and grandeur."[28] In him, who "in a sense is the most religious of philosophers,...Hellenic wisdom and reason speak their final word, and insure to humankind, apart from all supernatural assistance, and by the sole strength of their mind, the liberation of the soul and the most complete divine assimilation which could well be imagined."[29]

Judging from the *Enneads*[30]—the obscurity of which is proverbial—two parts can be distinguished in the philosophy of Plotinus. The first and more theoretical deals with the origin of the soul and of its descent into the body; thus, the first part prepares for the second, which is of a practical nature and points out the way that brings the soul back to the sovereign Good.

The universe, conceived of as eternal,[31] is organized along hierarchical lines into two very different worlds: the intelligible world and the sensory world. At the top of this whole hierarchy sits enthroned the One, the Being, the Origin, the first or sovereign Good, the King of all things, God. He is even "beyond being, also beyond action and beyond the νοῦς and thought"[32]: the Indeterminable by surplus of reality.[33]

The first Being, which is also the "first Living One,"[34] "could not remain in himself as if he were jealous of himself or powerless, since he is the power of all things;...but it is necessary that something come out from him."[35] While

---

[28] Othon Kiefer, *Plotin, Enneaden* (2 vols.; Leipzig, 1905), 1:15. Cf. page 20: "In this man a nostalgia for divinity was burning, such as one finds in no other philosopher of antiquity."

[29] Bremond, *La piété grecque*, 54.

[30] We know that Plotinus never published. Of the editions of his works, owed to his disciples, only that of Porphyry has come to us as a whole. The six *Enneades*, literally "novenas," i.e., "groups of nine treatises," the arbitrary division due to Porphyry, far from being a systematic exposition, appear rather as lectures, each of which is devoted to the study of one question. What makes the cohesion of it is the vision of the universe which controls the entire work. Cf. Bréhier, *La philosophie de Plotin*, 9-22.

[31] Cf. 3.7.6: ὥστε μηδὲ τὸν κόσμον ἀρχήν τινα χρονικὴν εἰληφέναι. We quote the *Enneades* according to the edition of É. Bréhier, *Plotin, Ennéades* (Collection des Universités de France; Paris, 1924-1931), for the first five, the only ones having appeared up to the present, and according to the edition of R. Volkmann, *Plotini Enneades*, vol. 2, (Leipzig, 1884), for the last four. The first numeral indicates the ennead, the second, the treatise; the third numeral indicates the chapter, the fourth, the line.

[32] 1.7.1.19-20: ἐπέκεινα οὐσίας. ἐπέκεινα καὶ ἐνεργείας καὶ ἐπέκεινα νοῦ καὶ νοήσεως. Cf. 5.4-5.

[33] 6.9.3. Cf. 5.4.1.

[34] 4.7.9.14-15.

[35] 5.4.1.34-38. According to Plotinus, the One begets, of necessity. "The Neoplatonic god always implies the image of this grand source of lasting and active life that Plotinus had the boldness to evoke, before Bergson idealized it as a vital surge." Éd. Krakowski, *Plotin et le paganisme religieux* (Paris, 1933), 287.

61   remaining unchanging, he thus engenders "an imitation and image" [μίμημα καὶ εἴδωλον] of himself,[36] namely, the Νοῦς, who is both intelligence and intelligible object [νοητόν].[37] Consequently, the Νοῦς is the "child" [παῖδα] of the Good,[38] a "second God" [θεὸς δεύτερος].[39]

From the Νοῦς proceeds the immaterial substance of the "universal soul," which "produces all the animals by breathing life into them."[40] Indeed, without dividing itself into parts, the universal soul spreads out and diversifies into the individual souls, which are the image of it insofar as, by illumination, they give the cosmos form in its details, as the universal soul gives it form in its whole. Being the same nature as the universal soul and not losing its union with it, the human soul is "a divine being [θεῖον],...the last god [θεὸς οὖσα ὁ ὕστερος]."[41] Nonetheless, the particular souls are distinguished from one another by their greater or lesser perfection, which depends on their proximity to the intelligible world.[42]

In that way, "the soul is...intermediary between the intelligible world and the sensory world, touching upon the first because, proceeding from it, it goes back to it in order to contemplate it eternally; and touching upon the second, because it arranges and organizes it."[43] As long as it remains docile in its
62   action, the sensory world is good and beautiful. But in reality, instead of unity and harmony, chaos and struggle, which entail becoming and perishing, reign there. This is because the bodies have matter for *substratum*, and *substratum* is "an unlimited and shapeless thing in itself,"[44] "complete indigence,"[45] the "first evil and evil in itself."[46] "If besides this evil there are bad things, this is either because they are mixed with evil, or because they tend toward evil or do evil."[47]

---

[36]   5.4.2.4-27.

[37]   5.4.2.

[38]   3.8.11.32-38.

[39]   5.5.3.3-4. In this third chapter, "very much marked with the religiosity of the Hellenistic mysteries," Plotinus compares the degrees of the hierarchy of beings with the increasingly sacred objects which appeared in the ritualistic processions. Cf. Bréhier, *Plotin*, 5:85. On the theodicy and divine hypostases of Plotinus, see also Jacques Barion, *Plotin und Augustinus* (Berlin, 1935), 53-58, 65-86, 89-98.

[40]   5.1.2.1-2. Cf. 5.1.7.36-41.

[41]   4.8.5.24-27.

[42]   4.4-6. Cf. 5.2.1 and 5.1.7.48, where it is said that "the divine things [τὰ θεῖα] settle on the soul."

[43]   Bréhier, *Histoire de la philosophie*, 1:459. Cf. Zeller, *Die Philosophie der Griechen* (4th ed.), 3:2:558-598. For Plotinus, souls are basically cosmic forces.

[44]   1.8.3.30-34.

[45]   3.5.9.50.

[46]   1.8.3.38-40. The problem of the first matter, purely metaphysical for Aristotle, becomes a problem of religious philosophy for Plotinus. Cf. R. Jolivet, *Essai sur les rapports entre la pensée grecque et la pensée chrétienne* (Paris, 1931), 102-138. R. Arnou, *Le désir de Dieu dans la philosophie de Plotin* (Paris, n.d. [1921]), 64-66.

[47]   1.8.3.33-34.

The particular soul, which, without leaving the intelligible world through its superior part, enters into a human body in order to arrange and illuminate it, could "remain entirely in the heights" [ἐν τῷ ἄνω],[48] that is, exclusively occupied with the contemplation of intelligible beings. But it is turned away from this vision by matter, by the necessities of the bodily life, which enslave it to the changes of the sensory world.[49] This is what Plotinus calls the "descent" [κάθοδος] of the soul.[50]

Consequently, a return to the superior world, which is the "homeland" of souls,[51] in other words, a "conversion" [ἐπιστροφή],[52] is essential. This conversion is possible because of the freedom which humankind enjoys.[53]

To show "the skill, the method, and the practice which lead where it is necessary to go," namely, "to the Good and to the first Principle,"[54] which is also "the end" of all things[55]—such is the goal and the contents of the practical philosophy of Plotinus. And the ascension of the soul toward God is made in two stages: purification [κάθαρσις] and union.

At face value, the soul, or rather its inferior part which "is in sympathy with the body and judges in agreement with it,"[56] is liberated from the sensory world. To that end, it must gather its thoughts, turn toward itself, toward the image, the mark of the Νοῦς and of the One whom it bears in itself.[57] This assumes that, by the practice of virtue, "the soul separates from the body," and becomes "absolutely impassive" [πάντως ἀπαθῶς ἔχουσα] and "pure" of all passions, no longer letting itself go toward the disorderly enticements of the flesh.[58]

Nevertheless, the individual's effort must not only aim at "being without fault [ἔξω ἁμαρτίας] but at being god [θεὸν εἶναι]."[59] Now, it is precisely "in

63

---

[48] 4.3.17.28-31.
[49] 4.3.12-18. In these chapters, the distancing of the soul from the intelligible world appears as a natural consequence of its incorporation. Further along, in the same *Ennead*, treatise 8, chapter 4, this same distancing is presented as a voluntary desertion, which consists in the love of the soul for the inferior world. But this is not the final thought of Plotinus. His hesitation is perhaps explained by the influence of the Platonic conception concerning the fall of the soul, from which he had not succeeded in wholly freeing himself. Cf. Bréhier, *Plotin*, 4:213-214; Arnou, *Le désir de Dieu*, 39; Jolivet, *Essai*, 131.
[50] 4.8.5.2.
[51] 5.9.1.16-22. In this passage, as elsewhere also, Plotinus makes allusion to Ulysses, whose return to Ithaca symbolizes for him the ascension to the divine life. Cf. 1.6.8 (below, 53-54).
[52] 1.2.4.16-18.
[53] See especially 3.3.4, where, contrary to Stoicism and astrology, Plotinus defends the existence in humankind of "a free principle." But some other expositions, e.g. 4.8.5, seem to show that he conceives of this liberty as a kind of spontaneity compatible with determinism. *Cf.* Jolivet, *Essai*, 134-138; Zeller, *Die Philosophie der Griechen* (4th ed.), 3:2:640-642.
[54] 1.3.1.2-3.
[55] Cf. 3.8.7; 6.7.25-26; 9.9. All things tend toward the Good; this is the universal eros, "the desire of God."
[56] 1.3.3.11-13.
[57] 6.9.7. Cf. 1.2.6; 1.6.9.7: Ἄναγε ἐπὶ σαυτόν; 5.5.5.
[58] 1.2.5.1-25. An impressive description of purification. It should be noted that according to Plotinus catharsis does not change the soul inwardly, the latter not being able to lose its natural purity or its natural perfection (cf. 3.6.5.14-20); at the very most it liberates it from its propensity toward the sensory.
[59] 1.2.6.2-3.

the flight from this world that Plotinus makes the likeness with God consist," this flight to the dear "homeland, of which we are natives and where the Father stays."[60] This means that once "released from the body" and exclusively "governed by reason and intelligence," the soul "makes use of the νοῦς [νοεῖ] and is thus without passion [ἀπαθής]. It is a state which can be called, in all truth, likeness with God [ὁμοίωσιν πρὸς θεόν], for the divine being is pure and his action [ἐνέργεια] equally so."[61] And so is the soul "which has become νοῦς."[62] Having reached this peak, the individual "is purely and simply a god, one of those gods who come after the First."[63]

Catharsis is therefore a real divinization. By eliminating impure elements from the soul, it gives back to the soul its primitive divine beauty, just as the work of the sculptor brings a beautiful statue out of marble.[64]

However precious the result thus obtained through purification may be, the completion of the ascension is still not necessarily reached. The second step, that of union, remains to be completed. In actual fact, not all can claim it. Only "the philosopher, the friend of the muses [μουσικός], and the lover [ἐρωτικός]" are capable of it.[65]

Once detached from sensory things and fixed in the intelligible world, and guided by superior dialectic, the soul of these privileged ones ascends toward the first Principle and the absolute One, who is "beautiful in himself."[66] The inner eye, sufficiently cleared and prepared by purification—"for, in order to contemplate, it is necessary that the eye be similar to and like [συγγενὲς καὶ ὅμοιον] the object seen"[67]—"suddenly senses the light," which comes from the One and which is the One. Thus "illuminated, the soul holds that which it cherishes," by virtue of an "intellectual contact" [νοερῶς ἐφάψασθαι]. "Such is the true end of the soul—the contact [ἐφάψασθαι] with this light, that is, the vision [θεάσασθαι] which the soul has, not by means of another light but by means of the very light which procures the vision for it."[68] This means that by its purification the soul finds itself "reduced to that trace of the One which constitutes its most intimate and lofty part, to that likeness which is in it and which it is. Then is the soul the pure likeness of God and brought into the presence of

---

[60]   1.6.8.21. Here the especially negative character of Plotinian ethics clearly appears. The distance of the sensory world is its essential element, since it has the conversion to the intelligible as a necessary consequence. Cf. Zeller, *Die Philosophie der Griechen* (4th ed.), 3:2:653-656.

[61]   1.2.3.15-22.

[62]   6.7.35 (ed. Volkmann 2:468, line 4). Cf. 4.4.2.24-32.

[63]   1.2.6.6-7: θεὸς μόνον· θεὸς δὲ τῶν ἑπομένων τῷ πρώτῳ.

[64]   Cf. 1.6.9.7-15.

[65]   1.3.1.9-10. Cf. 5.9.2.

[66]   5.9.2. This chapter is a transposition of the "ascension" described by Plato in the *Symposium*, 211c.

[67]   1.6.9.29-30. One recognizes here the ancient principle of the knowledge of the like by the like. Cf. above, 40.

[68]   5.3.17.28-35. For Plotinus, the luminous sensation is produced without intermediary by a contact of outer light with light supposedly interior to the eye. See Bréhier, *La philosophie de Plotin*, 162.

God, for at that time there is nothing more that separates them—according to the principle that incorporeals are separated only by their differences and that they are joined as soon as they are alike; the soul is as if absorbed by the One, and submerged and lost in the infinite vastness of his presence."[69]

This is the perfect union with God. It is less a "contemplation" [θέαμα] than "an ecstasy [ἔκστασις], a simplification [ἅπλωσις], a gift of itself, an impulse toward contact [ἔφεσις πρὸς ἀφήν], a rest [στάσις], and a dream of harmony, similar to the vision in the temple."[70] It is also and especially a state of ineffable bliss, comparable only to intoxication [μέθη] and the folly of love. Thrilled beside themselves to the point of losing thought and consciousness, without however being wiped out,[71] and united with God in such a way that "there is no longer anything between them, so that they are no longer two but that the two are one [ἓν ἄμφω],"[72] those who have reached the completion of the ascension "become god, or rather, are such already" [θεὸν γενόμενον, μᾶλλον δὲ ὄντα].[73]

Unfortunately, the ecstatic union, which divinizes as far as possible, in order to be a strenuous tension, could not last, as long as the individual "has not yet completely come out,"[74] namely, has not been delivered from the body. For a person is inevitably "again weighed down"[75] by sensory things, and then the divine light which was within is "somewhat faded."[76] This is a disappointing experience which Plotinus, often favored by ecstasy,[77] must have had himself.

"But a time will come when there will be the continuation of the vision [θέας] for the one who is no longer troubled by any problem coming from the body."[78] Indeed, death will procure for the soul worthy of it perfect and permanent divinization, along with the uninterrupted, unitive vision of the supreme Good, and a boundless and endless bliss.

The Plotinian ideal of deification reproduces the essential traits of Plato's, but it is enriched with numerous new elements borrowed especially from the Stoic and Neopythagorean tradition, and animated by a more fervent and quite eastern mysticism. It is particularly the loftiness of this ideal which explains "the long-standing sympathy that Neoplatonism aroused in Christian

---

[69] Arnou, *Le désir de Dieu*, 245; cf. 269-270; Bréhier, *La philosophie de Plotin*, 109.

[70] 6.9.11 (Volkmann 2:524:1-5). In the last part of the phrase, the allusion to the "vision" which crowned the rites of initiation is manifest.

[71] 6.7.35; Cf. Arnou, *Le désir de Dieu*, 241-258; Zeller, *Die Philosophie der Griechen* (4th ed.), 3:2:666-671. Bréhier, *La philosophie de Plotin*, 134, writes of the Plotinian ecstasy: "All moral and intellectual relationships which establish a thought and a person get lost in this contemplation." See also Krakowski, *Plotin*, 183-184.

[72] 6.7.34 (Volkmann 2:467:1-2).

[73] 6.9.9 (Volkmann 2:522:17-18).

[74] 6.9.10 (Volkmann 2:522:20-21).

[75] 6.9.9 (Volkmann 2:522:18).

[76] 6.9.9 (Volkmann 2:522:18-19).

[77] Cf. 4.8.1.1-11; Porph. *Vit. Plot.* 23 in Bréhier, *Plotin*, 1:27:15-18. According to Porphyry, Plotinus "four times attained," while Porphyry was with him, "the intimate union with the God who is above all things."

[78] 6.9.10 (Volkmann 2:522:21-23).

minds."[79] Most certainly, "the idea of a unique God that one can reach by contemplation and meet again by ecstasy, the concern to detach the spiritual life from the works of the flesh, asceticism, and charity, all prevailing features of the Neoplatonism of Plotinus,...connect profoundly and, so to speak, through the heart, the two doctrines, Christian and Neoplatonic."[80]

67   Nevertheless, "in its depths and by the bulk of its views, Neoplatonism proposed to justify something very suspicious,"[81] from the point of view of Christian thinkers. So it is "that there are some seeds of pantheism in the doctrine of Plotinus; and, in particular, there is necessity which rules over all that which the first cause produces."[82] Furthermore, Neoplatonism is "a full-scale naturalism"[83]: humankind are sufficient in themselves to purify themselves and to rise up to ecstasy.[84] However, while being the fruit of human effort alone, in actual practice the ecstatic union with God is reserved for an elite. Neoplatonism, an aristocratic doctrine, loses the interest of the πολλοί. Finally, in what strictly concerns our subject, the permanent union between the separated soul and the supreme Good, with the abolition of consciousness that it entails, looks too much like an obliteration of the human person due to a kind of pantheistic resorption of the soul into the One.

V

The implacable antagonism between Neoplatonism and Christianity, of which Plotinus was already aware,[85] had to be bluntly affirmed in the writings of his successors. However, the disciples of Plotinus hardly had the originality of his thought.[86]

The "Tyrian" Porphyry (d. circa 303-305), who was "the popularizer of Neoplatonic doctrine"[87] and a bitter enemy of Christianity, and with whom the tendency of making Plotinism a religion is already apparent, dreams of a divinization of humankind by means of a development of the spiritual life on the basis of "four elements," which are "faith, truth, love, hope."[88]

68   Iamblichus (d. circa 330), founder of Syrian Neoplatonism, transforms Plotinian philosophy into theurgy. According to him, individuals cannot be united with God by thought alone; in order to realize this union, they must have recourse to the sacred rites which "kindle" the benevolence of the

---

[79] De Labriolle, *La réaction païenne*, 227.
[80] Krakowski, *Plotin*, 221.
[81] De Labriolle, *La réaction païenne*, 227.
[82] R. Arnou, "Platonisme des Pères," *DTC* 12:2277.
[83] Arnou, "Platonisme des Pères," 2282.
[84] Cf. Arnou, "Platonisme des Pères," 2368-2372.
[85] Cf. Bremond, *La piété grecque*, 54-58.
[86] Cf. Krakowski, *Plotin*, 282: "Proclus, Iamblichus, Porphyry in the basic elements, in the vital substance, of their thought scarcely but repeat that of Plotinus."
[87] L. Vaganay, "Porphyre," *DTC* 12:2562.
[88] *Marc.* 24 (ed. Nauck [Leipzig, 1886], 289). Cf. Louis, *Doctrines religieuses*, 308-318.

gods,[89] the source of all good. Consequently, it is theurgy which is "the pre-eminent way to bliss, the way which leads the souls to the intellectual realization of the divine union. The priestly and theurgic gift of bliss is called a gate to God, the demiurge of the universe, or even the place or vestibule of the Good, and it has the pre-eminent strength to purify the soul; it then purifies the thinking so that it may participate in the Good and contemplate it [εἰς...θέαν] by freeing itself from all that is contrary to it; in the end, it unites to the gods, the source of all good things."[90]

Finally, Proclus (d. 485), the most representative leader of the Neoplatonic school of Athens, develops the triadic schema already sketched out by Iamblichus and thus gives Neoplatonism its most discerning form, but also its most rigid.[91] Again for him, "the goal which must be reached by the threefold way of purification, illumination, and union, by prayer and sacrifice, by the cathartic, the telestic, and theurgy, by the *logia* and hierarchy, is divinization."[92]

"There was in Greek culture and the religion which was, if not its soul, at least an integral part of it," writes Fr. Bremond,[93] a need for the divine and tran-   69
scendent, and a sense of insufficiency and human dependency. Starting from Socrates, philosophy will define this need as the desire of *divine assimilation*, the desire of being like the gods, perfect with their perfection, happy with their happiness,[94] and it will claim to satisfy this desire rationally.... But by its power-lessness to satisfy a need that it has made more conscious and more pressing, philosophy indirectly prepares for the gospel."

We could not characterize with a more succinct passage the Hellenic analogies, in their worth and in their deficiencies, which the fathers were able to recollect in meditating on the deification of the Christian.

---

[89] Iambl. *Myster.* 2.11 (ed. G. Parthey [Berlin, 1857], 96-97). Here we read: "It is not knowledge which unites [συνάπτει] the faithful [θεουργούς] to the gods; or else nothing would prevent the philosophers from possessing theurgic union with the gods. But in reality it is not so." What leads to the divine union are, on the contrary, the practice of the ineffable rites and the "power of the mysterious symbols known by the gods alone."

[90] *Myster.* 10.5 (291-292). Cf. Louis, *Doctrines religieuses*, 318-327.

[91] Cf. Zeller, *Die Philosophie der Griechen* (4th ed.), 3:2:850-851.

[92] H. Koch, *Pseudo-Dionysius Areopagita in seinem Beziehungen zum Neoplatonismus und Mysterienwesen* (Mayence, 1900), 190. Conforming to the Neoplatonic tradition, by λόγια Proclus means the oracles and the doctrines of the ancient "theologians" like Homer, Orpheus, Pythagoras, Plato, etc. See Koch, *Pseudo-Dionysius*, 41-43.

[93] Bremond, *La piété grecque*, 24.

[94] Cf. Kleinknecht, "θεός," 78: "We must attain to God's mode of being, not God to ours. Such is the specifically Greek experience of God."

BOOK ONE

THE PREPARATION

BOOK TWO

THE DOCTRINE OF THE GREEK FATHERS

CHAPTER ONE

THE OLD TESTAMENT

"Hellenic culture," as Maurice Croiset has said, "is rationalistic and aristocratic. It is the divinization of well-ordered appetites or of a rational rule of
desires and natural ambitions."[1] Very different, because profoundly religious, is
the culture reflected in the source par excellence of patristic Greek thought,
namely, the Holy Scripture, the teaching of which the fathers place well above
all human wisdom. Essentially religious also, consequently, is the ideal of
perfection advocated in the Holy Books.

Without doubt the Old Testament is still more or less imperfect in relation
to the destinies of humankind. But by recognizing in the destinies of humankind, from the first lines of Genesis, a likeness with the Creator, the Old Testament opens up some broad perspectives to religious reflection. Later, the
theocratic alliance gives rise to the idea of divine filiation, which, refined and
deepened by the prophets and in particular by the author of Wisdom, ends
up becoming the equivalent of deification and prepares for the Christian
ideal.

I

26 And Elohim said: "Let Us make man in Our image according to Our likeness,
and let them[2] have dominion over the fish of the sea, over the birds of the sky,
over the domestic animals, and over all the earth, and over the reptiles which
crawl on the earth." 27 And Elohim created man in His image, in the image of
Elohim He created them...[3]

The emphasis of this text strongly brings out the divine likeness of the first
human being. Because of this likeness, humankind exercises their dominion
over the earth and the animals which inhabit it. This amounts to saying that
humankind is the image of God and like His lieutenant on the earth by virtue of
faculties which place them above the animals, namely, intelligence and free will.[4]

Beginning with Saint Irenaeus, many fathers concluded from the account of
the forming of Adam that a certain deification of the latter exists. Distinguishing between image [εἰκών] and likeness [ὁμοίωσις], they understood this

---

[1] Maurice Croiset, *Histoire de la littérature grecque*, 4:327; quoted by Bremond, *La piété grecque*, 18.
[2] The Hebrew has the plural.
[3] Gen 1:26-27.
[4] Cf. P. Heinisch, *Das Buch der Genesis* (Bonn, 1930), 100-101; Hubert Junker, *Die Biblische Urgeschichte* (Bonn, 1932), 40; Éduard Koenig, *Die Genesis* (Gütersloh, 1919), 153-161; Jean Hempel, *Gott und Mensch im Alten Testament* (Stuttgart, 1936), 206.

latter item in the sense of a more perfect similarity, which would surpass by far what humankind possess in their nature.

In reality, the sacred writer employs the two terms like synonyms, perhaps with the slight difference that the second should clarify the first. This exegesis is confirmed by verse 27, in which the writer is content to say that "Elohim created humankind in His image."

In His partiality for the masterpiece of His creation, Yahweh had reserved for humankind a still more precious favor: the participation in the specific benefit of divinity, namely, "eternal life." To this end, He "made the tree of life to grow in the middle of the garden," the fruit of which possessed the virtue of bringing immortality. But this had to be a reward for an act of obedience; it was dependent on the observing of the precept not "to eat of the tree of the knowledge of good and of evil."

Deceived by the serpent, Eve first, and then Adam following, disdained the deification which was compatible with their created nature and which God had offered to them, and allowed themselves to go after the ambition of "being like Elohim," after the dream of a divinization which would be a perfect equality with God, not only in what concerns His eternal life but also as to His unlimited knowledge and absolute autonomy.[5] It was a culpable dream and was soon followed, moreover, by a sorrowful awakening. The forbidden fruit brought to the first parents a new consciousness, but it was the consciousness of their folly and of their weakness. In accordance with the divine threat, their offense had as its consequence their absolute banishment from the tree of life and, by that, from immortality.[6]

There is a junction here worth noting. Like the Greeks, the narrator of Genesis conceives of the divinization of humankind as, above all, an immortalization; likewise, he attributes an important role to knowledge as well. This is what the Hellenized author of Wisdom has well pointed out. Manifestly referring to our narrative, he in fact places the divine likeness of humankind in immortality: "For God," he writes, "has created man for immortality [ἐπ' ἀφθαρσίᾳ], and He has made them His image [εἰκόνα] from His own nature."[7]

This analogy between the Jewish and Greek conceptions of deification is nothing surprising since previously in primitive civilizations "a kind of eternity" is considered as an essential attribute of the supreme Being,[8] to which man aspires.

---

⁵ Cf. Charles Fruhstorfer, *Die Paradiesessünde* (Linz, 1929), 9.
⁶ Gen 2:8-3:24. Cf. Heinisch, *Genesis*, 113-130; Junker, *Die Biblische Urgeschichte*, 44-49; Koenig, *Die Genesis*, 216-270.
⁷ Wis 2:23. See below, 68.
⁸ Schmidt, *Origine et évolution de la religion*, 332.

II

Although lacking deification in the strict sense of the word, the oldest books 73
of the Old Testament are at least very firm on humankind's likeness with God.
This latter factor is to be clarified and enriched by the idea of divine filiation.

According to modern ethnologists, the concept of paternity as applied to the
Supreme Being and, consequently, the correlative concept of filiation as applied to human beings would seem to be extremely ancient.[9] There is nothing
surprising about the fact that we encounter these concepts among the Hebrews
as well, where as a matter of fact they occupy a considerable place. Indeed, the
writers of the ancient law—as, moreover, the Semites in general[10]—readily employ the image of filiation to convey the ties that join God's servants to Himself.
Nevertheless, the use of this metaphor brings out in the Old Testament some
important nuances, which become particularly perceptible in the book of Wisdom.

At this point, we do not have to dwell on the biblical passages where the
angels are called "sons of God."[11] It is sufficient for us to know that this appellation simply signifies that these supra-terrestrial beings live in the immediate
circle of the Lord and are, from His side, the object of a special affection and
concern.

The metaphor of filiation has an analogous sense when applied to people.
Frequently Yahweh Himself honors His people, taken as a whole, with the title
of "son." So it is that by the order of God Moses must speak to Pharoah: "Thus
says Yahweh: Israel is My son, My first-born."[12] In Hosea, God uses similar
language: "When Israel was a child, I loved him, and, from Egypt, I have sent
calls to My son."[13] Also, the sacred writers do not fail to call this filiation to 74
remembrance as much to Yahweh as to their compatriots. The author of the
prayer for the restoration of Israel, which is Psa 80, beseeches the "Shepherd of
Israel" in these words: "Protect that which Your right hand has planted and the
son that You have chosen!"[14] Speaking to all the people, Moses reminds them:
"You are children to Yahweh, your God."[15]

What exactly is the nature of the divine filiation of the chosen people as it
appears in the Old Testament?

---

[9] Cf. Schmidt, *Origine et évolution de la religion*, 329-330.

[10] Cf. Hubert Junker, *Das Buch Deuteronomium* (Bonn, 1933), 69.

[11] They are six in number: Job 1:6; 2:1; 38:7; Psa 29:1; 89:6; Gen 6:2. Concerning the last, very
controversial text, the ancient interpretation which saw angels in the *bene ha-elohim* has in its favor Jude
6-7. Less influenced by considerations of a dogmatic nature, this interpretation seems, besides, more
conformed to the particulars of the text.

[12] Exo 4:22.

[13] Hosea 11:1. Cf. Isa 1:2; 30:1, 9.

[14] Psa 80:15. Cf. Psa 72:15; Isa 64:7-11.

[15] Deut 14:1. It should be noted that the formula *bene elohim* is never applied to men. According to
Hosea 1:10, the new Israel will be called "son of the living God." Cf. Deut 32:5, 20. We would also be
able to add to the texts indicated all those in which Yahweh is called the Father of Israel. Cf. Hempel,
Gott und Mensch, 170-179.

Israel, insofar as being a people, is known as a "son" by Yahweh because God has given existence to him, guides him, and protects him with a paternal affection. Also, the image of the "son" is sometimes replaced by the analogy of the "spouse."[16] Both of these metaphors express a special bond of mutual adherence,[17] of tenderness, and of protection on the part of God, and of faithfulness and love on the side of the people.

Israel is the "particular people" of Yahweh "among all the peoples,"[18] according to the covenant.[19] In return, Yahweh is the God of Israel in a very particular way:[20] He makes the interests of His people His own interests; the enemies of Israel are His enemies;[21] and He promises to Israel a happy life and a bright future.[22]

75   This was, of course, on condition that the chosen people remained faithful to the commitments they had entered into with their God. Faithfulness was too often violated in spite of the preaching of the prophets. And these violations reached such a point that, facing the apostasy of so great a number of their compatriots, the prophets come to distinguish even within the people of God those who live according to the precepts of the Lord and "those whose heart walks after their idols." Only the first, the righteous, belong to God; whereas the ungodly are denied by Him.[23] The saints who will have a share in the divine promises will only be a minority, a "remnant of Israel,"[24] which will remain after the purifying chastisement reserved for the adulterous nation.

In this way, the prophets endeavor to make their compatriots realize that the fact of belonging to the race of Abraham is not sufficient for establishing the divine filiation and entitling them to the promised bliss, and that, furthermore and above all, the moral element of the faithful observation of the divine law is necessary, and to this Yahweh Himself has subordinated the realization of His promises.

These promises, moreover, do not exceed the scope of collective and earthly eschatology,[25] which hardly takes account of the individual. Later, in the book of Daniel and in the second book of the Maccabees, the hope of a resurrection

---

[16]   See in particular the oracles of Hosea and Jer 31:22.

[17]   In the Semitic languages especially, the image of filiation is of a standard usage for expressing any relationship of belonging (cf. Psa 89:22: "the son of iniquity"), but notably that which joins the faithful to their God. In the Bible itself, the Moabites are described as sons and daughters of Chemosh, their national god (Num 21:29); the foreign women with whom the Jews have entered into marriage are called the "daughters of a strange god" (Mal 2:11; Cf. Jer 2:28).

[18]   Exo 19:5. Cf. 6:7.

[19]   Cf. Exo 19:1–24:8; 34:10, etc.

[20]   Cf. Exo 20:1.

[21]   Cf. Exo 23:22.

[22]   See the Messianic promises, especially Amos 9:11-15; Hosea 1–3; Isa 54, 56–66.

[23]   Ezek 11:17-21. Cf. Isa 66:1-6.

[24]   Cf. Isa 6:13; 7:3 (a child of Isaiah is called "a remnant will return"); 10:20-23 ("the remnant of Israel"); 28:5-8; Micah 4:7; 5:6-7; Jer 4:27; Ezek 5:4, 12; 6:8-10; 9:2-6; 14:22; Zech 13:8-9.

[25]   Cf. Eccl 9:2-10; Job 14:13; Isa 38:18; Psa 6:5; 88:5, 10-12; Sir 17:22-23.

emerges, which would allow the already departed righteous, at the moment of the advent of the Messianic kingdom, to participate in it.[26]

Long before this, however, a slight tendency toward an individualistic conception of divine filiation may already be noted. Indeed, not only the people in His group but also some individuals are called "sons" by God.

This is the case for David and Solomon. Speaking of the first, Yahweh says in Psa 89:26: "He will call upon Me: You are my Father, my God, and the rock of my salvation. And I, I will make of him the firstborn." A similar promise is made by God on behalf of Solomon: "I will be for him a Father, and he will be for Me a son."[27]

Logically one ought to expect that the Messiah also is honored by God with the title of "son." This is what occurs at least once, in Psa 2, "the messianic psalm par excellence."[28] He Himself making known His rights to the kingship, the Messiah speaks here in this way: "Yahweh said to Me: You are My Son, I have begotten You today. Ask, and I will give You the nations for an inheritance, the ends of the earth for a domain."[29] According to the context, these verses refer to "the glorification of the Messiah and to the inauguration of His reign,"[30] to that day when the messianic King will be "begotten"; that is, He will become by a special title the Son of Yahweh.

This title of "son," conferred by God on the king and the Messiah, means that these privileges are grounds for partiality in God's view and that their bearers are His lieutenants on the earth, who have been invested with an exceptional dignity and authority by Yahweh.[31]

In a similar way, the judges are sometimes called *elohim*, gods. It is thus that in verse 6 of Psa 82, Yahweh addresses these words to the wicked judges: "I have said: You are all gods [*elohim*] and children of the Most High."[32] Here again, it is a matter of honorary designations which simply indicate that the judges "render justice in the name and place of God,"[33] and that they take part in the divine authority without, in spite of all this, their nature being changed in the least. Moreover, this is what Yahweh, the *Elohim* par excellence, reminds

---

[26] Cf. Dan 12:1-3; 2 Macc 7; 12:43-45; 14:46. The same idea perhaps appears already in what we call the *Apocalypse of Isaiah* 24–27, notably 26:19. See L. Dennefeld, *"Judaïsme," DTC* 8:1630; F. Noetscher, *Altorientalischer und alttestamentlicher Auferstehungsglauben*, (Würzburg, 1926), 154-159.

[27] 2 Sam 7:14. Cf. 1 Chron 17:13; 22:9; 27; 28:6.

[28] M.-J. Lagrange, "La paternité de Dieu dans l'Ancien Testament," *RB* 5 (1908): 492.

[29] Psa 2:7-8.

[30] J. Lebreton, *Histoire du dogme de la Trinité* (2 vols.; 7th ed. Paris, 1927), 1:134. The expression "son of God" is never applied to the Messiah.

[31] From the primitive period, a number of peoples have identified the Supreme Being with the tribal ancestor and have thus attributed a divine origin to their chiefs. See Schmidt, *Origine et évolution de la religion*, 323. Nothing of the sort is observed in Israel.

[32] See as well Exo 21:6; 12:7-8, 28; Psa 58:1. For this last text, see Fr. Zorell, *Psalterium* (Rome, 1928), 97; H. Herkenne, *Das Buch der Psalmen* (Bonn, 1936), 202.

[33] F. Vigouroux, *La Sainte Bible polyglotte* (Paris, 1903), 4:199. Cf. Thdt. *Ps.* 81 (PG 80:1528b-1529c).

them, and not without irony. As magistrates, they are "gods" in the sense that their sentences are without retort. They do not remain because of it the less mortal: "Nevertheless, you will die as men, you will fall as one of the demons."[34] Whatever many of the ancient exegetes may say about them, the titles of *elohim* and "children of the Most High," conferred here on the judges, do not thus have, in the least, the sense of a divinization by an assimilation of humankind to the divine nature.

All in all, whether it may be applied to the people as such or to some privileged member of the people, the analogy of divine filiation seems to express a rather external relationship, a favor which, as its principal goal, assures the salvation of the Jewish nation and thereby the triumph of its God.[35]

III

One must come to Wisdom to see that divine filiation takes on a clearly individual and transcendent sense.

It is not that the sage is unaware of the traditional conception of a collective divine filiation based upon the fact of membership among the people of God. Quite the contrary, the idea whereby Israel is "God's child"[36] seems to dominate the whole third part of his book, in which he describes the action of wisdom in history.[37]

But next to this conception emerges that of a personal filiation, which, if not entirely new,[38] expresses itself with a clarity until then unknown.

From the first part of his book, the sacred author takes up again, by dramatizing it, the discrimination of the prophets between righteous and ungodly Israelites.[39] He presents the wicked themselves and has them unfold *ex professo* their ideal of life and utter their hatred of the righteous person. While speaking concerning the righteous man, they say: "He boasts in having God as Father. Let us see therefore if what he says is true.... For if the righteous man is God's child [υἱὸς θεοῦ], God will take up his defense."[40] But in the day of judgment the ungodly are confounded and find themselves forced to acknowledge their

78

[34] Psa 82:7. With B. Duhm, *Die Psalmen* (vol. 14 of *Kurzer Hand-commenntar zum Alten Testament*; ed. D. K. Marti; Freiburg im Breisgau, 1899), and Herkenne, *Das Buch der Psalmen*, 281, we read *hashshedim*, "demons," instead of *hassarim*, "princes," of the Massoretic text.

[35] Cf. L. Dennefeld, *Le judaïsme* (Paris, 1925), 90-91.

[36] Wis 18:13. Cf. 12:7.

[37] Wis 10–19.

[38] Already toward the end of the Assyrian period, a tendency is noticed in Israel toward the individualization of religious hope, of piety in particular. See J. Hempel, *Gott und Mensch*, 134-162. In a general way, "Jeremiah and Ezekiel have expressly and solemnly established individualism as a principle of religion" (Dennefeld, *Le judaïsme*, 92).

[39] Wis 1–4.

[40] Wis 2:16-18.

error concerning the final lot of the righteous one who, after death, is "counted among the children of God."[41]

For the first time in the Bible the title of "God's child" is here clearly given to the righteous individual. Now, in order to be righteous in the eyes of our author, it is without doubt essential to have Abraham as father;[42] but this descent is surely insufficient: "God, in fact, only loves the one who lives with wisdom."[43] Consequently, only the person who possesses this practical wisdom, which is identified with the fear of the Lord and virtue, is pleasing to God, that is, righteous. In other words, righteousness is the perfect conformity of the human life to the requirements of the divine law.[44]

The wisdom exalted by pseudo-Solomon, because it is of fundamentally religious inspiration, is essentially different from Greek wisdom. Far from being the fruit of human effort alone, as the latter is, it is a gift of God, a reward for the moral purity acquired by the individual.[45] "Knowing," says Solomon, "that I could not obtain wisdom unless God granted it to me—and that the knowing from whom this gift comes was already from wisdom—I spoke to the Lord and I called upon Him."[46] Therefore, one is entitled to conclude— although this conclusion may not be formally drawn by the sacred writer himself—that the divine filiation of the righteous, like the wisdom which is its condition sine qua non, is a gift of the Lord.

Now this gift implies a genuine assimilation of a person to God, for it is basically just a participation in the wisdom which "is the breath of the power of God,[47] and a pure emanation of the glory of the Almighty; ...the brilliance of the eternal light, the spotless mirror of the activity of God, and the image of His kindness."[48] It follows that, without ceasing to be an outward tie of member-

---

[41] Wis 5:5. That the ungodly presented should be Israelites is what clearly arises from the context. Indeed, there they are described as "apostates" [τοῦ κυρίου ἀποστάντες}; they hate the righteous man because he "reproaches them for their sins against the law" (Wis 2:12).

[42] If, for our sage, all the Israelites are not righteous, he, however, does not seem to have acknowledged the existence of righteous ones outside of Israel.

[43] Wis 7:28.

[44] We have often observed that our author "nowhere gives a definition, properly speaking, of wisdom." He "is content to show its properties and effects" (E. Tobac, *Les cinq livres de Solomon* [Brussels, 1926], 140). It is nevertheless evident from the body of the book, in particular from chapters 1-8, that it is a virtue, both intellectual and practical, which leads individuals to their end. Thus from the first verses righteousness is identified with wisdom and the latter is opposed to iniquity (1:1-5). See Rodolphe Schuetz, *Les idées eschatologiques du livre de la Sagesse* (Strasbourg, 1935), 66-67.

[45] Wis 1:3-5. We can say that wisdom is "much more a reward than a free gift of God." P. van Imschoot, "Sagesse et Esprit dans l'A.T.," *RB* 47 (1938): 49.

[46] Wis 8:21. Cf. 9:6-18; 7:7.

[47] The author of Wisdom identifies wisdom with the spirit of God. Cf. Imschoot, "Sagesse et Esprit," 44-46.

[48] Wis 7:25-26. In verse 27 it is said of the divine wisdom that "through the ages it spreads into all the holy souls."

ship to the God of the covenant, divine filiation has become an inner grace which transforms the human souls and makes them "friends of God."[49]

This divine filiation and this friendship, assured to the righteous from the present life onward, will nevertheless attain to their full blossoming only in the hereafter.

Therefore, due to his psychology, refined through his contact with Hellenic culture, the author of Wisdom sees the immortal soul as the principal subject of human destiny. Consequently, with him the conception of salvation becomes individualistic. This allows him to free himself not only from the disappointing vision of Sheol,[50] which seems to exclude any idea of ultra-terrestrial punishments,[51] but also, although perhaps not completely, from the collective and terrestrial eschatology[52] and come to conceive of recompenses beyond the grave.

So for pseudo-Solomon, wisdom, which renders human beings like God from this life onward, will complete their divine likeness and their divine filiation in the other life by "assuring to them incorruptibility," for which they have been created.[53]

Now immortality "grants a place near God."[54] After death, in fact, "the souls of the righteous are in the hand of God" and "in peace."[55] "The righteous live eternally, and their reward is in the Lord; and the Most High takes care of them. This is why they will receive the kingdom of honor and the diadem of glory from the hand of the Lord."[56] They will be counted "among the children of God," and their "lot is in the midst of the saints."[57]

Whereas in the present life the divine filiation of the righteous seems to be of a purely moral nature, it blossoms out in the hereafter in this way: it even makes the separated soul actually participate in the specifically divine properties of blessed immortality, power, and glory. Is this not a genuine deification of the soul—even though it is not so described—to the entire extent in which its position as creature, which, of course, never disappears, allows?

[49] Wis 7:27; cf. 7:4, verses which recall Plato, *Leg.* 4.716: Ὁ μὲν σώφρων ἡμῶν θεῷ φίλος. See above, 41.

[50] The Sheol of the Hebrews resembles the Hades of Homer; we find it again in a similar way with the Babylonians. Cf. Noetscher, *Auferstehungsglauben*, 10-15.

[51] See above, 64.

[52] Cf. Wis 18:4; 19:22.

[53] Wis 6:18, combined with 2:23: "For God has created humankind for incorruptibility, and He has made them the image of His own nature." The two parts of this verse seem to be synonymous: by creating humankind for ἀφθαρσία, God made them His image. Thus, it is immortality—identical with incorruptibility—which causes humankind to be the image of God. See Tobac, *Les cinq livres de Solomon*, 131; R. Schuetz, *Les idées eschatologiques*, 44-47.

[54] Wis 6:19 (Greek text).

[55] Wis 3:1, 3. Cf. 4:7.

[56] Wis 5:15-16 (Greek text).

[57] Wis 5:5.

The similarity between the conception of salvation reflected in Wisdom and the Hellenic ideal of divinization is evident. In fact, in both there is the assimilation of the soul to God by means of wisdom and blessed immortality. However, the dissimilarities appear greater still. The most important consists in the fact that, in opposition to the Greeks, who expect everything by their own effort, the sacred writer sees wisdom and incorruptibility as divine gifts.

A second difference is quite obvious: for pseudo-Solomon, the divine likeness is not, as for the Greeks, the conclusion of a mystical ascension and union. With him, there is no trace of a mysticism of divinization; he was able to resist the fascination of Hellenistic mysticism, which was to so profoundly influence his compatriot Philo.

This shows that while being open to Hellenism, the sage did not allow himself to be controlled by it. Because of it, he was the more apt to fertilize the seeds of a doctrine of deification contained in the oldest books of the Old Testament and thus prepare the way for the Christian revelation.

CHAPTER TWO

EXTRA-CANONICAL JEWISH LITERATURE

82   At first sight, it is strange that assimilation to God by means of wisdom and blessed immortality, as explained by pseudo-Solomon, hardly found any echo in post-biblical Jewish literature. But looking at it more closely, we can easily explain the fact. Indeed, we notice at the start that Wisdom, the work of a Hellenized Jew who was probably from the Alexandrian community,[1] does not appear in the Palestinian canon of the Old Testament and, furthermore, that on a number of points Jewish thought developed differently in Palestine and within the Egyptian dispersion. It is at Alexandria, in the writings of Philo, that we see the appearing of what we could call the first Judeo-Hellenic mysticism of divinization.

I

    In Judaea, the exaggerated feeling of the divine transcendence—a feeling characteristic of post-biblical Judaism as a whole—develops to such a point that people let "the particular name of the God of Israel drop away" and distance God as much as possible from the world and from people.[2] Because of monotheistic scruples, the rabbis avoid calling the angels *elohim* or *bene elohim*, as found in Scripture.[3] If, on the contrary, the non-canonical authors conform
83 without hesitation to the biblical usage of naming Israel the "firstborn," the "son" of God, it is because the purely metaphorical sense of these names does not cause anyone misgivings.[4] Like the title *Father,* which is given to God but is absent from the pseudepigraphical writings, these terms even take on a personal and tender tone in the mouth of the rabbis, a tone that recalls Wisdom.[5] This does not prevent rabbinic exegesis from striving to make out of the divine likeness of humankind, which is clearly affirmed in Genesis all the same, a "likeness that is before Yahweh" and, eventually, a likeness that is with the angels only.[6]

---

[1] Cf. Tobac, *Les cinq livres,* 113-118; F. Feldmann, *Das Buch der Weisheit* (Bonn, 1926), 13-15.

[2] J. Bonsirven, *Le Judaïsme palestinien au temps de Jésus-Christ: La Théologie* (2 vols.; Paris, 1934-1935), 1:144, 155-159. Cf. Lebreton, *Histoire du dogme,* 1:146-147.

[3] Cf. Bonsirven, *Le Judaïsme palestinien,* 1:223-226.

[4] See, for example, 4 Ezra 6:55-59. Cf. Bonsirven, *Le Judaïsm palestinien,* 1:84-85.

[5] Cf. Bonsirven, *Le Judaïsme palestinien,* 1:138-139; Lebreton, *Histoire du dogme,* 1:143-146.

[6] See Koenig, *Die Genesis,* 158.

To this touchy monotheism is added an excessive cult of the law, which was considered as the unique rule of wisdom and justice, as well as of outward observances. It is an attitude which, by suppressing the need of imploring help from on high, breeds self-satisfaction and paralyzes any mystical impulse.[7]

Finally, the eschatological problem receives some solutions in Palestine that are very different from what pseudo-Solomon gives it. Being faithful to the traditional conceptions while developing them, the Palestinian Jews dream of a redemption that would be both the brilliant and permanent triumph of their nation and the decisive victory of the unique true God.[8] This national restoration, in which a more or less important part is given to the Messiah, would be carried out either in the present age, which would be expected to continue its course,[9] or in a marvellously transformed world.[10] According to *4 Ezra*, "one of the most beautiful and touching" of the Jewish apocryphal books, and one "which has enjoyed the greatest circulation of all,"[11] the reign of the Messiah would follow the universal resurrection, the final judgment, and the ultimate recompenses. For the righteous, the recompenses would consist in a blessed life in the terrestrial paradise, which, closed after the fall of our first parents, would be "opened" again.[12]

84

Although very incomplete, these pieces of information are sufficient to show that in the period that runs from the second century before Christ to the first century of the Christian era, the religious atmosphere in which Palestinian Judaism developed is unfavorable to any idea of and, even more, to any mysticism of divinization.

II

As we might expect here a priori, the soteriology of Wisdom reappears in the Hellenistic group of apocryphal books. Fourth Maccabees is the most important of them from our point of view.

---

[7] Cf. Bonsirven, *Le Judaïsme palestinien*, 2:158-162, 178-182, 314.

[8] Late Judaism still reinforced the connection that, from time immemorial, the Jews had established between the interests of their nation and those of God.

[9] Cf. *1 En.* 10.16–11; 90. Aside from contrary indication, we give the references according to the edition of E. Kautzch, *Die Apocryphen und Pseudepigraphen des Alten Testaments* (2 vols.; Tübingen, 1900).

[10] Cf. *1 En.* 45; 91.14-17.

[11] J.-B. Frey, "Apocryphes de l'Ancien Testament," *DBSup* 1:411. Cf. Bonsirven, *Le Judaïsme palestinien*, 1:19-21.

[12] *4 Ezra* 7:121-123; 8:52-54. Cf. Léon Vaganay, *Le problème eschatologique dans le IVᵉ livre d'Esdras* (Paris, 1906), 115. On the subject of the virtually inextricable *imbroglio* of messianic and eschatological conceptions that extra-canonical Jewish literature encompasses, see especially Bonsirven, *Le Judaïsme palestinien*, 1:307-541.

In this "very philosophic discourse,"[13] which was written at the beginning of our era by a Jew loyal to his faith but imbued with Stoicism,[14] the author sets out to show, as much by rational arguments as by examples drawn from Jewish history, that "pious reason [ὁ εὐσεβὴς λογισμός] is the sovereign of the passions."[15] "Pious reason" is nothing other than piety based upon the Jewish law and tradition.[16] Eleazar, who made this his life's rule until his heroic death, is called a "philosopher of a divine life."[17]

The belief in the immortality of the soul shows itself with perfect clarity in this
85   pseudepigraphical work. Furthermore, along with Wisdom, it is the only Jewish writing of that period to employ the terms ἀθανασία and ἀφθαρσία.[18] What sustains the seven Maccabee brothers and their mother in their dreadful ordeals is the hope of "eternal life according to the divine promise,"[19] that is, "the hope of a salvation with God."[20] The firm belief in "the immortality of their pious souls" renders the brothers "unanimous in their resolution to die for piety." They run to meet a painful death "as if they were on the way to immortality."[21]

Moreover, the expectation of the martyrs is not disappointed; their "victory was incorruptibility [ἀφθαρσία] in a long-lasting life."[22] With her sons, the heroic mother "has a stable dwelling-place in heaven;"[23] "they are near the divine throne and live through blessed eternity,"[24] being "made worthy of a divine portion."[25]

This divine portion is manifestly conceived of as a participation in immortality and the glory of God, in which pseudo-Solomon had placed the supreme salvation of the righteous.

Nevertheless, in 4 Maccabees—no more than elsewhere in Jewish literature, whether canonical or extra-canonical—there is no trace of a mysticism of divinization, or we could say of mysticism at all. This is perhaps explained by the fact that if Jewish piety oscillates between the fear of God and trust in Him, the first of these sentiments clearly predominated on the whole.[26]

---

[13]   4 Macc 1:1: φιλοσοφώτατος λόγος. We quote according to the edition of H. B. Swete, *The Old Testament in Greek* (Cambridge, 1901-1903), 3:729-762.

[14]   Fr. Bonsirven, *Le Judaïsme palestinien*, 1:326, describes him as a "Stoic author."

[15]   4 Macc 1:7-9. Cf. 1:32-35; 2:6, 21-23, etc.

[16]   Cf. 4 Macc 1:14-17; 13:16, where the author does not hesitate to speak of "divine reason" [τοῦ θείου λογισμοῦ]. Cf. 17:11: ἀγὼν θεῖος.

[17]   4 Macc 7:7: φιλόσοφε θείου βίου.

[18]   4 Macc 14:5-6 and 16:13 [ἀθανασία]; 17:12 [ἀφθαρσία]; 18:23 [ἀθάνατος applied to the soul].

[19]   4 Macc 15:3.

[20]   4 Macc 11:7. Cf. 9:8; 16:25: "They knew that those who die for God, live with God [ζῶσιν τῷ θεῷ], like Abraham, Isaac, Jacob, and all the patriarchs."

[21]   4 Macc 14:5-6.

[22]   4 Macc 17:12.

[23]   4 Macc 17:5.

[24]   4 Macc 17:18. Cf. 18:23.

[25]   4 Macc 18:3: θείας μερίδος κατηξιώθησαν.

[26]   Cf. Hempel, *Gott und Mensch*, 4-33, 273. See L. Dennefeld, "Chronique biblique (Ancien Testament)," *RevScRel* 17 (1937): 322-324. According to a feeling that is clearly expressed, as much in the Old Testament as in Israelite worship, human beings cannot see Yahweh without dying. Exo 33:18-23. However, see Exo 24:18-23 (Hebrew text).

It is true that a great number of exegetes, with whom Father Bonsirven sides, see an "admirable manifestation of mysticism"[27] in prophethood. But the result of the minutely detailed analyses embarked upon lately—most recently by Heschel[28] and Hempel[29]—seems to be that what we could call the prophetic rush of emotion is essentially different from the mystic ecstasy. Indeed, whereas in ecstasy—to point out only the most obvious difference—the soul withdraws from the world in order to immerse itself in God in an ineffable impulse of love, the seer feels overcome, often reluctantly,[30] by a divine influence which sets his own feelings, so to speak, in unison with those of Yahweh, with a view to an intervention in the religious, social, or political life of the period. Consequently, it will be necessary to wait for the Judeo-Hellenic syncretism of Philo in order to find a mysticism of divinization in a Jewish author.

III

A mystic more than a philosopher, Philo of Alexandria, the most remarkable of the Jews who apply themselves to harmonize their faith with Hellenic civilization, writes particularly to defend the Jewish religion. To this end, he presents the latter not only as the true wisdom that contains, implicitly at least, everything that is good in Greek philosophy,[31] but also as the unique "mystery" worthy of the phrase "the true spiritual religion of humanity,"[32] which alone is capable of leading humanity to the knowledge of God and, thereby, to salvation. "The preoccupations of Philo are, above all, moral and concern the ascension of the soul to the knowledge of God."[33] Consequently, we can understand the impression made on him by Hellenistic mysticism and his effort to incorporate it into his system[34]—as long as it is permissible to apply the term *Hellenistic mysticism* to a group of often incoherent ideas that are put forward

---

[27]   J. Bonsirven, *Le Judaïsme palestinien*, 2:159. In France, this opinion is upheld by Adolphe Lods, *Israël* (Paris, 1930), 347, 513-520. It could be claimed for Philo of Alexandria. See below, 77, n. 73.

[28]   Abraham Heschel, *Die Prophetie* (Krakow, 1936). Recension by Dennefeld, "Chronique Biblique," 319-322.

[29]   Hempel, *Gott und Mensch*, 104, 132, 273. It is significant that the Protestant Hempel is of the same opinion as the Jewish Heschel in saying that the prophetic experience is the opposite of a mystical union.

[30]   Cf. William Sanday, *Inspiration: Eight Lectures on the Early History and Origin of the Doctrine of Biblical Inspiration* (Being the Bampton Lectures for 1893), 150: "We never hear of a prophet *volunteering* for his mission. It is laid upon them as a necessity from which they struggle to escape in vain"; quoted in A. Condamin, "Prophétisme israélite," *DAFC* 4:424. Cf. Hempel, *Gott und Mensch*, 96-99.

[31]   With the aim of elevating Judaism above paganism, the Hellenistic Jews dreamed up the theory of theft, according to which Plato and the other Greek philosophers would have taken the best elements of their doctrines from the holy books of the Hebrews. This theory was adopted subsequently by a number of Christian authors. Cf. Ad. Scheck, *De fontibus Clementis Alexandrini* (Augsburg, 1889); Lagrange, *L'orphisme*, 187-189.

[32]   G. Bardy, "Philon le Juif," *DTC* 12:1444.

[33]   Émile Bréhier, *Les idées philosophiques et religieuses de Philon d'Alexandrie* (Paris, 1908), 137.

[34]   On Philo and Hellenistic mysticism, see Joseph Pascher, Ἡ βασιλικὴ ὁδός. *Der Königsweg zu Wiedergeburt und Vergottung bei Philon von Alexandria* (Paderborn, 1931).

without method and almost always in the course of an allegorical exegesis of the sacred books.[35]

Two governing ideas control the whole of Philonian theology and, by that very fact, Philonian mysticism as well. These are the divine transcendence and the necessity of intermediary beings between God and the world.

In order to safeguard the absolute purity and sanctity of "the Being" par excellence [τὸ ὄν],[36] Philo separates Him from the sensory world by the intelligible world, which alone was created directly by Him,[37] and places Him even above the latter.[38] But elsewhere, as a believing Jew, our theosophist does not hesitate to affirm that the supreme Being, while being withdrawn from the sensory universe, does fill it in order to preserve and govern it.[39]

However, as a rule Philo attributes the government of the world to a series of intermediaries. These unsubstantial beings seem to have arisen from a curious effort to combine the Stoic doctrine of the Logos with the Platonic theory of ideas and the biblical speculations on wisdom and the word.[40]

At the top of the intermediaries our author places the Logos, who is conceived sometimes as an abstraction and sometimes as a person. An intelligible Being, who is identical to the intelligible world or at least the model of that world,[41] and who is called "image of God and His angel,"[42] as well as "firstborn son" [πρωτόγονος υἱός] of God,[43] "second God" [δεύτερος θεός],[44] and even "God" without the article,[45] the "divine Logos"[46] is especially conceived of as a cosmic force. Being both model and agent of creation,[47] he is at the same time

88

---

[35]   Cf. Émile Bréhier, *Histoire de la Philosophie,* 1:438-439.

[36]   *Mut.* 27 (3:144). We quote according to the *editio minor* of Cohn, Wendland, and Reiter (Berlin, 1896-1915). The numeral that follows the title of the treatise indicates the paragraph of the text; the numerals in parenthesis indicate the volume and the page of the edition mentioned. Among the qualifiers that Philo attributes to God, we point out the principle ones: "uncreated [ἀγένητος], incorruptible [ἄφθαρτος], and unchanging [ἄτρεπτος]" (*Leg.* 1.51 [1:63]); "the first good and the most perfect" (*Spec.* 1.277 [5:57]). See the list drawn up by Drummond, *Philo Judaeus* (London, 1888), 2:63, reproduced in Lebreton, *Histoire du dogme,* 1:190.

[37]   Cf. *Leg.* 1.41 (1:60).

[38]   The image that Philo makes of the world is composed of three heavens stacked one upon the other: the heaven of the stars, that of the intelligible beings, and the heaven where God is enthroned. See Pascher, *Der Königsweg,* 15-16.

[39]   Cf. *Dec.* 53 (4:233). See Bréhier, *Les idées philosophiques,* 70-76.

[40]   Cf. Lebreton, *Histoire du dogme,* 1:198-209; Bréhier, *Les idées philosophiques,* 83-176.

[41]   See especially *Opif.* 24-25 (1:5-6). Cf. Bréhier, *Les idées philosophiques,* 89-97; Pascher, *Der Königsweg,* 25-26.

[42]   *Somn.* 1.239 (3:237). Cf. *Leg.* 3.96 (1:128): σκιὰ θεοῦ δὲ ὁ λόγος αὐτοῦ ἐστιν.

[43]   *Agr.* 51 (2:100) and in many other places, the list of which can be found in Lebreton, *Histoire du dogme,* 1:617.

[44]   *QG* 2.62, quoted in Eus. *Praep. ev.,* 7.13 (PG 21:545B).

[45]   *Somn.* 1.230 (3:235). Cf. Lebreton, *Histoire du dogme,* 1:239-240.

[46]   *Fug.* 5 (3:98): θεῖος λόγος.

[47]   *Cher.* 127 (1:197). Cf. *Leg.* 3.96 (1:128).

"the most firm and solid support [ἔρεισμα]" and the infrangible bond [δεσμός] of the universe."[48]

As the principal intermediary between God and the world from the physical point of view, the Logos is also such in the moral and religious sphere. Insofar as he is the divine Word revealed, He is, in fact, the messenger of God to human beings and the mediator between the creatures and the Creator.[49] In particular, he is "the royal way" [ὁδὸς βασιλική][50] that leads to "God, the first and only King of the universe."[51]

In his different functions, especially in those as humankind's Guide to God, the Logos is helped and sometimes even replaced by the other intermediaries, the most important of whom are Wisdom, the angels, and the powers, the latter not really being anything other than divine attributes.[52]

Like the author of Wisdom, Philo gives prominence to the biblical words according to which humankind is created in the image of God. But, and this is to be expected with his theory of intermediaries, our philosopher transforms the divine likeness of humankind into a similarity with the Logos: "Among the terrestrial things, nothing is more sacred or more like God [θεοειδέστερον] than humankind; for they are magnificent imprints of a magnificent image that was fashioned after the model of the ideal archetype."[53] Humankind is thus "the image of an image."[54]

By basing his case on the two different accounts of the formation of the first human being,[55] our exegete distinguishes between humankind that was made in the image and humankind that was formed from the ground. "The one who is fashioned," he explains, "is sentient and partakes of quality [μετέχων ποιότητος]; he is composed of a body and a soul, is male or female, and is mortal by nature [φύσει θνητός]. Humankind according to the image, on the contrary, is a kind of idea or type or mark [ἰδέα τις ἢ γένος ἢ σφραγίς], intelligible, incorporeal, neither male nor female, and incorruptible by nature [ἄφθαρτος φύσει]."[56] Having been made before the other, this one is a "generic human being" [τὸν γενικὸν ἄνθρωπον],[57] a "celestial human being" [οὐράνιος ἄνθρωπος].[58]

---

[48] *Plant.* 8-9 (2:126-127).

[49] See especially *Spec.* 1.116 (5:24); *Somn.* 2.188-189 (3:271-272).

[50] According to Num 20:17: A message from Moses to the king of Edom: "Please, let us pass through your country...we will follow the royal way..."

[51] *Post.* 101-102 (2:22-23). On the Philonian Logos, see Pruemm, *Der christliche Glaube,* 1:245-248.

[52] Cf. Bréhier, *Les idées philosophiques,* 112-157; Lebreton, *Histoire du dogme,* 1:198-209.

[53] *Spec.* 3.83 (5:147). Cf. *Opif.* 69 (1:18).

[54] *Opif.* 25 (1:6).

[55] Gen 1:26-27 and 2:7.

[56] *Opif.* 134 (1:38).

[57] *Leg.* 2.12-13 (1:81). Cf. *ibid.,* 1.31-43 (1:58-61). *Conf.* 114 (2:247), κατ᾽ εἰκόνα ἄνθρωπος is identified with the Logos.

[58] *Leg.* 1.31 (1:58).

Nevertheless, in the same treatise *(De opificio mundi)* in which he distinguishes so clearly between the spiritual and the sensory human being, Philo implicitly recognizes that the latter is also in the image of God. He explains in fact that the divine likeness of humankind is not sought in the body: "As God is not anthropomorphic [ἀνθρωπόμορφος], neither is the human body deiform [θεοειδές]." "But the image is expressed according to the νοῦς, the pilot of the soul," which "is, as it were, a god [τρόπον τινὰ θεὸς ὤν] for the one who bears it."[59] It is thus "according to the intellect [κατὰ τὴν διάνοιαν] that anyone may enter into a relationship with the divine Logos, who has become an imprint or a reflection of the blessed nature."[60] This was true especially for the first man. Having been formed by God directly, he was "perfect in soul and body" to a point far surpassing all his descendants.[61]

The divine element that the human soul bears in itself, due to the in-breathing and the divine contact [ἥψατο], renders the soul capable of knowing God. "Indeed, the human νοῦς would never have dared to rise up and grasp the nature of God [ὡς ἀντιλαβέσθαι θεοῦ φύσεως], had not God Himself raised it toward Himself in the measure in which the human νοῦς could be raised, and had not fashioned it according to the powers accessible to knowledge."[62] Hence, it is by utilizing the powers as so many steps that individuals progressively and ordinarily reach the knowledge of God, which is the most precious knowledge there is, since in it they find the height of their perfection and bliss.[63]

91   But very often the intelligence pays attention to inferior powers. A few persons succeed in contemplating the Logos, which is already "a great benefit,"[64] for they become "sons of the most holy Logos."[65] However, all those ones "only celebrate the small mysteries, since they are incapable of grasping the Being without an intermediary, that is, Himself alone, and can only do so through the works that He does, whether by creating or by governing."[66]

The ones who are "initiated into the great mysteries" are very exceptional. They are granted to penetrate into the absolutely divine sphere. Only the "entirely purified" soul can arrive there, which, "when it has gone beyond not only the multitude of numbers, but also the dyad bordering on the monad, soars up to the pure and simple Idea, and is perfectly self-

---

[59] *Opif.* 69 (1:18). Here and in 135 (1:39), where it is said that what God "has infused is none other than a divine intellect," Philo seems to identify this intellect with the νοῦς. Elsewhere, on the contrary, e.g. *Leg.* 1.33-40 (1:58-60), he clearly distinguishes them, since the νοῦς here is presented as "receiving" the intellect.
[60] *Opif.* 146 (1:42).
[61] *Opif.* 136-140 (1:39-40).
[62] *Leg.* 1.38 (1:59-60).
[63] Cf. *Spec.* 1.332 (5:69).
[64] *Fug.* 97 (3:115-116).
[65] *Conf.* 146 (2:247): παῖδες...λόγου τοῦ ἱερωτάτου. On the ascension to the Logos, see Pascher, *Der Königsweg*, 37-160.
[66] *Abr.* 122 (4:24).

sufficient."[67] This purification, in the first place, is of a moral nature; "the mystae worthy of the most holy mysteries are those who, being without ostentation and with modesty, practice genuine and sincere piety."[68] But at the highest degree, it becomes a "second birth" [δευτέρα γένεσις] or a "divine birth" (*divina nativitas*),[69] which mystically makes the initiates purely spiritual beings, or even transforms them into the Logos Himself,[70] that is, "divinizes" them.[71]

When these privileges—and truthfully, Philo knows only a single instance of them, namely, Moses initiated at Sinai by God Himself[72]—are grasped "by the divine *pneuma*," their human νοῦς finds itself "removed; for it is not permitted that the mortal live together with the immortal. Also, the fading out of reason and the obscurity that results from it engender an ecstasy and frenzy that are inspired by God [ἔκστασιν καὶ θεοφόρητον μανίαν]." For when "the human light has faded, the divine light rises up."[73] Then the initiate "soars [ὑπερπτῆναι] above all ideas and genera," and penetrates into "the invisible region," even to God Himself;[74] "for the gnosis and knowledge of God are the conclusion of the way."[75] "By this ascension, which takes place not in the air, nor in the ether, nor in the highest heaven, but above all the heavens, the holy soul is deified [*deificari*],"[76] that is, "transformed into a divine being to the point of becoming similar to God and truly divine."[77]

To listen to him, Philo would have made himself the experiment of a mystical deification of this kind. In his treatise, *De specialibus legibus*, he indeed writes:

> There was a time when, being devoted to philosophy and the contemplation [θεωρία] of the cosmos and of that which it contains, I received the magnificent intellect [νοῦς], which is so desired and truly beatifying. Ever immersed in the meditation of divine words and doctrines, which I enjoyed without ever having my fill of them, and far from thinking about base and earthly things, or from grovelling around in the glory of wealth or bodily pleasures, it seemed to me that

92

---

[67] *Abr.* 122 (4:24). We recall that this idea of a purification of the soul by "unification," i.e. by the reduction of the soul to its true nature or to its original simplicity, must have been strongly exploited by Plotinus. See above, 53-55.

[68] *Cher.* 42 (1:178).

[69] *QE.* 2.46-47, quoted in Pascher, *Der Königsweg*, 242-243.

[70] See Pascher, *Der Königsweg*, 143-160.

[71] *Leg.* 3.44 (1:115); the entirely purified soul is "divinized" [ἐκθειασθῇ].

[72] *Sacr.* 8 (1:201). Cf. *Gig.* 54 (2:52); *Plant.* 26-27 (2:29-130); Pascher, *Der Königsweg*, 238-239.

[73] *Her.* 264-265 (3:51). In this passage, Philo places mystical ecstasy and prophetic agitation on the same plane. In *Opif.* 71 (1:19), Philo calls the ecstasy a "sober drunkenness" [μέθη νηφάλιος].

[74] *Sacr.* 8 (1:201), combined with *Gig.* 54 (2:52). For Philo also, the initiation is made up of a symbolic voyage into a new world. Cf. Pascher, *Der Königsweg*, 13-23.

[75] *Deus* 143 (2:82). Cf. *ibid.*, 160 (2:86): the end of the "royal way" is "to meet the king" [ἐντυχεῖν τῷ βασιλεῖ]. See also *Det.* 89 (1:259).

[76] *QE.* 2.40, quoted in Pascher, *Der Königsweg*, 240.

[77] *QE.* 2.29, Pascher, *Der Königsweg*, 249-250: transmutatur in divinum, ita ut fiat Deo cognatus vereque divinus.

I was continually carried to the height in a kind of divinization of the soul [κατά τινα τῆς ψυχῆς ἐπιθειασμόν] and that I was turning with the sun, the moon, the entire sky, and the cosmos. Then, yes then, as I lifted my eyes above the ether and as if from an observation point aimed the eye of my mind [τὸ τῆς διανοίας ὄμμα], I contemplated the ineffable vision of all that is on the earth, and I considered myself fortunate to have escaped with all my strengths from the destiny of mortal life.[78]

93

There is no need to add that our mystic does not in any way intend to make the initiate a god, in the full sense of the term. Indeed, for him the absolute uniqueness of God is an inviolable dogma. "The true God is unique, but those who are called [gods], so to speak [ἐν καταχρήσει], are numerous."[79] For Philo, ecstasy divinizes in the sense that it makes the "mystae... intermediate beings, between the unbegotten nature and the corruptible nature [μεθόριον τῆς ἀγενήτου καὶ φθαρτῆς φύσεως],"[80] and, as a result, places them among the divine powers.[81] This does not prevent the initiates, when ecstasy has been passed through and "when they return from the divine things," from "becoming human again."[82] But the day will come in which death will permanently confirm them in the state of bliss that they had known in ecstasy.[83]

Thus, according to Philo, perfect deification is carried out by an intuitive knowledge of God, that is, a vision which takes place outside the νοῦς or, better still, over the νοῦς, due to a direct contact with divinity. This is all that is necessary for a properly mystical experience. Oddly enough, this mysticism appears as if it is both intellectualistic, since it ends up in an intuition of God, and irrational—the vision is achieved apart from reason. Using Philo's own expression, it is really a question of a "literary mystery concerning the Unbegotten and His powers" [τὸν ἱερὸν περὶ τοῦ ἀγενήτου καὶ τῶν δυνάμεων αὐτοῦ μύστην λόγον],[84] manifestly modelled on the mysteries made known to us by Hermetism.

94

On the other hand, the Philonian mystery seems to have exercised a profound influence on Plotinian mysticism. The two conceptions resemble each other so much that only a dependence of Plotinus upon Philo can explain their relationship.[85]

However, alongside some very marked similarities, there are some no less considerable differences, the principal ones of which are as follows:

---

[78]   *Spec.* 3.1-2 (5:129).

[79]   *Somn.* 1.229 (3:235). Cf. *Det.* 161-162 (1:276).

[80]   *Somn.* 2.234 (3:279). Of note is the very Platonic contrast between ἀγένητος and φθαρτός.

[81]   Cf. *Sacr.* 5-8 (1:200-201). Thus understood, deification seems to involve degrees and to be suitable also for those who are initiated only to the minor mysteries. According to the *Corp. herm.* (*Poimandres*) 1.26 (Scott 1:128), having arrived at the end of their ascension, the mystae "become powers and are in God" [δυνάμεις γενόμενοι ἐν θεῷ γίνονται]. See above, 32.

[82]   *Somn.* 2.233 (3:279).

[83]   Cf. Pascher, *Der Königsweg*, 251-252, 260.

[84]   *Sacr.* 60 (1:215).

[85]   Cf. Arnou, *Le désir de Dieu*, 259-263.

Philo supports his assertions by an allegorical—it would be more accurate to call it "fanciful"— exegesis of the holy books of his people. Plotinus, on the contrary, derives his theory of ecstasy from his philosophical principles.[86] In either conception, the mystical experience, in that it suspends the νοῦς, appears to suppress personal consciousness. Nevertheless, the Jewish theosophist unequivocally maintains the distinction between God and the soul in ecstasy, whereas the Greek philosopher seems to sacrifice this distinction.

One final trait, more than all the rest, contrasts the Philonian mysticism with that of Plotinus: if for the latter the contemplation of God, which is the supreme good of man, is accessible to human strength alone, then this contemplation assumes, in Philo, the coming of the divine mind into the soul. Consequently, the vision of God and, as a result, perfect bliss are a free gift, that is, a grace of God. As a result, Greek intellectualism and naturalism prove to be surpassed; divine revelation and grace as sources of knowledge and bliss are placed above reason. By endeavoring to infuse Hellenistic mysticism in this way with a Jewish soul, Philo has prepared the way for Christian mysticism.

---

[86] Cf. Arnou, *Le désir de Dieu,* 205-271.

CHAPTER THREE

THE NEW TESTAMENT

95   With the New Testament, we enter into a world very different from that of the Old. What constitutes the distinctive character of the Christian revelation in relation to the Jewish revelation is that the former revolves around the person of Jesus Christ, who is recognized by His believers not only as the Messiah predicted by the prophets, but also as the unique Son of God who was incarnated. As a result, a transcendent divine filiation appears, which the Old Testament had not imagined.

And yet, by His incarnation, the Son of God has become the brother of humankind in order to save them. To that end, He reconciles them to His Father, who consequently adopts them as children. Thus, by the appearance of Christ, the Judaic conception of divine filiation is transformed and raised up to a genuine participation. Barely sketched out in the Synoptics, this transformation becomes manifest in Saint Paul and Saint John.[1]

I

96   In the Synoptics, in order to express the relations between God and humanity, Jesus goes back to the metaphor of fatherhood familiar to the Old Testament, but He gives it a more complex and intimate sense.

God is first the Father of humankind insofar as He is the Creator and "Lord of the heaven and of the earth."[2] According to the covenant concluded with them, He is always, by a special title, the Father of the Jews.[3] But there is another divine filiation which, far from being based upon a privilege of race,[4] is of a purely spiritual nature, since it is a divine gift put within reach of all.

---

[1]   Here we need not enter into the discussion of problems of authenticity and historicity that have been raised about the writings of the New Testament, a discussion which, due to the efforts of A. Loisy (see especially: *Remarques sur la littérature épistolaire du Nouveau Testament* [Paris, 1935]; *Les origines du Nouveau Testament* [Paris, 1936]) and J. Turmel (notably: *Les écrits de Saint Paul* [4 vols.; 1926-1928], published under the pseudonym H. Delafosse) has recently experienced a revival in France. Furthermore, however great their importance to other points of view may be, these questions could only touch upon our subject from afar. Indeed, the New Testament writings are of interest to us here not as the personal work of some author or other, but as documents reflecting the faith of the first Christian generations.

[2]   Luke 10:21. Cf. Matt 6:25-34; 7:7-11; Luke 11:9-13; 12:22-31.

[3]   Cf. Matt 15:21-28; Mark 7:24-30. In this discussion with the woman of Canaan, Jesus adopts the Jews' manner of speaking, in calling the latter "children" and the Gentiles "the dogs." See also Matt 6:7-8, 31-33, where the Jews are contrasted with the Gentiles and where God is called the Father of the Jews.

[4]   Cf. Matt 8:11-13; Luke 13:28-29.

To obtain this spiritual filiation, human beings, who have been estranged from God by sin, must firstly renounce this by μετάνοια, that is, by a profound change of heart that includes the loathing of evil and the confident return to God.[5] Furthermore, they must "believe in the gospel"[6] and become "children of the kingdom"[7] as preached by Christ.

Not content to impose upon His disciples the practice of righteousness, the Savior calls them to perfection:

> I, on the contrary, say to you: Love your enemies and pray for those who perse-cute you, in order that you may be children of your Father who is in the heavens; for He makes His sun to rise over wicked and good, and makes it rain on just and unjust....Therefore, you also be perfect as your heavenly Father is perfect.[8]

This is a wonderful call that in its simplicity is infinitely more religious, more accessible to the masses, and hence more stirring than the aristocratic ὁμοιοῦσθαι τῷ θεῷ of Plato.

To imitate the heavenly Father's infinite kindness by a practice of charity which extends, if necessary, all the way to the love of enemies is the distinguishing feature of the perfect divine filiation.

Having become "members of [His] family,"[9] the disciples of Jesus enter into a special relationship of a love that is confident toward God;[10] they are the "blessed" of the Father, for whom the kingdom "has been prepared from the creation of the world."[11]

In this last text, it is a matter of the kingdom in its stage of completion, that is, of "eternal life"[12] "in the age to come."[13] The righteous "will shine there as the sun"[14] and "will have a place at the feast" with the patriarchs.[15] "They will be satisfied,...will see God,...will be called children of God."[16]

As we can see, the conception of divine filiation expressed in the Synoptics is in principle free from considerations of a racial nature. It also brings out an intimacy with which pseudo-Solomon was unacquainted. Finally, by present-ing divine filiation in its definitive stage as a sure participation in the unfailing glory and blessing of God, the Synoptics lead us to the threshold of the mystery

97

---

[5] See especially Luke 15:11-32 on the parable of the prodigal son; Luke 18:9-14 on the Pharisee and the publican.

[6] Mark 1:15. Cf. Matt 10:7; Luke 10:9, 11.

[7] Cf. Matt 13:37-39. In this passage, "the children of the kingdom" are the disciples of Christ who practice righteousness (v. 43). In Matt 8:11-12, by contrast, the same expression indicates the unbeliev-ing Jews who will be "cast into the outer darkness."

[8] Matt 5:44-48.

[9] Matt 25:31-46. Cf. Mark 3:35; Luke 8:19-21; Matt 10:32; 18:20.

[10] Matt 6:5-34; Luke 12:22-32.

[11] Matt 25:34.

[12] Matt 19:29; Mark 10:30.

[13] Mark 10:30; Luke 18:30.

[14] Matt 13:43, according to Dan 12:3.

[15] Matt 8:11. Cf. Isa 25:6; Matt 22:1-14; 26:29; Mark 14:25.

[16] Matt 5:6-9. Cf. Wis 5:5.

according to which a Christian is assimilated to the divine nature; and this is a mystery about which Saint Paul and Saint John have some more profound developments in store for us.

II

Indeed, the revelation of the mystery of deification owes its most decisive progress to Saint Paul. To be convinced of this, it is sufficient to compare Jesus' preaching on salvation according to the Synoptics with Saint Paul's doctrine on the Christ-Savior. So striking is the difference that some have wanted to make the apostle the creator of the "Christian mystery" of the redemption.[17] But if not its author, "he was certainly its most ardent preacher and first theologian."[18] By developing the initial elements of the primitive tradition concerning the economy of salvation unveiled by Jesus, Saint Paul actually worked out the first Christian theory of salvation. And the most personal element of Pauline soteriology is a mysticism of deification of which the glorious Christ is the center.

Like every doctrine of salvation, that of the apostle is controlled by the conception of overcoming evil, *in casu* of sin, which forms its point of departure. Not content to state the fact of sin, the apostle inquires into its historical origin, which he finds in the Genesis account of the disobedience of Adam. The first man's sin is the source of all the physical and moral miseries which weigh humanity down, namely, enmity with God, personal sin with its humiliating slavery, suffering, and especially death. This is according to a mysterious joint responsibility that exists by virtue of a divine arrangement between Adam and all of his descendants, whereby Adam is not only the first man, but the head and representative of humanity, which, because of this, he involves in his fall.

But here, after having temporarily given humanity up to its particular weakness, without however completely rejecting it, when the fullness of time comes, God sends His unique Son, clothed in human flesh, to humanity so that as a new Adam He might rectify the work of death of the first one. Adam and Jesus are thus, for Paul, the two pivots around which the religious history of humanity revolves. The first, the father of sinful humanity, is by antithesis the type, that is, the figure, of the second, who is the father of regenerated humanity.

Nevertheless, if it is true that Paul sees Adam, particularly, as the father of sin and death, he clearly says that the first man became such only after his fall. Without describing it directly, the apostle places the original condition of Adam in parallel with the state of justice and holiness brought by Christ, since he presents the latter's work as a renewal, a reconciliation,[19] and a restoration.[20] Furthermore, by saying that death has entered into the world only "through

---

[17] Cf. F. Prat, *La théologie de Saint Paul* (2 vols.; 7th ed.; Paris, 1923), 2:25-32.
[18] Rivière, *Rédemption: étude théologique*, 62.
[19] 2 Cor 5:17-20.
[20] Rom 5:15-21; 1 Cor 15:21-22.

sin,"[21] he implicitly recognizes the gift of immortality in the innocent Adam. By acknowledging in that way a basic identity between the two states, primitive and restored, Saint Paul seems to be suggesting that Adam was originally raised to a state of divine friendship and adorned with extraordinary gifts. This was to the point of possessing a likeness with God that was superior by far to what he held from his actual formation, according to which he was "the image of the glory of God."[22]

The privileges that our first father lost for himself and his posterity Christ has superabundantly restored to them. By dying on the cross, the God-Man destroyed sin and death; by resurrecting, He established a new life,[23] and became "the origin, the firstborn from among the dead,"[24] and "the firstborn within a large family."[25]

In order to share in this "newness of life,"[26] in this kind of "new creation,"[27] a person must be conformed to the image of Christ;[28] he must be "buried with Him by baptism into His death" and "grafted onto Him," so that, being "set free from sin"[29] and saved "by the washing of regeneration,"[30] he may live "to God in Christ Jesus."[31]

In this way, union with Christ is the condition and the means of the new life, 100 and thus of salvation. There is consequently nothing surprising in the fact that the expression "in Christ," or its equivalents, reappears so frequently under the apostle's pen.[32] More uncommon, but no less expressive, is the form "Christ in us."[33] Most certainly, the expression ἐν Χριστῷ sometimes expresses membership in the mystical body of Christ which is the church[34] and can, in several texts, be rendered by the adjective "Christian."[35] In the great majority of cases, however, it means that Christ is intimately joined to His believers, and that there exists between Him and them a genuine identity of life. Such at least, without a possible doubt, is the meaning of the expression "Christ in us."

---

[21] Rom 5:12.
[22] 1 Cor 11:7.
[23] Rom 6.
[24] Col 1:18.
[25] Rom 8:29.
[26] Rom 6:4.
[27] 2 Cor 5:17. Cf. Eph 2:4-10.
[28] Rom 8:29.
[29] Rom 6:1-10. We need not insist here on the measures of a moral nature that Saint Paul calls for, with justification by baptism in mind.
[30] Titus 3:5: διὰ λουτροῦ παλιγγενεσίας.
[31] Rom 6:11.
[32] We have counted up to 164 passages that contain it. See A. Wickenhauser, *Die Christusmystik des hl. Paulus* (Münster in Westphalia, 1928), 10; Prat, *La théologie de Saint Paul,* 2:476-480.
[33] Cf. Wickenhauser, *Die Christusmystik,* 21-25.
[34] So in Rom 16:7; Gal 3:28.
[35] Cf. Gal 1:22: "the churches of Judaea in Christ." See Wickenhauser, *Die Christusmystik,* 14-15; Prat, *La théologie de Saint Paul,* 2:476-480.

In brief, for Saint Paul Jesus' union with His believers is a fact. But what is its nature? It is surely a union of a moral nature, an identity of sentiments, and a conformity of thought, of will, and of action. Christians ought to have "the same sentiments with which Christ Jesus was animated"[36] and thus Christ will be "formed in them."[37]

But the reality that the Pauline expression covers is much richer. In fact, according to the apostle the glorified Christ, who has become a "life-giving spirit,"[38] is like an atmosphere in which the baptized ones are immersed[39]; He co-penetrates them to the point of being "one body" and "one spirit,"[40] and "one new human being"[41] with them. This means that baptism insures a direct contact between the glorious Lord and His believers. Now Christ is God, because in Him "dwells all the fullness of the deity bodily."[42] As a result, the sacrament of Christian initiation creates an immediate union between God and the individual, which is strengthened even more by the Eucharist.[43]

So, "for Saint Paul the Christian life is a divine life, in which the believer, as it were, appropriates the spiritual and divine nature of Christ to become a new person and arrive at perfection."[44] This objective union with the Lord need only be changed into experience in order to become mystical in the strict sense of the word.[45]

His own writings clearly prove that Saint Paul experienced such a transformation. In fact, for him the communion of life with his divine Master, so beloved, is not a speculative and abstract truth; it is a profoundly heartfelt and true-life reality, and the principle of his moral activity.[46] All his piety aims at intensifying this experience from which he draws the indomitable energy that, despite his physical weakness, makes him the most ardent and greatest of the apostles. This is because he feels "taken hold of by Christ"[47] as by an irresistible force,[48] by which he knows he is inseparably united with

---

[36]   Phil 2:5. Cf. Rom 6–7.

[37]   Gal 4:19. The Greek fathers connected their doctrine of the birth of the Logos in the heart of each believer with this text. See Hugo Rahner, "Die Gottesgeburt," *ZKT* 59 (1935): 333-418.

[38]   1 Cor 15:45.

[39]   This is the sense of the expression βαπτίζειν εἰς Χριστόν and other similar ones. Cf. Wickenhauser, *Die Christusmystik*, 65-66; Prat, *La théologie de Saint Paul*, 2:361-362.

[40]   1 Cor 12:12-13. Cf. Eph 2:16.

[41]   Eph 2:15. The Pauline conception of the mystical body assumes the intimate union of the individual Christian with the Lord. The mystical body is only the social aspect of this union. Cf. J.-B. Colon, "A propos de la 'mystique' de Saint Paul," *RevScRel* 15 (1935): 179-180.

[42]   Col 2:9-10.

[43]   Cf. 1 Cor 10:17; 11:27.

[44]   Colon, "La 'mystique' de Saint Paul," 171-172.

[45]   We call "mystical," in the strict sense only, the *"psychological* event" in which man thinks to directly and immediately arrive at God, in a word, "to experience" God, in whatever way this may be. Cf. A. Fonck, "Mystique," *DTC* 10:2600; Colon, "La 'mystique' de Saint Paul," 160-163; Anselme Stolz, *Theologie der Mystik* (Ratisbon, 1936), 13-16.

[46]   Cf. G. Staffelbach, *Die Vereinigung mit Christus als Prinzip der Moral bei Paulus*, (Freiburg im Breisgau, 1932).

[47]   Phil 3:12. It is not without reason that a recent author calls Paul "one who was possessed by Christ." See Henri Morice, *La vie mystique de Saint Paul* (Paris, 1932), 245.

[48]   2 Cor 5:14: *Caritas Christi urget nos.* Cf. 1 Cor. 9:16-19.

Him.[49] Strengthened by Him, he can do all things.[50] In a word, it is no longer   102
he, Paul, who lives, but it is Christ who lives in him.[51]

There is therefore in the apostle's doctrine concerning salvation through incorporation with Christ a mysticism of the divinization of Christians.[52] Is it necessary to add that, in the thought of Saint Paul, the mystical union which divinizes leaves the individual's personality intact, and that it could never become an absorption, that is, the return of a small stream of life to the great river so as to be lost and dissolved there?[53]

Incorporation with Christ has as a necessary consequence the joining of the Christian to the Father and to the Holy Spirit as well. The baptized ones are reconciled to God;[54] because of the gift of "adoptive filiation,"[55] they are the "children," the "heirs of God, and the co-heirs of Christ."[56] Furthermore, they are specially consecrated to the Holy Spirit. This One dwells in them;[57] together with Christ, He is like the motor of their salutary activity[58] and their new life. Indeed, the believer lives in the Spirit, just as he lives in Christ; in his soul the activity of the one is inseparable from that of the other. As the incorporation with Christ is a "pledge" of the "glory to   103 come,"[59] in the same way the gift of the Spirit is "a deposit" of the inheritance for the Christian.[60]

Under these conditions, we can say without exaggeration that, while being christocentric, Pauline mysticism does have the divine Spirit as its active principle.

---

[49]   Rom 8:35-39.

[50]   Phil 4:13.

[51]   Gal 2:20. Concerning this text, Fr. Lagrange speaks of an "explosion of mystical faith" (*L'orphisme*, 198).

[52]   Cf. Émile Mersch, *Le corps mystique du Christ* (2 vols.; 2d ed.; Paris, 1936), 1:190-191. The author draws the same conclusion from the Pauline doctrine of the mystical body.

[53]   See Wickenhauser, *Die Christusmystik*, 58-59. E. Jacquier, "Mystères païens (les) et Saint Paul," *DAFC* 3:595-596. Assuredly, it is difficult for us to conceive of the mystical union proclaimed by the apostle. Wickenhauser believes in finding analogies; for example, the ones of the indwelling of personified divine Wisdom in the soul of the righteous (cf. Wis 7:27–11) and of the devil's activity in sinners (52). Be that as it may, "the difficulty that a person of today might have in intellectualizing such a conception is not a sufficient reason for not recognizing it in the Scripture." E. Tobac, "Grâce," *DAFC* 2:338. Cf. Colon, "La 'mystique' de Saint Paul," 183.

[54]   Rom 5:10-11.

[55]   Gal 4:5. Cf. 3:26.

[56]   Rom 8:14-17. Since it is an assimilation to Christ which is the condition of our salvation according to Paul, Pauline mysticism is a union with Christ and not with God directly. See Wickenhauser, *Die Christusmystik*, 104.

[57]   1 Cor 3:16-17; 6:19; 2 Cor. 6:16; Eph 2:22.

[58]   Cf. Rom 8:14.

[59]   2 Cor 1:22; 5:5. Cf. Rom 8:18, 23-25.

[60]   Eph 1:13-14. Cf. 2 Cor 1:22; Rom 6; 8:11. See Colon, "La 'mystique' de Saint Paul," 329-332.

The inheritance to which Christians have right, and of which their present condition is like an anticipation, is eternal life. That is where their union with Christ and with God, which is being realized from this life onward, will be brought to the maximum intimacy; they will be "forever with the Lord."[61] He "will transform the body of our humiliation in order to render it conformed to the body of His glory."[62] Clothed with "a spiritual body"[63] and thus having become "incorruptible" [ἄφθαρτοι],[64] we will see God "face to face."[65] At that time our assimilation to the glorious Christ, in other words, our divinization, will reach its culminating point.

The Pauline conception of deification, namely, the participation in the specifically divine attribute of blessed incorruptibility,[66] is clearly related to the analogous ideas that we have encountered in Wisdom and the Synoptics. But the theology and, more especially, the mysticism of the apostle have this point in particular: they present divinization as the direct effect of the assimilating union with Christ that baptism brings about. This is something new not only compared with the Old Testament, but also in view of the first three gospels.[67] It is not that the mystical significance of baptism is necessarily a discovery of Paul, since the believers in Rome were already acquainted with it when the apostle entered into relations with them for the first time.[68] The novelty consists in the fact that, for the first time in the Scripture, this idea of salvation comes out, in the Pauline Epistles, of deification that is obtained by a mystical assimilation to the death and resurrection of the God-Savior—a conformity that is definitely produced by baptism.

From whence does this mysticism of divinization come, one which is already familiar to the Christians of the church in Rome when Paul writes to them? It is a problem as difficult as it is delicate, and for around fifty years it has been fascinating theologians, exegetes, and indeed even philologists, and has received the most conflicting solutions.[69]

104

---

[61]   1 Thes 4:17. To express the union of the believer with Christ in the hereafter, the apostle never employs the expression "in" Christ, but "with" Christ. See Wickenhauser, *Die Christusmystik*, 33-34, 113-114; 118-119; Colon, "La 'mystique' de Saint Paul," 343.

[62]   Phil 3:20.

[63]   1 Cor 15:44.

[64]   1 Cor 15:52.

[65]   1 Cor 13:12; 2 Cor 5:7.

[66]   Cf. 1 Tim 6:16, where God is called ὁ μόνος ἔχων ἀθανασίαν.

[67]   Fr. Pruemm, *Der christliche Glaube*, 2:291-293, endeavors to find the "foundation" of Pauline mysticism in the idea of the [vicarious] satisfaction that is manifested in Matt 20:28, in the "mysticism of suffering" [*Leidensmystik*] that would imply the invitation to bear the cross in pursuit of Christ (Matt 10:38), and even indeed in the Old Testament, where "from the protevangelium, there extends the theology of joint responsibility [*Theologie der Verbundenheit*] that there is between humanity and its future Savior." The "foundation," to tell the truth, is as feeble as it is fragile.

[68]   Cf. Rom 6:3, 6, 11, 16. See Wickenhauser, *Die Christusmystik*, 112; J.-B. Colon, "Paul," *DTC* 11:2448.

[69]   In Pruemm, *Der christliche Glaube*, 2:275-321, we find an exposition and closely reasoned discussion of the problem. Cf. Jacquier, "Mystères païens," 982-1014; W. Bousset, *Kyrios Christos* (2d ed.; Göttingen, 1921), preface.

As we have seen, to imitate the "passion" of a hero-savior in order to insure salvation is like the *leitmotiv* or "constructive principle"[70] of the mystery religions.[71] Without doubt—and what is about to be said of Paul also applies to the other missionaries who evangelized the pagans, in particular to those among them who had come from the Gentiles—"the apostle knew certain doctrines of the mystery religions; it could not be otherwise, because these ideas, we could say, were in the public domain; they were not secret. Furthermore, Paul, who was in frequent contact with converted pagans, some of whom had been initiated into the mysteries, must have learned the conceptions and rites of the mysteries from these converts—the conceptions in order to combat them, the rites in order to judge them."[72]

Consequently, we can realize that, while strongly insisting on the essential differences that contrast the Christian mysticism of baptism with the similar conceptions of pagan mysteries,[73] and while rejecting the hypothesis whereby Saint Paul would have made direct borrowings from these mysteries, a number of authors, even Catholic ones, consider that we do not have the right "to exclude the *possibility* that the missionaries (who had come from the Gentiles) would make use of the idea according to which the destiny of the mystes is combined with that of the god; and they would do this in order to explain to their hearers, by means that are borrowed from their way of thinking and of seeing, the significance of baptism for the one who receives it. This is perhaps in deliberate contrast with the pagan belief, as Saint Paul, for example, says in front of the Areopagus: 'What you worship without knowing is that which I announce to you' (Acts 17:23). Therefore, in our case, what the priests who initiate into the mysteries wrongly affirm concerning their gods (1 Cor 8:5) is fully realized in Christ. There would basically not be any borrowing from the mysteries (*keine sachliche Anleihe*) but simply the utilization of a set form of thought and expression, into which a new content is poured. It is like Paul also saying that to be baptized is to 'put on Christ' (Gal 3:27; Rom 13:14) and thus employing an image that was very widely used in ancient religions, and also familiar to the initiated ones of the mysteries."[74]

In short, the baptismal mystery of divinization would be "an attempt that was undertaken by Christians converted from paganism or by their missionaries to

105

---

[70] The expression is from Fr. Pruemm, *Der christliche Glaube*, 2:277: "Aufbauprinzip."

[71] See above, 29. Cf. A. J. Festugière and Pierre Fabre, *Le monde gréco-romain au temps de Notre-Seigneur* (Paris, 1935), 2:140.

[72] Jacquier, "Mystères païens," 1011.

[73] See in particular Wickenhauser, *Die Christusmystik*, 103-138; Heigl, *Antike Mysterienreligionen*, 60-68.

[74] Wickenhauser, *Die Christusmystik*, 112-113. The opinion of this author is summarized and adopted in B. Heigl, *Antike Mysterienreligionen*, 91-92.

preach Jesus and Christian piety to the Hellenized Gentiles in their own language."[75]

106   Be that as it may, it is certain that in the Pauline Epistles divinization is understood to be only through Christ. It is in the Savior that Christians are regenerated, that they are born new persons reproducing the ideal of perfection which is the Son of God incarnate, and that they thus become adoptive children of God. In brief, it is in Christ that a person is assimilated to God, that is, divinized.

III

No less brilliant a theologian and mystic, the author of the inspired writings which tradition identifies with Saint John the apostle also continues, in his way, the development of the Christian message. Along with Saint Paul, he sees salvation in a participation in the incorruptible and blessed life of God obtained by union with Christ; but he views the conditions of this union differently. So the Pauline idea of the glorious Lord who has become a life-giving spirit is not evident in his writings.[76]

The analogies of the "light" and the "life," which characterize the theodicy of Saint John,[77] also govern his soteriology. Since the fall of Adam, human beings have been plunged into "darkness,"[78] that is, "into evil,"[79] "because their deeds were evil."[80] They were also "in death,"[81] in the grip of divine wrath,[82] and under the rule of Satan.

107   In this world of death and of darkness, the "Logos,"[83] the "Only Begotten" of God,[84] through whom "everything has been made"[85] and in whom "was life,"[86] appears, having been "made flesh,"[87] as "the life"[88] and "the true light."[89] By His

---

[75]   J. Leipoldt, *Sterbende und auferstehende Götter* (Leipzig, 1923), 73. Cf. in the same sense, G. van Randenborgh, *Vergottung und Erlösung* (Berlin, n.d.), 115. The explanation of Leipoldt is viewed as a possibility by B. Bartmann, *Dogma und Religionsgeschichte* (trans. M. Gautier; Paderborn, 1922), 81-82. Dom O. Casel, in *Jahrbuch für Liturgiewissenschaft* 5 (1925): 232, admits as well that, from his way of expressing himself, Saint Paul could have been under influences that were foreign to Christianity. Faller, "Griechische Vergottung," 424-426, speaks of an "adaptation of the language of pagan mysteries to the Christian doctrine of divinization," an adaptation that would have begun with Paul and John.

[76]   The following exposition is inspired by both the fourth Gospel and the First Epistle of Saint John. From our point of view, these two writings form one unit.

[77]   Cf. 1 John 1:5: "God is light;" John 5:26: "The Father has life in Himself."

[78]   John 1:5; 3:19.

[79]   1 John 5:19. Cf. John 1:29.

[80]   John 3:19.

[81]   1 John 3:14. Cf. John 5:24.

[82]   John 3:36.

[83]   John prologue.

[84]   John 1:18.

[85]   John 1:3.

[86]   John 1:4.

[87]   John 1:14.

[88]   John 11:25.

[89]   John 1:9.

incarnation the "Logos of life"[90] becomes the source of divine and eternal life for people,[91] "the bread of life,"[92] and "the true vine," who imparts His sap to those who are joined to Him.[93]

Although he is especially preoccupied with emphasizing the life-giving function of the incarnated Word, the evangelist, for all that, does not forget the expiatory role of Jesus. He indeed is "the Lamb of God,"[94] who by His freely accepted death[95] becomes "a sacrifice of propitiation [ἰλασμός] for our sins."[96]

Finally, after His resurrection the glorious Savior completes His expiatory and enlivening activity by the gift of the Holy Spirit.[97]

In order to have a part in the divine life supplied by Jesus Christ, the individual must be united with Him by faith[98] and a new birth "of water and spirit."[99] This life-giving union of the Savior with His "disciples"[100] and "friends"[101] is consummated in the Eucharist, a new pledge of "eternal life."[102] Through Jesus, the believer is united with the Father and with the Holy Spirit as well.[103] Their mutual love establishes a kind of mystical identity between God, who is love, and the Christian soul, which practices charity.[104]

Being "born of God"[105] or "from above,"[106] and being in possession of a "seed" or of a "germ of God" that "remains in him,"[107] the baptized one is a "child [τέκνον] of God"[108] in the etymological sense of the word.

But although the believers possess eternal life or simply "life" from today onward[109] as well as divine filiation, these gifts will be revealed in all their splendor only in the "kingdom of God," that is to say, in heaven. There, the

---

[90]   1 John 1:1.

[91]   1 John 4:9. Cf. John 3:16; 4:10-14.

[92]   John 6:35.

[93]   John 15:1-8. The image of the vine expresses the same idea of an organic and life-giving union as the analogy of the body that was dear to Saint Paul.

[94]   John 1:29, 36.

[95]   Cf. John 10:11-18.

[96]   1 John 2:2; cf. 4:10; John 3:14-17; 11:51-52; Rev 1:5; 7:14; 22:14.

[97]   John 7:39; 16:7-14; 20:22-23.

[98]   John 3:36.

[99]   John 3:5; cf. 1:13.

[100]   John 13:35.

[101]   John 15:14-15.

[102]   John 6:32-58.

[103]   John 14:15-23.

[104]   1 John 1:3; 4:7-21.

[105]   John 1:13; cf. 3:5-8.

[106]   John 3:3, 7.

[107]   1 John 3:9.

[108]   John 1:12. Whereas Saint Paul employs the word υἱός to designate the quality of an adoptive son, Saint John exclusively makes use of the term τέκνον, meaning "one who has been begotten," derived from τίκτειν.

[109]   On the synonymy of these two expressions, see J.-B. Frey, "Le concept de vie dans l'évangile de Saint Jean," *Bib* 1 (1920): 52. In Saint John, the kingdom of the Synoptics and Saint Paul "has become life" (Tobac, "Grâce," 340).

friends of Jesus will not only be with Him forever to gaze upon His glory [δόξαν],[110] but in seeing God "as He is," they will be "like [ὅμοιοι] Him."[111]

Thus underneath the clothing of different analogies, the Johannine writings contain a teaching on the divinization of the Christian that in its broad outline agrees with that of Paul; in fact, with the two apostles it is through union with Christ that a person is filled with divine life. Although he speaks of it with less ardor than the apostle of the Gentiles, there is no doubt that the beloved disciple himself has lived in this union, and that for him as well it has become a mystical experience.

Along the way, we may have observed that the coupled concepts of "life and light" as applied to God, and also the idea of an assimilation to God, that is, of deification by the vision of God, which is expressed in the First Epistle of Saint John[112]—to point out only the most important contact points[113]—are also found in Hermetic literature.[114] Most certainly, the fundamental differences that separate this literature from the Johannine writings, as well as the very marked originality that characterizes each of these two groups of documents, absolutely exclude any direct dependence that we may place on whatever side. But here again it is not beyond possibility to explain the undeniable similarities by the influence that a common Hellenistic environment would have exerted on the two currents of ideas, Christian and pagan.

109

IV

In the rest of the New Testamental writings, the conceptions of salvation hardly exceed the level of the Synoptics. Only the Epistles of Saint Peter in places recall "the splendid flights of Saint Paul and Saint John."[115] The second of Peter's letters contains a passage that has become rightly famous, and which seems to sum up, by clarifying it, the soteriology of the two apostles. The text, which is unfortunately obscure and, consequently, very controversial, is as follows:

> Seeing that His divine power has granted to us everything for life and piety, by the knowledge [διὰ τῆς ἐπιγνώσεως] of the One who has called us by His own glory and virtue, by which precious and very great promises [ἐπαγγέλματα] have been granted to us, in order that by these you might become partakers of the divine nature [ἵνα διὰ τούτων γένησθε θείας κοινωνοὶ φύσεως], after you have escaped from the corruption [φθορᾶς] of lust [that is] in the world.[116]

---

[110]   John 3:3-5 combined with 17:24.

[111]   1 John 3:2. In this text, the divine likeness appears as an effect of the vision of God.

[112]   1 John 3:2, just quoted. Cf. John 6:40; 17:3, texts in which eternal life is presented as an effect of the vision or of the knowledge of the Father and of His Messenger.

[113]   See also other analogies in Bousset, *Kyrios Christos*, 154-177.

[114]   Cf. *Corp. herm.*, 1 (Poimandres). 9, where God is said "to be ζωὴ καὶ φῶς." See above, 31. Other examples in Bousset, *Kyrios Christos*, 174-175.

[115]   Tobac, "Grâce," 339.

[116]   2 Pet 1:3-4.

Is the *consortium divinae naturae* in question here gained from the time of this present life? Or is it rather the object of a promise, which is a goal to be attained only when we have left this corrupt world and have entered "into the eternal kingdom of our Lord and Savior Jesus Christ"?[117] This latter interpretation seems preferable.[118]

Whatever the moment of its realization, the partaking of the divine nature clearly appears to be a gift of God that is entirely free, yet conditioned by the moral effort of the individual; it is a grace of assimilation to God. It is not a matter of a simple "conformity"[119] of a moral nature only, which results, of course, from the imitation of God. Such a conformity is the indispensable condition but is not the essence of the partaking of the divine nature. Indeed, the latter consists in making people share in the "eternal glory,"[120] in the very life of God,[121] that is to say, in His blessed incorruptibility;[122] in brief, it consists in deifying them. We might well think that, along with Paul and John, our writer saw final divinization as an effect of the vision of God.

Has Peter acknowledged, with Paul and John, that from here on earth onward the Christian possesses, at least in the early stages, the partaking of the divine nature? Taken in themselves, Saint Peter's writings do not allow us to settle this question. Nevertheless, it does not seem rash to attribute to him an idea strongly implied by Saint Paul and Saint John, whereby the heavenly glory is only the blossoming of the new life with which the baptized are favored from the time of their earthly existence onward.[123] It is therefore probable that our author also makes the deification of the Christian begin from the present life.[124]

Consequently, there is nothing surprising in the fact that the fathers made a very special case of this text, utilizing it as one of the principle scriptural arguments in favor of their doctrine of divinization.

Therefore, if this latter term and its equivalents are absent from the New Testament, it is not less certain that the reality which they express is found there. Having been united with God, having become an adoptive child of God, living by a truly divine life, and assured of blessed incorruptibility, all by and in

---

117 2 Pet 1:11.

118 Cf. 1 Pet 1:3-5, 13.

119 Cf. 1 Pet 1:14-15: it is necessary to be "conformed" [συσχηματιζόμενοι] to Jesus Christ.

120 1 Pet 5:10.

121 1 Pet 4:6.

122 Cf. 1 Pet 1:23, where it is said that, in the Christian, the divine word is "a seed that is not able to be corrupted, but is incorruptible." See also 1:3-4; 5:4.

123 Fr. Lange, *De gratia*, 303, considers that in the text of Saint Peter the expression ἐπαγγέλματα ought to be translated by "promised things" rather than by "promises;" most probably the partaking of the divine nature would therefore be granted from this life (183). Even if we adopt the eschatological interpretation, as the author further writes, we can appeal to the biblical idea in which the gifts of the future glory are pre-formed in the gifts of grace.

124 Mysticism is absent from the Second Epistle of Saint Peter.

Christ, the Christian is assimilated to God and partakes of the divine nature as much as is possible for a human creature.

This is the "good news" that Christianity has come to announce to the world as the supernatural realization—by virtue of the incarnated Son of God—as much of Jewish aspirations to divine filiation as of the Greek ideal of deification.

The Greek fathers will continue the same gospel by adapting it to their environment and explaining it with the resources at their disposal. All will echo, although to different degrees, the Pauline doctrine that bases our salvation on the death of Christ. But several among them, preferring to develop the Johannine idea of the Logos as the incarnated source of the divine life, will insist on the incarnation as the principle of our divinization.

BOOK ONE

THE PREPARATION

Part I: HELLENIC ANALOGS
Part II: BIBLICAL AND JUDAIC PARTICULARS

BOOK TWO

THE DOCTRINE OF THE GREEK FATHERS

Part I: THE PERIOD OF FORMATION
Part II: THE PERIOD OF APOGEE
Part III: THE PERIOD OF CONSOLIDATION

Among the Greek fathers the seeds of a doctrine of divinization contained in the New Testament fell on a soil all the more fertile to receive them and make them fruitful due to the religious and philosophical conceptions which they held from Hellenism. Therefore, almost unanimously they were not satisfied with teaching the fact of the deification of the Christian, although sometimes they did this only implicitly. Rather, they applied themselves at an early stage to specifying its practical details.

This work of development, which stretches over approximately seven centuries, was accomplished in three stages. In the first stage (during the second and third centuries), the rough draft is drawn. In the fourth century, due to the substantial progress that the Alexandrians and the Cappadocians made in Christology and in the theology of the Holy Spirit, the doctrine blossoms greatly and reaches its peak. The third period (from the fifth to eighth centuries) reveals the doctrine of divinization being consolidated—in the realm of theology with Saint Cyril of Alexandria and in the field of mysticism with pseudo-Dionysius. Finally, the Damascene incorporates the essential elements of the teaching of his predecessors into his theology and leaves them to posterity.

BOOK ONE

THE PREPARATION

Part I: HELLENIC ANALOGS
Part II: BIBLICAL AND JUDAIC PARTICULARS

BOOK TWO

THE DOCTRINE OF THE GREEK FATHERS

CHAPTER ONE

EARLY SKETCHES

1. The Apostolic Fathers

In moving from the New Testament to the apostolic fathers, we notice that   116
the soteriological conceptions of these first, non-inspired witnesses of the
development of Christian doctrine in the early church are related to those of the
Synoptics. Only seldom do they rise to the height of the views of a Saint Paul or a
Saint John. This is doubtless due to the fact that, with the exception of Saint
Ignatius, they are of intellects that are not very speculative, being moralists
rather than theologians or mystics.

Nevertheless, all of them echo the New Testament revelation in which the
salvation offered by Christianity consists essentially in ἀφθαρσία or ἀθανασία,
terms synonymous with eternal life. And therein lies the practical equivalent of
deification—a term, moreover, that is absent from their vocabulary. Only the
bishop of Antioch shows himself to have been genuinely touched by Pauline
and Johannine mysticism.

It is only from then on, virtually, that the idea of the deification of humankind through Christianity is found among the apostolic fathers. Even so, in one
of them, Hermas, we encounter a case of divinization which, special and
exceptional though it is, nonetheless merits being pointed out.

I

According to the Didache, that "elementary handbook of religion" so appre-   117
ciated by the first Christian generations, it is through Jesus that God has made
"life and gnosis [γνῶσις]" known to humankind,[1] has revealed to them "gnosis,
faith, and immortality [ἀθανασία]," and has given them "nourishment and a
spiritual drink, as well as an eternal life."[2] This last item will be received at the
parousia. Indeed, it is then that the "immortal benefit" [τὸ ἀθάνατον][3] will be
granted to the "saints" as their portion. They alone will rise from the dead and
accompany the Lord who comes on the clouds from heaven.[4]

---

[1] *Did.* 9.3, (ed. F.-X. Funk, *Patres apostolici* [2 vols.; Tübingen, 1901], 1:22). The page numbers
which follow the succeeding references refer to Funk's edition. Its text is reproduced in H. Hemmer, *Les
Pères apostoliques* (4 vols.; Paris, 1907-1912). The work of Funk has been re-edited by K. Bihlmeyer, *Die
apostolischen Väter* (Tübingen, 1924).

[2] *Did.* 10.2-3 (22).

[3] *Did.* 4.8 (12).

[4] *Did.* 16.6-8 (36).

Such a conception of salvation very much emphasizes the element of immortality. Yet it is inferior to that of the Synoptics, in that we hardly see any emphasis on the divine filiation of the Christian.

This last idea takes up more space in the curious letter known as Barnabas, in which a conception of salvation is expressed that is richer than that of the Didache, although it is distorted by a particularly pronounced millenarianism.

"Before believing in God," writes the anonymous author who readily draws from the Pauline Epistles, "the tabernacle of our heart was transient and void...as well as being the habitation of demons, because we did that which was contrary to God." But "after having received the remission of sins and hope in the Name, we have become new, having been created as new a second time. This is why in our dwelling God truly dwells in us."[5] Such a transformation, carried out through baptism,[6] is "a restoration in the remission of sins," a second creation,[7] a "sanctification of the heart,"[8] which makes of us "children of God."[9]

"Those who hope in Jesus will live eternally."[10] Eternal life will be inaugurated after the resurrection[11] by the millennium, which the Son of God will come to establish in the seventh millennium. After having reigned for a thousand years, "He will put an end to all things; and this will be the beginning of the eighth day, which will mark the advent of a new world."[12]

Thus, according to pseudo-Barnabas the moral restoration of Christians, as well as their divine filiation, end up in an eternal life that is conceived of as an endless and happy existence, first in the present world and then in a renewed world. We are a long way here from the ideal of an assimilation to the "pneumatic" Christ, which was preached by Saint Paul.

II

Clement of Rome, who also likes to quote the apostle of the Gentiles, is the first among the apostolic fathers to insist on the divine likeness, which the Scriptures recognize in Adam.

Readily pausing to contemplate the work of creation and the divine power manifested there,[13] Clement does not miss the opportunity to present humankind as the masterpiece of God's hands and "as an imprint of His image":

---

[5] *Barn.* 16.7-8 (86-88). Cf. 1 Cor 3:16-17.
[6] *Barn.* 11.11 (74).
[7] *Barn.* 6.11 (56). Cf. 16.8 (88). Compare 2 Cor 5:17; Gal 6:15; Titus 3:5.
[8] *Barn.* 8.3 (62).
[9] *Barn.* 4.9 (48).
[10] *Barn.* 8.5 (62). Cf. 11.11 (74).
[11] *Barn.* 21.1 (94).
[12] *Barn.* 15.4-8 (82). In the six days of the creation Barnabas sees a symbol and a prediction of the duration of this world: "In six thousand years, the Lord will complete all things."
[13] See especially *1 Clem.* 20–33 (Funk 1:126-140).

After all the other ones, with His holy and spotless hands He formed the most excellent and the greatest [by intelligence] living being, the human being, as an imprint of His own image. For God speaks thus: "Let us make man in our image and in our likeness."[14]

119

This divine likeness is the distinctive feature not only of Adam but of all human beings. Certainly, the special manner of formation, which is described in the sacred text, remains the exclusive privilege of the first human being. Yet all the descendants share the gift of intelligence. Indeed, Clement seems to see in this the main element of the divine likeness.[15]

Concerning the position of fallen humanity with regard to salvation, our author, without referring to Adam's sin,[16] assumes that all men need to repent and that all are consequently sinners. But he also admits that all, even those who were "foreigners to God," could save themselves by μετάνοια.[17]

It is precisely the "gift of repentance" that Jesus has prepared for the whole world through the shedding of His blood—"precious to God" and "shed for our salvation."[18] Through this, above all, Jesus Christ is "Savior."[19] But He is also the Master of "the immortal gnosis," since

> through Him the Demiurge of the universe has called us from darkness to light, from ignorance to the full knowledge [ἐπίγνωσις] of the glory of His name....[20] Through Him we have our eyes concentrated toward the heights of the heavens; through Him we see as in a mirror His immaculate and noble face; through Him the eyes of our heart have been opened; through Him our slow and darkened intelligence opens up to the light; through Him the Master has desired to have us taste the immortal gnosis [τῆς ἀθανάτου γνώσεως].[21]

120

By calling the Christian doctrine an "immortal gnosis," Saint Clement is undoubtedly saying that this doctrine assures immortality. Indeed, he writes elsewhere that "great and glorious promises"[22] are in store for "those who have served the Demiurge in a saintly way and with the confidence of a perfect faith."

---

[14] *1 Clem.* 33.4-5 (140). In Funk and Bihlmeyer, 1:53, the words "because of intelligence" [κατὰ διάνοιαν] are removed because they are lacking in the ancient versions. But if it is not authentic, the addition is very much with the thought of the author.

[15] In the passage just quoted nothing gives us the ground to decide on a supernatural endowment for Adam, as, for example, J. Sprinzel does in *Die Theologie der apostolischen Väter* (Vienna, 1880), 145. This interpretation is contested by A. Struker in *Die Gottebenbildlichkeit des Menschen* (Münster in Westphalia, 1913), 7.

[16] Clement, who is nevertheless a "Paulinist," applies Wis 2:24, "through the devil's envy death entered the world," to the murder of Abel (*1 Clem.* 3:4–4.7 [102–104]). Generally speaking, we can say that the apostolic fathers do not speak of the fall of our first parents. Cf. A. Gaudel, "Péché originel," *DTC* 12:317-318.

[17] *1 Clem.* 7.5-7 (108).

[18] *1 Clem.* 7.4 (108).

[19] *1 Clem.* 59.3 (176).

[20] *1 Clem.* 59.2 (174).

[21] *1 Clem.* 36.2 (144-146). Notice the connection that our author establishes between gnosis and immortality.

[22] *1 Clem.* 34.7 (142).

They will rise from the dead like the phoenix[23] to a "life in immortality,"[24] which they will enjoy in "the kingdom of Christ,"[25] the "dwelling place of glory."[26]

So in the hereafter the elect will therefore possess immortality, being near God. Does he mean that they also partake of the very life of God in a more intimate way?

More than once Clement exalts the divine Parenthood.[27] But he conceives of it "as the relationship that links the Demiurge to His creatures rather than as the intimate bond of the divine adoption."[28] For Clement, the union that love establishes between God and humankind seems to be of a purely moral nature. This is the same as the union between Christ and the baptized one.

Our author certainly does not grow tired of pointing out the major role that the Lord plays in the life of His believers. All that God does for them is accomplished through the intermediary of the Savior. The expression διὰ Ἰησοῦ Χριστοῦ is repeated more than enough;[29] the expressions ἐν Χριστῷ Ἰησοῦ or simply ἐν Χριστῷ are less frequent.[30]

However, these expressions do not have the sense of an actual mystical union. In speaking of "our whole body in Jesus Christ,"[31] Clement is clearly thinking of the church, of which Christ is the principle of unity, and therefore of what will later be called "the mystical Body" of Christ. But in Clement the phrase ἐν Χριστῷ never expresses the idea of an intimate closeness of life, in the Pauline sense, between Christ and His believer. It can almost always be replaced by διὰ Χριστοῦ. And our author himself writes indiscriminately: "We have been called in Jesus Christ";[32] and "those whom God has called through Jesus Christ."[33] This shows that in Clement's thinking it is a matter here of mediation rather than of union. Nevertheless, in reading such passages of his letter—in particular, the magnificent chapter thirty-six—we believe that we are hearing a sort of faint echo of the elevations of the Apostle to the Gentiles.

Such fervor is absent from the piece of writing that we call *The Second Epistle of Clement,* the first known Christian sermon. The anonymous author, who considers himself to be among the ἄσοφοι,[34] strongly insists on bodily

---

[23]   Cf. *1 Clem.* 25–26 (132-134), where the legend of the phoenix is recounted with a good number of details.

[24]   *1 Clem.* 35.2 (142): ζωὴ ἐν ἀθανασίᾳ.

[25]   *1 Clem.* 50.3 (164).

[26]   *1 Clem.* 5.4 (104).

[27]   Cf. *1 Clem.* 19.2; 35.3; 62.2.

[28]   Lebreton, *Histoire du dogme,* 2:281.

[29]   *1 Clem.* 34 (144-146); 50.7 (164); 59.3 (176); 64.1 (182); 65.2 (184).

[30]   *1 Clem.* 32.4 (138): ἐν Χρ. Ἰ.; 43.1 (152): ἐν Χρ., etc.

[31]   *1 Clem.* 38.1 (146): Σωζέσθω οὖν ἡμῶν ὅλον τὸ σῶμα ἐν Χριστῷ Ἰησοῦ. Perhaps Fr. Mersch (*Le corps mystique du Christ,* 1:292) could have derived more profit from this text, although it was pointed out by him.

[32]   *1 Clem.* 32.4 (138). Cf. 44 (158).

[33]   *1 Clem.* 65.2 (184).

[34]   *2 Clem.* 19.2 (Funk 1:208).

immortality, guaranteed to Christians by the "Savior," who is "the author of in-corruptibility."[35]

Christ, "whom we should consider as a God,"[36] "has given us light. As a father, He has called us His children and saved us when we were perishing."[37] This means that all those who "keep baptism pure and spotless" will enter "into the kingdom of God"[38] to enjoy there the "rest of eternal life."[39] Thus, after the resurrection, our flesh will partake of the "incorruptible benefits [τὰ ἀγαθὰ ἄφθαρτα],"[40] that is to say, of "life and incorruptibility, by virtue of its union with the Holy Spirit,"[41] for "it is in this flesh that we will receive the reward [μισθόν]."[42]

Clearly expressed here is the idea that the final incorruptibility of the resur-rected baptized one is a direct result of the Holy Spirit's indwelling of the flesh of the Christian. At the same time, it remains the most precious fruit of the redemptive work of Christ.

122

III

Very different from the writings that we have just mentioned are the letters of Saint Ignatius. These "short notes, hastily written by a martyr who is march-ing to his death,"[43] reveal the novel and fervent personality of a theologian coupled with that of a mystic.

For the bishop of Antioch, as for Saint John, the positive aspect of the "econ-omy of God"[44] is summed up in the concepts of "life,"[45] "true life,"[46] "eternal life,"[47] and "incorruptibility and eternal life."[48] Having been prepared for by the prophets,[49] this "plan that was made by God"[50] was carried out by Jesus Christ by means of "His passion and His resurrection."[51]

---

[35] 2 *Clem.* 20.5 (210): τὸν σωτῆρα καὶ ἀρχηγὸν τῆς ἀφθαρσίας.

[36] 2 *Clem.* 1.1 (184).

[37] 2 *Clem.* 1.4 (184-186).

[38] 2 *Clem.* 6.9 (190-192). Cf. 7.6 (192) and 8.6 (194).

[39] 2 *Clem.* 5.5 (190). Cf. 7.7 (190).

[40] 2 *Clem.* 6.6 (190).

[41] 2 *Clem.* 14.5 (202): τοσαύτην δύναται ἡ σὰρξ αὕτη μεταλαβεῖν ζωὴν καὶ ἀφθαρσίαν, κολληθέντος αὐτῇ τοῦ πνεύματος τοῦ ἁγίου. Notice the force of this last expression: the Holy Spirit "clings" to the flesh.

[42] 2 *Clem.* 19.5 (194). Cf. 15.1 (202).

[43] Lebreton, *Histoire du dogme,* 2:282.

[44] Ign. *Eph.* 18.2 (Funk 1:226).

[45] Ign. *Eph.* 14.1 (224).

[46] Ign. *Eph.* 7.2 (218). Cf. 11.1 (222).

[47] Ign. *Eph.* 18.1 (226). Cf. 19.3 (228).

[48] Ign. *Pol.* 2.3 (288-290).

[49] Ign. *Phld.* 5.2 (268). Cf. 9 (272).

[50] Ign. *Eph.* 19.3 (228).

[51] Ign. *Phld.* 9.2 (272). Cf. Ign. *Rom.* 7.1 (258-260); Ign. *Smyrn.* 2 (276).

Salvation has thus been objectively carried out by Christ. Humankind
123 appropriates it through union with the Savior. And our author evidently sup-
poses that this union is realized by baptism, though he does not formally mention it anywhere.[52] Therefore, in his writings we do not find the baptismal
mysticism of Saint Paul. It is all the more strange, then, that he should insist
hardly any less than the apostle does on the union of the individual Christian
with Jesus Christ, as well as on the unity of all the baptized ones in the Lord.[53]
We ought to do "all our deeds," he writes to the Ephesians, "as though Jesus
was dwelling in us, in order that we might be His temples and that He Himself
might be in us as our God."[54] In brief, to lead a Christian life is to "live in
Jesus Christ."[55] Moreover, "by having Jesus Christ in them,"[56] Christians are
χριστοφόροι.[57] The Savior within us is not like a statue in a temple. On the contrary, He is "our inseparable life,"[58] "our eternal life."[59] The new life of the baptized one feeds on the Eucharist, which is the "flesh of our Savior Jesus
Christ,"[60] "a medicine of immortality, an antidote for us not to die but to live in
Jesus Christ forever."[61]

The union with Christ entails union with God the Father. Christians are
θεοφόροι,[62] and their bodies are the "temples of God."[63] Being "completely for
124 God"[64] and "full of God,"[65] they "partake" of Him.[66] Finally, just as the activity of
Christ in our souls cannot be dissociated from that of God the Father, it is
equally inseparable from that of the Holy Spirit.[67]

Nevertheless, as close as it may be here on earth, the fellowship of life which
exists between Christians and their God is destined to become even more intimate. Indeed, the supreme happiness, which was ardently desired by our
martyr and which he recommended to Polycarp, consists in "attaining to Jesus

---

[52] Barring error, Ignatius only speaks of baptism a single time, in passing in Ign. *Pol.* 7.1 (292).
[53] On the doctrine of the mystical body in Saint Ignatius, see Mersch, *Le corps mystique du Christ,*
1:294–305; P. Batiffol, *L'Église naissante et le catholicisme,* (9th ed.; Paris, 1927), 157-170.
[54] Ign. *Eph.* 15.3 (224-226).
[55] Ign. *Eph.* 20.2 (230). Cf. 8.2; 10.3; 11.1 (220, 222, 222).
[56] Ign. *Magn.* 12 (240).
[57] Ign. *Eph.* 9.2 (220).
[58] Ign. *Eph.* 3.2 (216).
[59] Ign. *Magn.* 1.2 (232).
[60] Ign. *Smyrn.* 7.1 (280). Cf. Ign. *Rom.* 7.3 (260).
[61] Ign. *Eph.* 20.2 (230): φάρμακον ἀθανασίας, ἀντίδοτος τοῦ μὴ ἀποθανεῖν, ἀλλὰ ζῆν ἐν Ἰησοῦ
Χριστῷ διὰ παντός.
[62] Ign. *Eph.* 9.2 (220). According to the superscription of the seven letters, Ignatius also had the
name θεοφόρος.
[63] Ign. *Phld.* 7.2 (270).
[64] Ign. *Eph.* 8.1 (218-220): ὅλοι ὄντες θεοῦ.
[65] Ign. *Magn.* 14.1 (240): θεοῦ γέμετε.
[66] Ign. *Eph.* 4.2 (216): θεοῦ μετέχητε.
[67] Cf. Ign. *Magn.* 13 (240). Saint Ignatius lays more stress on the role that the Spirit plays in the
church—particularly in the hierarchy of which He is the initiator—than in the soul of the believer.

Christ" or, more often, in "attaining to God."[68] This is the perfect and final union which, having only taken shape in this life, will be fully realized in the "kingdom of God."[69] There, after the "resurrection to Christ,"[70] the believers will have "a share in God"[71] and will possess "ἀφθαρσία and eternal life."[72]

For the bishop of Antioch, to attain to God, to be indissolubly united with Him, is the ideal terminus of the Christian life. By all accounts, this is not a matter of a simple moral assimilation through imitation. Such imitation is pre-supposed, since Christians have to be "imitators of Jesus Christ, as He Himself is of His Father."[73] But Saint Ignatius does not stop here. In his writings we defi-nitely find the mysticism of a Saint John and, even more, of a Saint Paul, who experientially realizes a direct union with Christ and, through Him, with God the Father and the Holy Spirit. To be convinced of this, we have only to read the following passage from the letter to the Romans: "My love [for the world] has been crucified, and there is no longer in me any fire that loves matter [πῦρ φιλόϋλον], but a living water that murmers in me and says to me from the depth of my soul: Come to the Father."[74] Or again, in the letter to the Philadel-phians we read: "My brothers, my love for you overflows, and it is an utmost joy for me to travail for your strengthening, yet not I but Jesus Christ."[75] Is this not the faithful echo of Saint Paul's word: "It is no longer I who live; it is Christ who lives in me"?

Following Paul and John, our martyr thus conceives of salvation as a taking hold of, that is, a possession of the human being by God and of God by the human being through Christ and the Spirit. This possession is not an absorp-tion but an elevation of humankind to a new existence in incorruptibility, or we may say, to a quasi-divine mode of being.[76] This means that the soteriology of Saint Ignatius is a doctrine, indeed even a mysticism of divinization, without the term.

125

---

[68] Cf. Ign. *Eph.* 12.2 (222): θεοῦ ἐπιτυχεῖν. See also Ign. *Magn.* 14 (240); Ign. *Rom.* 1.2 (256, etc.). For the expression Ἰησοῦ Χριστοῦ ἐπιτυχεῖν, see Ign. *Rom.* 5.3 (258).

[69] Ign. *Eph.* 16.1 (226). Cf. Ign. *Phld.* 3.3 (266).

[70] Ign. *Trall.* Inscription (242): ἐν τῇ εἰς αὐτὸν ἀναστάσει.

[71] Ign. *Pol.* 6.1 (292).

[72] Ign. *Pol.* 2.3 (288-290). If, under the pen of Ignatius, ἀφθαρσία ordinarily seems to refer to moral incorruptibility, that is to say, holiness, here the meaning of immortality is postulated by the addition of "eternal life." Cf. A. Lelong, *Ignace d'Antioche* (Paris, 1910), 3:33-34.

[73] Ign. *Phld.* 7.2 (270). Cf. 8.2 (270).

[74] Ign. *Rom.* 7.2 (260).

[75] Ign. *Phld.* 5.1 (266).

[76] Everything invites us to think that, in accordance with the Greek philosophical tradition, Ignatius has seen in ἀφθαρσία, and in ἀγεννησία, which establishes the former, the essential attributes of God (Cf. Ign. *Eph.* 7.2 [218], and the commentary on this text in Lebreton, *Histoire,* 2:314-316). For Ignatius, to become incorruptible must therefore have signified being assimilated to God and being divinized. But although it may be in the line of his thought, Ignatius does not draw such a conclusion anywhere.

IV

Whereas Saint Ignatius is a theologian and a fervent mystic, Hermas, the author of the pious novel that is entitled *The Shepherd*, is a moralist who, despite his visions, has nothing of the mystic in him. His dogmatic conceptions betray a disconcerting hesitancy and inconsistency. Consequently, we could have passed him over in silence had we not encountered in his work a case of divinization that is worthy of being noted.

The case is to be found in the parable of the vineyard and the explanations that are given for it.[77] The following persons are presented: the master of the vineyard, namely, the Creator; his son, who, for the author, is the Holy Spirit; the slave, who is "the Son of God," that is to say, Christ;[78] and the friends and advisers of the master, who are the first-created angels.[79] According to the parable itself and its explanation in the fifth paragraph, as a reward for the work that he has done in the master's vineyard, the faithful slave is set free and becomes coheir of the son, that is to say, of the Holy Spirit. Since he is distinguished from the other servants only by his zeal, the slave is seen as a simple person who becomes the Son of God by adoption.[80]

Such a conception must have shocked the Christian conscience of the time, which demanded that a person "should think of Jesus Christ as of a God."[81] Consequently, with a new explanation[82] the author endeavors to make his parable less unworthy of the Savior. At any rate, the slave here is Christ or, more precisely, the "flesh" of Christ, and in this flesh or human nature God made to dwell

> the Holy Spirit, who was pre-existing, who created the entire creation....This flesh, in which the Holy Spirit had fixed His dwelling-place, served Him wonderfully by walking in the paths of holiness and purity, without ever bringing the slightest stain on Him. Because of such a noble and chaste life, because of the part that it had taken in the labors of the Spirit and the help that it had given to Him in every circumstance, and because of its courageous and honourable conduct, God wanted to make this flesh the partner of the Holy Spirit [μετὰ τοῦ πνεύματος τοῦ ἁγίου εἵλατο κοινωνόν]....Therefore He took counsel from the Son and from His glorious angels to give a place of rest to this flesh, which had served the Spirit with an irreproachable faithfulness, not wanting it to look like the flesh had lost the reward for its services. For all flesh that will have served as a dwelling-place

---

[77]   Herm. *Sim.* 5.2-6 (Funk 1:530-542).

[78]   Cf. A. Lelong, *Le Pasteur d'Hermas* (Paris, 1912), 78: "In the Shepherd, we do not encounter the name of Jesus or that of Christ a single time; the Savior there is ordinarily called the Son of God."

[79]   Herm. *Sim.* 5.5.2-3 (538).

[80]   The efforts made by certain writers—for example by Lebreton, *Histoire du dogme,* 2:364-366—to prove, according to Herm. *Sim.* 5.2-3, the pre-existence of the slave who was in charge of the vineyard, at least in the form of an angel, do not appear convincing.

[81]   *2 Clem.* 1.1, quoted above, 103. However, it does not seem that Hermas was an isolated case, since even from the time of Saint Justin some Christians were doubting the pre-existence of Christ. Cf. Just. *Dial.* 48 (Otto 2:162-164).

[82]   Herm. *Sim.* 5.6-7.

for the Holy Spirit and will have been found to be without stain and without spot will receive a reward.[83]

We see that the adoption in the parable has become an "identity with the Holy Spirit" here in the explanation. After its resurrection and ascension the human nature, which was united with the Spirit during its earthly existence, is joined with this same Spirit. It enters, so to speak, into the divine family and becomes the Son of God, who "has received all power from His Father."[84] At that time the indwelling of the Holy Spirit gives way to identity with the Spirit.[85]

Therefore, according to Hermas, the man Jesus Christ would have been introduced into the divine sphere and honored with the name of Son of God as a reward and by way of a kind of adoption or assumption. In short, He would have been divinized.

But the Holy Spirit did not dwell solely in the flesh of Christ. He resides in the flesh of the righteous as well,[86] and there is nothing in the thought of Hermas to indicate that the two cases of indwelling may be different in kind. In both cases, the Holy Spirit is considered as an occupant within the soul and not as a principle of divine life.[87] Nevertheless, concerning the reward that awaits the righteous, Hermas only mentions the "kingdom of God."[88] He never speaks of identity with the Spirit in relation to the elect. Such an identity is the exclusive privilege of Christ—Christians will not be divinized like their Master.

All the apostolic fathers place the essence of Christian salvation in blessed incorruptibility or eternal life. In the writings of some of them we even see the beginnings of the idea according to which God alone is incorruptible by   128

---

[83] Herm. *Sim.* 5.6.5-7 (540-542). Certain writers regarded Herm. *Sim.* 5.6.4–7.1 as a gloss. Cf. Bousset, *Kyrios Christos*, 263.

[84] Herm. *Sim.* 5.6.4. This latter little phrase is seen only in the Latin version. See Funk, *Patres apostolici,* 1:540.

[85] It does not seem necessary to see "in this union of the flesh and the spirit a substantial and perpetual union, like that which is a necessary consequence of the incarnation" (Lebreton, *Histoire du dogme,* 2:317). Indeed, if such had been the thought of Hermas, would he have been able to assign the role of slave to Christ and to speak of the indwelling of the Spirit in the flesh of Christ as an accepted fact? Furthermore, would he have been able to recognize in such a flesh the possibility of sinning, as he evidently does?

[86] Herm. *Sim.* 5. 7.1 (542). Cf. Herm. *Sim.* 9.24.4 (620); Herm. *Mand.* 3.1.4 (472); 5.1.2-4 (482); 10.1.2 (498).

[87] Cf. Herm. *Mand.* 3.4 (472); Herm. *Sim.* 5.7. 2 (542).

[88] Herm. *Sim.* 9.12 (598–600). Cf. 15.2 and 16.2-4 (606 and 608).

nature, and humankind could become such only by way of a participation in divinity, that is, by a divinization.[89]

Now it is precisely on this point that some conceptions were about to manifest themselves in the church, and the church would not delay in rejecting them as heretical.

2. Heretical Gnosis

The writings of the apostolic fathers give only a very imperfect idea of the intense intellectual life which animated the church of the second century. In other respects we know that she numbered among her believers some vigorous thinkers. Several of these, prior to their conversion, seem to have been followers of one or others of the pre-Christian gnostic systems, or at least under their influence. The hermetic writings perhaps give us some idea of this pagan gnosis.[90] Convinced that they could incorporate the new elements that Christianity provided into their philosophico-mythological speculations and transform the faith of the common people into some superior knowledge, that is, into a "gnosis," these masters eventually compromised the very foundations of Christian doctrine. Such is the origin of innumerable systems that we include under the name of Gnosticism.[91]

129   Gnosticism is of interest to our subject insofar as all gnostic systems conceive of salvation as divinization or, to be more precise, as redivinization. The conception is so intimately bound to the fundamental doctrines of gnosis that without them we could neither present it nor understand it. Our study will focus on the school of Valentinus, "in which the gnostic movement attains its speculative peak and, at the same time, a spreading that few systems have known."[92]

I

Like every "gnosis," Gnosticism is a religion of salvation in which redemption depends on the knowledge [γνῶσις], gained through revelation, of God, of the meaning and goal of the cosmos, and of human life.[93] The systems that this generic name covers, as numerous as they are varied, have in common the fact that, following the trend of the time, they exaggerate the transcendence of God to the point of making Him an inaccessible and unknowable abstraction. Yet this abstraction is supposed to be capable of manifesting itself, of opening out into a series of emanations, growing increasingly weaker, called aeons.

---

[89] We must point out, as a curious item, a passage from *Diognetus*, in which it is said that the one who gives alms "becomes (the) god [θεὸς γίνεται] of those who receive (them)." This is a simple metaphor for saying that the one who gives is an "imitator of God." *Diogn.* 10.6; in Funk, *Patres apostolici*, 1:408.

[90] On pre-Christian gnosis, see especially Cerfaux, "Gnose préchretienne," 671-681.

[91] Cf. J. Tixeront, *Histoire des dogmes* (11th ed.; Paris, 1928-1931), 1:192-197.

[92] J.P. Steffes, *Das Wesen des Gnostizismus und sein Verhältnis zum katholischen Dogma* (Paderborn, 1922), 137-138.

[93] Cf. Leisegang, "Gnosis," *RGG* 2:1272.

Having emanated from the Father of all things, whose unbegotten essence is "incorruptibility and light,"[94] these beings are intermediary between God and matter. They make up the hierarchical whole of the *pleroma* or plenitude, doing so by couples, each of which forms a syzygy.

One of the inferior aeons, Achamoth, a runt of the aeon Sophia, having been driven out of the *pleroma*, produces other aeons that are evil like it and inferior to the aeons of the *pleroma*. One of these creates the material world, including humankind. This is the Demiurge of which Genesis speaks, the harmful God of the Old Testament.[95] Gnostic soteriology is grafted onto such a theogony and cosmogony.

130

II

Therefore, like everything that is outside of the *pleroma*, human beings do not owe their origin to the supreme God, but to the Demiurge who is merely an inferior aeon. The Demiurge made humankind "according to the image and likeness" [κατ' εἰκόνα καὶ ὁμοίωσιν].[96] This means that the Demiurge formed the "hylic" human according to image and the "psychic" human, on the contrary, according to likeness. However, without the knowledge of the Demiurge, his mother Achamoth deposited in certain men of her choice a pneumatic seed that makes them capable of receiving the perfect knowledge.[97]

This distinction between image and likeness, which according to Irenaeus was current in the Italic school of Valentinus, is found in this gnostic's eastern school. For example, we read in the *Excerpts from Theodotus*: "The hylic is according to the image; the psychic is according to the likeness of God; the pneumatic is according to the particular [essence]."[98] The hylics are the numerous humans with the "earthy and material soul that is devoid of reason [ἄλογον] and of the same substance [ὁμοούσιον] as the souls of beasts."[99] Cain is their

131

---

[94] Ptol. *Flor.* (PG 7:1289d): τοῦ δὲ πατρὸς τῶν ὅλων τοῦ ἀγεννήτου ἡ οὐσία ἐστὶν ἀφθαρσία τε καὶ φῶς αὐτό, ὂν ἁπλοῦν τε καὶ μονοειδές. We are not surprised to again find this classical thesis of Greek philosophy in the writings of the gnostics.

[95] See G. Bareille, "Gnosticisme" *DTC* 6:1434–1467, especially 1447–1453; Albert Ehrhard, *Die Kirche der Märtyrer* (Munich, 1932), 164–168; E. de Faye, *Gnostiques et gnosticisme* (Paris, 1913), 436–439; Steffes, *Das Wesen des Gnostizismus*, 137–184; Tixeront, *Histoire des dogmes*, 1:197–199.

[96] Cf. Iren. *Haer.* 1.5.5 (PG 7:500b).

[97] *Haer.* 1.5.6 (501).

[98] Clem. *Exc. 54* (edited by Otto Staehlin, *Clemens Alexandrinus* [Leipzig, 1890], 3:124-125): ὁ μὲν χοϊκός ἐστι "κατ' εἰκόνα", ὁ δὲ ψυχικὸς "καθ' ὁμοίωσιν" θεοῦ, ὁ δὲ πνευματικὸς κατ' ἰδίαν. The expression κατ' ἰδίαν—some read κατ' ἰδέαν—is rendered in various ways. Some like Struker, *Gottebenbildlichkeit*, 58, by taking it as an adverbial phrase, translate, "the pneumatic is a being to itself." Others, for example W. Capitaine, *Die Moral des Clemens von Alexandrien* (Paderborn, 1903), 131, comment: κατ' ἰδίαν, that is, οὐσίαν. This interpretation seems preferable because it permits us to translate the preposition κατά in a uniform manner in the three cases in which it is used. And this renders the phrase more homogeneous. Furthermore, it is quite natural for a gnostic, for whom the spiritual seed that is deposited in the pneumatic comes from the *pleroma*, to say of spiritual humans that they are "made according to the particular essence" of God.

[99] *Exc.* 50 (123). The term ἄλογος, "devoid of reason," here means that in the moral order of things the hylics behave as if they did not have reason. It has an ethical sense.

representative.[100] The human being who is made "according to the likeness of the Demiurge Himself is the one into whom the Demiurge has breathed and inspired something that is consubstantial with Himself [ὁμοούσιόν τι αὐτῷ]."[101] The psychic human being is within the hylic, "the divine soul hidden in the flesh" and for which the hylic soul serves, so to speak, as flesh.[102] It is a "nature that is endowed with reason and is righteous," in the manner of Abel.[103] Consequently, psychic humans are less numerous.[104] Finally, the pneumatic is that rare human who "has the pneumatic seed sown into the soul by Sophia," a seed that makes "the soul rational and heavenly..., full of spiritual marrow."[105]

There are thus three categories of human beings: the hylic, the psychic, and the pneumatic. The first—these are the pagans and the Jews—though they are "near God, are not consubstantial with Him" [παραπλήσιον μὲν, ἀλλ' οὐχ ὁμοούσιον τῷ θεῷ].[106] "Incapable of receiving the breath of incorruptibility," they inevitably perish, being eventually devoured, along with matter, by the fire that is hidden in the world. The psychics, namely, the faithful of the great church, are free to decide between the hylic or the pneumatic. By way of a "plain faith" and a good life, they can save themselves, but without ever obtaining "the perfect gnosis" [τὴν τελείαν γνῶσιν] or being able to penetrate the *pleroma*. At the consummation of all things they will enjoy [ἀναπαύσεσθαι] an inferior bliss with the Demiurge in the "intermediary place," that is to say, a place situated between the *pleroma* and the material world, "for nothing psychic enters into the *pleroma*."[107]

The pneumatics, that is, the gnostics, are incorruptible by nature. Whatever they may do, they are assured of their salvation. Indeed, whatever their "hylic actions" may be, they cannot lose their "pneumatic substance," no more than gold that has fallen into mud loses its glitter. For them, final salvation will consist in the release of the pneumatic element. Even their souls they will lay down, in order to become pure spirits and go back into the *pleroma* with Achamoth, where they will become the spouses of the angels.[108] Such a redemption is carried out exclusively by means of the gnosis which has been revealed by the Savior, one of the superior aeons who, with the appearances of a human, took the name of Jesus.[109] "To know the Father, until then unknown, to penetrate the mysteries of the sect, to believe in its secret traditions, to interpret as it does the

132

---

[100]   *Exc.* 54 (124).
[101]   *Exc.* 50 (123).
[102]   *Exc.* 51 (123).
[103]   *Exc.* 54 (124).
[104]   *Exc.* 56 (125): οὐ πολλοὶ δὲ οἱ ψυχικοί.
[105]   *Exc.* 53 (124).
[106]   *Haer.* 1.5.5 (500b).
[107]   *Haer.* 1.6-7.1 (504-513a).
[108]   *Haer.* 1.6.2 (505-508); 1.7.1 (512-513).
[109]   This conception seems to be at the base of the quite varied gnostic musings on the person of the Savior. Cf. A. Ehrhard, *Die Kirche der Märtyrer,* 169.

evangelical writings and the phenomena of nature, and to participate in its rites—such is the salvation that Jesus has brought us."[110]

In gnostic soteriology what impresses us at the outset is that it denies the universality of salvation. Only the pneumatics will obtain blessed incorruptibility. Furthermore, in the gnostic systems immortality is only window-dressing, because nothing belonging to human nature is made incorruptible. Indeed, it is exclusively the seed or the divine spark, which has fallen from the *pleroma* into humankind, that goes back into its homeland to enjoy there an immortality that it had never lost. Assuredly, this return appears to be a veritable redivinization of the "spiritual substance" [πνευματικὴ ὑπόστασις] that has been hidden in the pneumatic.[111] But from the gnostic point of view, there is not, nor is there any possibility of having, a deification of the human soul. And this is even more the case with the entire human being, since the gnostics deny the resurrection of the flesh, seeing in matter something that is essentially evil.

On this last point our authors remain in the traditional line of Greek philosophy. But they abandon this line when they make a cosmic event out of redemption, with no connection to morality, a notion that logically leads to fatalism. In short, in its soteriology, as well as in its entirety, Gnosticism proves to be not so much "an abrupt Hellenization of Christianity"[112] as a superficial Christianization of a Hellenistic "gnosis" that is fundamentally pagan.   133

Therefore one can realize that "the struggle against gnosis was the great doctrinal concern of the church in the second century."[113] But if for the church the gnostic movement constituted a more formidable peril than official persecution, it nonetheless remains the fact that the movement was indirectly useful to the church. This is because the defenders of orthodoxy were obliged to develop and clarify the traditional doctrine, a task facilitated by a considerably enriched vocabulary. Through such progress the conception of salvation, and with it the idea of divinization, could not fail to profit, as we will see in the writings of the apologists.

3. The Apologists

Whereas the apostolic fathers did not feel the need to rationally fathom their faith, the apologists endeavor to base it on reason and to justify it outwardly by interpreting it according to the philosophy of their time. To that end, they make a point of emphasizing all that the faith has in common with Greek

---

[110]   Tixeront, *Histoire des dogmes,* 1:201.
[111]   *Haer.* 1.6.2 (508).
[112]   Harnack, *Dogmengeschichte,* 1:250. A. Loisy seems to be closer to the truth when he writes, "In Gnosticism, it is...the gospel that is absorbed by pagan philosophy and mysticism." *Les mystères païens et le mystère chrétien* (Paris, 1930), 341.
[113]   Tixeront, *Histoire des dogmes,* 1:205.

thought and of presenting Christianity as a "philosophy," that is to say, "an investigation into the divine."[114] Such a preoccupation leads them to analyze, in particular, the notion of incorruptibility promised to the Christian and to compare this with the immortality of God, and all the more so because bodily ἀφθαρσία constituted a genuine stumbling block for every mind of Hellenic education. Proof of this is found in the fact that the gnostics denied it and limited natural incorruptibility, acknowledged in the pneumatic, to the divine element alone.

134

The apologists, on the contrary, keep the revealed doctrine of eternal life, which is guaranteed to every Christian worthy of that name, just as it stands. They ask from philosophy only the solution to the speculative problem raised by this dogma.

Now, from the time of Plato[115] and Aristotle[116] it was a standard thesis in philosophy that only the non-generated [ἀγέννητος] Being is also incorruptible [ἄφθαρτος] or immortal [ἀθάνατος] by nature.[117] Our authors, and all the Greek fathers following them, have no objection to adopting this principle. They conclude from it that the immortality that is destined for the righteous could only be a shared incorruptibility.

I

Saint Justin, "the most important" of the apologists of the second century,[118] understood and expounded to the greatest extent the fundamental harmony between the Christian religion and philosophy. He is the first Christian author to clearly set forth, by making it his own, the thesis of which we have just spoken. Indeed he writes, God alone "is unbegotten and incorruptible [ἀγέννητος καὶ ἄφθαρτος], and by this He is God, whereas everything else that comes after Him is begotten and corruptible."[119] Consequently, we should not say that the human soul is immortal, "because if it is immortal, then it is obviously also unbegotten." Furthermore, it would not sin nor would it be filled with folly.[120] Therefore, it is wrong to claim, as the gnostics do, that "the soul is incorruptible because it is a part [μέρος] and a breath [ἐμφύσημα] of God, and that, for this reason, He wanted to save what is His own and akin to Him [τὸ ἴδιον καὶ συγγενές]."[121]

---

[114] Just. *Dial.* 1, (ed. Th. von Otto, *Corpus apologetarum christianorum saeculi secundi* [9 vols.; Jena, 1851-1881], 2:4). Unless otherwise indicated, we quote the apologists according to this edition.

[115] See above, 39-41.

[116] See above, 45.

[117] Cf. Lebreton, *Histoire du dogme,* 2:635-640.

[118] Aimé Puech, *Les apologistes grecs du II͏ᵉ siècle* (Paris, 1912), 46.

[119] *Dial.* 5 (2:26).

[120] *Dial.* 5 (2:22-28).

[121] *Fr. res.* 8 (3:240).

However, when He created them, God intended to keep humans "sheltered 135
from corruption and punishment [ἀφθάρτους καὶ ἀτιμωρήτους], if they would
choose what pleases Him."[122] Unfortunately, "from the time of Adam, the
human race had fallen under the power of death and into the error of the
serpent, each one of them committing evil by his own transgression."[123] More
and more the demons were extending their dominion over fallen humanity,
especially by means of idolatry.[124]

Nevertheless, humankind was not abandoned by God, and this because "the
entire human race has something of the nature of His Word":

> Those who have lived according to the Word are Christians, even though they
> were regarded as atheists, such as, among the Greeks, Socrates, Heraclitus, and
> their fellows, and, among the barbarians, Abraham, Hananiah, Azariah, Mishael,
> Elijah, and so many others, the actions and names of whom it would be too
> lengthy to cite here.[125]

But these Christians before Christ had only a partial knowledge of the Word.[126]
This was more complete among the Jews, because the working of the Logos
was more manifest among them. He spoke to them through the prophets and
personally appeared to them as the messenger of God the Father.[127] The manifestation of the Word as Master and Savior is complete in Jesus, in whom He
"became human for our sakes, to take part in our ills and to heal us from
them."[128] "Through Him we have been called to a salvation that has been
prepared with the Father."[129]

For the righteous this "eternal salvation"[130] will consist in incorruptibility 136
and impassibility, which they will enjoy in the company of God.[131] And it will
be realized at the time of the *parousia* of Christ,[132] when He "will raise up the
bodies of all humans who have existed, clothe the righteous with incorruptibility, and send the wicked into eternal fire."[133] When the elect "have become
impassible and immortal like God," they will be "judged worthy of being called

---

[122]   *Dial.* 88 (2:322).

[123]   *Dial.* 88 (2:320).

[124]   Cf. J. Rivière, *Saint Justin et les apologistes du second siècle* (Paris, 1907), 220-226.

[125]   *1 Apol.* 46 (1:128).

[126]   *2 Apol.* 10 (1:224-226). In this passage, Justin maintains that, if the philosophers have said anything good, it is due to a parcel of the Logos [κατὰ λόγου μέρος]. But this does not prevent him from
adopting elsewhere (*1 Apol.* 44 [122-123]) the theory of plagiarism. See above, 73, n. 31.

[127]   *1 Apol.* 33 (102). Cf. *1 Apol.* 36 (106-108); *2 Apol.* 10 (224-226); *Dial.* 87 (2:316), etc.

[128]   *2 Apol.* 13 (238).

[129]   *Dial.* 131 (2:466).

[130]   *1 Apol.* 12 (36).

[131]   *1 Apol.* 10 (32).

[132]   *1 Apol.* 52 (138-140). With the whole of early tradition, Justin awaits the return of Christ as an
event in the immediate future. Cf. *Dial.* 32, 81.

[133]   *1 Apol.* 52 (138-140).

by Him His children." According to Psa 82:6, they will even be "gods and children of the Most High."[134]

By applying this verse to the blessed, Justin in an equivalent way is saying that the bestowing of incorruptibility is a kind of divinization.

II

Even more clearly than his master Justin, the impetuous and obscure Tatian presents the immortality that is destined for humankind as an assimilation to that of God.

According to him, humankind was made "the image of immortality [εἰκόνα τῆς ἀθανασίας]" by the heavenly Logos "in order that, just as incorruptibility belongs to God, they might possess immortality in the same way by participating in the portion of God [θεοῦ μοῖρας...μεταλαβών]."[135] And this divine portion that made humankind "the image and the likeness of God" was the superior or divine Spirit who had been given to the first humans, in addition to their souls, and who elevated them "above matter."[136]

137   Thus the divine likeness, which is constituted above all with ἀφθαρσία or ἀθανασία, terms that are evidently synonymous, had been bestowed upon the first parents from the time of their formation. But in them "the joining [συζυγία] of the divine Spirit" with the soul was not to last. The Spirit left the soul because it had refused to follow Him.[137] As a result, the soul became mortal.[138] For,

> in itself, the soul is not immortal but mortal. Nevertheless, it is capable of not dying as well. The soul dies and dissolves with the body if it does not know the truth. However, it resurrects with the body at the end of the world to receive death within immortality as a punishment. On the other hand, the soul that did acquire the knowledge of God does not die any more, although it was dissolved for a time.[139] Indeed, by itself it is only darkness, and nothing of light is in it. And

---

[134]   *Dial.* 124 (2:446-448).

[135]   Tat. *Or.* 7 (Otto 6:30).

[136]   *Or.* 12 (52). In chapters 12-13 of his "discourse" Tatian distinguishes between two kinds of spirits. The first is an inferior spirit, which is conceived of in the Stoic manner and which is "in the stars, the angels, the plants and the waters, and in humans and animals. And although it may be one and the same being, it has some differences in itself;" that is to say, it tells the difference between things (12 [56]). The second is a Spirit that is "superior to the soul, which is the image and likeness of God" (12 [52]); it is "heavenly" (20 [90]), "holy" (15 [66]), "divine" (13 [62]), and identical to the "Logos, who is the light of God" (13 [60]). Cf. Puech, *Les apologistes grecs*, 163.

[137]   *Or.* 13 (62). The conception of Tatian, according to which the divine Spirit forms a "syzygy," that is to say, a couple, with the soul is of gnostic inspiration. Cf. 15 (66): τὴν κατὰ θεὸν συζυγίαν (quoted below, 114). See above, 109.

[138]   *Or.* 7 (32).

[139]   Certain authors have interpreted this passage in the following sense: the soul dissolves, "that is to say, is separated from its body, but it does not die." Cf. Baur, "Untersuchungen über die Vergöttlichungslehre," 29. Such an interpretation is obviously erroneous, since Tatian himself says (*Or.* 15 [66]) that the soul—which is only the bond of the body for him—could not exist without the body. Cf. A. Puech, *Recherches sur le discours aux Grecs de Tatien* (Paris, 1903), 71.

it is certainly regarding this that it has been said, "Darkness does not receive the light." For the soul has not saved the Spirit, but the soul has been saved by the Spirit, and the light has received the darkness. Now the light of God is none other than the Logos; darkness, on the contrary, is the ignorant soul. And this is why, when left to itself, the soul inclines toward matter, which is down below and dies with the flesh. On the contrary, the soul that possesses the syzygy of the divine Spirit is not without aid. It climbs up to regions where the Spirit guides it, for He has His dwelling place on high, whereas the soul has its origin down below.[140]

Having been deprived of the divine Spirit, fallen humankind has ceased to be   138
the image of God; they "prevail over animals by articulate speech alone."[141] However, a "spark" [ἔναυσμα] of the superior Spirit has remained in the soul, which allows it to seek after God without, however, protecting it from falling into polytheism.[142] Fortunately the Spirit of God has united with the soul of a few righteous ones, such as the prophets, who announced hidden things to other souls.[143]

But now we must endeavor to recover what we have lost. We must "unite the soul with the Holy Spirit and form the couple that is according to God [τὴν κατὰ θεὸν συζυγίαν]."[144] Only this Spirit, that is to say, the Logos, who is the "first work of the Father,"[145] is capable of restoring to us the divine likeness that was lost. For it is through the intermediary of the Spirit, as of an ambassador, that God lives in men, as in a temple.[146] But this is on the condition that they die to the world and live for God through faith and penitence.[147] Thus, "the perfect Spirit is like a winged craft for the soul," which allows it to rise up to God.[148]

Having become the image and likeness of God again and possessing the Logos, who is the divine light, the Christian is capable of "seeing the perfect things."[149] Furthermore, at the end of the world and after the resurrection,[150] a "blessed immortality" [τὸ ἀθάνατον μετὰ ἀπολαύσεως]—"eternal life"[151]—will be his portion.

---

[140]   *Or.* 13 (58-62).

[141]   *Or.* 15 (70).

[142]   For Tatian, the fallen human being that is not raised is no longer truly human. Indeed, a man or a woman does rise up, contrary to the definition given by philosophers "in the voice of a crow" [κορακόφωνοι], according to which he or she is a "reasonable animal, capable of receiving intelligence and knowledge." Our author only wishes to call human "one who, by advancing beyond humanity, has gotten closer to God Himself" a true human being (*Or.* 15 [68]). By a fortunate inconsistency, our author nonetheless stands by the full freedom and responsibility of fallen humankind, contrary to the fatalists. See *Or.* 7 (30-32).

[143]   *Or.* 13 (62). Cf. 20 (90).

[144]   *Or.* 15 (66).

[145]   *Or.* 5 (22).

[146]   *Or.* 15 (68-70).

[147]   *Or.* 15 (70-72). Cf. 11 (50): Ἀπόθνησκε τῷ κόσμῳ...ζῆθι τῷ θεῷ.

[148]   *Or.* 20 (88).

[149]   *Or.* 13 (62).

[150]   Cf. *Or.* 13 (58-60).

[151]   *Or.* 14 (64). As a result of this passage there is a difference between ἀθανασία and τὸ ἀθάνατον. Whereas immortality can be good or bad, τὸ ἀθάνατον signifies the immortal "good," namely, blessed immortality.

139   What is striking in what Tatian imagines about incorruptibility, whether it be granted to the first human or promised to Christians, is that it is presented as an effect of the knowledge of God and conditioned, in turn, by the indwelling of the Spirit. On this latter point, our apologist is of the same opinion as the author of the sermon known as the Second Epistle of Saint Clement, who also attributes the immortality of the human flesh to the presence of the Holy Spirit.

III

Platonists though they be, but above all preoccupied with exalting the immortality that is assured by Christianity, Saint Justin and Tatian denied the natural incorruptibility of the human soul. In this matter they were obviously in error. Athenagoras was a better philosopher than they, and in the heading of his *Legatio pro Christianis* [Plea for the Christians] he labels himself "an Athenian, Christian philosopher."[152] He applies himself to "balance the Greek doctrine of the immortality of the soul and the belief in the resurrection of the body,"[153] which already entails a participation in the divine nature.

He also sees in ingenerateness, as well as in the incorruptibility and eternity which proceed from it, attributes that characterize divinity.[154] No created being possesses "perpetuity [διαμονήν] by virtue of his own nature." The angels themselves, "beings that are fully incorruptible and immortal..., were created immortal from the very beginning and remain so indefinitely by the sole will of the 140   Creator." In what concerns humans, "as to the soul, they possess unchanging perpetuity from birth; but as to the body, they will receive incorruptibility through transformation."[155]

Thus Athenagoras firmly maintains the immortality of the human soul, yet does so by presenting it as the effect of a special divine arrangement. This is already an improvement over Saint Justin and Tatian. However, he does not distinguish, any more than they do, between the "perpetuity" of God, which is eternity itself, and the "perpetuity" of the soul, which could only be an immortality.[156] This is why our philosopher feels obliged to deny that the soul possesses immortality κατὰ τὴν οἰκείαν φύσιν.

---

[152]   Athenag. *Leg.* inscription (Otto 7:2).

[153]   Puech, *Les apologistes grecs*, 199.

[154]   *Leg.* 4 (20): τὸ μὲν γὰρ θεῖον ἀγένητον εἶναι καὶ ἀΐδιον, νῷ μόνῳ καὶ λόγῳ θεωρούμενον, τὴν δὲ ὕλην γενητὴν καὶ φθαρτήν. The reading ἀγένητον, "not having become," adopted as well by J. Geffken, *Zwei griechische Apologeten* (Leipzig, 1907), 123, is suggested by the γενητήν which follows. *Codex Parisinus 451* has the reading ἀγέννητον, "unbegotten." The question of orthography is secondary here, the thought of the author not being doubtful: he wishes to say that God is without origin.

[155]   *Res.* 16 (252).

[156]   Later on, following Boethius, some will distinguish *aevum* [αἰών] or *sempiternitas*, which is a shared eternity, from eternity itself, which God alone possesses. Cf. Boeth. *Consol. Philos.* 5.6 (PL 63:858–862).

Be that as it may on these finer points of a philosophical nature, Athenagoras testifies in turn that Christians await a second life after this life. It will be either better, with the possession of heaven, or worse, with the agony of fire. The heavenly bliss is reserved for the righteous. After the resurrection they will be near to God and with God, and the soul will be imperturbable and impassible. They will not be as flesh, though they will have it, but as spirits. And that is precisely where the superiority of humankind over the animals lies. Having been endowed with intelligence, and bearing in themselves the image of their Creator, human beings do not perish like the beasts,[157] but are assimilated to God in the hereafter.

IV

In contrast to Athenagoras, Theophilus of Antioch is a resolute adversary of philosophy. The author of the three books entitled *To Autolycus,* he sets forth views on the immortality for which Christians hope that recall the conceptions of Justin and Tatian.

Theophilus insists on the divine likeness of humankind. Adam, whose formation was the only work that the Creator judged to be worthy of His own hands,[158] was made "according to the image and the likeness" of God. Not only our first ancestor, but every person without exception "is the work and the image" of God.[159] And following Saint Paul[160] our apologist quotes the famous passage of Aratus, according to which "we are of the race of God."[161] But he does not specify upon what such a kinship is based.

However, besides an ill-defined likeness between God and the first human being, there was above all this difference, namely, that humankind was not immortal by nature. God, on the contrary, "is without origin because He is not created [ἄναρχος δέ ἐστιν, ὅτι ἀγένητός ἐστιν]. He is immutable since He is immortal,"[162] and He has need of nothing.[163] If therefore God had made humankind

> immortal from the beginning, He would have made them God. On the other hand, if He had made them mortal, God would have seemed to be the cause of their death. Consequently, He made them neither immortal nor mortal, but... capable of both. If humankind turned toward the things of immortality, by observing the precept of God, they would receive immortality from Him as a reward and would become god [γένηται θεός]. On the contrary, if they turned to the works of death by disobeying God, they themselves would be the cause of their own death. For God made humankind free and independent.[164]

---

[157] *Leg.* 31 (162-164), combined with *Res.* 12 (234-236).

[158] Theoph. *Autol.* 2, 18 (Otto 8:108).

[159] *Autol.* 1.4 (14).

[160] Cf. Acts 17:28.

[161] *Autol.* 2.8 (70).

[162] *Autol.* 1.4 (12). The form ἀγένητος is suggested by the quotation of the Sibyl, which is in 2.36 (164); there such a reading is guaranteed by the meter of the verse.

[163] *Autol.* 2.10 (78).

[164] *Autol.* 2.27 (130-134). Cf. 2.24 (124).

Therefore, the first human, to whom God had "given the incentive for progress," was called to grow, to become perfect [τέλειος], "indeed even God by assumption [Θεὸς ἀναδειχθείς],[165] and thus to go up to heaven..., being put in possession of eternity [ἀϊδιότητα]."[166]

142   But having become unfaithful to this calling, Adam was lost through sin.[167] Following his disobedience, he endured labor, suffering, and sorrow, eventually falling under the dominion of death,[168] and "the whole human race" with him.[169]

Yet God did not disassociate Himself from humanity. He "gave it a law and some holy precepts." Whoever "observes them can be saved, partake of resurrection, inherit incorruptibility,"[170] and "obtain eternal life."[171] And when the chosen ones have put off that which is mortal and put on incorruption, they will see God according to their own merit [κατ᾽ ἀξίαν]. Having become immortal, they will see the Immortal One.[172] In this way, in spite of sin, the original divine plan will be realized.

For the first time, and with perfect clarity, Theophilus expresses the idea by which humans become God through receiving immortality; in other words, they are divinized. Only the word itself is lacking. According to our apologist, the immortality that deifies is the blessed incorruptibility or eternal life in heaven, which God reserves for the resurrected Christians. Thus it is, and will always remain, a divine gift, and it will never become an incorruptibility "by nature" or absolute incorruptibility like that of God. And, in saying that the human who has been made immortal becomes God, Theophilus takes care to specify: "God by assumption."

❧

All the apologists teach that the eternal life that is offered by Christianity could only be a shared immortality. Moreover, all of them suggest what Theophilus states formally, namely, that such a partaking of divine incorruptibility implies an assimilation to God and therefore a divinization, even though none of them employ this term.[173]

143   The deification of the Christian, as our authors suggest it, is distinctly eschatological. This does not assume any less of an earthly preparation, which

---

[165] Literally, "an assumed god," (*deus assumptus*).
[166] *Autol.* 2.24 (124).
[167] *Autol.* 2.24 (124).
[168] *Autol.* 2.25 (128).
[169] *Autol.* 2.29 (138).
[170] Cf. 1 Cor 15:50: "...nor does the perishable inherit the imperishable."
[171] *Autol.* 2.27 (134).
[172] *Autol.* 1.7 (24).
[173] Tatian employs the term θεοποιεῖν when he reproaches the Greeks for "divinizing the elements of the world" in *Or.* 18 (6:82).

above all consists in the acquisition of the knowledge of God and in a perfect life.[174] In this preparation, the part assigned to the free will is major; on this, human destiny seems to primarily depend. Nonetheless, the prevenient activity of the Word is implied everywhere and is often affirmed. But since religion for the apologists is above all a knowledge of divine things, and since they see in sin ignorance and error particularly, they view the role of the Logos mainly as that of an agent of revelation, that is, as a *didaskalos*. And the Word would have exercised the role of One who enlightens even before His incarnation. We may even wonder whether the apologists made an essential distinction between His activity before and after this event. The specifically redemptive work of Christ is mentioned only by Justin.[175] Under these conditions, it seems difficult to see in the earthly preparation that has to precede the eschatological deification of the Christian anything other than a transformation of a moral nature.

All things considered, what we find in the writings of the apostolic fathers and the apologists are rough sketches of a doctrine of deification. Although these rough sketches lack neither value nor interest when taken in themselves, they derive all their importance from the fact that they will be the starting point of a considerable development to be inaugurated by Saint Irenaeus.

---

[174] See, for example, the praise that Athenagoras gives for virginity, which "draws one closer to God" (*Leg.* 33; [7:170–174]).

[175] Cf. Rivière, *Rédemption: étude historique*, 112–116.

Chapter Two

INITIAL DEVELOPMENTS

1. The Christian Tradition: Saint Irenaeus

144   Too exclusively conceived of as an eschatological divinization, the soteriology of the apologists does not sufficiently integrate the teaching of Saint Paul and of Saint John, for whom the baptized one lives by the very life of Christ and by His Spirit from this life onward. It is precisely this doctrine that the first exegetes and theologians take up again, led by Saint Irenaeus. Thus, they not only complement the apologists; at the same time, they set against the Gnostic delusions the authentically Christian notion of assimilation to God, that is, of deification beginning from this life, due to the incarnation of the Word and the indwelling of the Holy Spirit in the soul of the righteous, and being completed in the hereafter through the actual gift of bodily incorruptibility.

I

Following Saint Paul, the bishop of Lyon develops his soteriology, in which divinization occupies a special place, by starting from the parallel between Adam and Jesus Christ. In the latter we again find "what we had lost in Adam, namely, the image and likeness of God."[1] "This phrase," observes Rivière, "gives us the general principle and a kind of summary of the redemptive theology of
145   Saint Irenaeus."[2] The phrase also shows that he conceives the divine similitude of the Christian to be the type of divine likeness that he attributes to Adam. And the interest that the study of the original state arouses in the understanding of Christian grace comes from this.

Our doctor does not grow weary of repeating that humankind has been made "according to the image and likeness of God."[3] He often treats these two expressions as synonyms. This is the case when he writes: "[God] impressed His own likeness on His creature, that we might truly see that this creature is the image of God."[4] The same synonymy still appears to be implied each time

---

[1]   Iren. Haer. 3.18.1 (PG 7:932). Unless otherwise indicated, the writings of the fathers are quoted according to Migne.

[2]   Rivière, Rédemption: étude historique, 121.

[3]   Cf. for example Haer. 3.18.1 (932); 3.22.1 (956); 23.1-2 (960-961); 4.38.3-4 (1108-1109); 5.1.3 (1123).

[4]   Epid. 11 (PG 12:762). We quote the Epideixis according to the French translation by Joseph Barthoulot, in Patrologia orientalis 12:749-800, by checking it against the English translation that precedes it, as well as against the German translation of S. Weber, Irenäus (Kempten-Munich, 1912).

one of the two terms is utilized by itself, without being contrasted with the other, in order to express the similitude between God and humankind in a general way. This results from the following passages:

> By saying "according to the image of the Creator," he [Saint Paul] has shown the recapitulation of humankind who, at the beginning, was made according to the image of God.[5]

> Humankind is a mixture of a soul and a flesh, and has been formed in the similitude of God [*qui secundum similitudinem Dei formatus est*].[6]

By accepting the perfect synonymy of *imago* and of *similitudo* in the text of Genesis, Saint Irenaeus is, moreover, only following the Scripture itself[7] as well as tradition. Consequently, it is all the more surprising to encounter passages in his writing in which he contrasts these two words, one with the other, with a clarity that excludes any doubt. When describing the perfect person, this is what he teaches:

146

> When this Spirit [of God], which has been blended with the soul, unites with the flesh, then, because of the outpouring of the Spirit, a person has become spiritual and perfect. And this is the one who is made in the image and in the similitude of God. On the contrary, if the Spirit is absent from the soul, such a person is truly animal and, having remained carnal, will be imperfect, since this one indeed has the image in the flesh, but does not possess the similitude in the Spirit....In fact, the flesh by itself is not the perfect person, but the body is a part of the person; nor is the soul anymore on its own, but is the soul and is a part of the person; neither, finally, is the Spirit, because it is called Spirit and not "man". It is the blending and the union of all three of these elements that constitutes the perfect person.[8]

The perfect person, who is therefore Adam before his fall, is consequently composed of three parts: the *plasma* or the flesh—which is also called the body— the soul, and the Spirit. That which is "formed in the image of God" is the flesh and, in our text, is clearly distinguished from the soul. The "animal and carnal" person "possesses the image in the *plasma*."[9]

In the face of such precise assertions, it seems difficult not to recognize that, for Irenaeus, "the εἰκών is above all realized in the body."[10]

[5] *Haer.* 5.12.4 (1155). Cf. 4.20.1 (1032).
[6] *Haer.* 4. Preface 4 (975). Cf. 5.1.1 (1121). Not without reason does Struker, *Gottebenbildlichkeit*, 89-90, feel that, in all the passages in which the Latin translator employs the term *similitudo* to express the divine likeness of humankind, when taken in the broad sense, the original Greek did not have ὁμοίωσις, but ὁμοιότης. Cf. *Haer.* 3.21.10 (955); 3:22:1 (956).
[7] Cf above, 61-62.
[8] *Haer.* 5.6.1 (1137-1138).
[9] *Haer.* 5.6.1 (1137-1138). Cf. 5.1.3 (1123).
[10] Harnack, *Dogmengeschichte*, 1:589.

How then can we reconcile such a conception with the doctrine of the absolute spirituality of God, so very firmly upheld by our doctor?[11] A passage from the *Demonstration* seems to contain the key to this enigma. In chapter 22, after quoting the passage Gen 9:1-6, a quotation which ends with the phrase, "for God made humankind in His image", Irenaeus comments: "The image of God is the Son in whose likeness humankind has been made. And this is why He [the Son] has appeared at the end of time, namely, to show that His image is like Himself."[12] Now if, for the bishop of Lyon, "to be made in the image of God" is nothing other than "to be made in the image of the Son" incarnate, we can understand how, in the passage from *Against Heresies* quoted above, he could see "the image of God" being initially realized in the human body, since the human body, according to Irenaeus, was formed after the type of the body of the Logos, which had been incarnated from all eternity and was ideally present with the Creator.

147

What we are really saying is that the image of God or of the Son is "initially" realized in the human flesh, in order to show that it is not the body alone that is an image of God. Indeed, Saint Irenaeus elsewhere discerns a twofold similitude of natural humankind in relation to God:

> As for the man, He formed him with His own hands, by taking of the purest and the finest earth and mingling His strength with the earth, in due proportion. Furthermore, He impressed His own traits onto His work, so that even the visible [in the man] might be deiform; because having been [thus] fashioned, the man was placed on earth as the image of God. And in order that he might become living, He blew on his face the breath of life, so that, both by this breathing-upon and by his formation, the man might be like God. And he was free and self-sufficient, since he was made by God to have control over all the beings that would be on the earth.[13]

Hence, in their body already human beings are the image of God, or, more precisely, of the incarnated Logos, since the body has been fashioned according to the God-Man, the ideal type of all humanity.[14] They are such in the soul as well, insofar as, by the soul, they are free and masters not only of their own actions, but also of the whole creation.[15] Moreover, this divine similitude,

---

[11] Cf. X. Le Bachelet, "Dieu," *DTC* 4:1036-1039.

[12] *Epid.* 22 (767). As is already the case for Philo, the likeness of Adam with God, which is maintained in the biblical account, becomes in the writings of Irenaeus a likeness with the Logos. Cf. above, 75.

[13] *Epid.* 11. The translation of this passage that is given by Fr. Barthoulot, 762, differs notably both from the English translation, 667-668, and from the German translation of Weber, *Irenäus*, 591. We owe the translation that we give to the kindness of our colleague, Mr. Karst, Professor of Armenian at the University of Strasbourg.

[14] Cf. *Haer.* 5.6.1 (1136): "Glorificabitur autem Deus in suo plasmate, conforme illud et consequens suo puero adaptans." [And God will be glorified in His created thing, fitting it to be conformed to, and following after, His own Son.] See also 5.16.2, quoted below.

[15] Struker, *Gottebenbildlichkeit*, 99, has indeed seen the assertion of a "twofold element in the natural divine likeness" of humankind in our text. But being unable to explain it, he eliminates this passage as an interpolation. We think that we have shown that it is not necessary to resort to such an expedient.

based on the intelligence and free will of humankind, is affirmed on several   148
occasions by Irenaeus in his main work. Contrasting humankind to beings that
are deprived of reason, he writes for example: "Human beings who are rational
and thereby similar to God, were created free in the will, and self-sufficient."[16]

The fact that this is the whole person, body and soul—taking no account of
the Spirit,[17] who is the image of the Logos—clearly results from another text in
which the distinction that is made in humankind between εἰκών and ὁμοίωσις
is expressed.

> So this means that this Word was revealed when the Word of God became
> human, being Himself assimilated to humankind and assimilating humankind to
> Himself. And this was in order that humankind might become more dear to the
> Father, due to their likeness with the Son. In the past, it was indeed said that
> humankind was made in the image of God, but this was not manifest. Actually,
> the Word was still invisible by whose image humankind had been made. This is
> why they easily lost the similitude [ὁμοίωσιν]. But when the Word of God became
> flesh, He strengthened both, because He revealed the true image by becoming
> Himself what was His image, and He firmly restored the similitude by making
> them with Himself like [συνεξομοιώσας] the invisible Father, through the visible
> Word.[18]

Therefore, having become visible through His incarnation, the Logos
showed that humankind was truly in His image. Consequently it is by means
of their nature that humankind is the image of the Word. And this is why they
did not lose the εἰκών through original sin any more than they could have lost   149
the human nature.[19] The ὁμοίωσις, on the contrary, was erased by the sin of
Adam.

However great the difficulties of interpretation may be, due to the imprecision of the thought and even more of the vocabulary of Saint Irenaeus, it is
certain—and this is the main point for us—that each time he brings εἰκών
together with ὁμοίωσις, the bishop of Lyon sees the divine image realized in
the very nature of humankind. Therefore the εἰκών is seen as something that is
natural to humankind, incapable of being lost, and common to all.

---

[16] *Haer.* 4.4.3 (983). Cf. 4.37.4 (1102); 4.38.4 (1109), where the divine similitude of human beings is situated in their free will.

[17] Cf. *Haer.* 5.12.2 (1152-1153), where Irenaeus distinguishes between the "πνοὴ ζωῆς, which
makes humankind psychological," that is to say, gives them the rational soul, and "the life-giving Spirit,
which perfects them by making them pneumatic." But in this passage our doctor only seems to recognize the "breath" in Adam and seems to refuse him "the spirit" which, nevertheless, he formally attributes to him elsewhere.

[18] *Haer.* 5.16.2 (1167, 1168).

[19] Cf. E. Klebba, *Die Anthropologie des hl. Irenäus* (Münster in Westphalia, 1894), 24-26. The author
mistakenly understands in εἰκών not only human nature but also the preternatural gifts with which
Adam was adorned.

The first human being thus possessed both the εἰκών and the ὁμοίωσις. The latter was lost through disobedience—*similitudinem facile amisit*. But the Word of God "firmly restored the likeness by making humankind like the invisible Father."

It follows from this that the divine likeness of Adam, when it is distinguished from the state of image, was something spiritual that he could lose without ceasing to be a human being. Being added to and being superior to the natural similitude, his divine likeness was the effect of the possession of the Spirit of God—*similitudinem assumens per Spiritus*.[20] This is because the Spirit had given "the robe of holiness"[21] to Adam and had made a perfect person out of him. But He did not make him with an absolute perfection that excludes any progress, but with a relative perfection. For humankind was destined to "progress peacefully and rise up toward the perfect, that is to say, to draw closer to the Unbegotten [τοῦ ἀγεννήτου]. Indeed, the Unbegotten is perfect and He is God." At the end of such an ascension, Adam would have seen God. "Now the sight [ὅρασις] of God brings ἀφθαρσία, which in turn gives a place that is near to God."[22] Thus the Creator did not make a god out of the man from the very beginning, because he might have been incapable "of bearing the power of divinity." It was necessary for this one first of all to become truly human, and god only afterwards by acquiring perfection, that is to say, incorruptibility, by virtue of the vision of God.[23]

Progressive deification was therefore the aim that was presented for the working life of our first ancestor. But far from realizing this, through his rebelliousness Adam lost for himself and his descendants the gifts that he had only received on a precarious basis—the Spirit and thus the ὁμοίωσις with God.[24]

II

After a suitable preparation[25] and at the end of times, the Son of God became human, in order to give back to us what we had lost in Adam. Indeed, the work of perfect restoration postulated a God-Man:

> The Word of God became human and the One who is the Son of God became the Son of Man, united with the Word of God, in order that humankind might receive adoption and become sons of God. For we could not receive incorruptibility and immortality in any other way than by union with incorruptibility and immortality. But how could we have been united with incorruptibility and immortality, if incorruptibility and immortality had not first become what we are, in order that what was corruptible might be swallowed up by incorruptibility,

---

[20] *Haer.* 5.6.1 (1138), quoted on page 121.

[21] *Haer.* 3.23.5 (963).

[22] Cf. Wis 6:19.

[23] *Haer.* 4.38.3-4 (1108-1109). On the "spiritual childhood" of Adam, see A. Verrièle, "Le plan du salut d'après saint Irénée," *RevScRel* 14 (1934): 515-518.

[24] Cf. Gaudel, "Péché originel," 325-326.

[25] *Haer.* 4.11.2 (1011).

what was mortal might be swallowed up by immortality, and in order that we might receive the adoption of sons?[26]

Elsewhere the same doctrine is condensed into this succinct expression:

Qui [Jesus Christus] propter immensam suam dilectionem factus est quod sumus nos, uti nos perficeret esse quod est ipse.[27]

This means that the Savior "recapitulates" all of humanity in His Person and thus becomes for it a new Adam who, by uniting humanity with His divinity, gives immortality back to it and, with immortality, the divine likeness that was lost:

When [the Son of God] was incarnated and became human, he recapitulated in Himself the long succession of human beings [*longam hominum expositionem in seipso recapitulavit*], giving us salvation outright [*in compendio*], in order that we might regain in Jesus Christ what we had lost in Adam, namely, the image and the likeness of God.[28]

He was therefore uniting humankind with God....If humankind had not been united with God, they would not have been able to partake of incorruptibility [οὐκ ἂν ἠδυνήθη μετασχεῖν τῆς ἀφθαρσίας].[29]

In these passages we see a physical or mystical conception of deification beginning to emerge for the first time.[30] According to this theory, which springs from the Johannine idea of the Logos as the principle of life, human nature is immortalized and thus divinized by the very fact of the intimate contact that the incarnation establishes between it and the divine nature of the Word.

But if the incarnation plays the major role here, to the point of seeming to be sufficient for salvation on its own, the doctor of Lyon does not at all underrate the redemptive value of the death of Christ. In a number of passages, he actually presents as the fruit of the passion the same benefits, in particular, immortality, that he attributed to the incarnation earlier:

Through His passion the Lord destroyed death, dispelled error, exterminated corruption, and abolished ignorance; He manifested life, revealed the truth, and conferred incorruptibility.[31]

This is nothing other than biblical realism, above all, Pauline, and traditional realism, according to which our redemption is carried out through the

---

[26] *Haer.* 3.19.1 (939-940). Cf. *Haer.* 3.18.7 (937); 4.33.4 (1074). In these passages, Saint Irenaeus starts from the deifying work of the Savior in order to establish both His divinity and His humanity.

[27] [Jesus Christ, who because of His immeasurable love, became what we are, in order that He might cause us to be what He is Himself.] *Haer.* 5. preface (1120).

[28] *Haer.* 3.18.1 (932). Cf. *Haer.* 3.21.10–3.22 (954-960); 4.20.4 (1034).

[29] *Haer.* 3.18.7 (937).

[30] Cf. Tixeront, *Histoire des dogmes,* 1:265; 2 (9th ed., 1931):149; Richard, *Le dogme de la Rédemption,* 84.

[31] *Haer.* 2.20.3 (778). Other references are in Rivière, *Rédemption: étude historique,* 123-126. Cf. F. Vernet, "Irénée," *DTC* 7:2472-2474.

expiatory sacrifice of Jesus Christ.[32] But nowhere does Irenaeus show how this sacrifice harmonizes with the efficiency that he elsewhere ascribes to the incarnation as such.

Of course, however great the virtue that he recognizes in the salvific work of Christ may be, the bishop of Lyon is far from thinking that nothing more remains to be done by a person with a view to divinization. On the contrary, according to him only the believers who "are united with the Word of God the Father" will obtain incorruptibility.

Indeed, this is what Irenaeus firmly teaches regarding the heretics who only see Christ as a mere man. He writes concerning them:

> Stubbornly persisting in the bondage of the ancient disobedience, they die, still not being united with the Word of God the Father [*nondum commixti Verbo Dei Patris*] and still not having obtained freedom through the Son....They are deprived of His gift, which is eternal life. And since they do not want to receive the Word of incorruptibility, they remain in the mortal flesh and are subjected to death because they do not accept the antidote of life.[33]

The deifying union with the incarnated Logos and His Spirit takes place through faith, love, and the customary practice of sacraments, such as baptism and the Eucharist.[34] By these means the divine operation renews humankind "in the image and the likeness of God"[35] and restores to them the ὁμοίωσις τῷ θεῷ that was lost through sin.

III

153   Of what exactly does the superior divine likeness that is granted to the Christian consist? Its origin is certainly the Holy Spirit:

> By the outpouring of the Spirit, humankind has become spiritual and perfect, and this is what is in the image and in the likeness of God. But if in a person the Spirit is absent from the soul, such a person will be imperfect...not possessing the similitude in the Spirit.[36]

Assertions of this kind frequently recur in the writing of our author.[37] Moreover, for him this indwelling of the Spirit of God in humankind was not the exclusive privilege of Adam, before the arrival of Christ. The prophets and the righteous ones of the Old Testament were blessed with it as well.[38] In brief, there is no doubt that, following Saint Paul, the bishop of Lyon teaches the

---

[32]   Cf. Tixeront, *Histoire des dogmes*, 2:149, 265-266; Vernet, "Irénée," 2470; Bernard Bartmann, *Précis de théologie dogmatique* (trans. M. Gautier; 8th ed.; Mulhouse, 1935), 1:436.

[33]   *Haer.* 3.19.1 (938c-d).

[34]   Cf. Vernet, "Irénée," 2492-2495.

[35]   *Haer.* 5.36.3 (1224). Cf. *Epid.* 97 (799).

[36]   *Haer.* 5.6.1 (1138). See above, 121.

[37]   Cf. *Haer.* 5.9.1-3 (1144-1146); 4.20.4, 6 (1034, 1036); 5.8.1 (1141); 5:10.1 (1150); 5:12.2 (1152-1153); *Epid.* 7 (760).

[38]   *Epid.* 49 (781); 73 (791). Cf. *Haer.* 3.21.4 (950); 4.20.8 (1037-1038).

special indwelling of the Holy Spirit in the soul of the Christian and, through this, in the body. More precisely, the flesh of the righteous is possessed by the divine Spirit; and in accordance with the apostle this flesh must be "a pure temple so that the Spirit of God may take delight in it, like the husband takes delight in the wife."[39] Irenaeus did not speculate on the practical details of this special presence of the Holy Spirit in the baptized one.

Beside the personal gift of the Holy Spirit, our doctor seems to acknowledge in the righteous the presence of a kind of "spiritual nature that is related to the divine Spirit and created by Him, and which has become the personal property of humankind."[40] Strucker infers this from the following passage in *Against Heresies*:

> Once the number that He has fixed in advance by His decree has been fulfilled, all those who are enrolled in the book of life will rise again, with their own bodies and their own souls and their own spirits [ἴδια πνεύματα], in which they pleased God. But those who deserve punishment will be about to suffer it, with their own bodies and their own souls, in which they stood away from the grace of God.[41]

154

By so assigning to each of the elect his "own spirit," exactly like his "own" body and soul, Irenaeus would lead us to believe that the πνεῦμα in question is the personal and exclusive property of the human being, just like the body and the soul, without however belonging to the human nature, since the reprobates are deprived of it.[42] Klebba, on the contrary, considers that the expression ἴδιον πνεῦμα refers to the Holy Spirit Himself, "insofar as He has been given to human beings, kept intact by them, and has thus become their own." The adjective "own" would simply indicate the personal and varied measure according to which the Spirit is possessed by human beings.[43]

If either of these interpretations is possible in itself, the first has in its favor the fact that our doctor himself seems to distinguish between *spiritus hominis* and *Spiritus Dei* in another passage of *Against Heresies*:

> Si enim substantiam tollat aliquis carnis, id est plasmatis, et nude ipsum solum spiritum intellegat, iam non spiritualis homo est, quod est tale, sed spiritus hominis aut Spiritus Dei.[44]

In the same passage, commenting on 1 Thes 5:23—"May the God of peace Himself sanctify you wholly, and may all that is in you, that is, the spirit, the

---

[39] *Haer.* 5.9.4 (1146-1147). Cf. *Haer.* 5.9.3 (1145): *caro a Spiritu possessa.* See Klebba, *Anthropologie,* 166-169.
[40] Strucker, *Gottebenbildlichkeit,* 106.
[41] *Haer.* 2.33.5 (834).
[42] *Haer.* 2.33.5 (834).
[43] Klebba, *Anthropologie,* 181.
[44] [For if anyone would take away the substance of the flesh, that is, of the created thing, and simply understand only the spirit itself, such a thing is no longer a spiritual human being, but would be the spirit of the human being or the Spirit of God.] *Haer.* 5.6.1 (1137).

soul, and the body, be kept blameless until the day of the coming of our Lord Jesus Christ"—Saint Irenaeus writes:

> And what reason did he thus have to implore—with a view to the coming of the Lord—a full and complete perseverance for these three components, namely, the soul, the body, and the spirit, unless it is because he knew that the believers' unique and actual salvation consists in the re-establishment and mingling of these three things?[45]

155

It seems difficult to identify the *spiritus* of this text with the Holy Spirit, since it is a question here of its salvation, like that of the body and of the soul. On the contrary, everything invites us to see here a spiritual reality that is distinct from the divine Spirit and inherent in humankind. But a little further on, Irenaeus once more gives the impression that "the spirit of the human being" for him is identified with "the Spirit of God," when he writes:

> Perfecti igitur, qui et Spiritum in se perseverantem habuerint Dei, et animas et corpora sine querela servarint.[46]

The commentary that Irenaeus makes regarding the comparison of the wild olive tree and the cultivated olive tree, which was used by the apostle, supplies Struker with a novel argument in favor of his thesis. Just as the wild olive tree, after being grafted and without changing its nature, is inwardly improved, as its fruits prove, likewise "a genuinely intrinsic though not substantial change" should take place in those who receive the Spirit of God and bring forth His fruits.[47]

This argumentation both explains and brings out again the real thought of our doctor and would seem to be confirmed by a series of other indications leading in the same direction.

Thus, the bishop of Lyon often says that, for the Christian, the Holy Spirit is the origin, the source of divine life: *qui (Spiritus Patris) emundat hominem et sublevat in vitam Dei.*[48] This new life "does not come from us or from our nature, but it is given according to the grace of God"; it is a partaking of the divine life itself.[49] Superior to the natural life—it will later be called "supernatural"—does this life not assume a spiritual *substratum* in humankind, that is, a *spiritus hominis* that has been produced by the Holy Spirit and, consequently, is distinct from Him?

156

---

[45]   *Haer.* 5.6.1 (1138b).

[46]   [So then, they are the perfect who both have had the Spirit of God remaining in them and have preserved their souls and bodies blameless.] *Haer.* 5.6.1 (1138b-c).

[47]   Struker, *Gottebenbildlichkeit*, 107.

[48]   [...who (the Spirit of the Father) purifies human beings and raises them up to the life of God.] *Haer.* 5.9.2 (1144). Cf. *Haer.* 5.9.3-4 (1145-1147).

[49]   *Haer.* 2.34.3-4 (836-837). Here we have *in nuce* the distinction between nature and grace. But far from insisting on such a distinction, Irenaeus and the Greeks in general indicate the continuity between the two orders instead; "nature hardly appears as more than an imperfect partaking of God whose grace perfectly achieves the similitude, so to speak, following the same line" (M.-J. Congar, "La déification dans la tradition spirituelle de l'Orient," *VSpir* 43 [1935]: [99]-[100]).

Moreover, the divine action on humankind is compared by Saint Irenaeus to that of a minter and of an artist: "By the Spirit we receive the image and the inscription of the Father and of the Son."[50] So we should offer to the divine artist a malleable heart and should carefully guard the masterpiece that He is forming in us.[51] These images of an inscription and of a masterpiece produced in us, along with that of the "robe of holiness," strongly suggest that our doctor has caught a glimpse within the Christian of the presence of a "spirit of the human being." It is a spiritual gift, distinct from the divine Spirit, but produced by Him and inseparable from Him, which elevates to a superior mode of existence and activity, to the point of rendering the human being like the divine persons,[52] a gift that would essentially constitute the divine ὁμοίωσις of the regenerated human being. Subsequent theology will not have any trouble in recognizing habitual or sanctifying grace here.[53] In brief, we can say without anachronism that, in a certain way, Saint Irenaeus anticipated the distinction between uncreated Gift and created gift.[54]

Therefore we find in the writings of the bishop of Lyon, the idea, at least implied, according to which the ὁμοίωσις—that superior likeness that exists between God and redeemed humankind—is conditioned by the possession of the person of the Holy Spirit, and constituted by a created grace that transfigures humankind and makes them like the three trinitarian persons. By assimilating them to the incarnated Logos who is the "child" of God by nature, this grace makes the baptized ones the adopted children of God.[55] The Scripture even goes as far as calling them "gods"; because the word of Psa 82:6, "I said: You are gods and all of you children of the Most High," applies "to those who have received the grace of adoption by which they cry: Abba, Father."[56]

157

IV

As precious as it may be, the gift of the divine ὁμοίωσις granted to the Christian from the time of this life onward is only a seed. Even though it develops in advance here below, it will only blossom in full in the hereafter. Undoubtedly, Irenaeus calls "perfect" the person who is filled with the Holy Spirit; but for him, it is not a question of an absolute perfection. On the contrary, like that of Adam before the fall, this gift remains capable of an unlimited progress: *homo*

---

[50] *Haer.* 3.17.3 (930).
[51] *Haer.* 4.39.2 (1110).
[52] The Holy Spirit transforms humankind to His own image (*Haer.* 5.9.3 [1145]): "by assuming the quality of the Spirit," humankind becomes "conformed to the Word of God" (*Haer.* 5.9.3 [1145]); this One, finally, "makes humankind like the invisible Father" (*Haer.* 5.16.2 [1168]. Cf. *Epid.* 5 [758-759]).
[53] Cf. Lange, *De gratia*, 187.
[54] Consequently, it seems at least exaggerated to pretend, as J. Turmel does in *Histoire des dogmes* (Paris, 1935) 4:465, 451, that the fathers "were only acquainted with uncreated sanctifying grace" and that, "until the 13th century" this "alone will be what exists."
[55] Cf. *Haer.* 5.6.1 (1137); 3.6.1 (861); 5.12.2 (1152).
[56] *Haer.* 3.6.1 (861).

viator "will make progress slowly and will walk toward the perfect, that is to say, approach the ἀγέννητος."[57] "Now we only receive from the Spirit of God a certain amount, with a view to perfection and the preparation for incorruptibility, little by little making us accustomed to take hold of and to bear God." But "the complete grace of the Spirit" which will be given to us by God "will make us perfect according to the will of the Father, because it will make humankind in the image and in the likeness of God."[58]

Now, with Saint Ignatius and the apologists—and we could add the gnostics—our doctor sees in ἀγεννησία, with ἀφθαρσία which proceeds from it, the distinctive element of the divine essence, perfection, and the "glory" of divinity.[59] Only God is incorruptible by nature, in the strict and complete sense. However some creatures have part in the "glory of the Unbegotten," insofar as, "taking on the virtue of the Uncreated," they endure forever.[60] Such is the case of the human soul.[61] Humankind, on the contrary, that compound of body and soul, belongs to corruption. But after the resurrection and the general judgment,[62] God will have them partake of the privilege of incorruptibility. This participation will be the result of the vision of God, which by pure kindness the Father will grant to the elect. In fact, "those who see God are within God, and partake of His splendor."[63] Having been made "immortals by vision,"[64] the blessed possess the ὁμοίωσις τῷ Θεῷ to the highest degree: they will be divinized to the farthest extent possible.

Consequently, although Saint Irenaeus never uses the terms θεοποιεῖν and θεοποίησις, his soteriology does imply a doctrine of deification.

⸉⸊

Two features especially characterize the doctrine of Irenaeus. First of all, the distinction that it makes between the εἰκῶν and the ὁμοίωσις in redeemed humankind. We have seen that this distinction is found for the first time with the gnostics, but with Irenaeus it appears with very different characteristics. In fact, rejecting the gnostic concept of the ὁμοίωσις as a divine seed which, forming the essence of the pneumatic, is a gift of nature in this one and consequently incapable of being lost, the bishop of Lyon identifies the ὁμοίωσις with the

---

[57] *Haer.* 5.38.3 (1108).
[58] *Haer.* 5.8.1 (1141-1142).
[59] Cf. *Haer.* 2.24.2 (835); 4.38.3 (1108): παραμονὴ ἀφθαρσίας δόξα ἀγεννήτου.
[60] *Haer.* 4.38.3 (1107-1108).
[61] *Haer.* 2.24 (834-837). Cf. Klebba, *Anthropologie,* 108-111. In that which concerns the natural immortality of the soul, Irenaeus thinks like Athenagoras. See above, 116-117.
[62] We know that Saint Irenaeus lapsed into the millenarianist error. According to him, the earthly kingdom of Christ, of a duration of one thousand years, should be inaugurated by the resurrection of only the righteous (*Haer.* 5.28-36). See Vernet, "Irénée," 2503-2505.
[63] *Haer.* 4.20.5 (1035b).
[64] *Haer.* 4.20.6 (1036a). Cf. the whole of 4.20.

possession of the Holy Spirit and His gifts. In this, he is manifestly inspired by the Pauline doctrine of the divine Spirit, the source of new life in the Christian.[65]

This fundamental difference carries along several others with it. For Irenaeus, ὁμοίωσις is an accidental perfection only, a divine grace added on top of the human nature. Far from being the inborn and exclusive privilege of a specific category of men, the pneumatics, the superior likeness is within the reach of all, although only those who cooperate with the divine working may acquire it. For ever since the sin of Adam, human beings are born devoid of the ὁμοίωσις. Having been regained, this item can be lost again: when they disobey God, they ruin it, just like our first ancestor did, and thus commit veritable suicide.[66] This means that, far from being above good and evil, as the gnostics dream, the spiritual ones remain subject to all the demands of the divine law and fallible.

But what ensures to Saint Irenaeus a special place in the history of the doctrine of divinization is that he is the first one to attempt a theological interpretation of the fact of deification, to try to specify its conditions and point out its origin, starting sometimes from the incarnation and sometimes from the death of Christ. In doing so, he has shown the way for subsequent development.

2. Christian Gnosis: Clement of Alexandria

Being above all a person of tradition, Saint Irenaeus refutes Gnosticism by setting against it the doctrine commonly received in the church. The excesses of heretical speculation inspire him with a marked distrust for any attempt to transform Christianity into a "philosophy." Thus he writes:

> It is better to know absolutely nothing, not even one, of the causes of all things that have been made, and to believe in God and to persevere in love, rather than, being puffed up by this knowledge, to fall from the love which enlivens humankind; [it is better] not to search for any other knowledge apart from Jesus Christ, Son of God, crucified for us, than to fall into gossiping and ungodliness, brought about by the subtlety of questions.[67]

However, such distrust was not shared by all the Christian doctors of the period. In Alexandria, at the end of the third century, an attempt of great scope takes shape, considerably greater than that of certain apologists such as Saint Justin, with the view of presenting Christianity as "the true philosophy,"[68] which "is not a knowledge born of human speculation, but a higher religious understanding, due to a privileged revelation;...an intuition which initiates those who enjoy it to mysteries forbidden to the crowd, transforms their

---

[65] When he grants the deification of the perfect human being, Irenaeus refers expressly to the apostle. Cf. *Haer.* 5.6 (1136-1139).
[66] *Haer.* 4.39.1 (1109-1110).
[67] *Haer.* 2.26.1 (800b-c).
[68] Clem. *Strom.* 2.22 (PG 8:1080b). Cf. *Strom.* 2.2 (933c-d).

moral and religious life, rescues them from the servile condition common to everyone, makes them friends of God, equal or even superior to the angels."[69] In brief, represented in particular by Clement of Alexandria and Origen,[70] these thinkers set a Christian gnosis in opposition to the Gnosticism that had become particularly dangerous in the Egyptian metropolis, with the goal of more effectively combatting it. This was a conception of Christianity whereby salvation is obtained due to a more profound and learned knowledge of the Christian faith. Because salvation itself here has deification as the terminus, this gnosis is a gnosis of divinization.

According to Clement, philosophers such as Plato and the Stoics are in agreement with the writers of the Old and New Testaments in placing the sovereign good of humankind in their assimilation, as perfect as possible, to God:

> The assimilation [ἐξομοίωσις] to the λόγος ὀρθός, as far as possible, is the aim....The assimilation to God, with a view to becoming as righteous and holy in prudence as possible—such is the goal of faith.[71]

161   Once again it is the Hellenic ideal of the divinization of humankind that our author takes up for his own use, but he infuses into it a Christian soul. In fact, he presents deification as the exclusive work of the incarnated Logos, beginning with baptism and finishing in heaven.

I

By virtue of their formation, human beings already possess a certain similitude with God. Indeed, according to Wisdom, "God created us for incorruption and made us in the image of his own eternity."[72] Contrary to what the gnostics dream therefore, a human being is a creature, neither a fragment of God nor consubstantial with Him. The image and likeness of God, humankind are such not "in the body," but "according to the νοῦς and reason."[73] This means that "the human νοῦς is the image of the image..., the image of God being the divine and kingly Logos, the impassible man [ἄνθρωπος ἀπαθής]."[74]

---

[69] J. Lebreton, "Le désaccord de la foi populaire et de la théologie savante dans l'Église du 3ᵉ siècle," *RHE* 19 (1923): 493.

[70] Certain indications lead us to think that a certain teacher of Clement—perhaps Pantaenus—already endeavored to work out a Christian gnosis. Cf. Lebreton, "Le désaccord," 493-494; G. Bardy, "Aux origines de l'école d'Alexandrie," *RSR* 27 (1937): 72-77.

[71] *Strom.* 2.22 (8:1084-1085). The ὀρθὸς λόγος is the upright reason of the Stoics, accepted by Clement as the regulating principle of morality. Cf. *Strom.* 5.14 (9:140b). See A. de La Barre, "Clément d'Alexandrie," *DTC* 3:179-180. The second phrase of our quotation reproduces Pl. *Theaet.* 176b. See above, 41.

[72] *Strom.* 6.12 (9:317c). Cf. *Paed.* 1.3 (8:257a-b); *Ecl.* frg. 17 (ed. O. Staehlin, GCS 3:141). In this last text, Clement expressly denies any pre-existence of humankind, so also of the human soul. Cf. Jean Hering, *Étude sur la doctrine de la chute et de la préexistence des âmes chez Clément d'Alexandrie* (Paris, 1923), 28-34.

[73] *Strom.* 2.19 (8:1048b).

[74] *Strom.* 5.14 (9:140). Philo already calls humankind "image of an image," namely, of the "divine Logos." See above, 75-76.

Clement points out the distinction that certain Christians at his time were making between the image and the divine likeness in humankind, and which he manifestly makes his own: "Are there not among us some who think that humankind have received the image [τὸ κατ᾽ εἰκόνα] by virtue of their very origin, whereas they are going to receive the likeness [τὸ καθ᾽ ὁμοίωσιν] later through perfection?"[75] This means that Adam in fact "was not created perfect, but capable of gaining virtue, because the capacity for its acquisition leads toward virtue. Now God would have us save ourselves by ourselves."[76] Thus the salvation of humankind will not at all be the effect of a natural determinism, as the gnostics would want it to be, but the fruit of his free will. Nonetheless, we can say that "Adam was perfect as to his formation, because nothing was lacking to him of that which characterizes the human idea and form."[77]

162

By his creation then, our first ancestor possessed only the image of God that is inherent in the human nature and therefore incapable of being lost. He did not yet have the divine likeness, which is something superior to the status of image, something added on top of the nature. Adam however was endowed with immortality[78] and was leading a happy life in paradise.[79]

Due to his disobedience,[80] the first man "exchanged an immortal life for a mortal life, but not forever."[81] The sin of Adam inaugurates a period of darkness[82] and death for all of humanity, which increasingly sinks into corruption and the slavery of sin.[83] However, in spite of everything, the Logos does not abandon them: He is not only the Creator of human beings, but also their enlightener, their teacher and Savior.[84] For all those who lived before His incarnation He has prepared some appropriate means of salvation: for the Jews, it is the law; for the Greeks, philosophy.[85] But only after He became human did the Logos reveal the complete truth. Thus, the incarnation is the crowning achievement of the salvific work accomplished by the Word. It encompasses humanity completely in a single economy of salvation.[86]

163

---

[75]   *Strom.* 2.22 (8:1080c). Cf. *Paed.* 1.12 (8:368b).

[76]   *Strom.* 6.12 (9:317b).

[77]   *Strom.* 4.22 (8:1360b).

[78]   Immortality is the only privilege exceeding the natural order which Clement points out in Adam. Since for him, the soul is naturally immortal (see N. Le Nourry, *Dissertationes in Clem. Alex.* 2.8.3 [PG 9:1155c-d] and 2.18.1 [1289-1291]), it is bodily immortality which he thus acknowledges in the first human being. See also Capitaine, *Clemens*, 118-121.

[79]   *Prot.* 11 (8:228c).

[80]   The sin of our first parents was "to let themselves be led to the procreation of children sooner than they should have been." *Strom.* 3.18 (8:1205b). Cf. Gaudel, "Péché originel," 330.

[81]   *Strom.* 2.19 (8:1041b). Like Irenaeus, Clement believes in the final salvation of Adam.

[82]   Cf. *Strom.* 6.16 (9:360a).

[83]   Cf. *Paed.* 3.12 (8:672c): τὸ μὲν γὰρ ἐξαμαρτάνειν πᾶσιν ἔμφυτον καὶ κοινόν.

[84]   See La Barre, "Clément," 160-161.

[85]   *Strom.* 7.2 (9:413c-416b). Cf. *Strom.* 6.5-6 (261-269).

[86]   *Strom.* 6.13 (9:328b). Cf. *Protr.* 11 (8:228).

II

The salvation brought by Christ is deification: "The Logos of God has become human in order that you may learn from a human being how humankind can become god."[87] "By His heavenly doctrine He deifies humankind" [οὐρανίῳ διδασκαλίᾳ θεοποιῶν ἄνθρωπον].[88]

Clement is the first one who uses the term θεοποιεῖν to refer to the deifying action of the incarnated Logos in the Christian. Used with increasing frequency, this verb, with a substantive θεοποίησις, will henceforth be standard among the Greek fathers.

Being the supreme goal of all divine education and the final purpose of humankind, deification is realized by degrees or steps. A continuous ascension must lead a person by "an initial salutary change, from being a Gentile to faith," and by "a second, from faith to gnosis. The latter, ending in love, then unites friend with Friend, the one who knows with the One who is known."[89]

It is true that, according to the *Paedagogus* "faith is already the perfection of doctrine;" for "nothing is lacking to faith, since it is perfect and full by itself." One can say, in fact, that the regenerated ones are "perfect as much as it is possible to be in this world":[90]

To have believed and to have been regenerated is already perfection in life.[91]

Having been baptized, we are enlightened; having been enlightened, we are adopted; having been adopted, we are made perfect; having been made perfect, we are immortalized. "I said," it is written, "You are gods and all of you children of the Most High."[92]

Nothing more is lacking than "the possession of eternal life."[93] Moreover there is no distinction of classes among Christians:

It is thus not true that some are gnostics, others psychics, in the same Logos; but all those who have been stripped of carnal desires are equal and pneumatic in the eyes of the Lord.[94]

When reading these enthusiastic descriptions of the grandeur of "Christian childhood," we must not lose sight of the fact that, in the passages in question, Clement is fighting against the gnostic theory which establishes a difference of nature between psychics and pneumatics. To that end, with the utmost energy he denies any original and essential difference between baptized ones. Furthermore, we should remember that in his *Paedagogus* our doctor is speaking to

164

---

[87]   *Protr.* 1 (8:64d).
[88]   *Paed.* 1.12 (8:368a-b).
[89]   *Strom.* 7.10 (9:481a).
[90]   *Paed.* 1.6 (8:286a. Cf. 280b): "Having been regenerated, we immediately received perfection."
[91]   *Paed.* 1.4 (8:281b).
[92]   *Paed.* 1.4 (8:281a).
[93]   *Paed.* 1.4 (8:286a).
[94]   *Paed.* 1.4 (8:288a-b).

neophytes, to whom he endeavors to give as lofty an idea as possible of the state of perfection which results from baptism.

In the *Stromata*, however, inspired by Rom 1:17, Clement clearly distinguishes a twofold faith: the "common faith" [κοινὴ πίστις] and an "increased and perfected" faith.[95] The first is that of simple believers who know God, accept the facts contained in the revelation, and do not in any way practice unrighteousness.[96] The more perfect faith is "the magnificent and excellent gnosis of the truth."[97] The one who possesses it, "the gnostic," is "the only truly pious man;" he is "the true Christian" [ὁ τῷ ὄντι χριστιανός].[98]

III

On several occasions, notably in the sixth and seventh *Stromata*, Clement sketches the portrait of the gnostic, the philosopher, the perfect Christian, in whom he hails the flower of Christianity, the ideal which "epitomizes all the aspirations of a noble heart and enthusiastic piety."[99] In such a one he sees the deifying action of the Logos revealed in the most brilliant way. Therefore, it is in the gnostic, above all, that we must study this action.

How may gnosis be reached?

On more than one occasion, our doctor presents gnosis "as the result of a secret tradition, passed on under the cover of an esoteric method and the discipline of secrecy."[100] Thus, having called to mind his teachers, he writes:

> Those ones preserved the genuine tradition of the blessed teaching, received directly from Peter and from James, from John and from Paul, the holy apostles, the child receiving it from a parent—but few were like their parents—and, with God, they came to us also, in order to pass on to us these ancient and apostolic seeds.[101]

Rarer and fainter in the earlier *Stromata*, assertions in favor of this esoteric tradition become more frequent and definite in the later *Stromata*.[102] It would seem, then, that toward the end of his life, when he composed the later *Stromata*, Clement "gave way to the enthusiasm of his masters for a life free from passions, fixed in perpetual contemplation, raised above humanity. And this very high ambition, not without illusion, entails some very serious consequences in its conception of Christianity, and particularly of the relationships of faith and gnosis."[103] This was, in fact, to distinguish within Christianity two classes of distinctly separate believers: an elite of initiated ones, the gnostics,

165

166

---

[95] *Strom.* 5.1 (9:12a).
[96] *Strom.* 5.1 (9:9-13). Cf. 7.2 (408b).
[97] *Strom.* 5.1 (9:13c).
[98] *Strom.* 7.1 (9:401b).
[99] E. De Faye, *Clément d'Alexandrie* (2d ed; Paris, 1906), 313.
[100] La Barre, "Clément," 191.
[101] *Strom.* 1.1 (8:700a).
[102] See, for example, *Strom.* 6.16 (9:356b); 6.7 (284): Gnosis, "passed on and made known by the Son of God," "passed on orally [ἀγράφως] by the apostles, by tradition has come down to a small number of men."
[103] Lebreton, "Le désaccord," 497.

and a mass of simple believers who could not attain to the religious knowledge and the complete divinization reserved for the gnostics. This was to compromise the inner oneness of the Christian church.[104]

More numerous, however, especially in the *Paedagogus* and the earlier *Stromata*, though not completely lacking in the later ones,[105] are passages where the gnosis which divinizes is presented as an organic blossoming of faith, and consequently as a perfection to which every believer in principle can and should aspire.[106] In fact, only an elite arrives there, for it presupposes an arduous training, a long preparation, intellectual as well as moral. And first the candidate for gnosis or Christian philosophy must acquire all knowledge, including practical wisdom, "for it is impossible for the ignorant to be able to philosophize, as long as they remain such."[107] No less indispensable is moral discipline. In their constant prayer, the future gnostics "first of all ask for the remission of their sins; then [for the grace] to sin no more; next [for the grace] to do good..."[108] They will work continuously, not to curb their passions, but to eradicate them;[109] to gain all the virtues: beside faith, hope and love which are the foundation of gnosis,[110] especially those of strength and of continence.[111] In a word, only "a second conversion"[112] is "the kingly way"[113] which leads from simple faith to gnosis.

Even then the grace of God is necessary, for gnosis is above all the work of Christ, the divine teacher, in the soul which is intimately united and perfectly submissive to Him.[114]

The result of this second conversion is marvelous: "The gnostics possess perfect knowledge and virtue: they know all, they achieve all, they understand all. All of their actions are uprightness itself; there is more passion; transfigured

---

[104] Is it necessary to explain this evolution by the increasing influence that Gnosticism and the pagan mysteries would have exerted on Clement? In view of the constant hostility of our doctor toward these two religious currents, such an explanation hardly seems probable. It is more worthwhile to suppose that, in growing old, Clement allowed himself to be won over by an excessive mystical enthusiasm, a phenomenon which, moreover, is not rare. Cf. Bardy, "L'école d'Alexandrie", 77. The writer judges that, in the last *Stromata*, Clement "follows the natural bent of his spirit."

[105] Cf. above, 134.

[106] Did Clement realize the contradiction in which he was becoming involved by adopting, if not simultaneously, at least successively, both of these two conceptions? It does not seem so, since nowhere does he appear preoccupied to harmonize them. Furthermore, our catechist is nowhere near a contradiction.

[107] *Strom.* 2.9 (8:980c-981a). Cf. 6.8 (9:284 ff.); 6.10 (300c ff.); 6.15 (340). How far one is from Matt 11:25!

[108] *Strom.* 6.12 (9:324a).

[109] *Strom.* 2.20 (8:1048-1049). The gnostic must τὴν ἐπιθυμίαν ἐκκόπτειν.

[110] *Strom.* 4.7 (8:1264c-1265b).

[111] *Strom.* 2.20 (8:1048b ff.) In that which concerns continence in marriage, see *Strom.* 2.23 ff. (1085c ff.) and *Strom.* 3 in its entirety, where Clement defends the excellence of marriage against the Encratites.

[112] *Strom.* 7.10 (9:481a), quoted above, 134.

[113] *Strom.* 7.12 (9:501b): ἡ ὁδὸς βασιλική, an expression clearly borrowed from Philo. See above, 75.

[114] *Strom.* 7.10 (9:477-484). Cf. 2.22 (8:1084a); 5.11 (9:109b); De Faye, *Clément*, 285-286; Idem, *Origène* (3 vols.; Paris, 1923-28), 3:207.

in God they pray to Him unceasingly; their lives are a perpetual feast. The gnostics are apostles; they are priests, who constitute not only the elite, but the real hierarchy of the church."[115] In brief, these Christian philosophers have realized their destiny, which is to be not only in the divine image but also and especially in the divine likeness:

> It is this one who is according to the image and the likeness, the gnostic, who imitates God as much as it is possible, omitting nothing of that which leads to the possession of the ὁμοίωσις.[116]

> The likeness [ἐξομοίωσις] with the Savior God is the lot of the gnostic who has become perfect as much as is permitted to human nature.[117]

An adoptive child of God,[118] the gnostic is "the equal of angels";[119] according to Psa 82:6, this one has even "become god,"[120] "a god walking about in the flesh" [ἐν σαρκὶ περιπολῶν θεός].[121] So according to the heavenly doctrine of Christianity, the gnostic for Clement is a deified human being.

168

IV

What exactly does the divinization of humankind, their assimilation to God by means of gnosis, consist of?

The meaning of the word *gnosis* in the writings of Clement is very complex. Indeed, he distinguishes a gnosis of natural order[122] and a gnosis which is inspired by faith [πιστὴ γνῶσις].[123] The latter itself is subdivided into gnosis which all possess [ἡ κοινὴ ἐν τοῖς κοινοῖς], by which one knows "that there is a unique God," and another, higher gnosis which alone makes the perfect Christian.[124]

"The gnosis based on faith is the scientific proof of the truths passed on in true philosophy."[125] This definition, as well as many others given by Clement, clearly brings out the fact that the intellectual element is essential in gnosis. By their knowledge, the gnostics embrace not only τὰ ὄντα, that which really is,[126] but even τὰ νοητά, the intelligible world:[127]

---

[115] Lebreton, "Le désaccord," 499-500. Cf. *Strom.* 6.9-13 (9:292-329).
[116] *Strom.* 2.19 (8:1040b).
[117] *Strom.* 6.12 (9:325b). Cf. 2.22 (8:1080c); 7.3 (9:417a).
[118] *Strom.* 7.13 (9:516a).
[119] *Strom.* 7.10 (9:481a).
[120] *Strom.* 4.23 (8:1360a). Cf. 7.10 (9:480a-b).
[121] *Strom.* 7.16 (9:540b).
[122] *Strom.* 6.1 (9:209b-212a).
[123] *Strom.* 2.11 (8:984b).
[124] *Strom.* 4.15 (8:1304a-b).
[125] *Strom.* 2.11 (8:984b).
[126] *Strom.* 6.8 (9:292a).
[127] *Strom.* 6.8 (9:289b). Cf. 6.1 (209c). Without acknowledging Plato's world, Clement employs the term which expresses it. But he has difficulty in finding a new content for it, as the text which follows shows.

By knowledge, they penetrate the heaven [τέμνει τὸν οὐρανόν], and after passing through all the pneumatic essences and every principality and power, they attain to the highest thrones, tending uniquely toward the One to whom their thoughts aspired.[128]

169

The gnostics are even "initiated into the blessed vision face to face" [πρόσωπον πρὸς πρόσωπον τὴν μακαρίαν θέαν μυηθῇ].[129] This is contemplation which is carried out "according to the bare operation of the soul"[130] or "with the νοῦς alone" [φιλῷ τῷ νῷ],[131] that is to say, without the aid of the body.[132] It is an ἐποπτεία θεοῦ like that of the mysteries.[133] Therefore, however indispensable human effort may be in rising to this supreme gnosis, the latter remains "a grace which comes from God by the Son;"[134] for "only divinity possesses wisdom by nature."[135]

Being a divine grace is a specific characteristic which distinguishes the gnosis of Clement, like that of Philo before him moreover, from the vision of ideas dear to Plato, whom it elsewhere recalls so strongly.[136] To this first difference is added another, still more important one: the gnosis of the Alexandrian doctor is at least as much moral as intellectual. It is not only knowledge, but equally action, life, and virtue, even "virtue par excellence."[137]

Two traits especially characterize the moral physiognomy of the gnostic: impassibility [ἀπάθεια] and love [ἀγάπη].

The "apathy" of Clement, clearly modelled on that of the Stoics,[138] is neither insensitivity nor apathetic indifference. Rather it is a kingly independence, a perfect freedom of spirit and of heart with regard to all benefits other than gnosis.[139] By this, and by preserving the gnostic from all sin,[140] "the impassibility gained by asceticism makes the gnostic, as far as possible, like the One who possesses ἀπάθεια by nature."[141]

170

---

[128]   *Strom.* 7.13 (9:516a). Cf. 6.8 (289b).

[129]   *Strom.* 6.12 (9:324b).

[130]   *Strom.* 6.1 (9:209c).

[131]   *Strom.* 5.11 (101b-104a).

[132]   Cf. again *Strom.* 5.11 (9:109).

[133]   *Paed.* 1.7 (8:313b). Cf. *Strom.* 5.11 (9:108-109). One is tempted to call this vision of God a "mystical" knowledge, but it is not certain that Clement is thinking here of an experiential laying hold of God. See Fonck, "Mystique," 2604-2605.

[134]   *Strom.* 5.11 (9:109b). Moreover, according to Clement, all knowledge comes to humankind by the Logos. See De Faye, *Clément,* 266. Here again the influence of Philo is evident.

[135]   *Strom.* 2.9 (8:980c).

[136]   Cf. *Strom.* 5.14 (9:204).

[137]   De Faye, *Clément,* 291.

[138]   The Stoic influence, not only on the terminology, but on the moral conceptions themselves of Clement could not be disputed. It is more of a principle adopted by him—as the following: "actions follow gnosis, just like shadow the body"—and it clearly shows that his morality is intellectualist, like that of the Stoics, whereas Christian morality is not. See De Faye, *Clément,* 292-299; Bréhier, *Histoire de la philosophie,* 1:507-508.

[139]   Cf. *Strom.* 4.22 (8:1345d-1348a; 1356a-b). One finds here the marvellous expositions on the disinterestedness of the gnostic.

[140]   Cf. *Strom.* 2.6 (8:961b); 4.5 (1233b); 4.18 (1320-1328); 6.12 (9:321c).

[141]   *Strom.* 7.3 (9:417a). Cf. 4.23 (8:1356d); 6.9 (9:293b).

Gnosis ends in ἀγάπη, "the most holy love which is superior to all knowledge."[142] Love "is the essential moving force of a truly gnostic soul. It should not be sufficient for wise Christians," says Clement, "to avoid doing evil; they should do good, and they should do this good neither through fear nor through hope of reward, but exclusively through love."[143] Their love for God causes them to accept suffering and even martyrdom;[144] it urges them to work for the salvation of their brothers and sisters,[145] to forgive wrongs and to love their enemies.[146] But the most precious blessing of love consists in uniting the soul with Christ[147] and through Him, with God. In the gnostics, ἀγάπη is no longer a desire, "for they already possess, as much as is possible, the very object of their desire,"[148] "being intimately joined to God by love."[149] This union floods the soul with a perpetual joy, which delights without ever satiating.[150]

From the emphases with which Clement exalts the love which unites the gnostic with God and the resulting happiness, we perceive that he is speaking from experience. Thus the union with God which he magnifies is a real-life union, and therefore mystical.

171

Because it is knowledge and impassibility, gnosis makes human beings like God, who alone possesses wisdom and *apatheia* by nature; because it is love, finally, it completes this likeness in the mystical union.

V

Is the assimilation of the gnostic to God advocated by our doctor of a purely moral and mystical nature? Is it simple imitation which, while going beyond the human capacities and being a divine grace, does not affect a person's actual nature? Or indeed does it assume in us some element, a superior principle inherent in the soul? Our catechist does not seem to have anticipated this problem.

It is true that some believe they have discovered allusions to sanctifying grace in a number of passages where Clement speaks of righteousness as of a mark or seal of the soul, which constitutes its real beauty.[151] However, we should not lose sight of the fact that the righteousness in question is not that of any of the baptized, but the perfection which only the gnostic can reach. Furthermore, in the texts that one may cite, nothing proves that the "characteristic

---

[142] *Strom.* 7.11 (9:493c).

[143] De Faye, *Clément,* 302. Cf. *Strom.* 4.22 (8:1345b).

[144] *Strom.* 7.11 (9:492b-496b).

[145] Cf. *Strom.* 7.1 (9:405a-408a).

[146] *Strom.* 2.18 (8:1028-1040).

[147] *Strom.* 7.10 (9:481a)· "The perfection of the gnostic soul...is being with the Lord." Cf. Capitaine, *Clemens,* 154-155.

[148] *Strom.* 6.9 (9:293).

[149] *Strom.* 6.12 (9:324b-325b). Ἀγάπη here is called θεοφοροῦσα καὶ θεοφορουμένη. The expositions on love recall the First Epistle of Saint John. See above, 89.

[150] Cf. *Strom.* 6.9 (especially 9:296b-297b).

[151] See especially *Strom.* 6.12 (9:325a-b); 4.18 (8:1325a). Cf. de La Barre, "Clément," 162 and 190.

quality"[152] of this perfection is a physical *habitus*; on the contrary, it seems that our author has seen here a mark of a purely moral nature, like that which characterizes the damned.

In brief, if Clement knows of a divine aid which, acting upon our superior faculties, produces many effects in them which surpass their native capacities, he does not seem to have suspected in the Christian the existence of a divine gift which raises, which divinizes the very essence of the soul.

172   So sublime is the ideal of deification proposed by the Alexandrian doctor that he himself had to recognize that on earth only Christ realized it perfectly.[153] Others will arrive there only after the resurrection.[154] The souls of the believers who are not yet completely purified will attain to such through various punishments; even after their purification, there remains for them "the tremendous sorrow from the fact that, having been found deserving of another dwelling place, they are not gathered together with those who have been glorified because of righteousness."[155] The portion of the pure souls will be as follows: immediately after separation from the body,[156] they will be established in the "supreme place of rest," near to the Lord, and enjoy in an unfailing way the eternal contemplation of God, face to face,[157] and, by that, an unutterable joy.[158] Finally, by uniting the beatified soul with the glorified body, resurrection will result in the divinization of the entire person.

☙

Like Saint Irenaeus, Clement places the terminus of salvation in the ὁμοίωσις τῷ θεῷ. For both of them, this is a loftier likeness than the similitude between God and humankind, by virtue of the very nature of the latter. It is a likeness based on a participation, as perfect as possible, in specifically divine benefits, a participation granted to humankind by pure kindness.

But when specifying these divine benefits thus partaken, the two writers
173   manifest notable differences. For the bishop of Lyon, the ὁμοίωσις, conditioned here below by the indwelling of the Holy Spirit, seems to be strictly constituted by a created gift which makes the righteous one a friend and adoptive child of God. Both of these graces are found, although to different degrees, in every true Christian. In the other life, the divine likeness of the elect will consist above all in their partaking of the blessed incorruptibility of God.

---

[152]   *Strom.* 6.12 (9:325a-b): χαρακτεριστικαὶ ποιότητες. We especially stress this expression.

[153]   *Strom.* 4.21 (8:1340b).

[154]   Cf. *Paed.* 1.6 (8:284b). According to Clement, unbelievers and sinners will not rise from the dead, because they have already been judged (*Strom.* 2.15 (8:1008b) and because their souls have already been condemned "to the torment of eternal fire" (*Quis div.* 33 [9:640a]. Cf. *Strom.* 5.14 [9:132b-133a]).

[155]   *Strom.* 6.14 (9:332a-b).

[156]   *Strom.* 4.4 (8:1228b). Cf. 4.7 (1256b).

[157]   *Strom.* 7.10 (9:480b-481a).

[158]   Cf. *Protr.* 12 (8:237), where a poetic description of the heavenly joy is read.

According to Clement, the real and full ὁμοίωσις τῷ θεῷ is essentially the effect of gnosis; more precisely, it is gnosis. As its name indicates, gnosis is mainly knowledge, contemplation, and therefore intellectual assimilation to divinity which from here below, according to certain texts, would reach intuitive vision. At the same time the gnosis of Clement is a moral assimilation through *apatheia* and love.

Such a conception, inasmuch as the divine likeness is the privilege here of a spiritual aristocracy, is inspired by Platonism and Stoicism more than by Christian revelation. Clement's thought is very different from the thought of Irenaeus and comes closer to that of the apologists. It especially exhibits affinities with Hellenistic mysticism as it appears in Hermetic literature. Even if it is unlikely that Clement knew the Hermetic treatises which we still possess, the evolution of the ideas manifested there could hardly have remained unknown to him.[159] However, his Christianity preserved him from the pantheistic tendencies which dominate Hermetism, whereby ultimate human happiness would consist in absorption by the first principle. Indeed, our doctor firmly maintains the distinction between God and the perfect human being.[160] In so doing, at the same time, he goes against Stoic tendencies to identify the soul with divinity.   174

The fact that the idea of immortality only plays a secondary role with Clement is not surprising in a disciple of Plato who recognizes in the soul a natural incorruptibility and sees in the gnosis which is vision the final purpose of humankind. It is all the more significant that Clement, guided by his Christian sense, maintained the dogma of the resurrection, although actually, in his thought as a whole, this dogma figures somewhat as an erratic block.

Is it not equally a fact that due to philosophical influences the Alexandrian doctor mentions the Logos almost exclusively as an intermediary between God and humanity, and he only attributes a very insignificant role to the Holy Spirit in the work of salvation?[161]

In short, we can say that for Clement of Alexandria, Christianity is "a mystery similar to those of the pagans, but more truthful and certain."[162] For simple believers it is a mystery of worship in which they find their salvation. On the contrary, for perfect Christians, the gnostics, it is a literary mystery[163] which divinizes them.

---

[159] Clement knows "somes books of Hermes" and lists forty-two of them (*Strom.* 6.4 [9:253a-256a]). But there it is a matter of Egyptian writings in use within the priestly schools. Concerning the Hermetic writings such as ours, Scott (*Hermetica*, 1:87-90) estimates that Clement either did not have any knowledge of them or knew of them, but, regarding them as recent, did not take any of them into account.

[160] Cf. *Strom.* 7.3 (9:417a); passage cited above, 138; 6.9 (293). See Faller, "Griechische Vergottung," 427-428.

[161] Cf. La Barre, "Clément," 159-160; Capitaine, *Clemens*, 104 and 334.

[162] Festugière, *L'idéal religieux*, 133.

[163] For the expressions "mystery of worship" and "literary mystery," see above, 35.

3. Christian Gnosis: Origen

Interesting and original though it may be, the conception of Christianity worked out by Clement does not seem to have exercised a considerable influence on Christian thought. Without doubt, this is because his relatively chaotic work was supplanted by the more systematic and penetrating work of Origen. It is through the agency of the latter that the Christian gnosis of Alexandria came to influence subsequent theology.

I

175   Origen, in fact, takes up again Clement's idea of Christianity as a mystery, a gnosis which deifies man. But by placing it in a new framework, he gives this idea a distinctive physiognomy. The new framework is the cosmology of our doctor which, with its implied anthropology, forms the basis of his soteriology and therefore of his doctrine of deification.

For Origen, human souls are intelligences [νόες] which were created pure by God, but which degraded due to a failure, or "cooled off," as the etymology of the Greek word ψυχή suggests. Concerning those who have fallen from the love of God, it must be said without hesitation that they have cooled off from their love and have become cold."[164] For having thus lost "this natural and divine warmth and being cooled off from its more divine and better state," the soul has received the name of ψυχή in Greek.[165]

Nevertheless—and this is where the indestructible optimism of the Alexandrian doctor is apparent—evil, that non-being,[166] could not triumph permanently. Indeed, freedom has remained for the fallen intellects, and by it they can be restored to the state of fervor in which they found themselves in the beginning.[167] With a view to this restoring, the "visible world has been formed" as a place of purification.[168] The failed intelligences—which is all of them with the exception of that which became the soul of Jesus[169]—have been clothed with a body, more or less luminous or opaque, according to the degree of their defection.
176   In this way, the souls have entered into appropriate bodies and have been called human beings.[170]

II

In order to explain the unenviable state of present humanity, Origen the philosopher would probably have been content to cite his theory of the

---

[164]   Or. *Princ.* 2.8.3 (PG 11:222b).

[165]   *Princ.* 2.8.3 (11:222c-d). In this place, Origen seems to be inspired by Aristotle, *De an.* 405.b.23-30, where the philosopher has ψυχή derive from ψυχρός.

[166]   *Comm. Jo.* 2.7 (14:136a). Origen deduces this negative notion of evil from the very Platonic identification of τὸ ὄν with τὸ ἀγαθόν adopted by him.

[167]   *Princ.* 2.8.3 (11:221c-222a).

[168]   *Princ.* 3.5.4 (11:328-330). Cf. 2.2.2 (187); *Comm. Jo.* 19.5 (14:568-569).

[169]   *Princ.* 2.6.5-6 (11:213-214). Cf. 4.31 (504-506).

[170]   *Princ.* 1.7.4 (11:173). For Origen, the stars are the fallen spirits clothed in luminous matter.

pre-existence of souls and their fall into the suprasensitive world, a hypothesis which he futhermore believes to find suggested in the Holy Scripture.[171] But when he was acting as an exegete and preacher, our doctor could not but take into account the scriptural material, which attaches the decline of humanity to a sin of the first man.

Concerning the original state and role of Adam, we find in the immense work of the Alexandrian catechist the most disparate views. Sometimes, speaking as a Platonist, Origen sees a stain for the soul in the single fact of being united with the body:

Quaecumque anima in carne nascitur iniquitatis et peccati sorde polluitur.[172]

Sometimes, in preaching to the people, he interprets the biblical account of the formation of Adam as a historical document. Lastly, writing elsewhere for the scholarly world, he allegorizes the same account to the point of "substituting for the historical person of the first man a philosophical view of humanity."[173]

From this imbroglio of incoherent interpretations there seems to emerge, nevertheless, the fundamental idea of a privileged state for our first parents, in comparison with us. Adam's privileges, our exegete points out, include the sojourn in Paradise, incorruptibility or immortality,[174] and also a certain uprightness or relative perfection.[175]

177

Following the example of Clement, Origen distinguishes between εἰκών and ὁμοίωσις in our first ancestor. If Adam was in the image of God because of his reasoning soul,[176] he still had to acquire the divine likeness [ὁμοίωσις] by means of his free activity, by the "imitation of God."[177] To that end, it would have sufficed for him to turn completely toward the One in whose image he had been made and to lay down every inclination toward matter.[178] This shows that in the thought of our author, ὁμοίωσις τῷ θεῷ did not in any way consist in the extraordinary gifts of the original state.

Having responded to the divine advances by an act of disobedience, Adam lost his privileges for himself and for his descendants. Led by his bad example,

---

[171] Cf. *Hom. Jer.* 2.1 (13:277). Methodius of Olympus quotes a series of scriptural texts in which, by virtue of his allegorical exegesis, Origen would discover his theory of pre-existence. See especially *Res.* 1.55-58 (ed. Bonwetsch, GCS, 313ff).

[172] [Every soul that is born in the flesh is defiled by the filth of iniquity and sin.] *Adnot. Lev.* 8.3 (12:496a). Cf. *Hom. Luc.* 14 (13:1834b); *Cels.* 7.50 (11:1494).

[173] A. Slomkowski, *L'état primitif de l'homme dans la tradition de l'Église avant saint Augustin* (Paris, 1928), 54.

[174] *Comm. Rom.* 10.14 (14:1275a).

[175] *Comm. Jo.* 13.37 (14:464a-b). Cf. *Comm. Rom.* 3.3 (933b).

[176] Cf. *Hom. Gen.* 1.13 (12:93-96); *Cels.* 4.83, 85 (11:1156-1157, 1160).

[177] *Princ.* 3.6.1 (11:333c). Cf. *Cels.* 4.30 (1072b): "God made man in the image of God, but not right away in the likeness." It happens, however, that the terminus of the image represents the superior likeness. Cf. *Princ.* 4.37 (11:412c).

[178] *Comm. Jo.* 20.20 (14:621b).

and seduced more and more by the devil and concupiscence, humanity sank still further into a universal moral decay.[179]

III

In spite of everything, in intelligence and free will fallen humankind possesses the means of returning to the Creator[180] and of obtaining the divine likeness, but not, however, without the assistance of God.

178   Now, "from time immemorial, by His Word,...God has brought back to the right way those who have given ear to His words."[181] From before His incarnation, the only begotten Son, the "mediator between people and the light," has "enlightened all creation."[182] Is it not due to a participation in this "light of the cosmos" that human beings are reasoning [λογικοί]?[183] But those were only partial, incomplete revelations. Only in the incarnated Logos is the final and perfect revelation accomplished.[184]

Therefore, for our doctor the teaching activity of the Logos seems to be the principal part of the redemptive work of Christ. Assuredly, this "was considered by Origen more or less from every angle, and in his vast commentaries he had occasion to bring to light all its results."[185] Thus for him Jesus is Redeemer in the etymological sense of this term, because He redeems us from the devil, who became our master on account of our sins.[186] He is our Savior and also our Lord, who, insofar as He was both a priest and sacrificial victim, offered to His Father His body and blood as a true propitiatory sacrifice in order to reconcile human beings to God.[187] Nonetheless, the impression predominates that for our catechist Christ is mainly Savior because He is the enlightener, the teacher of humanity, the διδάσκαλος θείων μυστηρίων:[188]

179   In Him the divine nature and the human nature have begun to be closely joined together [συνυφαίνεσθαι] in order that, by its closeness with what is more divine [τῇ πρὸς τὸ θειότερον κοινωνίᾳ], the human nature might become divine, not

---

[179]   Cf. Gaudel, "Péché originel," 333-338.

[180]   Cf. *Princ.* 2.8.3 (11:222). One of the principal ideas of Origen is that of a union, a fundamental harmony between God and the world of intelligences. It is a union which, even if it was able to be disrupted for a time, must inevitably be restored sooner or later. This is the key to the whole soteriology of Origen and especially to his doctrine of apocatastasis. Cf. *Princ.* 3.6.1 (11:333-334); *Comm. Jo.* 1.40 (14:93).

[181]   *Cels.* 4.3 (11:1032c). Cf. *Princ.* 1.2.7 (135-136). See C. Verfaillie, *La doctrine de la justification dans Origène d'après son commentaire de Épître aux Romains* (Strasbourg, 1926), 41-50.

[182]   *Princ.* 1.2.7 (11:135c).

[183]   *Comm. Jo.* 1.42 (14:96-97). Attracted by the play on words, Λόγος-λογικός, here Origen seems to forget his theory of pre-existence whereby souls are νόες, thus intelligent by nature.

[184]   *Comm. Jo.* 19.1 (14:524-537).

[185]   Tixeront, *Histoire des dogmes*, 1:315.

[186]   Cf. *Comm. Matt.* 16.8 (13:1397b); *Comm. Rom.* 2.13 (14:911c.) See J. Rivière, *Le dogme de la rédemption: études critiques et documents* (Louvain, 1931), 165-212. According to the author, the "ransom" would only be a metaphor which expresses the "costly way of our redemption."

[187]   *Comm. Rom.* 3.8 (14:946-950). Cf. *Hom. Num.* 24.1 (12:756-759).

[188]   *Cels.* 3.62 (11:1001b).

only in Jesus, but also in all those who, with faith, embrace the life which Jesus taught and which leads to friendship and closeness with God.[189]

This passage, where we can believe we are hearing an echo of the physical theory of divinization, clearly shows that for Origen the deification of humankind is the aim of the divine pedagogy, of which the incarnation is the decisive stage.

IV

The first step toward this deification is faith, an active faith which is confirmed by a Christian life.[190] The latter presupposes the receiving of baptism, the sacrament which remits sins for those who turn away from them.[191] However, if faith with baptism is sufficient for salvation, it is far from perfection. Following Clement, our doctor distinguishes two classes of Christians, and this distinction "is major" in his teaching.[192]

First of all, there is the mass of simple believers who as "friends of the letter"[193] content themselves with the somatic sense of the Scriptures, with the "shadow of the mysteries of Christ."[194] These *simpliciores*[195] "know nothing but Jesus Christ and Jesus Christ crucified, considering that the Logos becoming flesh is the main thing for the Logos, and knowing Christ only according to the flesh."[196] They are the flock "that Christ pastures because of their mild, meek, but not very intelligent nature."[197] They are the Corinthians, for whom only the infants' milk is suitable.[198] However, our theologian takes care to declare that even these simple ones, by their morality and strength of soul, surpass by far the wisest of the pagans.[199]

But in particular, there is the elite of the perfect, to whom goes all of Origen's preference. Being "more intelligent,"[200] they grasp the mysteries of analogy, the pneumatic sense of the Scriptures, "the eternal or spiritual Gospel,"[201] and like the Ephesians, can receive the food of the strong.[202] These

180

---

[189] *Cels.* 3.28 (11:956d). Cf. (956a).

[190] Cf. *Comm. Jo.* 19.6 (14:569b).

[191] Cf. *Comm. Jo.* 6.17 (14:253-257); *Hom. Luc.* 21 (13:1855b).

[192] G. Bardy, "Origène," *DTC* 11:1514. Sometimes Origen divides Christians into three groups in conformity with the three senses which he distinguishes in the Scripture: somatic, psychic, and spiritual. Cf. *Hom. Rom.* 6.14 (14:1102); *Cels.* 6.13 (11:1309-1312). But more often than not, he only mentions two classes.

[193] *Hom. Gen.* 13.3 (12:232c).

[194] *Comm. Jo.* 1.9 (14:36d).

[195] *Princ.* 3 2.1 (11:305b).

[196] *Comm. Jo.* 2.3 (14:113).

[197] *Comm. Jo.* 1.30 (14:77a).

[198] *Hom. Ezech.* 7.10 (13:726-727). Cf. *Comm. Jo.* 5.8 (ed. Preuschen, GCS, 105), where Origen does not hesitate to speak of a πίστις ἄλογος καὶ ἰδιωτική!

[199] *Cels.* 1.13 (11:680). Cf. 7.44 (1485a).

[200] *Comm. Jo.* 1.30 (14:77a).

[201] *Comm. Jo.* 1.9 (14:36d).

[202] *Hom. Ezech.* 7.10 (13:727a): solidus cibus mysticus.

τελειούμενοι[203] "partake of the Logos;"[204] they rise up to gnosis. Toward them the Word no longer acts as a simple shepherd, but as a king[205] and a husband.[206]

Just as in the temple of Jerusalem a person entered by degrees into the Holy of Holies, likewise the real disciple of Jesus rises up to divine wisdom by degrees. Guided by "the Only-Begotten of God" and making use of palpable things, the gnostic first acquires the knowledge of the intelligible cosmos, then that of the Logos, to finally arrive "at the contemplation of the essence, or of the power which is beyond the essence, and of the nature of God."[207] This "gnosis of God goes beyond human nature";[208] it is a gift "that God grants to those who have made themselves capable of receiving it."[209]

The knowledge of the Father, which constitutes "the perfect gnosis" [ἡ γνῶσις τελεία], is therefore "the greatest good." And it is from this that all His glory comes to the Son.[210] This is even to the point that the Logos "would not remain God, if He did not persist in the uninterrupted contemplation of the paternal depths."[211]

In an analogous manner, "the νοῦς which is purified and raised above all material things in order to have a clear vision of God is deified in its vision [ἐν οἷς θεωρεῖ, θεοποιεῖται]." This is what happened to Moses when he conversed with God. For if the Scripture says that a ray of glory rested on his face, this is a trope for showing that his νοῦς had been divinized.[212]

The Logos is consequently the archetype of all that have been deified through a participation in the deity of the "God by Himself" [τὸ αὐτόθεος]. He is the archetype of the "gods who are formed according to the true God, like images of a prototype."[213]

---

[203] *Comm. Jo.* 13.14 (14:420c).

[204] *Comm. Jo.* 2.3 (14:113a).

[205] *Comm. Jo.* 1.30 (14:76-77). Cf. 1.22 (57c).

[206] *Comm. Cant.* 17 (11:472b). In his commentary on the Song of Songs, Origen sees in the wife sometimes the church, but more often the soul taught by Christ, the husband. Cf. Rahner, "Die Gottesgeburt," 351-358.

[207] *Comm. Jo.* 19.1 (14:536): ἵν' οὕτως ἔλθη ἐπὶ τὸ ἐνιδεῖν τῇ οὐσίᾳ, ἢ τῇ ὑπερέκεινα τῆς οὐσίας δυνάμει καὶ φύσει τοῦ θεοῦ. The expression ἐπέκεινα οὐσίας, applied to God, is often encountered in Plotinus. See above, 51. Cf. *Cels.* 7.46 (11:1488-1489).

[208] *Cels.* 7.44 (11:1484c).

[209] *Cels.* 6.13 (11:1309). Cf. *Comm. Jo.* 32.18 (14:820c).

[210] *Comm. Jo.* 32.18 (14:817).

[211] *Comm. Jo.* 2.2 (14:109b): λόγος...οὐκ ἂν μείνας θεός, εἰ μὴ παρέμενε τῇ ἀδιαλείπτῳ θέᾳ τοῦ πατρικοῦ βάθους. This conception appears less strange when one remembers an analogous idea of Plato. Indeed, according to this, "it is because the cosmic gods contemplate the unchanging Forms that they enjoy immortality," that they are really gods (Festugière, *Contemplation et vie contemplative selon Platon*, 455). The text of Origen becomes even more clear when we compare it with passages in which Plotinus describes the second god, the Noῦς, and the relationship which the latter maintains with the One. Cf. Arnou, "Le Platonisme des Pères," 2333-2336.

[212] *Comm. Jo.* 32.17 (14:816-817). We have seen that already, for Philo, Moses is the type of the deified human being. See above, 77.

[213] *Comm. Jo.* 2.2 (14:109). Cf. *Cels.* 3.28 (11:956d); Justn. *Orig.* in J.D. Mansi, *Sacrorum conciliorum nova et amplissima collectio* (Florence, 1759-1781), 9:525e.

This closeness established between "the partaking of divinity," which is distinctive to the divine Noῦς who is the Logos, and that granted to the human voῦς seems difficult to defend from the viewpoint of orthodoxy. Far from help-   182 ing to specify the nature of the participation which divinizes humankind, he only manages to complicate the problem. Judging by what he writes about it at the end of his *Peri Archon*, Origen would have only imagined an assimilation of a moral nature, obtained by the practice of all the virtues: whereas the virtues "are in God by virtue of His substance *(per substantiam)*," they can only be found in humankind due to a "hard-working imitation of God."[214]

Yet there is more. The gnosis which deifies the perfect Christian is no longer a purely speculative knowledge. According to Origen, all true knowledge presupposes the union of the one who knows with the object known, for "to know is to mingle and to unite." Divine gnosis, then, must of necessity be completed in the union with God.[215]

Our doctor exalts the unitive gnosis with a lyricism which barely yields to the transports of Clement. He sees in it the wine of the true vine which gladdens the human heart. By gnosis the Logos gladdens our heart, that is to say, our thinking faculty, "by rescuing us from human things, by filling us with enthusiasm, and by making us drunk with a drunkenness which is not unreasonable but divine."[216] These metaphors show that for Origen it is a matter of a mystical union proceeding all the way to ecstasy. Consequently, one understands that perfect gnosis re-heats the soul, giving back to it the warmth, the loss of which had caused its fall, and re-establishes it in its original state of intelligence:

> Nourished by wisdom, the intellect *(mens)* is perfectly restored anew to the image and likeness of God, just as humankind was made in the beginning.[217]

Here the original relationship of the soul with God reappears: in the superior   183 part of their being, humankind are "accepted into the order of angels,"[218] become children of God, and are deified.

V

However great and persevering the efforts of the gnostics may be, their knowledge here below remains a faint outline "to which, in the future life, will be added the beauty of the perfect image."[219] After they die, they will first be

---

[214] *Princ.* 4.37 (11:412c).

[215] *Comm. Jo.* 19.1 (14:529c-532). In order to show that the real knowledge requires union, Origen is not afraid of appealing to the biblical euphemism: "Adam knew Eve, his wife" for him means that Adam really knew Eve only after being united with her.

[216] *Comm. Jo.* 1.33 (14:77-80). Cf. *Princ.* 2.11.3 (11:242), where the expression *divinae sapientiae pocula* is found.

[217] *Princ.* 2.11.3 (11:242d).

[218] *Princ.* 1.8.4 (11:180a-b).

[219] *Princ.* 2.11.4 (11:244a).

taught about everything which takes place on the earth, and then "initiated into the knowledge of the stars."[220] Finally, "the already perfected understanding will attain to perfect gnosis, contemplating face to face the reasons for things" and feeding on this contemplation. But the nourishment par excellence of the elect will consist in the "vision of God, a nourishment having its own measures, appropriate and adapted to this created nature."[221] At the moment of the apocatastasis,

> there will be no more than one occupation for those who, due to the Logos, have reached up to God, namely, that of contemplating God, in order that, having been formed in the gnosis of the Father, all become sons completely, just as now only the Son knows the Father... None, indeed, whether apostles or prophets, know the Father unless they have become one with Him, just as the Son and the Father are one.[222]

Then the saints will see the Father as the Son sees Him, without an intermediary. The end will be when the Son hands over the kingdom to His God and Father, and when God becomes "all in all."[223]

If one is to believe Saint Jerome,[224] our theologian would have given a pantheistic sense to this expression of Saint Paul,[225] by acknowledging that the beings end in merging with the divine substance. But on this point, the testimony of the learned exegete seems more than suspect. In the first place, this is because the Alexandrian doctor acknowledges the resurrection.[226] It is true that he only attributes to the resurrected ones ethereal, spiritual bodies.[227] But however delicate one conceives these bodies to be, they necessarily prevent those clothed with them from merging with the absolutely spiritual, divine essence. And this because it is hardly likely that Origen, who never wearies of repeating that "the end is always like the beginning,"[228] had conceived of the apocatastasis as an abolition of the original distinction between God and the created intellects.

In brief, under the pen of our exegete, the Pauline expression "God will be all in all"[229] simply signifies that at the consummation of everything all reasoning creatures will go back into the original order of submission and moral union

---

[220] *Princ.* 2.11.5-6 (11:244-246).
[221] *Princ.* 2.11.7 (11:248). According to Origen, the separated soul rises up to God by an ascension which resembles that which leads to earthly gnosis.
[222] *Comm. Jo.* 1.16 (14:94c-52a).
[223] *Comm. Jo.* 20.7 (14:588a).
[224] Jer. *Epist.* 124.10.14 (PL 22:1069, 1071-1072).
[225] 1 Cor 15:28.
[226] *Princ.* Preface, 5 (11:118a-b). Cf. 3.6.6 (338-340); *Cels.* 5.17ff. (11:1205ff).
[227] Cf. Bardy, "Origène," 1546-1547. On this point of the resurrection, the influence of faith on the Origenist thought is particularly noticeable, since the logic of his system ought to have pushed Origen to a denial of any bodily resurrection.
[228] Cf. *Princ.* 1.6.2; 3.5.4 (11:166b, 329a), etc.
[229] On the meaning of this verse, see Colon, "La 'mystique' de saint Paul," 345-349.

with God. This will be the apocatastasis, namely, the re-establishment of the original harmony by the destruction of everything that had troubled it.[230]

The divinization of the most noble part of the human being, having begun in this life by the gnosis, and fully realized in the hereafter due to the vision of God, is thus, for Origen, the terminus of salvation offered by Christianity. This is, in short, the conception of Clement, but with important particulars, moreover, which have not really improved upon it.

By reducing the role of love in gnosis, Origen further reinforces its intellect-ualist character, already exaggerated by Clement. In conformity with his theo-ries of pre-existence and apocatastasis, he conceives of the final deification of humankind as a simple restoring of the human νοῦς into its original, "divine" state—one might as well say as a redivinization. So untraditional a conception can hardly have favored the progress of the doctrine of divinization.

Here there are grave errors due to philosophical influences. These could not however, on the whole, change the fundamentally Christian inspiration of the gnosis of Origen. This inspiration is clearly revealed in the place reserved for human freedom, in the central role assigned to the incarnated Logos, in the preponderance granted to the divine initiative in the work of salvation, and finally, above all, in the firmness with which the distinction between God and the deified creature is maintained. If the Origenist gnosis can be called a mysti-cism, it is certainly not a mysticism in the Neoplatonic sense, but a Christian mysticism of divinization.

---

[230] Cf. *Comm. Jo.* 1.16 (14:49c). The apocatastasis is for Origen only a conclusion of his optimistic conception of creation. He can only acknowledge that the original harmony which had united the spiri-tual creatures with God may have been eternally compromised by that non-being which is evil.

CHAPTER THREE

ATTEMPTS AT SYNTHESIS

1. Saint Hippolytus

186   The founders of the school of Alexandria are in agreement with the most brilliant representative of the tradition of the churches of Asia Minor in affirming the fact of the divinization of the human being by Christianity. But as soon as they begin to explain the nature and conditions of this deification, fundamental differences reappear which characterize the two doctrinal currents that they embody, one rather positive and conservative, the other particularly speculative and progressive. Under these conditions, an attempt at synthesis was essential. It was attempted more or less consciously by two Greek-speaking fathers, each of whom has left important theological works: Saint Hippolytus of Rome and Saint Methodius of Olympus.

I

In what is left to us of his numerous works, the "first western exegete"[1] only speaks in passing about the original state of humanity and the salvation brought by Christ. But these sporadic passages are sufficient to show that in the divinization of the human being he saw the supreme goal of creation as well as of redemption.

187   God formed humankind in His image[2] without, however, making gods of them, but He reserved for them the possibility of becoming gods by their faithfulness. The human body "was not mortal by nature, but became such by disobedience."[3] This does not mean, however, that humankind are failed gods, as certain gnostic musings seem to suggest. They are just as the creator wanted them:

> After this, He created the head of the universe, forming him out of every compound substance. He did not end up wanting to make a god or an angel—I am not misleading—but a human being. In fact, if He had wanted to make him god, He could have done it; you have the example of the Logos. Wanting you to be human, He made you human. If, however, you also want to become god, obey the One who has made you and do not resist Him now, in order that having been

---

[1]   É. Amann, "Hippolyte," *DTC* 6:2487.
[2]   Cf. Hipp. *Haer.* 10.34 (ed. P. Wendland, GCS 3:293, lines 12-13; PG 16:3454). In what concerns the works of Saint Hippolytus, Migne's edition is very insufficient. This is why we are quoting according to the corpus of Berlin. As far as possible, we reference Migne as well.
[3]   *Comm. Dan.* 2.28; (1a:94:21-24).

found faithful in the little things, you can receive great things from Him. The Logos alone is [descended] from God; this is why He is God, being God's substance [οὐσία ὑπάρχων θεοῦ]. The world, on the contrary, is [derived] from nothingness. This is why it is not god; it is susceptible to being dissolved, when the Creator wants.[4]

The fact that our doctor sees immortality as the element which deifies humankind seems to emerge from this rather obscure passage. Why then does he not want to admit that Adam was divinized, since he was created incorruptible? It is doubtless because our first ancestor only possessed incorruptibility precariously, and that only the permanent possession of this quality, promised for his faithfulness, would have made him a god. In reality, due to his disobedience, Adam was condemned to death.[5]

Nevertheless, humankind has never been abandoned by God: 188

> From earliest times, a law was imposed on humankind by the ministry of just people. Closer to us, by Moses, a pious man and beloved of God..., a law full of holiness and righteousness was given. But it is the Logos of God that governs all; the firstborn Son of the Father, the voice which, before the morning star, brings the light...[6]

> This Logos, the Father sent later... We know that He took a body from a virgin, bore the old human person, after having newly formed it [διὰ καινῆς πλάσεως]; He passed through all the ages of life in order to become Himself the law for every age, to offer to everyone His own humanity as a pattern and to demonstrate through Himself that God has done nothing evil, that humankind are masters of themselves, capable of wanting and of not wanting, having both in their power.[7]

In these lines, the redemptive action of the Word is described as above all a work of pedagogy, which seems to reveal the influence of the apologists. But one discovers here, as well, a fleeting allusion to the physical theory of deification, which our doctor, moreover, as a faithful disciple of Saint Irenaeus[8], seems elsewhere to make his own. By his incarnation, he writes, the Son of God "re-formed Adam, the first man, in Himself."[9]

> The Logos of God, being without flesh, clothed Himself in holy flesh taken from the holy virgin, like a fiancé with his wedding robe, weaving it for Himself in the suffering of the cross, in order to unite our mortal body with His power, to mingle

---

[4] *Haer.* 10.33; (3:290:1-9; PG 16:3450a-b). For the translation of passages taken from the *Haer.* we have made use of A. Siouville, *Philosophoumena* (2 vols.; Paris, 1928).

[5] Cf. fragment of a treatise *On the Song of Moses [Canticum Mo.]* (1b:83:10).

[6] *Haer.* 10.33 (3:290:20-25; PG 16:3450c).

[7] *Haer.* 10.33 (3:291:14-25; PG 16:3451b-c).

[8] Cf. H. Achelis, "Hippolytstudien," *Texte und Untersuchungen* 16.4 (Leipzig, 1897), 27.

[9] *Comm. Dan.* 4.11 (1a:214:5-6). Cf. *Antichr.* 26 (1b:19:1-2; PG 10:748c): ἀναπλάσσων δι' ἑαυτοῦ τὸν Ἀδάμ.

the corruptible with the incorruptible, the weak with the strong, and to save lost humankind.[10]

189 We recognize here, formulated with a certain reserve perhaps, the thought of the doctor of Lyon, according to which, by virtue of the contact which takes place in the incarnation between the divine Word and the human nature, the whole of humanity is healed, immortalized, and consequently deified. Furthermore, this does not hinder Saint Hippolytus, on occasion, from presenting our deification as the effect of the death of Christ.[11]

II

Deification, however, is not the exclusive work of the Savior: a person needs to appropriate the fruits of redemption through the intermediary of the church, which continues on earth the action of Christ by continually engendering the Logos in souls.[12] To this end, it is necessary that a person submit to the direction of the Word and endeavor to be made like God by the knowledge of God and the imitation of Christ. Then the inhabitation of the Holy Spirit in the human flesh will ensure to it immortality.[13]

However, the saints who make up the church[14] will actually obtain incorruptibility only at the end of time, after the universal judgment. Those who die beforehand remain, for the time being, in Hades, the righteous ones separated from the sinners, each receiving the deposit of their eternal recompense.[15] On the day chosen by Him, God will resurrect all bodies for the great judgment. After this, the righteous will immediately enter into the heavenly kingdom.[16]

190 There complete deification awaits them. In a few rapid strokes, Hippolytus sketches a striking picture of this in the eloquent call addressed to the pagans at the end of his *Refutation of All Heresies*:

All of you hasten, and let us instruct you about the true God and His well-ordered creation. Do not become attached to the sophisms of skillful speech, nor to the vain promises of heretical plagiarists, but to the sublime simplicity of truth without conceit. By recognizing this truth, you will escape from the coming threat of the fire of judgment, from the dark spectacle of gloomy Tartar, not brightened by the voice of the Logos, from the crackling of inextinguishable flames of Gehenna's pool....And from all this you will escape by having known the true God. You will

---

[10] *Antichr.* 4 (1b:6:20–7:2; PG 10:732).

[11] Cf. *Antichr.* 26 (1b:19:3-4; PG 10:748d); *Comm. Dan.* 2.36 (1a:112:12-13); *Fr. Gen.* 24 (1b:60:9-12).

[12] Cf. *Antichr.* 61; (1b:41:17-42; PG 10:780-781). See also H. Rahner, "Die Gottesgeburt," 347-350.

[13] Cf. Πρὸς βασιλίδα τινά, frg. 4-6 (1b:252).

[14] Cf. *Comm. Dan.* 1.14 (1a:24:8-9); *Haer.* 9.12 (3:250; PG 16:3386-3387).

[15] Cf. A. D'Alès, *La théologie de saint Hippolyte* (Paris, 1906) 200-201. In the Hades of Hippolytus, there is no place for a purgatory.

[16] *Comm. Dan.* 4.14 (1a:222:7-12). This text gives the impression that Hippolytus has become liberated from the chiliastic dreams that his master Irenaeus had brought along from the East. Cf. D'Alès, *Saint Hippolyte*, 198 ff.; Amann, "Hippolyte," 2511.

have your body immortal and incorruptible, likewise the soul, and you will receive the kingdom of the heavens. You who, living on this earth, have known the heavenly King will be the intimate friend of God and the coheir of Christ, being no longer subject either to the desires of passions or to sicknesses. For you have become god [γέγονας γὰρ θεός]. All the hardships that you endured being human, God sent to you because you are human; on the other hand, all the good things which are natural to God, God has promised to give to you when, begotten to immortality, you will have been deified [ὅταν θεοποιηθῆς, ἀθάνατος γεννηθεῖς]. By obeying his holy precepts, by making yourself good by the imitation of His goodness, you will be like Him [ὅμοιος], having been honored by Him. For God is not poor, who has made even you god, with a view to His glory.[17]

Thus only after resurrection in the hereafter will the Christian be deified, according to Hippolytus, due to a participation in the absolutely divine benefits, first and foremost the divine impassibility and incorruptibility.

In short, on the subject of deification, the Roman doctor takes up again the main ideas of Saint Irenaeus. Like the latter, for him "salvation consists in divinizing our nature," and he gives "to the incarnation the dominant role."[18] But to judge by the rest of his work, the thought of the disciple on this point is, by far, not as profound, rich, and finely shaded as that of the master. Thus, Hippolytus did not seem to have contemplated in the soul of the righteous one living on earth the existence of a beginning of the heavenly deification. On the other hand, we must acknowledge that he did bring the conception of Irenaeus closer to that of the apologists and the Alexandrians by attributing a more considerable role to the intellectual element in the process of our divinization.

191

2. Saint Methodius of Olympus

The theology of the greatest of the Alexandrians—and, therefore, his doctrine of deification—contained so many elements foreign to the ecclesiastical tradition and unassimilable by it that eventually a reaction had to take place. Surprisingly, "even toward the end of the third century, with the exception of a few fleeting shadows, the reputation of Origen's orthodoxy does not seem to have suffered much. But at that moment some direct attacks took place against certain of his opinions."[19]

Among Origen's adversaries in this period, one of the foremost is Saint Methodius, bishop of Olympus in Lycia.[20] He especially attacks the Origenist

---

[17] *Haer.* 10.34 (3:292:11–293:15; PG 16:3454).

[18] Rivière, *Rédemption: étude historique,* 129.

[19] Tixeront, *Histoire des dogmes,* 1:477–478.

[20] In his writing on the worship of images, which was honored by a public reading at the second Council of Nicaea (787), John of Thessalonica invoked as patristic authorities, Basil and Athanasius, followed by "Methodius the Great [ὁ μέγα Μεθόδιος]" (Mansi, *Sacrorum conciliorum nova,* 13:165b).

192   theory of the pre-existence of souls, which he contrasts with the traditional conception of the human composite. The body, he writes, is not "an instrument of torture or a prison,"[21] "a bond, a snare, a shackle," inflicted on the soul at its incorporation to punish it for a disobedience which it would have committed in a former life.[22] "A human being is by nature...the composite of a soul and a body, which are united to constitute the unique form of the beautiful."[23] The body is thus "a co-worker [συνεργόν] for the soul, either in good or in evil."[24]

In fighting ardor, Saint Methodius even goes as far as maintaining that souls are not "incorporeal," as Origen, following Plato, had claimed.[25] They are, on the contrary, "reasoning bodies [σώματα νοερά], endowed with members visible to the eyes of reason." The fact is that "God alone is declared the unbegotten nature [ἀγένητος], exempt from need and suffering, being incorporeal."[26]

Consequently, we understand that, for our author, the deification of the Christian is above all a return to the incorruptibility originally granted to the first human being.

I

When Saint Methodius speaks of the original state of Adam, he takes up again the idea of Saint Irenaeus in which we were all contained in our first father, and constantly identifies us with our first parents. So it is that he does not hesitate to write that we lived in paradise "in the protoplasts, apart from concupiscence."[27] This particularly complicates the study of the conception which the bishop of Olympus derives from the original state.

193   At least one point is incontestable: with tradition, our doctor acknowledges "deiformity and divine similitude" in the first man.[28] First of all, humankind are the image of the Logos by their reasoning and free soul.[29] In addition to this, the entire human form is the image, not of the incarnate Logos, as Saint Irenaeus wanted it, but of God Himself.[30] This was true especially for Adam, since he had been made immortal also in his body:

---

[21]   Meth. *Res.* 1.5 (ed. Bonwetsch, GCS 27:227, lines 5-9). The remark made on the subject of the edition of the works of Hippolytus contained in Migne counts as well for the writings of Methodius.

[22]   *Res.* 1.54 (27:310-313).

[23]   *Res.* 1.34 (27:272:7-9). Cf. 1.5-6; (27:226-228).

[24]   *Res.* 1.31 (27:267:21-23).

[25]   *Res.* 3.17-18 (27:414-416). This passage constitutes an indirect testimony in favor of the opinion according to which Origen taught the perfect spirituality of the soul. On this point, Rufinus seems to have distorted the thought of his master. Methodius is consistent with himself, when he attributes the νοερὰ σώματα to the angels as well (*Res.* 3.15 [411:25-26]).

[26]   *Res.* 3.17-18 (27:415:11-15).

[27]   *Res.* 2.1-2; (27:329-333).

[28]   *Res.* 1.35 (27:274:4-5). Cf. *Symp.* 3.3-4 (27:29-31; PG 18:64-68).

[29]   *Symp.* 6.1 (27:64:14-20; PG 18:112-113). Cf. *Res.* 2.24 (27:380:4-5); *De autex.* 16 (27:186:11-13).

[30]   *Res.* 3.15 (27:411).

Did not God, the craftsman par excellence who can make all things even by drawing them out of nothing, of necessity have to make humankind, His reasoning statue, absolutely imperishable and immortal...by forming them in His image and in His likeness, humankind, the glory of the world [τὸν κόσμον τοῦ κόσμου], for whom the world was made?[31]

By comparing these lines with a passage of the *Symposium*, where, following the example of Saint Irenaeus, the bishop of Olympus makes a general distinction between εἰκών and ὁμοίωσις in humankind, one has the impression that Methodius considered the state of divine image to be constituted in Adam by his intelligent and free nature, whereas his divine likeness consisted in exemption from corruption.[32]

This impression is reinforced by another text of the *Symposium*, in which the ὁμοίωσις is formally attributed to every soul coming into this world. Extolling with enthusiasm the beauty of these souls, the virgin Agatha expresses herself in this way:

It is by being endowed with an indescribable beauty, related to and similar to Wisdom, O Virgins, that we all come into this world. Indeed, souls resemble their Father and Creator the most when they reflect immaculately the idea [made] according to the likeness [τὴν καθ᾽ ὁμοίωσιν ἰδέαν] and features of that vision which God contemplated when He created them with an immortal and imperishable form, and when they preserve these qualities.[33]

194

The divine likeness identified with incorruptibility, which is attributed here to every human soul at the time of its entry into this world, must *a fortiori* be acknowledged in the soul of innocent Adam. But our first ancestor received it only in a precarious way. In fact, the protoplast, like a clay vessel quite freshly coming from the hands of a potter, "had not yet arrived, like a shell of terra cotta, at being made firm and petrified by immortality." This is why "sin, like water coming down drop by drop, has dissolved it."[34]

The first and most serious consequence of Adam's disobedience was concupiscence: "Emptied of the inspiration of God, we have been filled with hylic concupiscence, which the deceitful serpent blew into us."[35] As a result, evil has settled down firmly in the human flesh, which it has made its dwelling place.[36]

---

[31] *Res.* 1.35 (27:275:3-10). Note in the passage the very Christian conception, that humankind are the center and purpose of the world, whereas, for the Greek philosophers, humankind are only a detail of the cosmos.

[32] *Symp.* 1.4-5 (27:12:20–13:16; PG 18:44-48). The author here writes in distinctive terms, clearly imitating Plato (see above, 41): ὁμοίωσις γὰρ θεοῦ φθορᾶς ἀποφυγή.

[33] *Symp.* 6.1 (27:64:8-14; PG 18:113a-b).

[34] *Symp.* 3.5 (27:31:14-18; PG 18:68b).

[35] *Res.* 2.6 (27:339:15-16).

[36] *Res.* 2.2 (27:333:4-8). Following the example of Saint Paul, the bishop of Olympus speaks of evil as a reality being able to subsist by itself. But clearly he is thinking of concupiscence, the cause of moral evil.

Therefore humankind was driven away from paradise so that they might not eat of the tree of life and so that "evil might not become immortal."[37] God thus made "tunics of skin" for them; that is, He, "as it were, wrapped them with mortality."[38] For "death was invented as a means of improvement," comparable to the blows by which one corrects careless schoolboys.[39] This means that sin, deep-rooted in the body, dies only "if it is killed along with the body."[40]

195   Even more fragile than in Adam is the native beauty of the divine likeness in his descendants, because the demons' envy aroused by it is aided by human concupiscence, so much so that, before the coming of Christ, "all were captured and subjugated" by the devil. None of the ancients was pleasing to the Lord, but all of them were involved in transgressions, the law being powerless to deliver mankind from corruption."[41]

II

By sending His Son, God has imparted a new strength to the natural good which is in us, but which up to then was overcome by concupiscence.[42] For "Christ has not come to transform or change human nature, but to bring it back to what it was at the beginning before falling—to immortality."[43]

In order to realize this divinization of humankind, the Logos did not unite with any human nature whatever, but with that of Adam himself, miraculously re-formed in the womb of the Virgin:

> Let us therefore examine how right Paul was in referring Adam to Christ, by seeing in him not only a type and an image, but by thinking that Christ became exactly what Adam was, because upon this one has come the Logos who is before the ages. Indeed, it was right that the Firstborn of God, His first offspring, His Monogene, His Wisdom, mingling with the protoplast, the first and the firstborn of humankind, became human....So therefore God, taking up again His work of the beginning and re-forming it once again with the Virgin and with the Spirit, fashions the same [being], just as at the beginning, when the earth was virgin and not yet plowed, He took of the dust and formed out of it, without seed, the most intelligent animal.[44]

If our doctor insists so much on the identity of the human nature assumed
196 by the Word with that of Adam, it is because, according to him, the perfection

---

[37] *Res.* 1.39 (27:283:15-16).

[38] *Res.* 1.38 (27:281:13-14). This is an interpretation directed against Origen, who had seen in the "tunics of skin" the corporeity with which the souls would have been clothed after their fall. Cf. 1.39, etc.

[39] *Res.* 1.38 (27:280:1-3).

[40] *Res.* 1.40 (27:285:2-4).

[41] *Symp.* 10.1 (27:122:3-7; PG 18:192-193).

[42] *Res.* 2.8 (27:344:16-18).

[43] *Res.* 1.49 (27:303:6-8). Cf. *Porph.* 1.3 (27:503:13-22).

[44] *Symp.* 3.4 (27:30:16–31:9; PG 18:65-68). Cf. 3.5-6 (27:30:31-33; PG 18:68-69).

of the redeeming work required that identity. Indeed, the sentence of perdition had to be lifted by the one who had provoked it; the devil had to be defeated

> by the one whom he had prided himself on having subjugated by his deceit; for it was not right that sin and condemnation be removed in any other way, unless it is that this same man, because of whom this word was pronounced: "You are earth and you will return to the earth," by a new struggle, might erase the curse which, because of him, had been extended to all; so that, just as in Adam at the beginning all died, so also once again all will be made alive in Christ, who has assumed Adam.[45]

So, by taking the human form, the Word made us capable "of once again taking hold of the divine form [τὴν θείαν μορφήν],"[46] that is to say, the incorruptibility which divinizes us.[47]

In these developments, Saint Irenaeus would have recognized his physical theory of deification, although the bishop of Olympus has complicated it with an unacceptable speculation about the identity of the body of Christ with that of Adam.[48]

Is there the need to add that Methodius does not conceive of divinization as a purely physical process, any more than Irenaeus and the whole tradition? On the contrary, he often comes back to the indispensable human cooperation. It is necessary to die and resurrect with Christ, in order to live by His life; it is necessary for the church to give birth to us "until Christ be begotten and formed in us, in order that each of the saints, through the participation in Christ, may be born a Christ."[49] For to reproduce in one's own life the traits of the earthly life of Jesus "is to form oneself exactly in the divine likeness [καθ' ὁμοίωσιν θεοῦ]."[50] The imitation of Christ is the condition of our deification.

197

III

However, this imitation involves some degrees,[51] and only an elite is capable of reaching the goal, of rising to perfection.

---

[45] *Symp.* 3.6 (27:33:7-16; PG 18:69b). This passage excludes any symbolic interpretation according to which Adam would symbolize only the human nature taken by the Word, an interpretation attempted by J. Farges, *Les idées morales et religieuses de Méthode d'Olympe* (Paris, 1929), 127. Tixeront, *Histoire des dogmes,* 1:494, on the contrary, recognizes that "Methodius pushes things so far that he seems to identify Christ with the person of the first Adam."

[46] *Symp.* 1.4 (27:12:23–13:2; PG 18:44d).

[47] Cf. *Res.* 3.23 (27:420:25–421:6).

[48] Certain bold expressions of the doctor of Lyon could have suggested this curious theory to Methodius. Cf. *Haer.* 3.21.10 (PG 7:9). The term ἀναπλάσσειν also used by Saint Hippolytus with reference to the incarnation (see above, 151, n. 9), does not in his writings have the same realistic sense as with Methodius.

[49] *Symp.* 8.8 (27:90:12-14; PG 18:149c). This is the central thought of the *Symposium.* Cf. Rahner, "Die Gottesgeburt," 359-364.

[50] *Symp.* 1.4 (27:13:2-11; PG 18:44d-45).

[51] *Symp.* 7.3 (27:73-75; PG 18:116-117).

Clement and Origen, one remembers, identified perfection with gnosis. While highly appreciating the knowledge of the Scriptures and the understanding of the divine truths, to the point of making it a condition of faith and, especially, of virginity,[52] it is in this last item that Saint Methodius sees the Christian ideal. Did he not even write that, "by order of Christ, virginity replaced the law and became the queen of human beings"?[53]

Thus, for the bishop of Olympus, virginity is not merely the virtue of complete integrity, but the consecration, freely[54] made to the Lord, of the entire person, body and soul, for the whole life.[55] As such, it rescues a person from the domination of the devil and of concupiscence;[56] it allows one to keep intact the original beauty of the soul[57] and assures immortality.[58] By transforming a person to the image of the divine Husband, virginity, and that "alone, renders the one who possesses it, who has been initiated to its pure mysteries, like God."[59] Thus, above all, it is the divine gift[60] of virginity that immortalizes humankind, and by that deifies them.

To the chosen souls, who give themselves to Him without reservation, Christ grants His partiality: He makes them His beloved spouses[61] and His helpers in the birth of the believers;[62] He makes them, in advance, "dwell with Him in heaven":[63]

198

> Light and endowed with powerful wings, they succeed in casting a glance toward the supra-earthly region of life and see from a distance what no other person has gazed upon: the actual fields of incorruptibility, all sprinkled with flowers, of an unspeakable beauty. Always turned toward these places, they meditate unceasingly on the wonders there. So they consider what one regards here as beautiful as of little value: wealth, glory, nobility of birth, marriage; for them, nothing is equal to the supra-earthly benefits. Much more, if out of revenge one wanted to cast their bodies to ferocious beasts or into fire, they are ready to endure tortures with indifference, so great is their thirst for these benefits and the fascination which they exercise over them, to such a point that, while still being in this world, they seem to be no longer of the world, but already, by their spirit and the rush of their desires, to belong to the company of those who are in the heavens. Indeed, it is not in the nature of the wing of virginity to dwell at length

---

[52] Cf. *Symp.* 1.1 (27:8-9; PG 18:37b-40); 5.4 (27:57:9–58; PG 18:101-104); *Lepr.* 1.2; (452).

[53] *Symp.* 10.1 (27:122:7-8; PG 18:193a); cf. 9.4 (27:118-119; PG 18:185-188).

[54] Cf. *Symp.* 3.14 (44-45; PG 18:84-85). To those who, after having chosen virginity, feel incapable of maintaining it, Methodius recommends getting married.

[55] *Symp.* 5.1-6 (27:53-60; PG 18:97-109).

[56] *Symp.* 10.1 (27:121:23–122:15; PG 18:192-193).

[57] *Symp.* 6.2 (27:65:8-17; PG 18:113-116).

[58] *Symp.* 4.2, 4 (27:46:9-12, 27:49:19-20; PG 18:89a, 92b).

[59] *Symp.* 8.1 (27:81:5-6; PG 18:137c).

[60] *Symp.* 3.14 (27:44:1-2; PG 18:84c).

[61] *Symp.* 7.1-2 (27:72:9–73:18; PG 18:125b-128c).

[62] *Symp.* 3.8 (27:37:3-15; PG 18:72-76). This passage recalls the spiritual birth of which Plato speaks in his *Symposium*, 209.

[63] *Symp.* 4.2 (27:47:16-17; PG 18:89a).

on the earth, but to rise on high into the pure ether and toward a life in the near-ness of angels.[64]

In language full of lyricism, where the Platonic inspiration is evident,[65] we see in Methodius a mystic, who, in a kind of ecstasy, believes that he achieves, from this life, direct union with the glorious Christ and "glimpses the divine things [ἰνδάλλοντο τὰ θεῖα]."[66] This is, basically, Origen's mysticism of deification, which Methodius has adapted to his ideal of virginity by stressing the purity of the gnostic. It is with this difference though: the bishop of Olympus does not employ the terminology characteristic of the doctrine of divinization.   199

IV

The assimilation of the believers to Christ will be consummated in the future age. Contrary to Origen, our doctor affirms the identity of the resurrected bodies with those which we bear in this world.[67] The bodies of the righteous ones will be transformed into impassible and incorruptible bodies, into "pneumatic" bodies, "assimilated" to the glorious body of the resurrected Christ,[68] because they have been penetrated and governed by the Holy Spirit.[69] In that way, having participated in the struggles of the soul, the flesh will share in its triumph as well.

After the world will have been overwhelmed and burnt by fire descending from above, to be "purified and renewed" by it,[70] the resurrected saints will cele-brate "the millennium of rest with Christ, which we call the seventh day, the true Sabbath."[71] Then, having been transformed "in grandeur and angelic beauty," they will enter into heaven.[72] The virgins, rising "above the heavens," make their way "into the very house of God,"[73] "as into a nuptial chamber," to enjoy there the "vision of the Father"[74] and lead "a chorus of harmonious celebration in glorifying   200
God."[75]

---

[64] *Symp.* 8.2 (27:82:11–83:9; PG 18:140-141).

[65] See the references to the writings of Plato in Bonwetsch, GCS 27:82-83.

[66] *Symp.* 8.2 (27:83:16; PG 18:141a).

[67] See especially the third book of *Res.* (27:388-424).

[68] *Res.* 3.11 (27:407). Methodius expresses doubts on the subject of the resurrection of sinners. But he is convinced that, if they do resurrect, the bodies of the wicked also will be incorruptible, but not transfigured.

[69] *Res.* 3.16 (27:413:5-11). Text extracted from the series of pseudo-Oecumenius, the tradition of which is subject to caution.

[70] *Res.* 1.47 (27:297:12–298:2).

[71] *Symp.* 9.5 (27:120:14-15; PG 18:189a); cf. 9.1-2 (27:113-116; PG 18:177-185); *Res.* 1.55 (27:313:6-11); G. Bardy, "Millénarisme," *DTC* 10:1760-1763.

[72] *Symp.* 9.5 (27:120:19-21; PG 18:189b).

[73] *Symp.* 9.5 (27:120:21-26; PG 18:189b).

[74] *Symp.* 7.3 (27:74:5-6; PG 18:128d).

[75] *Symp.* 8.3 (27:84:22-26; PG 18:144a).

☙

In his conception of the deification of the Christian, Saint Methodius brings in, to a notably greater extent than Saint Hippolytus, both the physical theory outlined by the doctor of Lyon and the gnosis of the Alexandrians, indeed even the mysticism of Origen. However, it was not without imprinting a personal mark on the borrowings that he makes. Assuredly, the preciseness which he adds to the theory of Irenaeus, by saying that the Logos has taken the body of Adam, is not an advance. On the other hand, credit remains to him for being one of the first to discern the main antichristian elements in the Origenist gnosis and to fight them, while maintaining the gnostic ideal. And who would dare blame the bishop of Olympus for the fact that, in accomplishing this very delicate task, he could not himself remain without fault?

Nevertheless, more than anyone before him, Methodius succeeded in uniting Christian tradition and Hellenic speculation in his conception of divinization. By that, he heralds and prepares for the blossoming of the doctrine of deification in the great patristic age.

BOOK ONE

The Preparation

Part I: Hellenic Analogs
Part II: Biblical and Judaic Particulars

BOOK TWO

The Doctrine of the Greek Fathers

Part I: The Period of Formation
Part II: The Period of Apogee

Chapter 1: The Great Doctrinal Syntheses:
Saint Athanasius

Chapter 2: The Great Doctrinal Syntheses:
Saint Gregory of Nyssa

Chapter 3: Occasional Attestations:
The School of Alexandria

Chapter 4: Occasional Attestations:
The School of Antioch

Part III: The Period of Consolidation

CHAPTER ONE

THE GREAT DOCTRINAL SYNTHESES: SAINT ATHANASIUS

From the first three centuries onwards, the idea of the deification of human- 201 kind through Christianity occupies an increasingly important place in the thoughts of the Greek fathers, and for an elite, at least, it seems to have been a strong point. In the fourth century, due to some particularly favorable circumstances, and especially to the theological work of Saint Athanasius and Saint Gregory of Nyssa, this advancement would reach its culminating point, ending in some great doctrinal syntheses.

The theme of divinization must have been very common at that time in the churches of the East, since Athanasius bases upon it one of his principal arguments for the perfect divinity of the Son of God in his struggle against the Arians. Thus he writes in his *On the Councils of Ariminum and Seleucia:*

> If the Logos had also been God by participation, and not consubstantial divinity and the image of the Father by Himself, He would not have been able to deify, being Himself deified. For it is not possible that one who only possesses by participation communicate to others what he has thus received, because what he does not have from himself, but from the giver, and what he has received, is barely sufficient for himself.[1]

The same argumentation recurs constantly in the *Orations against the Arians* 202 and, later, is applied to the Holy Spirit in the letters to Serapion directed against the Pneumatomachi. It follows that, for the Alexandrian doctor, the divinization of the Christian is not a more or less secondary and casual element, as with the majority of the earlier fathers, but the central thought of his theology.

It is true that with Athanasius we would search in vain for a systematic and well-balanced exposition on the matter. However, by grouping together the main texts from numerous ones in which he touches on it in passing, we can obtain a collection which reflects in a sufficiently precise way his conception concerning the fact, the conditions, and the nature of divinization.

I

Clearer than anyone before him, Athanasius conceives of redemption, and in that framework deification, as a restoration of the original state of Adam. Even clearer still, he identifies this state with that of restored humankind. This

---

[1] Ath. *Syn.* 51 (PG 26:784b).

explains the particular attention which he pays to the divine likeness of our first ancestor, the prototype of our divinization.

On several occasions, our doctor analyzes the original state directly. In the two works of his youth, which form one unit, *Against the Pagans* and *On the Incarnation*, he speaks about this state as a Platonic philosopher and apologist, whereas in his *Orations against the Arians* he deals with them rather as a theologian.

We do not need to dwell for long on the highly idealistic portrait that Athanasius, when still a simple deacon, draws of innocent Adam. He makes the ideal gnostic out of him, who, "being raised above the sensory things and every physical imagination" and "thus released from every obstacle to the gnosis of the divine, contemplates unceasingly the image of the Father in its own purity, the God-Logos, according to the image of whom he was made,"[2] and lives "as a god, like the divine Scripture says" in Psa 82.[3] Thus for him, the original state of Adam included the likeness with the Logos and, by this, with God, as the most precious of divine gifts, a similitude which was for our first ancestor the source of the knowledge of God, of happiness, and of incorruptibility.[4]

203

Some twenty years later in his controversies with the Arians, the bishop of Alexandria, without saying it formally, introduces substantial modifications to his youthful conception relating to the original state.

Thus in his *Orations against the Arians* he distinguishes between the divine act by which humankind are created and the divine act by which they are adopted. Concerning Mal 2:10 ("Has not one and the same God created us? Is there not one and the same Father for us all?")[5] he writes:

> In this passage as well, he [the prophet] has again placed the words "He has created" first and the "Father" second, in order to also show that by virtue of our origin and according to our nature we are creatures and that our Creator is God through the Logos; that we are taken as children later and that our Creator at that time becomes our Father as well. The word "Father," and not that of "Creator," relates thus to "child," while "child" refers to "Father." This is so that it would be thus manifest that we are not children by nature [μὴ εἶναι ἡμᾶς φύσει υἱούς], but really the Son who is in us, and that in His turn God is not our Father by nature, but Father of the Logos, who is in us, in whom and because of whom we cry, "Abba Father!"[6] In the same way the Father, on His side, calls children those in whom He sees His Son and says [concerning them], "I have begotten." For *to*

---

[2] *C. Gent.* 2 (25:5-8b). The speculations which this passage contains recall certain conceptions of Philo (see above, 75-76) and betray some Neoplatonic influences.

[3] *Inc.* 4 (25:104a-c).

[4] Athanasius here takes up again the idea dear to Clement and Origen, according to which the divine gnosis is generatrix of immortality.

[5] In our editions, the order of the two parts of the verse is reversed. The order followed by Athanasius is that of the *Codex Alexandrinus*, which he used. It is pointless to reply to the weakness of an argument so basically fragile.

[6] Cf. Rom 8:15. It should be noted that, according to the apostle, it is in the Spirit that "we cry, 'Abba! Father!' "

beget indicates a child, whereas *to make* signifies works. So this is why we are not first begotten, but made. Indeed it is written, "Let us make humankind." But later, after receiving the grace of the Spirit, we are also said to be "begotten."[7]

204

Adopted children and images of God, we are not such, consequently, as creatures in our "natural being" [τὸ κατὰ φύσιν];[8] we become such uniquely by a special "generation" which consists in the coming of the Logos into us:

> If we have been made in the image, if we are described as the image and glory of God,[9] it is not because of us; but it is because of the image and true glory of God living in us, who is His Logos, having later become flesh for us, that we possess the grace of this designation.[10]

This is to set down quite clearly the distinction in principle between the "natural being" in humankind and grace. But for our theologian the "natural being" is less the sum of the elements which constitute human nature than the actual quality of being a creature, of being "fluent and subject to dissolution" without the support of the Logos, who alone makes beings remain alive.[11] Nonetheless, since even to the fallen human being he attributes a spiritual and immortal soul, endowed with reason and freedom, Saint Athanasius must have considered these gifts as virtually inseparable from human nature. But his philosophical views on human nature, considered in itself, did not allow him, unlike a large number of earlier fathers, to recognize in the natural endowment of the soul an initial similitude with God, namely, the state of image, the εἰκών, and to distinguish it from a superior, divine likeness, the ὁμοίωσις. Thus, he knows only a single divine likeness of humankind, that which results from the indwelling of the Logos in us and which he calls a "grace."

205

Our doctor has manifestly attributed this grace to Adam. The final conception which he developed of the divine similitude of the first human being can consequently be summarized in this way: by His substantial presence, which, according to points given in the letters to Serapion, implies that of the Father and of the Holy Spirit, the Logos has transfigured the soul of Adam to the point of making of it His own image; through this He has assured to him, with the divine sonship, incorruptibility and a happy life in intimacy with God. It is easy to see that Saint Athanasius ascribes to our first ancestor the traits of the ideal Christian, such as he conceives of one.

---

[7] *C. Ar.* 2.59 (26:273).

[8] *C. Ar.* 2.58 (26:272a).

[9] Cf. 1 Cor 11:7.

[10] *C. Ar.* 3.10 (26:334a). Cf. 1.37 (89b).

[11] Cf. *C. Gent.* 41 (25:81c). See A. Gaudel, "La doctrine du Λόγος chez saint Athanase," *RevScRel* 11 (1931): 4-14. Following Philo, the apologists, and the early Alexandrians, Athanasius distinguishes two acts or two aspects in the creative function of the Logos: on the one hand, He derives them from nothingness; on the other hand, He co-penetrates them in order to arrange them and to keep them in existence. See also *Inc.* 11-13 (25:113c ff).

According to Plato, *Tim.* 53b, the chaotic state is natural to "everything from which God is absent." Cf. Diès, *Autour de Platon,* 565.

By transgressing the precept of God, Adam separated from, emptied himself of, the Logos. With the knowledge of the divine, he also lost incorruptibility and fell under the law of corruption and death. Now, "by the disobedience of Adam, sin invaded all of humankind,"[12] and, with sin, all its deadly consequences.

Nevertheless, even in this state humankind lost neither the power to know God, nor the freedom. So our doctor does not hesitate to declare on occasion that by virtue of these faculties, the human νοῦς has the possibility of re-establishing within it the image of the Logos obliterated by sin,[13] or even that, by conversion [μετάνοια], humankind can recover the divine filiation which they lost.[14] More often though, notably in his theological treatises, the bishop of Alexandria proclaims that only the Logos was able to restore the image in fallen humankind.[15]

In actual practice, human beings only abused the gifts which had remained to them and fell into an ever deeper corruption.[16] In order to re-create humankind in the divine image, it was necessary for the Logos, the image of the Father, to intervene by taking a mortal body.[17] Not content to re-establish humanity in its original state, Jesus Christ brought to it a grace of divinization much more precious than even that of the beginning.[18]

206

II

The deification of fallen humankind as the goal of the incarnation is something that Saint Athanasius does not cease to repeat:

[The Logos] became human, in order that we might be divinized.[19]

[The Son of God] became human, in order to divinize us in Himself.[20]

The bishop of Alexandria never wearies of showing the Arians that if Christ is not God, humankind has not been redeemed; for "a creature would not have united the creatures with God,"[21] and in order to deify it is first of all necessary to be God.[22]

This presupposes that the Arians and catholics agreed in seeing divinization as the goal of the incarnation. However, in this sense the latter has not only made it possible but has actually realized it. "In the very existence of the

---

[12] *C. Ar.* 1.51 (26:117c).
[13] *C. Gent.* 34 (25:68c).
[14] *C. Ar.* 1.37 (26:89b).
[15] Cf. *Inc.* 13 (25:117c).
[16] *Inc.* 12 (25:116-117).
[17] *Inc.* 13 (25:117-120).
[18] *C. Ar.* 2.67 (26:289c).
[19] *Inc.* 54 (25:192b): Αὐτὸς γὰρ ἐνηνθρώπησεν, ἵνα ἡμεῖς θεοποιηθῶμεν.
[20] *Ep. Adelph.* 4 (26:1077a): Γέγονε γὰρ ἄνθρωπος, ἵν' ἡμᾶς ἐν ἑαυτῷ θεοποιήσῃ.
[21] *C. Ar.* 2.69 (26:293a). Cf. *C. Ar.* 2:67 (289c).
[22] *C. Gent.* 9 (25:21a).

God-Man, the redivinization of humanity was in principle accomplished. It is in the constitution of the person of Christ that, for Athanasius, redemption has its center of gravity: due to the indwelling of the Logos in humanity, the latter has been penetrated by the divine life. Such is the fundamental thought of the soteriology of our Saint, in which he manifestly depends on Saint Irenaeus."[23]

In fact, under the pen of our doctor, the physical conception of deification, which the bishop of Lyon outlined, expands and takes on the appearance of a true synthesis. Here, beside the incarnated Logos, who of course plays the major role, a considerable place is reserved for the deifying action of the Holy Spirit.

207

The patriarch of Alexandria clearly explains that by the intimate contact which the incarnation produces between the divine Logos and human nature, the latter is deified:

> The Logos is not one of the created beings, but on the contrary the very Demiurge of these. This is why He took the created, human body, that, having renewed it as the Creator, He might divinize it in Himself and usher us all into the kingdom of the heavens, according to the likeness with Him [καθ' ὁμοιότητα ἐκείνου]. United with a creature, humankind would not have been divinized again, if the Son was not true God. Humankind would not have drawn closer to the Father, if the One who had put on the body had not been His natural and genuine Logos. And just as we would not have been delivered from sin and the curse, if the flesh put on by the Logos had not been by nature a human flesh—for we have nothing in common with a foreign being—in the same way humankind would not have been deified unless the One who became flesh is of the Father by nature and was His genuine and very own Logos. This is why the contact [συναφή] was thus made, in order that the human nature might be united with the divine nature and that the salvation and deification [θεοποίησις] of the former might be assured. Thus those who deny that the Son is by nature of the Father and that He is the characteristic of His essence are also denying that the Son took a real human flesh from Mary, forever virgin.[24]

In another passage, we find the idea whereby to divinize man, the Savior had to unite in Himself the divine nature with the human nature. This union alone could fill the human nature with divine strength in order to heal and immortalize it:

> If the works of the divinity of the Logos had not been accomplished through the body, humankind would not have been divinized; in the same way, if one does not think the Logos to be what is characteristic of the flesh, humankind would not have been completely delivered....Now since the Logos became human and appropriated what is of the flesh, the body is no longer touched because of the Logos who is in him and who has taken everything away. In fact, from that time on human beings no longer remain sinful and dead, according to their own

208

---

[23] H. Straeter, *Die Erlösungslehre des hl. Athanasius* (Freiburg im Breisgau, 1894), 140.
[24] *C. Ar.* 1.70 (26:296a-b).

passions; but, being resurrected by the power of the Logos, they remain forever immortal and incorruptible....We will no longer die in Adam, according to our first birth; but, our carnal birth and all our carnal infirmities being thenceforth transferred onto the Logos, we are resurrected from the earth; the curse resulting from sin has been lifted by the One who, in us, was made a curse for us.[25]

Expositions of this kind, more or less extensive, are frequently found in the writings of Athanasius,[26] giving the impression that, for our theologian, the Logos has assumed the human nature as such, or to redeem all humanity. There is a particularly vivid impression when one reads texts such as the following:

> Just as the Lord, by putting on the body, has become human, so we human beings, assumed by His flesh, are divinized by the Logos and from now on have as our inheritance an eternal life.[27]

> Given that all human beings have been lost by the transgression of Adam, the flesh of the latter has been saved and delivered, in the first place, since it has become the body of the Logos Himself; and then we, united in one body [σύσσωμοι τυγχάνοντες], are saved according to this same body.[28]

In these affirmations, however formal, some only wish to see "an abuse of Platonic language."[29] Such an interpretation empties the texts in question of their convincing force and of their profound significance. Therefore, it seems preferable to acknowledge that Saint Athanasius has really conceived of human nature in the way of a concrete reality, as a kind of "generic human being," to employ an expression of Philo,[30] in which all individuals participate, but in such a way that the accidental properties, the "figures and qualities,"[31] play the role of what we call the principle of individuation. This would explain why, while seeing in Christ the whole of humanity, the bishop of Alexandria attributes to the incarnated Logos a strictly individual body and soul, which belong exclusively to Him.[32]

Nonetheless, one would hesitate to attribute to the great doctor a realism so foreign to our conceptions if elsewhere in the writings of Athanasius it did not manifest itself with a clarity which excludes any doubt.

For example, in the second of the *Letters to Serapion concerning the Holy Spirit* he writes:

209

---

[25] *C. Ar.* 3.33 (26:383a-396a).

[26] Cf. for example, *Inc.* 44; *C. Ar.* 2.67 ff.; *Ep. Epict.* 9.

[27] *C. Ar.* 3.34 (26:397a-b). Cf. 1.46-50 (105-117).

[28] *C. Ar.* 2.61 (26:277b).

[29] Tixeront, *Histoire des dogmes* (9th ed.), 2:151. The same explanation in Straeter, *Erlösungslehre*, 175.

[30] See above, 75.

[31] Cf. *Syn.* 53 (26:788b-c).

[32] Cf. G. A. Pell, *Die Lehre des hl. Athanasius von der Sünde und Erlösung* (Passau, 1888), 125-133; Straeter, *Erlösungslehre*, 175.

> With the beings to which we are similar, we have identity as well, and we are consubstantial with them; being thus human beings and having identity, we are consubstantial one with another.[33]

A little further along, Athanasius establishes a parallel between the consubstantiality of human beings and that of the Trinitarian persons:

> Just as we would not call our fathers [our] creators [ποιητάς], but [our] generators [γεννήτορας], and just as nobody would say of us that we are creatures of our fathers, but indeed [their] children by nature and [that we are] consubstantial with the fathers; in the same way, if God is Father, He is surely Father of a Son by nature [who is] consubstantial [with Him],... every son being consubstantial with his father.[34]

Now, since our author conceives of the consubstantiality of the divine Persons as a numerical identity of essence,[35] we are forced to conclude that he has acknowledged the numerical unity of nature for human beings as well.

But in order to clearly understand his realist language concerning the incarnation, we must remember moreover that Saint Athanasius, "up to the end of his life, confused the two terms οὐσία and ὑπόστασις."[36] Through lack of as important a distinction as this, it was difficult for him to specify—as Saint John Damascene will do later—that the deification of the human nature does not automatically entail that of the persons. Still, the fact is that he presents individual divinization as the result of the combined action of the subject, Christ, and the Holy Spirit.

III

In his two apologetic treatises, the patriarch of Alexandria has only the incarnated Logos play a part, as the agent of our deification. But already in the *Orations against the Arians* he mentions the cooperation of the Holy Spirit. Eventually, the nature of this cooperation becomes clear in the four letters to Serapion against the Pneumatomachi, in which our doctor defends the divinity of the Spirit by means of the same principles which served him in establishing that of the Son. Thus the deifying action of the Holy Spirit, undoubtedly recognized by his adversaries, supplies him with one of his best arguments:

---

[33] *Ep. Serap.* 2.3 (26:612b):Ὧν ἐσμεν ὅμοιοι, καὶ τὴν ταυτότητα ἔχομεν τούτων, καὶ ὁμοούσιοί ἐσμεν· ἄνθρωποι γοῦν ὅμοιοι καὶ ταυτότητα ἔχοντες, ὁμοούσιοί ἐσμεν ἀλλήλων.

[34] *Ep. Serap.* 2.6 (26:617a-b): ... οὕτως, εἰ Πατὴρ ὁ θεός, πάντως Υἱοῦ φύσει καὶ ὁμοουσίου ἐστὶ Πατήρ. Cf. *Syn.* 53 (26:788b-c), where the author declares in a general way that "on the subject of essences, it is not of similitude, but of identity, that it is necessary to speak" [ἐπὶ γὰρ τῶν οὐσιῶν οὐχ ὁμοιότης, ἀλλὰ ταυτότης ἂν λεχθείη]. Indeed, he continues, "a human being is said to be similar [ὅμοιος] to a human being, not according to essence, but according to form and figure [κατὰ τὸ σχῆμα καὶ τὸν χαρακτῆρα], for through essence they are of same nature [ὁμοφυσεῖς]."

[35] Cf. *Syn.* 48 (26:780a-b): ἀνάγκη...κατὰ τὴν οὐσίαν νοεῖν καὶ τὴν Υἱοῦ καὶ Πατρὸς ἑνότητα... Ὁ δὲ Υἱὸς ἐκ τῆς οὐσίας ὢν γέννημα, οὐσίᾳ ἕν ἐστιν αὐτὸς καὶ ὁ γεννήσας αὐτὸν Πατήρ. See Tixeront, *Histoire des dogmes*, 2:71-72.

[36] Tixeront, *Histoire des dogmes,* 2:75.

211   It is by the Spirit that we are all said to have a share in God....Now, if by the participation of the Spirit we become partakers of the divine nature, it would be folly to say that the Spirit is of the created nature and not of the divine nature. This is also why those in whom He is are divinized [θεοποιοῦνται]. Now, if He divinizes, there is no doubt that His nature is that of God.[37]

The patriarch of Alexandria deduces that the Spirit contributes to our deification from the Trinitarian principle according to which "there is nothing which happens and is not carried out by the Logos in the Spirit."[38] Now, he argues, since there is only "one sanctification," it must "come from the Father by the Son in the Holy Spirit [ἐκ Πατρὸς δι' Υἱοῦ ἐν Πνεύματι ἁγίῳ]."[39]

On the general function of the Spirit, Athanasius explains himself in this way:

The Spirit is a holy oil and seal [χρίσμα καὶ σφραγίς]; in Him, the Logos anoints and seals all things....Now the holy oil contains the fragrance of the one who anoints,... the seal, the shape of the one who seals....Therefore it is right that, having been thus marked, we also become partakers of the divine nature, as Peter said,[40] and that, in like manner, all of creation partakes of the Logos in the Spirit.[41]

But beside that of the incarnated Logos, what exactly does the action of the Holy Spirit in our deification consist of? This role is basically identical to the one which the Third Person of the Trinity played in the incarnation. And yet it is precisely in the Holy Spirit that the Logos has assumed the human nature.

When the Logos descended into the holy virgin Mary, the Spirit came into her at the same time, and it is in the Spirit that the Logos developed and adapted His body, wanting through Himself to unite and offer the creation to the Father.[42]

212   Uniting in this way the human nature with the Logos, the Spirit was at the same time uniting with Him humanity, indeed, the entire creation:

It is thus in the Spirit that the Logos glorifies creation and, by deifying and adopting it [θεοποιῶν καὶ υἱοποιῶν],[43] leads it to the Father. But the one who unites creation with the Logos could not be part of the created, neither could the one who confers on creation the filial quality be foreign to the Son. If this was the case, it would be necessary to find another spirit, in order that, in it, the first might be united with the Logos. This is absurd. The Spirit is not, consequently,

---

[37]   *Ep. Serap.* 1.24 (26:585c-588a).

[38]   *Ep. Serap.* 1.31 (26:601a).

[39]   *Ep. Serap.* 1.20 (26:577c). Cf. 1.24 and 30 (585-588 and 597-600); 3.5 (632-633). The phrase "from the Father by the Son in the Holy Spirit" will become standard in the Greek church for expressing the respective role of each of the persons of the Trinity in creation and sanctification.

[40]   2 Pet 1:4.

[41]   *Ep. Serap.* 1.23 (26:585a-b).

[42]   *Ep. Serap.* 1.31 (26:605a). Elsewhere, *Inc.* 8 (25:109c), it is the Logos alone who prepares His body within the Virgin. Text quoted above, 173.

[43]   These two terms are here manifestly synonymous.

part of the created things, but He is characteristic of the divinity of the Father, and in Him the Logos deifies the creatures.[44]

So the divinization of humankind is presented as a gift of the whole Trinity: coming from the Father as from the source of all good, it is directly conferred on us by the Logos, yet in the Holy Spirit:

> What the Spirit distributes to each comes from the Father through the Son. This is why what is given through the Son in the Spirit is a grace of the Father.[45]

In brief, we are divinized by the intimate union with the Holy Spirit, which unites us with the Son of God and, through this One, with the Father.

IV

Taking literally the texts in which he puts forward his physical theory of divinization, some have maintained that Saint Athanasius concentrates the whole redemptive work in the very act of the incarnation and that he sees in our deification the result, so to speak, of a mechanical process, namely, of the "physical contact of the divine and the human in Jesus Christ."[46] Such is, in fact, the conception which Harnack ascribes to our doctor.[47]

Nothing prevents us from recognizing that, in his zeal to prove the divinity of the Savior by the efficiency of the incarnation, and ill-served by a generic realism of Platonic origin, the bishop of Alexandria was engaged in speculations which, in the very least, call for some correctives. As regards the latter, moreover, he himself provides the essential elements.

Thus, and in this he is echoing tradition, Athanasius recognizes in the human life of Christ[48] a certain redemptive value, in the sense that it completed the efficacy of the incarnation. In order to deliver us completely from our natural weaknesses, the incarnated Logos assumes them Himself; in order to divinize the human life in its various stages, He lived it personally.[49]

In this connection, our doctor reserves a separate place for the death of Christ in the work of salvation, as the means of atoning for our sins, of satisfying in our place the law of death brought by God to paradise, and thereby of returning to us the lost incorruptibility.[50] But he does not synthesize these various elements with the deifying role of the incarnation.

---

[44]   *Ep. Serap.* 1.25 (26:589b).

[45]   *Ep. Serap.* 1.30 (26:600b).

[46]   Rivière, *Rédemption: étude historique,* 147.

[47]   Harnack, *Lehrbuch der Dogmengeschichte* (4th ed.), 2:160-161.

[48]   Given his way of thinking and his dominant preoccupation—the defense of the perfect divinity of Christ—one can understand that the human life of Jesus hardly held the attention of Saint Athanasius, and, one can say, of the Alexandrians in general.

[49]   Cf. *C. Ar.* 3.33, quoted above, 167-168; *C. Ar.* 3.53 (26:433c-436a).

[50]   *Inc.* 6-9 (26:105c-112b). See below, 173, where an excerpt of this passage is quoted. Cf. J. Rivière, *Rédemption: étude historique,* 151; idem, *Le dogme de la rédemption: étude théologique* (3d ed.; Paris, 1931), 94-95; Tixeront, *Histoire des dogmes,* 2:149-152.

As for "mechanical" deification, the whole moral doctrine and, even more, the very life of the saintly bishop prove that such a more or less magical conception was foreign to him. In fact, just as Athanasius, despite his realism, recognizes in every person a full and complete moral autonomy, in the same way his physical theory of divinization does not prevent him from subordinating the deification of the individual to personal effort.

214 In fact, according to him, only Christians are deified, and in order to become Christian, faith and a serious conversion are indispensable.[51] Moreover, Harnack himself concedes that the Athanasian idea of divinization "is not completely naturalist" and that it includes "a restoration of the innermost being of the human being as well."[52]

However, this inner change, including faith, still does not make the Christian; one must receive baptism. Only by this is a person "united with divinity,"[53] regenerated and renewed "in the state of image,"[54] made a child of God thenceforth,[55] and thus deified.

But baptismal holiness can be lost.[56] To preserve it, one must consistently imitate the virtue and perfection which our pattern Christ possesses according to His divine nature.[57]

In practice, the deification of the Christian is therefore, above all, the work of the incarnated Logos and of His Spirit, to whom the initiative goes back completely;[58] but it is, at the same time, the fruit of a person's moral activity.

V

Although our doctor nowhere analyzes the concept of deification, the explanations that he devotes to its fact and conditions permit us to discover its main elements.

215 More clearly than the previous fathers, Saint Athanasius identifies divinization and divine filiation. He employs as synonyms the terms θεοποιεῖν and υἱοποιεῖν, which express the Christian's assimilation and intimate union with God due to the presence in that one of the Logos and of His Spirit. Assimilation, not identification, specifies the bishop of Alexandria, for the deified are children of God by adoption, by grace alone; they will never become children by nature, like the incarnated Logos:

> Only One is Son by nature; the others of us become children as well, not however like Him, by nature and in reality, but according to the grace of the One who calls

---

[51] Cf. *Inc.* 30 (25:148b), 50-51 (185-188).
[52] Harnack, *Dogmengeschichte*, 2:162.
[53] *C. Ar.* 2.41 (26:233b).
[54] *Inc.* 14 (25:120d). Cf. *Ep. Serap.* 1.22 (26:581-584).
[55] *C. Ar.* 1.34 (26:84a). Cf. *C. Ar.* 33 (80-81); *Ep. Serap.* 1.19 (573c-576a).
[56] *C. Ar.* 3.25 (26:376c).
[57] *C. Ar.* 3.18-22 (26:360-369).
[58] Cf. *Inc.* 50-51 (25:185-188).

us. While being people of the earth, we are called gods, not like the true God or His Logos, but just as God has wanted, who has given this grace to us.[59]

What deifies human beings and makes them children of God is their union with the Trinity. It is a primordial grace which implies a series of other blessings, such as a "heavenly life," "power over demons," the particularly precious gift of "the gnosis of the Father and of His Logos,"[60] and finally incorruptibility. On the latter, our doctor lays particular stress:

> Although He is powerful and the Demiurge of the universe, [the Logos] prepared for Himself, in the Virgin, the body as a temple and appropriated it as an instrument [ὄργανον] in order to manifest Himself and to dwell in it. Taking thus from our own a similar body [ἀπὸ τῶν ἡμετέρων τὸ ὅμοιον λαβών], and since we all had been subjected to the corruption of death, delivering it to death on behalf of all, He offered it to the Father. All this He did through love on behalf of human beings, in order that, all dying in Him, the law of corruption brought against them might be broken, as though having exhausted its holding-power over persons like [Him]. They having been turned over to corruption, He restores them thus to incorruptibility and brings them back from death to life, by an appropriation of the body and the grace of resurrection, destroying death in them, like a straw in fire.[61]

216

More than once, Saint Athanasius speaks of the defeat and powerlessness of death, indeed even of "death's death,"[62] in very expressive terms:

> For sure, given that the universal Savior has died for us, we, the believers in Christ, will now no longer die as in the past according to the threat of the law, for that condemnation has ceased.[63]

As he himself explains subsequently in this text, the bishop of Alexandria means by this that death is only a temporary dissolution for the disciple of the Christ, and thereby it has lost its terror.[64] In other words, Christians are so assured of their incorruptibility that they possess it, so to speak, right here and now.

Therefore, in the deified Christian the original state of humanity, with its union with God, its knowledge of God, and its immortality, finds itself magnificently restored, and this in a more stable fashion than at the beginning. This restoration is particularly complete with those who, by their escape from the world and practice of virginity, devote themselves to a life entirely in God.[65]

---

[59]   C. Ar. 3.19 (26:361c-364a). Cf. C. Ar. 3.24-25 (373-376); Decr. 31 (25:473c-d).

[60]   Ep. Aeg. Lib. 1 (25:540a).

[61]   Inc. 8 (25:109c-d). Cf. C. Ar. 3.33 (26:393-396).

[62]   Inc. 27 (25:141c).

[63]   Inc. 21 (25:132c).

[64]   Inc. 27 (25:141d).

[65]   This is the monastic ideal which Saint Athanasius celebrates in his Life of Anthony, destined to exercise as profound an influence in the East as in the West. With Saint Methodius, our doctor sees in virginity a specifically Christian virtue. Cf. Inc. 51 (25:185d-188a); Vit. Ant. 79 (26:953). See Straeter, Erlösungslehre, 180.

They are short of nothing more than paradise; but even this will one day be advantageously replaced by the heavenly kingdom.

VI

Indeed, in heaven, whose doors have been reopened by the resurrected Christ,[66] the divinization of the Christian will find its climax.

217   After "the second appearing of Christ among us, that glorious and truly divine event,"[67] resurrection will take place. The same body that we have borne during our earthly life will resurrect to be united again with our soul.[68] The body of the righteous will be like that of the glorious Christ, namely, immortal and impassible.

> From mortal, it has become immortal; being psychic, it has become pneumatic; and born of the earth, it has gone through the heavenly gates.[69]

But how is the incorruptibility of the resurrected bodies obtained? By a physical transformation of the human flesh as Bornhäuser thinks?[70] This is without any doubt, even though such a change seems to have been conceived of by our doctor as a simple effect of the presence and knowledge of the Logos, gifts which the resurrected ones inamissibly possess and which assure for them a stability in being such that there is no room for corruption there.

This explanation is suggested by two opinions of Saint Athanasius which complement one another. According to the first, if he had kept the divine similitude by the contemplation of God, Adam "would have blunted natural corruptibility and would have remained incorruptible."[71] According to the second, this quality would come to certain other beings from their knowledge of the Logos:

> Neither the sun, nor the moon, nor the skies, nor the stars, nor the water, nor the ether have wandered out of order; but, due to the knowledge of the Logos, their Demiurge and King, they remain just as they were created.[72]

---

[66] *C. Ar.* 1.41 (26:97b). Cf. *Ep. fest.* 5.3 (25:1380d-1381a).

[67] *Inc.* 56 (25:196a-b).

[68] Cf. *Vit. Ant.* 91 (26:972b).

[69] *Ep. Epict.* 9 (26:1065b). Cf. *C. Ar.* 3.34, (26:397a-b); 3.33 (393-396).

[70] K. Bornhäuser, *Die Vergottungslehre des Athanasius und Johannes Damascenus* (Gütersloh, 1903), 43-44.

[71] *Inc.* 4 (25:104c).

[72] *Inc.* 43 (25:172b-c): Ἀμέλει, οὐχ ἥλιος, οὐ σελήνη, οὐκ οὐρανός, οὐ τὰ ἄστρα, οὐκ ὕδωρ, οὐκ αἰθὴρ παρήλλαξαν τὴν τάξιν, ἀλλ' εἰδότες τὸν ἑαυτῶν δημιουργὸν καὶ βασιλέα Λόγον μένουσιν ὡς γεγόνασιν.

It goes without saying that, in the resurrected ones, incorruptibility is   218
accompanied by impassibility, both of which are indispensable conditions of
"eternal" bliss[73] in the house of God, where perfect "concord"[74] and "supreme
joy and exaltation" are reigning.[75]

The assimilation of the whole person to the glorious God-Man, the most
intimate union with the Logos and, through Him, with all the Trinity in the
heavenly bliss, such is, according to Athanasius, the complete and permanent
deification of the Christian.

What is particular to Saint Athanasius concerning the divinization of the
Christian is that in order to explain its conditions, without renouncing the
intellectualism of the school of Alexandria, he has been inspired less by the
gnosis of Clement and Origen than by the conception of Saint Irenaeus.
However, by enriching the latter with numerous elements borrowed from the
former and developing it by means of a philosophical idea—the realist concept
of human nature—the patriarch of Alexandria has not only marked it with the
stamp of his powerful personality, but has raised it to the level of a genuine
theory, of a doctrinal synthesis.

---

[73] Cf. *Ep. fest.* 14.2 (25:1419d).

[74] *Ep. fest.* 9.8 (25:1395a-b).

[75] *Ep. fest.* 1.10 (25:1366b). Cf. 19.8 (25:1429a). In his strictly theological writings, Athanasius
hardly makes allusion to heavenly blessing. In his festal or paschal letters, on the contrary, he speaks of
it often enough, but in passing, without ever treating this point of doctrine *ex professo*.

CHAPTER TWO

THE GREAT DOCTRINAL SYNTHESES:
SAINT GREGORY OF NYSSA

219   After Saint Athanasius, Saint Gregory of Nyssa is the witness par excellence of the Greek doctrine of divinization. In his *Great Catechism*, a "genuine little theological survey"[1] intended for Christian teachers, this most speculative of the fourth century Greek fathers not only gives it its most systematic and philosophical form, but makes it the unique base of his soteriology. However, the relatively brief exposition of the *Catechism* needs to be supplemented by the teaching contained in the other writings of the saint, notably, in what concerns our subject, his small anthropology entitled *On the Making of Man*.

More than any other father, the bishop of Nyssa appears preoccupied—especially when he addresses himself to the Gentiles—with supporting the truths of the faith on what he calls the "common fundamentals" [κοιναὶ ἔννοιαι],[2] which are principles borrowed by preference from Neoplatonism and Stoicism and out of which he constructs something of a framework for his religious philosophy. The principal ideas that dominate the Gregorian conception

220   of *theopoiesis* are notably the transcendence of the "Most High, who is inaccessible because of the loftiness of His nature,"[3] and His goodness. In accordance with his lofty idea of "the Being who possesses existence by virtue of His own nature,"[4] Saint Gregory proclaims as the supreme rule of our belief that nothing should "be contrary to the idea that one must have of God."[5] Now it would be unworthy of God, who is "the nature of good"[6] and even "above all good,"[7] to think that He may have created for any motive other than that of manifesting His wisdom and His goodness, especially toward humankind

---

[1]   F. Cayré, *Précis de patrologie* (Paris, 1927), 1:415.

[2]   Gr. Nyss. *Or. catech.* 5 (PG 45:20d). One critical edition of the discourse with French translation has been published, in the collection *Textes et documents*, by L. Méridier: *Grégoire de Nysse: discours catéchétique* (Paris, 1908). Where there is a difference between the text of the edition of Migne and that of Méridier, we follow the latter, especially as the first is often obviously faulty. In order to establish the translation of the excerpts which we are quoting, we have been aided by that of Méridier.

[3]   *Or. catech.* 27 (45:72b).

[4]   *Vit. Mos.* (44:333a-b): τὸ ὄν, ὃ τῇ ἑαυτοῦ φύσει τὸ εἶναι ἔχει, a definition which seems to be inspired by Aris. *Metaph.* 12. (a). 6 (1071 b: 19-20). Cf. Endre v. Ivanka, "Vom Platonismus zur Theorie der Mystik," *Schol* 11 (1936): 163-195. On the concept of God according to Gregory, see Jean Bayer, *Gregors von Nyssa Gottesbegriff* (Giessen, 1935).

[5]   *Or. catech.* 27 (45:72d). Cf. 9 (40d); 16 (49c); 20 (57a).

[6]   *Anim. et res.* (46:93b).

[7]   *Hom. opif.* 16 (44:184a): θεὸς...παντὸς ἀγαθοῦ...ἐπέκεινα ὤν. This phrase recalls Plotinus. Cf. Bayer, *Gregors von Nyssa Gottesbegriff*, 29-30.

whom He has called to know Him and become His friend in order to share in His bliss.[8] It is also unworthy of God to acknowledge that evil, which takes humankind away from His purpose, comes from the Creator, that the Being Himself would not end up by overcoming the evil which does not have its own existence,[9] or finally, that divine wisdom would not triumph over human folly:

> It is, in fact, impossible that what changes be stronger and more durable than the One who is always unchanging in Himself and firmly strengthened in the good.[10]

Already by these principles we can foresee that, in his conception of the original state, the doctor from Nyssa will exceed even the idealism of Saint Athanasius.

I

The Logos created humankind "in the superabundance of His love,...in order to make them partakers of the divine benefits."[11]

The actual formation of humankind was conceived of by our doctor in a very original fashion, and this was not without influence on his doctrine of deification. According to him—and he takes care to let the reader know that he is expressing a simple hypothesis—

> in the first creation, by the divine providence and power, all of humanity was included....All the fullness of the human race [ὅλον τὸ τῆς ἀνθρωπότητος πλήρωμα] was contained as if in one body, by the provident power of the God of the universe. This is what the account teaches when it says that God made humankind and that He made them in the image of God....All the nature thus, as much that of the first ones as of the last, is one image of the One who is.[12]

This ideal humanity, which seems to have existed only in the divine thought, possessed the perfect likeness with God, to the point of not being sexed, "sexual difference being unknown to the divine nature."[13] Without sin humankind would not have needed marriage in order to multiply; they would have been propagated in the mysterious way of the angels.[14] But foreseeing that human beings would abuse their freedom and would thus lose the angelic life, and not willing that "the throng of human souls remain incomplete," God "introduced to humankind, instead of the noble angelic way of propagation,

---

[8] Cf. *Vit. Mos.* (44:429c-d).
[9] *Or. catech.* 7 (45:32c). Cf. 21 (60a-b).
[10] *Hom. opif.* 21 (44:201b-c).
[11] *Or. catech.* 5 (45:21a).
[12] *Hom. opif.* 16 (44:185b-c). Cf. 22 (204-209).
[13] *Hom. opif.* 16 (44:181b, 185d).
[14] *Hom. opif.* 17 (44:189a). Gregory is certain that the angels are propagated, but he admits to being incapable of saying how.

that of the beasts and animals without reason."[15] And so our first parents were created sexed.

For this reason, the divine likeness possessed in a perfect fashion by the ideal human being—manifestly modeled on "the human being in the image," "the generic human being" of Philo[16]—has undergone an obscuring in historical humankind. These ones nevertheless retain the state of the divine image, since they also participate, though to a lesser degree, in the divine perfections:

222

> God...has not shown the half of the power of His goodness by granting one of His benefits and refusing, through jealousy, the partaking of another. On the contrary, the perfection of goodness consists in this: on the one hand, to make humankind pass from non-being to existence; on the other hand, to endow them richly with benefits. Now, since the list of [divine] perfections taken individually is long, it is not easy to enumerate them. This is why the [biblical] account sums up everything in a comprehensive word when it says that humankind was made in the image of God. This, indeed, amounts to saying that God made human nature the participant in everything good. If therefore divinity is the fullness of benefits and humankind His image, it is by the possession of every good that the image has the similitude [τὴν ὁμοιότητα] with the archetype. Thus there is in us every kind of beauty, every virtue and wisdom, and everything which can be conceived of as perfect.[17]

But any participation presupposes "an affinity with the object participated in."[18] Divinity is essentially "mind and reason" [νοῦς καὶ λόγος].[19] These perfections should consequently be granted to humankind before any other benefit:

> The Creator...has given to the human nature other benefits through liberality [ἐκ φιλοτιμίας]. Of the νοῦς and the intelligence, on the contrary, one cannot say, strictly speaking, that He has given them, but that He has shared [μετέδωκε] them by conferring on the image the glory which is characteristic of His nature.[20]

223   It is the νοῦς, in fact, which is quite particularly "made in the image of the sovereign beauty,...and adorned by the likeness [τῇ ὁμοιώσει] with the prototypal beauty, like a mirror is adorned by the form of the one who is reflected in it."[21]

The free will necessarily goes together with the intelligence:

---

[15]   *Hom. opif.* 17 (44:189c-d). Cf. F. Hilt, *Des hl. Gregor von Nyssa Lehre vom Menschen* (Cologne, 1890), 16-19.

[16]   See above, 75. Cf. Slomkowski, *L'état primitif de l'homme*, 16, 106-108; Arnou, "Le Platonisme des Pères," 2346-2347.

[17]   *Hom. opif.* 16 (44:184a-b). These developments recall certain passages from Saint Methodius (cf. above, 154-156) by whom, moreover, Gregory often seems inspired.

[18]   *Or. catech.* 5 (45:21d).

[19]   *Hom. opif.* 5 (44:137b).

[20]   *Hom. opif.* 9 (44:149b), insofar as it is a "specific property of human nature," the νοῦς could not be refused to humankind (*Apoll.* 22 [45:1169a-b]). Cf. *Hom. opif.* 8 (44:145c); *Virg.* 12 (46:369b). In these two latter texts, humankind is defined as λογικὸν ζῷον.

[21]   *Hom. opif.* 12 (44:161c-d).

The One who made humankind with a view to participation in His own good things...could not deprive them of the most beautiful and precious of benefits. I speak of the grace [χάριτος][22] of independence and freedom. In fact, if some necessity dominated human life, the image would be false on this point, being altered by something dissimilar to the archetype. How does one call a being subjected and enslaved to necessities the image of the sovereign nature? That which has been assimilated in every point to the divine had to possess autonomy and independence absolutely in its nature for participation in good things to be the prize for virtue.[23]

Inherent in the human nature, intelligence and free will consequently constitute a primordial likeness of humankind with God, an inamissible likeness and, as it were, a foundation of the subsequent likeness which, by pure liberality, God added to the first. Indeed, comparable to a painter who scrupulously gives the portrait the features and the colors of the original, the Creator has adorned His image with His own beauty, conferring on it, instead of colors,

purity, impassibility, beatitude, freedom from all evil, and all the gifts of this kind, by which the likeness with the divine [ἡ πρὸς τὸ θεῖον ὁμοίωσις] is transmitted to human beings. It is with flowers of this kind that the Demiurge has stamped our nature with His own image.[24]

Among these privileges, some relate to the human body, others to the soul. The body, with its upright posture directed to the sky, indicating already the royal dignity of humankind and their dominion over the other earthly beings,[25] has received the particularly precious gift of immortality.   224

Eternity being also one of the inherent benefits of the divine nature, it was absolutely necessary that the constitution of our nature should not be devoid of it, but might possess immortality in itself, so that it might know, by the power which is in it, what is above it, and might desire divine eternity.[26]

Since Saint Gregory is firmly convinced of the natural incorruptibility of the soul,[27] obviously he is thinking here of bodily immortality. This also emerges from the fact that he attributes to our first parents freedom from everything which leads to death:

---

[22]   The fact that our doctor calls free will a grace and yet elsewhere (e.g. *Virg.* 12 [46:372b-c]; *Anim. et res.* [46:148a, 369b]) he describes the original state, considered in its entirety, to be "in conformity with nature" [κατὰ φύσιν], demonstrates the difficulty of finding with him our categories of natural and supernatural. Cf. Tixeront, *Histoire des dogmes,* 2:139.

[23]   *Or. catech.* 5 (45:24c-d).

[24]   *Hom. opif.* 5 (44:137a-b).

[25]   *Hom. opif.* 7-8 (44:140d-149a).

[26]   *Or. catech.* 5 (45:21d).

[27]   Cf. *Anim. et res.* (66:18f). See Hilt, *Gregor von Nyssa,* 34-35. In *Virg.* 12 (46:369d), our doctor writes, furthermore, that "God did not create death." Cf. *Hom. Cant.* 12 (44:1020c).

In the first life, of which God Himself had been the Demiurge, there was, as is proper, neither old age, nor infancy, nor sufferings arising from numerous illnesses, nor any other bodily misery.[28]

Due to this "bodily impassibility" [ἀπάθεια τοῦ σώματος], humankind appears not to have had need of material food, for the fruits of paradise, mentioned in the biblical account, should be understood in a spiritual sense.[29] In any case, Adam was free from dissolute passions; in other words, he possessed ethical impassibility, which is "related to purity and in which beatitude unquestionably resides."[30]

225 In brief, "before the transgression, the man was similar to the angels."[31] He enjoyed not only "the company of angelic powers"[32] but also intimate dealings with his Creator, indeed the vision of God.

Not yet covered with the skins of mortality,[33] the first man beheld the face of God in all freedom; he was not yet judging the good by taste and sight, but was uniquely enjoying the Lord.[34]

The original condition of our first parents, then, could not have been higher and happier: in them human nature was truly "assimilated to the sovereign dignity,"[35] thus deified, "as far as possible."[36]

What this reservation *as far as possible* implies, the bishop of Nyssa explains more than once with all desirable clarity. "Human beings are a copy [μίμημα][37] of the divine nature,"[38] they partake "of the properties of divinity;" but will never be able to obtain "the identity of nature" [τὴν τῆς φύσεως ἰδιότητα][39] with God. The archetype, the "uncreated," is "unchanging by nature," whereas the image, the "created," "having existence from a change, is subject to alteration and does not remain absolutely in existence."[40]

---

[28] *Anim. et res.* (44:148a). Cf. *Virg.* 12 (44:369b).

[29] Cf. *Or. catech.* 5 (45:24a); *Hom. opif.* 19 (44:196c-d). These two passages are characteristic of the allegorical exegesis of Gregory.

[30] *Or. catech.* 35 (45:92b). Cf. 6 (45:25-29); *Virg.* 12 (46:369ff.).

[31] *Hom. opif.* 17 (44:189b). It goes without saying that, according to Gregory, our first parents were exempt from sexual desires.

[32] *Ps.* 6 (46:508b-c).

[33] Here again the influence of Methodius is evident. Cf. above, 156.

[34] *Virg.* 12 (46:373c). Gregory seems to have supposed that, during their stay in paradise, our first parents were not using their bodies. In that which concerns their "face to face vision of God," see also *Or. catech.* 6 (45:29b-c); *Beat.* 3 (44:1225d-1228a).

[35] *Or. catech.* 6 (45:28b).

[36] *Hom. opif.* 12 (44:161c).

[37] An expression which one encounters, in an analagous sense, already with Philo and with Plotinus. Gregory seems here to be inspired by the latter. See H. Willms, *Philo von Alexandreia*, Part One of Εἰκών. *Eine begriffsgeschichtliche Untersuchung zum Platonismus* (Münster in Westphalia, 1935), 8, 14-24, 56; Arnou, *Le désir de Dieu*, 123.

[38] *Or. catech.* 21 (45:57d). Cf. *Hom. opif.* 16 (44:184c).

[39] *Anim. et res.* (46:41c).

[40] *Hom. opif.* 16 (46:184d), combined with *Or. catech.* 21 (45:57d). For this last text, we follow the edition of Méridier, *Grégoire de Nysse*, 102.

Therefore, giving way to their innate tendency to change, deceived more-   226
over by the jealousy of an angelic power "in charge of maintaining and governing the earthly sphere,"[41] humankind sinned and turned away from God.
Having thus become "their own murderer,"[42] they fell from the deiform state in
which the divine love had created them.

II

"The eating" of the forbidden fruit "has become, for human beings, the
mother of death."[43] Assuredly Adam did not die at once; but he fell into an
earthly and animal state,[44] and his body was shrouded with mortality.[45] Furthermore, this mortality, together with the loss of impassibility and the other
ensuing evils,[46] is no less than a remedy for sin, for death allows God to dissolve
the sensory part of the human being in order to purge it of the evil which had
entered it through sin and restore it through resurrection to its original form.

But if bodily death did not immediately follow Adam's offense, spiritual
death was instantaneous. It consists, in fact, in "the separation of the soul from
the real life,"[47] that is to say, from God.[48] As a result, humankind lost "the   227
deiformity of the soul,"[49] "the grace of the image which was their own by nature
[τῆς οἰκείας αὐτῷ κατὰ φύσιν εἰκόνος τὴν χάριν], in order to be transformed
into the depravity of sin."[50]

By writing that humankind "ceased to be the image of the incorruptible
God,"[51] does our doctor intend to say that they had been deprived of their intelligence and of their liberty, perfections in which he nevertheless saw an initial
divine likeness? One would think that Gregory anticipated this difficulty, for
he takes care to add this explanation: "by falling into the mire of sin," humankind obscured the deiform beauty of the soul, the imitation of the prototype,

---

[41] *Or. catech.* 6 (45:28a-d). The "angelic powers," who cooperate in the organization and government of the universe, remind us of the servants of the Demiurge who are mentioned in Pl. *Tim.* 40-41.

[42] *Or. catech.* 6 (45:29b).

[43] *Hom. opif.* 20 (44:200d).

[44] See J.-B. Aufhauser, *Die Heilslehre des hl. Gregor von Nyssa* (Munich, 1910), 80-82; K. Holl,
Amphilochius von Ikonium (Leipzig, 1904), 202.

[45] *Or. catech.* 8 (45:33b-d). Adopting the exegesis of Saint Methodius, our doctor thus interprets
the text of Genesis according to which "the Lord covered the first human beings with tunics of skin."

[46] *Or. catech.* 8 (45:36c-37c). Cf. *Or. catech.* 5 (24b-d). In the eighth chapter of his *Great Catechism*,
Saint Gregory presents death as a remedy for sin invented after the original fall. In a number of other
places in the same work (e.g. 13 [45a]; 16 [52b]; 33 [84a]) death appears as natural to the human being,
since "birth and death are characteristic of the carnal nature."

[47] *Or. catech.* 8 (45:36b).

[48] *Infant.* (46:173d-176a). Cf. *Apoll.* 54 (45:1256c-d).

[49] *Or. catech.* 6 (45:29c). Cf. *Hom. Cant.* 8 (44:944d-945a): by sinning "humankind put off the
divine form [τὸ θεῖον εἶδος]."

[50] *Virg.* 12 (46:372b). This is one of the texts which show that, for Gregory, the nature of innocent
Adam was the genuine human nature. Same conception with Basil. Cf. below, 190.

[51] *Virg.* 12 (46:372b).

just as iron is darkened by rust."[52] This beauty has not entirely disappeared; it is only obstructed and concealed by the stain of evil or the flesh.

By this restriction, Gregory no doubt intends to maintain in fallen humankind the superior faculties mentioned earlier and to have the darkening of the divine image consist especially in the loss of bodily incorruptibility and of impassibility.

But just as in the gospel parable the woman seeks for the lost coin, we must likewise recover "the image of the King, which is not absolutely lost but hidden under the filth" of sin. This is for us "to restore the divine image to its original splendor."[53]

Does this mean that humankind could save themselves? And does it mean that, consistent with his maxim whereby the good must necessarily triumph over evil, Gregory recognized in human nature, which in its very depths 228 remained good even after Adam's offense, the power to raise itself again by its own means? He was too fundamentally Christian not to proclaim, along with ecclesiastical tradition, the necessity of a Redeemer who could only be God:

> To whom would be fitting the lifting up of the one who had fallen, the returning of the one who had been lost, the directing of the one who had gone astray? To whom, if not to the absolute Master of nature? To that one alone, indeed, who originally had given the life, was it at once both possible and fitting [δυνατὸν ἦν, καὶ πρέπον ἅμα] to restore the lost life as well.[54]

III

Undoubtedly, God could have saved humankind "while remaining in *apatheia*" and without "leaving the heights of His glory" simply by a decree of His will.[55] But He chose the "long way around," which included the incarnation of His Only Begotten, and this was for various reasons, the main one of which is this:

> [God] mingled with our nature in order that, by virtue of its mingling with the divine, our nature might become divine.[56]

> The God who was manifested mingled with the perishable nature, so that by His participation in divinity, humanity might be divinized at the same time [συναποθεωθῇ τὸ ἀνθρώπινον].[57]

On the reality of this deifying mingling, Saint Gregory explains himself in greater detail in his *Against Eunomius*:

---

[52] *Virg.* 12 (46:372b). Cf. *Beat.* 6 (44:1272a-c).

[53] *Virg.* 12 (46:372d, 373a-c).

[54] *Or. catech.* 8 (45:40c). Cf. *C. Eun.* 12 (45:889b); *Apoll.* 51 (45:1245b).

[55] *Or. catech.* 15 (45:48b-c).

[56] *Or. catech.* 25 (45:65d). The suitabilities of the incarnation are explained in chapters 15-25.

[57] *Or. catech.* 37 (45:97b). In place of the reading συναποθεωρηθῇ in Migne's edition, which is manifestly faulty (cf. 35 [45:85d-88a]), we adopt that of συναποθεωθῇ, according to Méridier, *Grégoire de Nysse*, 182.

We are saying that the unbegotten God, who by Himself has created the universe—now one of His works, namely, the human nature, rushing toward evil, had fallen into the corruption of death—by Himself has again raised it to immortal life and this He did by the man in whom He dwelt, by assuming in Himself all of humanity [ὅλον ἀναλάβοντα πρὸς ἑαυτὸν τὸ ἀνθρώπινον]. He has mingled His life-giving power with the mortal and perishable nature, and, by union with it, He has changed our mortality in grace and strength of life. And we are saying that the mystery according to the flesh of the Lord consists in this: the immutable takes residence in the mutable, in order that, by changing for better the inferior element and delivering it from the malice which had been mingled with the mutable nature, He might wipe out the evil in the nature, consuming it in Himself.[58]

229

Assumed by the Logos in the incarnation, the human nature has actually been deified. Moreover, the last text indicates how.

What exactly therefore is the real sense of this passage, which so closely recalls the analogous texts of Saint Athanasius examined above?[59] Opinions are divided. Some see here only "realistic images" chosen to describe "the link placed by the incarnation between the human race and the incarnated Word."[60] Others, on the contrary, consider that according to a realist conception of the generic essence of Platonic origin, Gregory would have actually admitted that the Logos has assumed "the human nature...humanity in its totality [*das ganze Menschliche*]."[61]

The saintly doctor himself supplied the necessary elements to conduct this debate. In fact, in *That There Are Not Three Gods*, in which, responding to the difficulties presented by Ablabius, he endeavors to establish the uniqueness of the divine οὐσία in the trinity of ὑποστάσεις, Gregory clarifies his conception of the generic essence. In substance he writes: "One must confess only one God according to the testimony of the Scripture," and not three Gods, because the οὐσία of the three persons is unique,[62] just as the human essence also is unique; for in different human beings, "such as Peter, James, and John, there is only one humankind."[63] Yet if the Scripture "permits speaking of human beings in the

230

---

[58] *C. Eun.* 51 (45:700c-d). Cf. (708); *Or. catech.* 16 (45:52): in this passage, our divinization is attributed both to the incarnation and to the resurrection; *Hom. Cant.* 2 (44:801a); *Apoll.* 16 (45:1153a-c); *Chr. res.* 1 (46:601b).

[59] See above, 166-168.

[60] Arnou, "Le platonisme des Pères," 2347. Holl, *Amphilochius von Ikonium*, 222-225, while recognizing that the bishop of Nyssa shows an excessive realism when he wants to establish the uniqueness of the divine essence, refuses to admit what this realism has enjoyed in the Gregorian conception of the incarnation. Gregory would visualize humanity as being one, as a result of his own ideas on the divine power and providence.

[61] Harnack, *Dogmengeschichte*, 2:166, following Herrmann, *Gregorii Nysseni sententiae de salute adipiscenda* (Halle, 1875), 16-27 and A. Ritschl, *Die christliche Lehre von der Rechtfertigung und Versöhnung* (2d ed.; Bonn, 1882) 12-14. Among Catholics, the realist interpretation is accepted by Hilt, *Gregor von Nyssa*, 68.

[62] *Tres dii* (45:117-120).

[63] *Tres dii* (45:132b).

plural, it is because, by this figure of language, nobody would suppose a host of humanities [πλῆθος ἀνθρωποτήτων]; nor would they think that a multitude of human natures [πολλὰς ἀνθρωπίνας φύσεις] is indicated because the word *nature* is expressed in the plural."[64] The same doctrine is in *De communibus notionibus.*[65]

In the face of such clear assertions, there is no longer any room for doubt: the bishop of Nyssa conceives of the generic essence in the way of a concrete reality, as a kind of universal nature, the individuals of which would only be hypostases differentiated by their "properties" [ἰδιότητες].[66] Obviously, in this he is wrong to confuse abstract essence and concrete essence, but he is right to affirm that the divine essence is necessarily unique and concrete.[67]

231

Besides, the excessive realism of Gregory of Nyssa is an increasingly recognized historical fact.[68] It also seems quite incontestable that this realism is at the root of his physical theory of deification, which served the saint both in affirming the individuality of the human nature of Christ and in maintaining that, in His incarnation, the Logos assumed *the* human nature, the entire humanity, deifying it through this assumption.

In brief, the physical conception of divinization outlined by Irenaeus and developed by Athanasius reaches its most accomplished expression with Gregory of Nyssa.

IV

Accordingly, of course, Harnack repeats the reproach that he already made against Saint Athanasius, now aiming it at the bishop of Nyssa: conceiving of deification "as a strictly physical process."[69] It is a reproach as much exaggerated in the second case as in the first.

It is true that in notably larger measure than the patriarch of Alexandria, Gregory makes the physical conception the core of his speculations concerning redemption. Assuredly, he does not ignore the traditional doctrine of

---

[64]   *Tres dii* (45:132d).

[65]   Cf. *Comm. not.* (45:184a, 185a-b). In this last place one reads: Τὸ κοινὸν γὰρ τῆς οὐσίας σημαίνει τὸ ἄνθρωπος, καὶ οὐκ ἰδικὸν πρόσωπον, Παύλου φέρε εἰπεῖν, ἢ Βαρνάβα. Above, the author writes: "Peter, Paul, and Barnabas are, as to essence, human being, only one human being [κατὰ τὸ ἄνθρωπος, εἷς ἄνθρωπος], and in this same sense, according to the essence "human being," they cannot be several [καὶ κατὰ τὸ αὐτὸ τοῦτο, κατὰ τὸ ἄνθρωπος, πολλοὶ οὐ δύνανται εἶναι]. We call them several through abuse of language, not in the proper sense [καταχρηστικῶς, καὶ οὐ κυρίως]; but the wise could not prefer some abusive language over the proper expression."

[66]   *Tres dii* (45:120b).

[67]   Cf. Gaston Isaye, "L'unité de l'opération divine dans les écrits trinitaires de saint Grégoire de Nysse," *RSR* 27 (1937): 422-439.

[68]   Cf. Th. de Régnon, *Études de théologie positive sur la sainte Trinité* (4 vols.; Paris, 1892), 1:376-380; Tixeront, *Histoire des dogmes,* 86-87; Cayré, *Précis de patrologie,* 1:425; P. Godet, "Grégoire de Nysse," *DTC* 6:1851; O. Bardenhewer, *Geschichte der altkirchlichen Literatur* (5 vols.; Freiburg im Breisgau, 1912), 3:212.

[69]   Harnack, *Dogmengeschichte,* 2:166.

salvation through the death of Christ, since he makes short allusions to it.[70] But never does he formally connect it to our deification. Nonetheless, just like Athanasius, our doctor subordinates individual divinization, not only to the moral effort of the subject, notably to his free "acceptance of the [evangelical] message"[71] and his renunciation of sin,[72] but also to the receiving of baptism and the Eucharist.

232

Being an imitation of the death and resurrection of the Savior[73] by "the presence of the divine power, [baptism] lets that which has been born in the corruptible nature pass to incorruptibility".[74] In other words, "salvation...is realized by purification in the water. Now whoever has been purified partakes of purity, but the true purity is divinity." Thus the good which results from baptism is related to the divine[75]: the baptized one receives God and this One is in the baptized one. United with Christ by spiritual regeneration, human beings become children of God. "After being stripped of themselves, they put on the divine nature [τὴν θείαν ἐπενδύεται φύσιν]."[76]

However, since they are composed of a soul and of a body,

> those who are on the way to salvation must necessarily unite, through both, with the Guide who leads toward life. The soul, once mingled to this One by faith, finds there the starting point of its salvation. Indeed, the union with life includes the participation in life. The body, on the contrary, participates in the Savior and mingles with Him in another way.[77]

After tasting evil, which like a poison penetrating the whole body has dissolved our nature, "of necessity we had need of that which reunites its separated elements." The remedy which we need

> is precisely that body which proved to be stronger than death and which was for us the beginning of life. Just as a little leaven, according to the word of the apostle, is assimilated into all the dough, so the body made immortal by God, once having entered into ours, transforms it and changes it completely into itself,...into its own nature [πρὸς τὴν ἑαυτοῦ φύσιν].[78]

In order to permit us to partake of His body "raised to the divine dignity," Christ instituted the Eucharist, by means of which He, like a seed, is put into

233

---

[70] Cf. *Or. catech.* 16 (45:52). The death of Christ appears here as a condition or an occasion rather than as a means of our salvation, insofar as it allows the Savior to unite, in a definitive fashion, what it had separated. For the allusions contained in the other writings of Gregory, refer to Rivière, *Rédemption: étude historique,* 156-159. It is to be noted that *De occursu Domini* is subsequent to the bishop of Nyssa. Cf. Bardenhewer, *Geschichte,* 3:208.

[71] *Or. catech.* 31 (45:77b-c). Cf. 30 (45:76c-77b).

[72] *Instit.* (46:292a).

[73] *Instit.* (46:292a).

[74] *Or. catech.* 33 (45:84d). Cf. 34 (86).

[75] *Or. catech.* 36 (45:92d-93a).

[76] *C. Eun.* 3 (45:609). To be combined with *Or. catech.* 45 (45:104b).

[77] *Or. catech.* 37 (45:93a-b).

[78] *Or. catech.* 37 (45:93a-b).

the body of the believers. By this union He makes them partakers of incorruptibility; in other words, He deifies them.[79]

As disputable as it may be, this theory, which assigns to baptism the role of deifying the soul and to the Eucharist that of immortalizing the body,[80] has the advantage of showing to what extent Gregory is preoccupied with making the human flesh benefit from the divinizing operation of the incarnated Word. It also shows that, in practice, the saintly doctor saw deification as the result of both divine action and human effort.

V

Among the divine perfections in which the Christian participates, the bishop of Nyssa—as, moreover, most of the Greek fathers—grants the first place to incorruptibility. In this he seems to see the essential element of our divinization.

However, immortality itself is for him only an effect of our union with God. Just as the decline of humankind was a result of their separation from God, in the same way their recovery is carried out by their return to the Creator. Due to its assumption by the Logos, the human nature is filled with divine strength, healed, and immortalized.

Being united with the Word, the Christian also enters into communion with the other two divine persons, who are inseparable from the Logos.[81] Thus the entire Trinity lives in the righteous one.[82]

234   By the progressive practice of virtue, the Christian's union with God must unceasingly grow in intensity all the way to ecstasy. In its "constant ascension toward God,"[83] the soul finds a help in virginity which, if not indispensable, is at least invaluable. It frees the soul "from all that is foreign to it" and brings it back "to what is proper to it and in accordance with its nature,"[84] so that "the beauty of the soul reappears," and with it, the divine image in its original purity. By contemplating itself, the soul thus purified "beholds unceasingly the immaterial Good."[85]

---

[79] *Or. catech.* 37 (45:93b-97b). Cf. Hilt, *Gregor von Nyssa*, 204-213. The ancient idea that the eucharistic bread is a φάρμακον τῆς ἀθανασίας is thus found incorporated in the Gregorian doctrine of divinization.

[80] Nevertheless, according to *Or. catech.* 33 (45:84d)—quoted on page 185— it is baptism which "lets the corruptible nature," i.e. the human body, "pass to incorruptibility."

[81] *Or. catech.* 2-3 (45:17-20).

[82] *Beat.* 4 (44:1248a). Cf. *Instit.* (46:296c).

[83] *Hom. Cant.* 12 (44:1025d): ἡ ἄπαυστος πρὸς αὐτὸν [θεὸν] πορεία.

[84] *Virg.* 12 (46:372c). Like Plato and especially Plotinus, our doctor conceives of the purification of the soul as a deposing of what is foreign to it and, consequently, as a return of the soul to itself, to its natural state. With Saint Methodius, he sees in virginity the ideal of Christian perfection.

[85] *Virg.* 12 (46:372c). One finds again with Saint Gregory the images, dear to Plotinus, of the soul as a mirror of God which, in order to reflect His image, must be pure, and of the eye of the soul which, in order to see God, must be clear.

Not content with this mediate and analogical knowledge of God,[86] however, and following Moses, whose life symbolizes humankind's ascension toward God,[87] the soul which endeavors to climb "the mountain of *theognosis*"[88] rises to the heights of contemplation,[89] at least for a short while. In this vision of God it makes use of neither its senses nor even its intelligence.[90]

"Risen in spirit by the power of the Spirit, coming out, so to speak, from itself, carried off in blessed ecstasy, [the soul] sees the inconceivable and the incomprehensible Beauty."[91] It "touches the Logos by a kind of incorporeal and spiritual contact."[92] "Clinging to the Lord, it becomes one spirit with Him, according to the word of the apostle."[93] Then, with the spouse of the Song of Solomon, it can say: "I am my beloved's and my beloved is mine."[94] It is an ecstatic union that is a real intoxication of the soul, yet "a divine and sober drunkenness" [θεία καὶ νηφάλιος μέθη].[95]

However, this mystical taking hold of is far from being an understanding of God. Even in ecstasy, "to see" God is "not to see Him": He remains both "in light and in obscurity," because He is seen without being comprehended.[96]

The fact remains that, "having come out from themselves and having been released from the material world," the mystics "return in some way, through impassibility, to paradise"; they rediscover the perfections of the original state and are "assimilated to God" [ὁμοιωθεὶς τῷ θεῷ][97] as far as possible in this world. In other words, they reach the highest degree of deification.

VI

However, inseparable union with God and the gift of actual incorruptibility are "reserved for the time to come."[98] When the number of the souls predetermined by God has been reached, the whole universe will be transformed in an

---

[86] There is controversy on the question of whether the "seeing" of God to which, according to Gregory, the soul can ascend from this life onwards is a mediate or immediate knowledge. See F. Diekamp, *Die Gotteslehre des heiligen Gregor von Nyssa* (Münster in Westphalia, 1896), 90-101; H. Koch, "Das mystische Schauen beim hl. Gregor von Nyssa," *TQ* 80 (1898): 397-420; J. Stiglmayr, "Die Schrift des hl. Gregor von Nyssa 'Über die Unsterblichkeit,'" *ZAM* 2 (1927): 346-347; v. Ivanka, "Vom Platonismus zur Theorie der Mystik," 163-195. It seems to us that the bishop of Nyssa accepts both a mediate knowledge (cf. *Virg.* 12 [46:372c], text cited above; *Beat.* 6 [44:1269c-d, 1272b-c]; see Bayer, *Gregors von Nyssa Gottesbegriff,* 38-44) and a mystical taking hold of.
[87] The influence of Philo is evident here.
[88] *Vit. Mos.* (44:372d).
[89] *Vit. Mos.* (44:373c).
[90] *Vit. Mos.* (44:373d). Cf. (376d-377a).
[91] *Virg.* 10 (46:361b). Cf. (368d).
[92] *Hom. Cant.* 1 (44:780d): Ἔστι δέ τις καὶ ἁφὴ τῆς ψυχῆς, ἡ ἁπτομένη τοῦ λόγου, διά τινος ἀσωμάτου καὶ νοητῆς ἐπαφήσεως ἐνεργουμένη.
[93] *Hom. Cant.* 1 (44:772d). This text refers to Eph 4:4.
[94] *Hom. Cant.* 15 (44:1093c-d).
[95] *Hom. Cant.* 10 (44:989b-992a). Cf. *Ascens.* (46:692b). See above, 77 (Philo), 147 (Origen).
[96] *Vit. Mos.* (44:376c-377c). Cf. *Beat.* 6 (44:1263b-c). See Koch, "Gregor von Nyssa," 406-408.
[97] *Hom. Cant.* 1 (44:772d-773a).
[98] *Or. catech.* 35 (45:88d).

236 instant. The trumpet will burst forth, "the sound of which will awaken, as from sleep, the deceased part of the human race; the part still in life, on the contrary, will be suddenly changed with a view to incorruptibility just as those who have been through resurrection."[99] Besides immortality, human nature will share in "glory, honor, power, and total perfection, in such a way that its life will no longer be subjected to physical conditions but changed into a spiritual and impassible state."[100] Saint Gregory seems even to have accepted that the resurrected body will be asexual, therefore, just as God had originally conceived of it.[101] In brief, the glorious body will be "adorned with divine qualities."[102]

Those who have been purified from this life onwards will enter right away into "the possession of the benefits that are in God,"[103] namely, "eternal life, the kingdom of the heavens, a happiness and joy without end."[104]

But one day, after "a healing...that could not take place without sufferings,"[105] all the reasoning beings, including the demons,[106] will have a share in this supreme and permanent deification of the righteous. This will be "the restoration," the re-establishment "in the blessed state, divine and free from all affliction."[107] Then "God will be all in all,"[108] and from the whole of creation, purified and brought back to Him, will arise "a chorus of thanksgiving."[109]

❧

237 Divinization as the goal of Christian salvation has thus become for Gregory of Nyssa the crux of all his theology, controlling in large part his views on humanity and the redemptive work of the incarnated Logos.

It is the union of human nature with divinity that deifies, a union established by the incarnation and sealed by the resurrection. This union is extended to individuals through baptism and the Eucharist, and is carried by ecstasy to the maximum intensity attainable here below.

In his conception of the deifying ecstasy, our doctor is clearly influenced by the unitive gnosis of his master Origen, but also by the mysticism of Philo and

---

[99] *Hom. opif.* 22 (44:205d-208a).

[100] *Anim. et res.* (46:156a, 157a). Cf. *Or. catech.* 16 (45:52b-c).

[101] *Mort.* (46:533a). Cf. Hilt, *Gregor von Nyssa,* 231-236.

[102] *Anim. et res.* (46:157a).

[103] *Anim. et res.* (46:152a). Cf. (156b-d); *Or. catech.* 35 (45:92b).

[104] *Ordin.* (46:553a).

[105] *Anim. et res.* (46:160b-c). Cf. (92a-b): in the other world, purification is carried out by the fire of shame and remorse (97bff.).

[106] Cf. *Or. catech.* 8, 26, 35.

[107] *Or. catech.* 35 (45:92a-b).

[108] *Anim. et res.* (46:104a). Cf. 1 Cor 15:28.

[109] *Or. catech.* 26 (45:69b).

of Plotinus.[110] Indeed, following the latter, he accepts that the ecstatic union is accomplished not by the νοῦς, as Origen thinks, but outside of or beyond the νοῦς by means of a mysterious contact of a spiritual nature. His Christian faith, however, has protected him from the danger of following Plotinus all the way to conceiving, with him, of the mystical union as an absorption of humankind by God.

Assuredly, such assertions by Gregory—in actual fact, of excessive boldness—seem to lead in this direction. So it is that he speaks of "a mixing of the human soul with the divine" [τῆς ἀνθρωπίνης ψυχῆς ἡ πρὸς τὸ θεῖον ἀνάκρασις][111] in order to characterize the ecstatic union. And though the term ἀνάκρασις "in common usage indicates the mixing of liquids and the reduction of their properties, the one by the other,"[112] language inaccuracies of this kind must be interpreted in the light of the general teaching of the bishop of Nyssa, who is openly opposed to any kind of pantheism.[113]

Consequently, we can hail Gregory of Nyssa as one of the initiators of Christian mysticism. In the evolution that the latter went through from Origen to pseudo-Dionysius, he emerges as the most important stage.   238

With Athanasius and Gregory of Nyssa, the doctrine of divinization reaches its greatest blossoming. In its physical conception, especially, it arrives at its peak with Gregory. It will not be long, though, before a certain subsiding is evident.

---

[110] For the dependence of the bishop of Nyssa on Philo and Plotinus, see esp. Koch, "Gregor von Nyssa."

[111] *Hom. Cant.* 1 (46:772a). Cf. *Anim. et res.* (46:93c), where the author speaks of the soul united with God in heaven: προσφύεταί τε αὐτῷ [sc. θεῷ] καὶ συνανακιρνᾶται.

[112] Godet, "Grégoire de Nysse," 1851.

[113] With the passage, *Or. catech.* 25 (45:65d), quoted by Harnack, *Dogmengeschichte,* 2:168-169, in order to justify the reproach of pantheism that he raises against Gregory, we can contrast *C. Eun.* 4 (45:628d), in which any pantheistic emanatism is positively rejected. Cf. Bayer, *Gregors von Nyssa Gottesbegriff,* 56-65.

CHAPTER THREE

OCCASIONAL ATTESTATIONS: THE SCHOOL OF ALEXANDRIA

239   The other great theologians of the fourth century who represent the school of Alexandria or are related to it are in agreement with Athanasius and Gregory of Nyssa in seeing in divinization the flower of Christian salvation. However, unlike these two, with whom this doctrine opens up into extensive syntheses, the others speak of deification in explicit terms, but only in an occasional way and without utilizing the physical theory.

1. Saint Basil

A man of action more than of speculation and preoccupied above all with the struggle against Arianism, Saint Basil does not hesitate to make the now traditional idea of divinization his own; but in employing the terminology which is particular to this theme, he seems to show a certain reserve. This is perhaps explained by the fact that a non-scriptural vocabulary is involved here.

In his turn, the bishop of Caesarea places the purpose of humankind in their assimilation to God: "To assimilate us to God, as much as is possible with the human nature, is what is intended for us."[1] It is a sublime destiny, but founded in the very essence of humankind. Indeed, insofar as they are the image of God

240   by intelligence and freedom,[2] they bear in themselves the natural desire of what is lovely. "Now what is properly lovely and worthy of love is the good. But God is good. Therefore, by tending toward the good, all beings are seeking for God."[3] Furthermore, the contemplation of God and the intimate union with Him are "the blessed purpose" of humankind.[4]

Such were precisely the benefits which our first parents enjoyed before their sin, namely, "intimacy with God and union with Him through love [ἡ προσεδρεία τοῦ θεοῦ, καὶ ἡ διὰ τῆς ἀγάπης συνάφεια]"[5]:

> There was a time when Adam lived on high, not as to place but by the elevation of his spirit, when newly enlivened, gazing upon heaven, delighted with that which he was beholding, he had been carried away by love for his Benefactor, who had

---

[1] Bas. *Spir.* 1.2 (32:69b).

[2] Cf. *Hom.* 9 (*In Illud: Quod Deus non est auctor malorum*).6 (31:344b); *Hom. Ps.* 48.8 (29:449b-c); *Reg. fus.* 2.3 (31:913b).

[3] *Reg. fus.* 2.1 (31:912a).

[4] *Spir.* 8.18 (32:100c), combined with 16.38 and 19.49 (137c and 157a), where it is said that the blessed life of the angels consists in the vision of the face of the heavenly Father and in familiarity with God. Cf. *Hom. Ps.* 33.7 (29:368-369).

[5] *Hom.* 9.6 (31:344b).

favored him with the enjoyment of an eternal life and had placed him in the delights of a paradise, who had granted to him a principality like that of the angels, and the power of living like the archangels and of hearing the divine voice. In addition to all that, under the protection of God, he was enjoying divine benefits.[6]

Adam did not persevere in this state of divinization: "Soon having more than enough of all his blessings, having grown insolent in his satiety," he was separated from God, "thus giving himself to death."[7] Moreover, his soul "was polluted so that it turned away from what was natural to it."[8]

In order to approach God again, humankind had to be purified from the stain of sin and, "by coming back to the native beauty [πρὸς τὸ ἐκ φύσεως κάλλος ἐπανελθόντα], to render, so to speak, to the royal image its original form through purity."[9]   241

Being incapable of recovering the lost divine likeness by themselves,[10] they have need of a Savior who surpasses their nature, who will be "not a simple man, but a God-Man." In brief, they need the Word, the incarnate Son of God, "who alone is able to offer to God an expiation for us all"[11] and "to deify the human race."[12]

The deifying work, accomplished by Christ, especially by His passion and death,[13] is continued and completed by the Holy Spirit, whose role consists, in general, in perfecting all that the Father carries out through the Son.[14]

The divine Spirit perfects the soul which is made worthy by being purified entirely. He is imparted to it in the measure of its faith and its capacity, while infusing into each soul sufficient grace. By raising it to a very heavenly life, He deifies the soul:

Like the sun when it encounters a clear eye, [the Holy Spirit] will show you in Himself the image of the Invisible One. In the beatifying contemplation of this image, you will see the unutterable beauty of the Archetype. Through Him is the ascension of hearts, the directing of the weak, the completion of the progressing ones. It is He who, by shining in those who have been purified from every blemish, renders them spiritual [πνευματικούς] by communion with Him. And just as bright and translucent bodies, when a ray touches them, become shining in their

---

[6] *Hom.* 9.7 (31:344c).

[7] *Hom.* 9.7 (31:344d-345a).

[8] *Hom.* 9.6 (31:344b): ἐκακώθη δὲ ἡ ψυχὴ, παρατραπεῖσα τοῦ κατὰ φύσιν.

[9] *Spir.* 9.23 (32:109a).

[10] *Hom. Ps.* 48.3 (29:440a).

[11] *Hom. Ps.* 48.4 (29:440b-c).

[12] Text taken from a summary of faith, preserved in Latin only, attributed to Basil and Gregory of Nazianzus (30:834a). One would be able to see an allusion to the physical theory of deification in the following text of Saint Basil: "How would the fruit of the incarnation reach us, unless by its union with divinity, our body had become stronger than the dominion of death?" (*Ep.* 262.1 [32:973b-c]). But it seems doubtful that the union with divinity which renders us immortal is here conceived of as an effect of the incarnation as such.

[13] Cf. Rivière, *Rédemption: étude historique*, 172-174.

[14] *Spir.* 16.38 (32:136-140).

242 turn and emit another brightness, in the same way the souls which bear the Spirit [αἱ πνευματοφόροι ψυχαί], illuminated by the Spirit, not only become spiritual themselves, but also pour forth grace upon others. From that comes the fore-knowledge of future things, the understanding of mysteries, the discovery of that which is hidden, the distribution of gifts, the heavenly life, choruses with the angels, joy without end, perseverance in God, likeness with God, and finally, the height of desirable things, deification [θεὸν γενέσθαι].[15]

Further on in the same treatise *On the Holy Spirit*, our doctor specifies that in the process of our divinization the divine Spirit "plays the role of form." Regarding the traditional expression ἐν Πνεύματι, Basil, in fact, writes:

The more I ponder over this simple and short syllable *in,* the more I discover in it multiple and varied meanings, each of which finds its application in the Holy Spirit. It is said that form [εἶδος] is in matter [ὕλη], power in what receives it, disposition in what is affected by it, and so on. Therefore, insofar as He perfects the reasoning creature,...the Holy Spirit plays the role of form [τὸν τοῦ εἴδους λόγον ἐπέχει]. For whoever no longer lives according to the flesh but is moved by the Spirit of God, whoever is called child of God and is conformed to the image of the Son of God is called spiritual.[16]

In this passage—which Petau did not fail to find[17]—utilizing Aristotelian terminology, Basil clearly says that the divine Spirit lives substantially in us and constitutes, through Himself, the definite cause of our divine adoption, of our deification.

Having become "children of God," the righteous "are worthy of being described as gods."[18] "But if humankind is called god, as is the case in the text 'I have said, You are gods,'[19] that is done by grace....For God alone is God by 243 essence. In saying 'alone,' I am designating the essence of God holy and uncreated."[20] Whereas the Holy Spirit, who "deifies others" [τὸ ἑτέρους θεοποιοῦν], possesses deity by nature, humankind, who are "deified by grace" [ὁ χάριτι θεοποιούμενος], continue to "belong to the nature subject to change which, by negligence, sometimes abandons the good."[21] In contact with the divine Spirit, the soul meanwhile is, so to speak, transformed into God, a little like iron, which placed in the midst of fire, becomes fiery through the most intimate contact with it. Without ceasing to be of iron, it "receives in itself the whole nature of fire and changes into fire as to color and activity."[22]

---

[15] *Spir.* 9.22-23 (32:108c-109c). For the translation of this passage, we have drawn our inspiration from É. Amann, *Le dogme catholique dans les Pères de l'Église* (Paris, 1922), 176-177.

[16] *Spir.* 26. 61 (32:180bc).

[17] Cf. Petau, *Dogmata theologica, De Trin.,* l. 8, c. 5, 14 (ed. Fournials; Paris, 1865-1867), 3:475-476.

[18] *Hom. Ps.* 7.4 (29:237b). Cf. *Eun.* 2.4 (29:580b): "The perfect in virtues are worthy to receive the qualifier *god* [τῆς τοῦ θεοῦ προσηγορίας ἠξίωνται]."

[19] Psa 82:6.

[20] *Ep.* 8.3 (32:249c).

[21] *Eun.* 3.5 (29:665b-c).

[22] *Eun.* 3.2 (29:660b). Employed by Basil in order to illustrate the action of the Holy Spirit in the angels, this comparison is clearly applicable as well to souls deified by the Spirit.

Among the benefits the participation in which divinizes humankind, the bishop of Caesarea seems to have ranked first stability in being. According to him, "those who are not united with God, the true Being, by faith" but give themselves over to the falsehood of idolatry "are called non-existents" by the Scripture. Concerning those, on the contrary, who are united by gnosis with Him who is, it says that they "are" in the strongest sense of this term.[23] This means that they possess an existence like that of God, being assured of eternal life and blessed immortality.[24]

The heavenly bliss will consist in "the contemplation of things which really exist,"[25] in the first place, of "the face of the Father, who is in the heavens."[26] This vision will forever strengthen the chosen ones in good and in bliss.[27] After the resurrection, and transformed "from animal into spiritual,"[28] the body also will have a share in divinization.   244

2. Saint Gregory of Nazianzus

Although basically identical to that of Basil, the conception of divinization reflected in the writings of Saint Gregory of Nazianzus is perhaps a little more elaborate, because far from imitating the reserve of his friend, Gregory displays a genuine fondness for the terminology of *theopoiesis*.

Influenced in larger measure than Basil by the school of Alexandria, and by Origen in particular, the "theologian" among the Cappadocians insists more on the relationship between God, the Νοῦς μέγας,[29] and the human νοῦς. Most certainly, Gregory is not afraid, on occasion, to call the entire human being, that ζῷον λογικόν,[30] that "compound of dust and breath," an "image of the immortal."[31] But making his thought clear, he writes elsewhere that "the flesh is inferior by far to what is according to the image"[32] and that it is in the soul that

---

[23] *Eun.* 2.19 (29:612b-c). Basil makes allusion to the address of the Epistle to the Ephesians, which he read in this form: τοῖς ἀγίοις οὖσιν, καὶ πιστοῖς ἐν Χ.᾿Ι. Not having observed that it is a question here of a circular letter and that, after οὖσιν, the name of the church in which it was read should have been inserted—for example, "to Ephesus," as our current text bears, or "to Laodicaea," as Marcion read (cf. Prat, *La théologie de Saint Paul*, 1:8-9; E. Mangenot, "Éphésiens [Épitre aux]" *DTC* 5:170-179)—our doctor takes the word οὖσιν in the absolute, metaphysical sense.

[24] *Ascet.* 1 (31:872a).

[25] *Ep.* 8.12 (32:265c).

[26] *Spir.* 16.38 (32:137c).

[27] *Spir.* 19.49 (32:157a). In this passage, Basil speaks of angels; but what he says here applies as well to the chosen ones.

[28] *Spir.* 18.69 (32:197a).

[29] Gr. Naz. *Carm.* 5.2 [The first numeral is that of the poem; the second numeral indicates the verse.] (37:424). Cf. *Carm.* 10.651 (727).

[30] *Or.* 32.9 (36:184c).

[31] *Carm.* 8.74-75 (37:452).

[32] *Carm.* 10.33 (37:467).

we bear "the image of the sovereign God,"[33] in this "divine and incorruptible soul," "a breath of God,"[34] "a spirit [πνεῦμα] having emanated from the invisible divinity," indeed "a divine particle."[35]

245   To judge from certain passages, our doctor seems to see in the soul [ψυχή] only "the life-giving nature which bears" life and with which "λόγος and νοῦς have been mingled."[36] This is to such a point that he wonders whether the soul, which "comes to us from above," is wholly "a divine emanation [θεία τις μεταρροή]," or only "the νοῦς, the leader and pilot of the soul,"[37] this νοῦς which is "an inward and unlimited sight."[38] Clearly it is in the νοερὰ ψυχή, that is to say, in the νοῦς, where, if not exclusively at least principally, Gregory places the divine image.[39]

Several expressions employed here by our theologian—who is at the same time a poet—resemble the emanatistic language of the Neoplatonists.[40] However, the general doctrine of the bishop of Nazianzus obviously guards against the temptation to press these poetic images. He expressly teaches, in fact, that outside of the Trinity there could not be divine emanations: "By saying God, I am saying Father and Son and Holy Spirit, the Deity not spreading beyond these three Persons, in order that we do not introduce a throng of gods."[41] In other words, by his bold language he does not at all intend to affirm consubstantiality, but simply a relationship between the divine Νοῦς and the human νοῦς: "The intellectual and perceptible natures are related to divinity only by the νοῦς."[42]

Because of this relationship, the soul tends toward God, "although bound to an inferior element."[43] Further, it has only "a single natural task [ἓν ἔργον αὐτῇ φυσικόν]: to rise on high and to be joined with God, always to have its gaze completely turned toward what is related to it, by the least possible serving of the passions of the body, which goes toward the earth and drags downward."[44]

246   This is the ideal life of innocent Adam, "deified by his propensity toward God [τῇ πρὸς θεὸν νεύσει θεούμενον]."[45] This means that our first ancestor,

---

[33]   *Carm.* 10.111-114 (37:688).

[34]   *Carm.* 8.1-3 (37:446-447). Cf. *Carm.* 1.156 (534); 14.76 (761).

[35]   *Carm.* 8.70-77 (37:452): Humankind bear in themselves θείαν μοῖραν. Cf. *Carm.* 10.135 (37:690); *Carm.* 88.158-163 (37:1441); *Or. de amore pauper.* 7 (35:865c).

[36]   *Carm.* 34.23-24 (37:947).

[37]   *Carm.* 10.59-62 (37:685).

[38]   *Carm.* 34.27 (37:947).

[39]   *Or.* 38.11 (36:321c-d).

[40]   See above, 52, for what is said of the emanation from the universal soul and of particular souls according to Plotinus. He calls the souls "particles" [μοίρας], having come from God. *Enn.* 5.1.1 (ed. Bréhier, 5:15, lines 1-3).

[41]   *Or.* 45.4 (36:628c).

[42]   *Or.* 45.6 (36:629c).

[43]   *Or.* 2.17 (35:425c).

[44]   *Carm.* 10.59-67 (37:685).

[45]   *Or.* 38.11 (36:324a). Cf. *Or.* 45. 7 (36:632b). *Or.* 45.3-9 is a reproduction of *Or.* 38.7-13, with some slight modifications.

being perfectly instructed in the secrets of the visible universe, was moreover an "initiated one of the intelligible world,"[46] indeed even "a brilliant initiated one of God and of divine things [μύστης τε θεοῦ θείων τε φαεινός]."[47]

Is this to say that Gregory attributes to Adam the vision of God, as some have thought?[48] The first of the passages just cited permits us, perhaps, to decide this question.

There the author grants to our newly created first ancestor, among other qualificatives, the following: "seer of the visible creation, initiate of the intelligible creation [ἐπόπτης τῆς ὁρατῆς κτίσεως, μύστης τῆς νοουμένης]." And we recall that in the language of the mysteries, a person is called "initiate" who has been initiated into the "small mysteries," whereas the title of "seer" is reserved for the candidate whose initiation was completed by the "great mysteries."[49] It seems probable, consequently, that our speaker may have made use of this precise terminology, well-known to his listeners, to imply that, if Adam was a "seer" with regard to the visible creation, he had, in contrast, only received a first initiation into the knowledge of God and the intelligible world, and the θεωρία, the contemplation of God, was to pass to him as a reward, only after the test had been undergone victoriously.

This exegesis is confirmed by the fact that Gregory places the original sin in the premature desire of Adam, still too simple and too eager to enjoy the θεωρία, allegorically designated by "the tree of gnosis."[50] The vision of God was not therefore part of the original deification.

By his disobedience the first man fell from his initial perfection, since he 247 "was separated from the tree of life, from paradise, and from God; he was covered with tunics of skin, which perhaps signify the most coarse, mortal, and repudiated flesh."[51]

In order to eradicate sin and to bring humankind back to the original divine likeness, God at first used various means, such as the word, the law, the prophets, and calamities. But, having become increasingly acute, especially following idolatry, the sickness demanded a more powerful remedy.

> This remedy was the very Logos of God. The eternal, the invisible, the incomprehensible, the immaterial, the beginning of beginning, the light of light, the source

---

[46] *Or.* 38.11 (36:324a).

[47] *Carm.* 1.161 (37:535).

[48] Slomkowski, *L'état primitif de l'homme,* 77, translates the last passage cited: "Adam contemplated God and was initiated into the divine things."

[49] See above, 20-21.

[50] *Or.* 38.12 (36:324b-c). To be noted is the allegorical interpretation of "the tree of the knowledge of good and of evil" of Gen 2:9.

[51] *Or.* 38.12 (36:324c). Cf. *Carm.* 8.105-118 (37:454-455). The influence of the exegesis of Origen is visible here. Cf. above, 156, note 38. But seeing that he does not admit the pre-existence of souls, Gregory has the opinion of the master undergo an important modification: the tunics of skin do not signify the flesh, *period*—as Origen thought—but an increased weight of the flesh which our first parents already possessed.

of life and immortality, the imprint of the archetype, the immovable seal [σφραγίς], the perfectly-resembling image, expression and logos of the Father [ὁ τοῦ Πατρὸς ὅρος καὶ λόγος], He moves towards His own image and bears the flesh for the sake of the flesh, mingles with a soul endowed with reason for the sake of my soul, and, purifying the like by the like, becomes human in all things, except sin....I had participated in the image and I have not preserved it. He participates in my flesh in order to save the image and to immortalize the flesh. He establishes a second likeness much more magnificent than the first....The present state is more divine than the preceding one and more sublime for those who are endowed with reason.[52]

At first glance, one might think to hear in this text an echo of the physical theory of divinization. But here the bishop of Nazianzus especially wants to show, contrary to the Apollinarists, that in order to save us, the Logos had to assume the complete human nature, body and soul. "For what has not been assumed has not been healed, that alone which is united with God being saved."[53] The incarnation is a remote cause of the redemption, insofar as it allows the Savior to give in ransom body for body, soul for soul;[54] salvation itself is consequently realized directly by the passion and the death of Christ.[55] Its fruits are applied to the individual by "spiritual regeneration," which the Lord works by His Spirit in the person who is involved in it.[56]

This means that since the ascension, the Holy Spirit is present in the righteous "no longer by His power only [ἐνεργείᾳ], as in the past, but by His essence [οὐσιωδῶς], if it is permitted to speak in this way."[57] He divinizes the believer by so manifesting His perfect divinity:

248

If the Spirit is of the same order as I, how does He deify me, or how is He able to unite me with divinity?[58]

If the Spirit ought not to be worshipped, how does He make me divine [θεοῖ] by baptism?[59]

If the Holy Spirit is not God, how is He first deified Himself and how does He afterwards deify me His equal?[60]

---

[52] *Or.* 38.13 (36:325); repeated in *Or.* 45.9 (633b-636a). Cf. *Carm.* 1.117ff. (37:531ff.).

[53] *Ep.* 101 (37:181): Τὸ γὰρ ἀπρόσληπτον ἀθεράπευτον· ὃ δὲ ἥνωται τῷ θεῷ, τοῦτο καὶ σῴζεται. This soteriological principle recurs often with Gregory.

[54] Cf. for example *Carm.* 10.5-9 (37:465): "When God became human, humanity became god...in order that, restoring that which He had granted by that which He has assumed, He would remove all condemnation and would kill the murderer by the one who has died."

[55] See Rivière, *Rédemption: étude historique*, 174-179. The same idea is often affirmed in the poems, for example: *Carm.* 2.1-2, 75f. (37:401, 407); 6.75-78 (435-436); 9.75-84 (462-465); *Carm.* 1.162ff. (535ff.).

[56] *Or.* 41.14 (36:448b).

[57] *Or.* 41.11 (36:444c).

[58] *Or.* 31 (*theol.* 5). 4; (36:137b): Εἰ τέτακται μετ' ἐμοῦ [τὸ Πνεῦμα], πῶς ἐμὲ ποιεῖ θεόν; ἢ πῶς συνάπτει θεότητι;

[59] *Or.* 31.28 (36:165a). Cf. 31.29 (168a).

[60] *Or.* 37.12 (36:252c): Εἰ μὴ θεὸς τὸ Πνεῦμα τὸ ἅγιον, θεωτήτω πρῶτον, καὶ οὕτω θεούτω με τὸν ὁμότιμον.

However, we receive from this life on only the firstfruits of the full and permanent θέωσις, which in the hereafter will be the prize for a life in accordance with true philosophy:[61]

> To become god, having been made a god, it is true [θεὸς θετὸς μὲν], but filled
> with the supreme light, of which we only taste the firstfruits here below, and even   249
> at that, with smallness: such will be the reward for your sorrows.[62]

More than once, Gregory apologizes for the boldness of his language with expressions such as: "if I dare to speak in this way,"[63] in order to clearly indicate the fact that, even deified, humankind could never cross the barrier which separates them from the Trinity.[64] Far from being an identification, divinization is only an assimilation. By being joined together with the soul as intimately as possible, God imparts to it His own life— "the contemplation of the holy and royal Trinity that is completely mingled with the whole νοῦς"[65]—and by that His own happiness; for "it is in knowledge that beatitude consists" [τὸ γνῶναι μακαριότης].[66]

Deification will finally spread to the resurrected body:

> Just as, by reason of their natural union, the soul participates in the tribulations of
> the body, in the same way it will impart to it also its enjoyments, after having entirely
> absorbed it into itself [ὅλον εἰς ἑαυτὴν ἀναλώσασα] and after having become one
> being with it, namely, spirit and god, the mortal and the fallen having been
> swallowed up by life.[67]

Let us conclude: Basil and Gregory of Nazianzus are unquestionably witnesses of the doctrine of divinization. However they could not be ranked among the representatives of the physical theory.[68] This we would expect to see reappear with the last important leader of the school of Alexandria, since   250 Didymus was one of the direct disciples of Athanasius and was placed by him at the head of the famous school.

---

[61]   Cf. *Or.* 21.2 (35:1084c).

[62]   *Carm.* 10.140-143 (37:690). Cf. *ibid.*, 97-99 (454): In the last day, a human being will set out from here "a god toward God."

[63]   *Or.* 11.5 (35:837c). Cf. *Or.* 14.23 (888a).

[64]   Cf. *Or.* 23.11 (35:1164a-b).

[65]   *Or.* 16.9 (35:945c).

[66]   *Or.* 23.11 (35:1164b).

[67]   *Or.* 7.21 (35:784a).

[68]   The same observation is asserted for several other fathers of the fourth century, as for Eusebius of Caesarea and Saint Cyril of Jerusalem. In *Comm. Ps.* 82.6 (PG 23:988b), Eusebius explains that the God who comes in the midst of the judges is the Son of God who, imitating the generosity [ἀφθονία] of the Father, imparts to all His divinity and calls them all gods and sons of the Most High. Elsewhere he strongly insists on the distinction between the true Son of God and the multitude of those who are called "by the name [ἐπίκλην] sons and gods" (*Eccl. theol.* 1.10, GCS 4: *Eusebius* [ed. E. Klostermann; Leipzig, 1906], 69). Regarding the same verse, Saint Cyril observes, in his turn, that the saints are said to be gods, but that they have not been "begotten" in the same way as the Son of God. This One is Υἱός φυσικὸς, ἄναρχος, whereas the Christians are sons insofar as having been promoted from servitude to the grace of adoption (Cyr. H. *Catech.* 11.4 [PG 33:693-696]; cf. *Procatech.* 6 [344-345]).

3. Didymus the Blind

It is above all as a theologian of the Trinity, or more precisely of the Holy Spirit, that Didymus[69] speaks of divinization. He links it, moreover, as with salvation in general, to the work of Christ, not, however, to His incarnation as such but to His death.[70] In other words, the physical conception of deification is foreign to him and, on this point, he is closer to Basil than to Athanasius.

Concerning the actual divinization of each believer, Didymus prefers to attribute it to the divine Spirit. Following the already traditional method, he uses the deifying action of the Spirit as an argument to affirm His divinity:

> How, according to the heretics, is the One who deifies us [ὁ ἡμᾶς θεοποιοῦν] not God?[71]

> If by baptism, together with God the Father and His Son, the Holy Spirit brings us back to the first image; if, by imparting Himself to us, He brings about our adoption and our divinization [διὰ τῆς μετουσίας αἴτιον ἡμῖν υἱοθεσίας καὶ τοῦ γίνεσθαι θεούς ἐστιν];[72] and if no creature possesses the power to adopt and to deify [θεοποιεῖν]; how is He not true God?[73]

251

In this last passage, Didymus seems to identify the divine adoption with deification, which he presents as a return to the original divine likeness,[74] all of these effects being due to our union with God.

Didymus often harks back to the deifying power of this union. Commenting on Psa 116:11, "Everyone is a liar," he writes:

> They who are still ruled by the human passions are called human beings. The individual, on the contrary, who has already been raised above carnal desires and who, for the sake of the perfection of the νοῦς, has come near to the condition of the angels, when one speaks of human beings, is manifestly distinguished from others. He is indeed truthful who says: "I have said, You are gods." This is especially so, if the same appellation is appropriate for others as well as for David. Now those who, in order to be intimately united with God by virtue, do not die as human beings, having in them the living God, are also "children of the Most High."[75]

---

[69] Although born before the Cappadocians, Didymus survived them and was under their influence. See G. Bardy, *Didyme l'Aveugle* (Paris, 1910), 232. This is why we are placing him after the Cappadocians.

[70] Cf. Jean Leipoldt, *Didymus der Blinde*, TU (new ser.) 14:3 (1905), pp. 78-79, 83; Bardy, *Didyme l'Aveugle,* 138-141.

[71] Didym. *Trin.* 2.25 (39:748d).

[72] Cf. *Exp. Ps.* (39:1481c), where Didymus writes that every saint is a god by participation in the Logos-God.

[73] *Trin.* 3.2 (39:801d-804a). The term *to deify* or its equivalents are again found in *Trin.* 2.14 (716a) 3.16 (868b-c); *Exp. Ps.* (1553d), etc.

[74] Cf. *Trin.* 2.12 (39:680a-b); *Exp. Ps.* (1505c).

[75] *Exp. Ps.* (39:1553d). Cf. (1477d), where the author speaks of those who are "deified according to virtue" [τοῖς κατ' ἀρετὴν θεοποιηθεῖσι].

Regarding the classic text of 2 Pet 1:4, our doctor explains that the participation in the divine nature of which the apostle speaks, is the union of the human being with the Father and the Son, brought about by the faith of baptism.[76]

Thus inaugurated, the deifying union with God must be intensified by the practice of virtue,[77] especially of gnosis, the virtue par excellence,[78] for perfect gnosis "unites and mingles the one who knows with the one who is known"[79] to the point that the soul which possesses it becomes the "spouse" of Christ.[80]

252

Incorruptibility, in which lies the main element of our divinization, is assured to us from this life on due to the inhabitation of the Trinity in our souls,[81] but it will only become effective in the other world. After the dissolution of "this house of the dense body, the soul is transported to the heavenly region, called eternal home, not made by human hands." It will nevertheless regain its body, which will become "heavenly" and "spiritual." Indeed, at the resurrection, "when we will put on immortality, life will not destroy our tent, but absorb it, the quality ensuing from life having become stronger than that which makes us mortals."[82] Thus we will be deified, body and soul.

The fathers who in the fourth century embody the doctrinal movement called the school of Alexandria all bear witness to the existence and vitality in the Greek church of the idea that the Christian is deified. They have in common this as well, that they are interested in this idea less for itself than for the arguments it furnishes them in favor of the divinity of the Logos and of the Holy Spirit. All of them, finally, see union with God, established by baptism and perfected by gnosis, as the indispensable condition of divinization, which they conceive of, above all, as a return to original incorruptibility.

This ideal of deification is also attested, although only in an equivalent way, by the representatives of the school of Antioch.

---

[76] *Trin.* 1.15 (39:304b). Cf. 2.1, 12, 14 (453a, 688a, 716a). In this last passage, the author says of baptism that it "immortalizes us and deifies us" [ἀπαθανατοῖ καὶ ἀποθεοῖ ἡμᾶς].

[77] *Exp. Ps.* (39:1477d), just cited.

[78] *Fr. Pr.* (39:1624a). Cf. Bardy, *Didyme l'Aveugle,* 156-160.

[79] *Fr. Ps.* (39:1624b). The influence of Origen is clearly manifested in this passage as well as in those which refer to gnosis.

[80] *Fr. Pr.* (39:1628b).

[81] On this inhabitation of the Trinity in us, see Th. Schermann, *Die Gottheit des Heiligen Geistes* (Freiburg im Breisgau, 1901), 210-217.

[82] *Fr. 2 Cor.* (39:1704a-d). Cf. *Fr. Judae* (39:1818c).

CHAPTER FOUR

OCCASIONAL ATTESTATIONS: THE SCHOOL OF ANTIOCH

253   The intellectual mysticism and allegorization of the Alexandrians greatly favored the development of the doctrine of divinization, as we have seen; the moralism and literalism of the Antiochenes hardly inclined them to share these views. Nonetheless, the theme of *theopoiesis* is found again with the latter as the essential base underlying the biblical analogies of the divine likeness and filiation.

1. Saint John Chrysostom

A moralist and director of souls more than a theologian and theoretician, Saint John Chrysostom never ceases preaching an ideal of perfection to the believers of Antioch and Constantinople. This ideal is none other than the return to the state of divine likeness in which Adam was created, a return made possible by Christ.

I

Like the Alexandrians, Chrysostom dwells at great length on the biblical expression "made according to the image" in order to claim from it, as well as from the context, some points on the original perfection of our first ancestor. In this it seems, he draws inspiration, by preference, from his master Diodore of Tarsus.[1]

254   According to John, this expression means that God established humankind as masters of everything that exists on the earth; nothing in the world is superior to them, and everything is placed under their dominion.[2] However, it is not a matter of a "dignity of essence" [οὐσίας ἀξία] but of a "similitude of dominion." Indeed, the Scripture does not say "according to the image of the form" but "according to the reason of the dominion"; this is why it adds: "And that they may have dominion..."[3]

Combining 1 Cor 11:7, "A man ought not to have his head veiled, since he is the image and reflection of God; whereas the woman is the reflection of man,"

---

[1]   Judging at least from a fragment of Diodore on Gen 1:26, reproduced in PG 33:1564c-1565a, and from the testimony of Theodoret of Cyrrhus, *Qu. 1 in Gen.* (80:108c-109a).

[2]   Chrys. *Hom. Gen.* 8.3 (53:72). Cf. *Stat.* 7.2 (49:93).

[3]   *Hom. Gen.* 9.2 (53:78). Cf. 10.3 (85). This is an exegesis directed against the anthropomorphites. Of note is the concern to interpret the sacred text by itself.

with Gen 1:26, our orator shows that only the man is in the image, he alone being made to be in control, whereas the woman must be subject to him.[4] But she participates in the dominion of the man[5] as well as in his dignity.[6]

Until their sin, Adam and Eve "lived in paradise like the angels; they did not burn with desires; they were not besieged by other passions, neither were they subject to the necessities of nature. Having been created fully incorruptible and immortal, they had no additional need of the covering of clothing."[7] This is because "the war of passions had not yet broken out"[8] and "the members of the body were in the service of the powers of the soul and subject to its will."[9] Our first parents "did not know they were naked; moreover, they were not naked, for the glory from above covered them more than any garment."[10]

Furthermore, Adam was favored with an "ineffable wisdom and with the charisma of prophecy."[11] But the most precious of the blessings which he received was intimacy with his Creator:

255

> He enjoyed an intimate company with God and took delight in the confidence [παῤῥησία] in Him. And while the angels trembled, while the cherubim and seraphim did not even dare to look Him in the face, he conversed with God as a friend with his friend.[12]

Dominion over the earth, impassibility, immortality, and divine friendship—such are the main elements of the divine likeness with which Adam was originally adorned. And in the divine plan this perfection could only be "the magnificent prelude, the splendid portico, and the beginning which leads to a better life" still.[13]

In what concerns the state of innocence, we see that our doctor hardly moves away from the traditional current. Nevertheless, while standing closer

---

[4] *Hom. Gen.* 8.4 (53:73).

[5] *Hom. Gen.* 10.4 (53:86).

[6] *Hom. Gen.* 16.2 (53:127). Cf 16.4 (130).

[7] *Hom. Gen.* 15.4 (53:123). Cf 16.4 (130); *Stat.* 11.2 (49:121).

[8] *Paenit.* 5.1 (49:307). Cf. *Hom. Gen.* 15.4 (53:124), where it is said that Adam was "like an earthly angel" [ἄγγελος ἐπίγειος]. The same expression frequently recurs, e.g., *Hom. Gen.* 16.1 (126); 16.6 (133).

[9] *Hom. Gen.* 12.5 (53:103).

[10] *Hom. Gen.* 16.5 (53:131).

[11] *Hom. Gen.* 16.5 (53:132). Cf. 14.5 (116-117); 15.3-4 (122-124). "Few Greek fathers have insisted with as much force on the wisdom of Adam as the archbishop of Constantinople." Gaudel, "Péché originel," 351.

[12] *Hom. Gen.* 16.5 (53:132). The term παῤῥησία, which we have encountered often already, expresses the assurance which the conviction of being in grace with God gives. In his study *Saint Jean Chrysostome, maître de perfection chrétienne* (Paris, 1934), Louis Meyer sees here "the most constant sign of an advanced supernatural state" (182, 111-112, 197). The author—whose book is not without merit—constantly attributes to Chrysostom our categories of nature and super-nature. In so doing, does he not expose himself to the criticism which he addresses to a historian for whom Chrysostom would place perfection in the love of God: "This interpretation of the great Greek orator's thought seems to us controlled rather by current theology than by the texts of Chrysostom"?

[13] *Praes. imp.* 1 (63:474). Cf. *Exp. Ps.* 135.1 (55:401).

to the Scripture and being less of an intellectualist, his optimism barely yields to that of the Alexandrians.

Deceived by the misleading hope of reaching the highest dignity, our first parents transgressed the divine precept. Immediately "they were deprived of the glory which surrounded them" and were driven out of paradise; furthermore, they lost the angelic life, the kindness of God, familiarity with Him, παῤῥησία, immortality, and were covered with shame and misery.[14] This was so because "by becoming mortal, the body, of necessity, also received concupiscence, passion, sadness, and all the other weaknesses."[15]

However, although the disobedience of Adam was complete, "God, in His love for human beings and overcoming our offenses by His goodness, did not remove from him every honor; nor did He deprive Adam of all dominion," since He left him power over the animals, which "are necessary and useful" to him.[16] Thus, partially at least, humankind kept the state of image.[17] The divine likeness, on the contrary, disappeared. But it can be recovered. This is precisely the goal of all our activity, the ideal that we must pursue without ever growing weary.[18]

II

How and by what means can this task be realized?

When speaking as a moralist concerned with defending free will and rousing his listeners to personal effort, Saint John exalts human liberty as if, due to reason which guides it, it was almighty in the moral domain.[19]

But, complementing the teaching of the moralist, the exegete strongly brings out the weakness of human nature when left to itself and the necessity of a redemption carried out by God. Thus in his eleventh homily on Saint John, he writes:

---

[14]   *Hom. Gen.* 16 (53:125-134).

[15]   *Hom. Rom.* 13.1 (60:507). To be noted is the connection established here between incorruptibility and impassibility.

[16]   *Hom. Gen.* 9.5 (53:79). A little earlier, in the same homily, John recognizes in the human being, "that amazing animal, reasoning and animated" (7.6 [53:68]), the faculty of subduing even lions (9.2 [53:78]). This shows that he basically sees the dominion over the animals, which constitutes the state of image, as an effect of human reason. But nowhere, unless we are mistaken, does he present the latter item as the element which renders us like God. Is that a manifestation of the anti-intellectualism of the Antiochenes?

[17]   Cf. *Hom. Gen.* 9.4 (53:79). Certain contrary assertions need not be taken literally. Cf. *Hom. Gen.* 23.5 (53:203); *Diab.* 1.2 (49:247). So the exaggeration is apparent when the orator, in this last passage, declares that "whatever they possessed, humankind lost" through sin.

[18]   Cf. *Hom. Gen.* 9.2 (53:78).

[19]   Cf. *Hom. Gen.* 9.2 (53:78). In this passage, John declares that the virtues, which when practiced render us like God, are in conformity with human nature. In *Hom. Gen.* 11.4 (95), he says that "God granted to us a reason which is sufficient and which is capable, if we want to apply ourselves a little in this, of controlling each of the passions which may arise in us." Our doctor has been manifestly influenced by Stoic morality. Cf. Meyer, *Saint Jean Chrysostome*, 108-118; G. Bardy, "Jean Chrysostome," *DTC* 8:678-679.

Indeed, it had really fallen, fallen with an incurable fall, and it needed this power-ful hand and this alone. For there was no other possibility of raising it up, unless He who had made it at the beginning held out His hand to it.[20]

Since the old law with its sacrifices, "which did not remove the stain of the soul, but was still concerned with the body," had been incapable of carrying out this restoration,[21] the divine Logos "took on our flesh, solely out of love, and through pity for us,"[22] in order to die for us, to deliver us from all evils, and cause us to participate in His benefits.[23]

The first of these benefits and the source of all the others is the divine filiation, in which the Christian participates by adoption:

> [The Logos] became Son of Man, while being true Son of God, in order to make children of God out of the children of human beings.[24]

Is this not the counterpart of the word of Athanasius: "The Logos of God became human in order to make us gods"?

The divine adoption is dependent on baptismal regeneration,[25] which unites and assimilates us to the natural Son of God to the point of transforming us into Jesus Christ. Regarding Gal 3:27, "As many of you as were baptized into Christ, you have clothed yourselves with Christ," reinforcing again the realism of his preferred master, John writes: 258

> If Jesus Christ is the Son of God, and if you have put Him on, having the Son in you and being assimilated to Him, you have been raised to one and the same rela-tion, one and the same form....You are all in Christ Jesus; that is to say, you only have one form, one figure, that of Jesus Christ.[26]

This assimilation is also increased through the Eucharistic communion. In a moving passage, the "doctor of the Eucharist" makes Christ Himself say:

> For you I was covered with blows and spittle; I divested Myself of My glory, I left My Father and I came to you, you who abhorred Me, fled from Me, and would not even hear My name. I pursued you, I ran after you, in order to hold you, and I united with you and bound you to Myself. "Eat Me," I said, "and drink Me." Is it not enough that I possess your firstfruits in the heavens?[27] Does that not satisfy the desire? I also descended to earth, not only to mingle Myself with you, but to intertwine Myself with you; I am eaten, I am broken into pieces, in order that the

---

[20] *Hom. Jo.* 11.2 (59:80). Cf. Meyer, *Saint Jean Chrysostome*, 80-82, 118-120, 186-190.

[21] *Hom. Heb.* 15.2 (63:119-120).

[22] *Hom. Heb.* 5.1 (63:47).

[23] Cf. *Comm. Gal.* 4.1 (61:657). That which saves us is the death of Christ whose incarnation is only a condition. Cf. *Hom. Gen.* 3.4 (53:57). See Rivière, *Rédemption: étude historique,* 180-186.

[24] *Hom. Jo.* 11.1 (59:79).

[25] Cf. *Catech. illum.* 1.3 (49:227): The washing of regeneration "does not only clean out the vessel, but recasts it again totally"; *Hom. Col.* 7.3 (62:346); *Hom. Tit.* 5.3 (62:692).

[26] *Comm. Gal.* 3.5 (61:656). Sometimes Chrysostom attributes the union with Christ to faith only; but in his thought faith is inseparable from baptism. Cf. *Hom. Heb.* 6.2 (63:56).

[27] I.e., His resurrected body.

mingling, the blending, the union may be profound. The things which one unites remain—each in itself; I, even I, as if one tissue with you [συνυφαίνομαί σοι]. I no longer want anything between the two of us: I desire that the two may be one."[28]

When he explains the necessity of this bodily union, our doctor concurs with Gregory of Nyssa. According to John, the material part of our being, emptied of life and doomed to death due to sin, needs to receive the ferment of a body that is pure and full of life in order to become capable of eternal life. The Eucharist is therefore, above all, a φάρμακον ἀθανασίας, which gives us the heavenly gift of bodily immortality.[29]

259

No less precious, however, are the effects which the communion produces in the superior part of our being.

> [The eucharistic blood] revives the flower of the royal image in us;...it is the salvation of our souls; by it, the soul is purified, beautified, ignited; by it, our νοῦς becomes brighter than fire, our soul more magnificent than gold. This blood has been shed and has opened heaven for us....Let us suppose, as if it were possible, that someone plunges a hand or tongue into molten gold; it would suddenly be gilded. As great, perhaps even greater still are the effects which the present gifts have on the soul.[30]

Due to our union, to our assimilation to Christ, we have become children of God.[31] But it is not a question here of a natural filiation like that of the Logos, who is the result of a generation "according to substance." Ours is due to a generation "according to dignity and grace"; it is the effect of an adoption.[32]

The Old Testament, it is true, already had a kind of divine filiation. But

260

it was a verbal honor; here reality is added. Concerning the first, it is written: "I have said, you are all gods and children of the Most High."[33] Concerning the second, on the contrary: "They have been born of God."[34] How and in what way? By the washing of regeneration and by the renewal of the Holy Spirit. And the former, after having been called children, still had a spirit of servitude, for they were so honored by this name while remaining slaves. We, on the contrary, having become free, have then received this honor, not in name, but in reality....This means that,

---

[28] *Hom. 1 Tim.* 15.4 (62:586). Cf. *Hom. Matt.* 82, 5 (58:744); *Hom. 1 Cor.* 8.4 (61:72-73), etc. See A. Naegele, *Die Eucharistielehre des hl. Johannes Chrysostomus* (Freiburg im Breisgau, 1900), 232-303. It goes without saying that "the ultra-realism" of John—the expression is that of P. Pourrat, *La théologie sacramentaire* (Paris, 1910), 8—calls for correctives. What is broken up in the communion is not Christ, but the eucharistic species.

[29] Cf. *Hom. 1 Cor.* 24 (61:201); *Hom. Eph.* 3.4 (62:28).

[30] *Hom. Jo.* 44.3 (59:261-262). In *Hom. Heb.* 16.2 (63:125), our orator says that the blood of Christ mixes with the very essence of the soul, and "renders it strong and pure and leads it to an ineffable beauty." Elsewhere, *Hom. Eph.* 3.4 (62:28), he does not hesitate to declare that the body of the Lord "is completely dissolved in the soul" [εἰς ἐκείνην [ψυχὴν] ὁλόκληρος ἀναλύεται].

[31] Cf. *Hom. Gal.*, comm. 4.1 (61:65).

[32] *Hom. Jo.* 3.2 and 25.1 (59:39, 154).

[33] Psa 82:6.

[34] John 1:13.

having been begotten again, one could say re-formed [ἀναστοιχειωθέντες], we
have thus been called children.[35]

In this passage, Chrysostom quotes the famous verse six of Psa 82, but in order
to apply it—unlike the other fathers—exclusively to the Jews and not to the
Christians. We might say that he purposely avoids speaking of divinization, in
order to confine himself to the image of filiation, all the riches of which he endeavors, moreover, to bring out.

III

As adopted children of God, endowed with new life and animated by the
Holy Spirit, Christians are able to practice all the virtues. Therefore they must
always make perfect their likeness with God.

In his youth, Saint John seemed to have placed this ideal of higher perfection in an angelic life. By that, he means a life of solitude, of detachment from
the things of this world, and of asceticism; in brief, a virginal existence,[36] as far
as possible independent from the conditions of the bodily life and entirely consecrated to the love and praise of God. This is manifestly the monastic ideal
then popular in Syria.[37]

Later on, after Chrysostom had become a priest and bishop, the ideal of
"angelization," without disappearing totally, is progressively supplanted by
another. The goal to attain always remains the assimilation to God:

> Here is the peak of highest virtue and what helps arrive at the very summit of ben-
> efits: to make ourselves like God as much as is possible for us [τὸ πρὸς θεὸν
> ὁμοιωθῆναι, κατὰ τὸ ἐγχωροῦν ἡμῖν].[38]

But the means of arriving there have changed: it is no longer the escape from
the world but the practice of virtues, notably of love, which is the "root of benefits, the perfect mistress of philosophy."[39] It is, above all,

> what draws closer to God; all the other virtues are inferior to it, being all charac-
> teristic of human beings, such as the battles which we are engaged in with concu-
> piscence, and the war which we sustain against intemperance, avarice, or anger.
> To love, on the contrary, is what we have in common with God.[40]

To love whom? God, without any doubt; but our orator thinks especially of
love for our neighbor. "It is in the imitation of the divine love for human

261

---

[35] *Hom. Jo.* 14.2 (59:93).

[36] Cf. *Hom. Gal.*, comm. 5.6 (61:674). With Gregory of Nyssa, our moralist considers that, without
sin, virginity would have been the normal state of humanity. See A. Moulard, *Saint Jean Chrysostome, le
défenseur du mariage et l'apôtre de la virginité* (Paris, 1923), 65.

[37] On the return to the angelic life, see Meyer, *Saint Jean Chrysostome*, 199-206.

[38] *Exp. Ps.* 134.7 (55:398). Cf. *Hom. Matt.* 52.4 (58:523).

[39] *Hom. Gal.*, comm. 5.6 (61:674). For our author, true philosophy is the practice of Christian
virtue. Cf. Meyer, *Saint Jean Chrysostome*, 186-192.

[40] *Laud. Paul.* 3 (50:483). Cf. *In illud: Domine, non est in via eius* 4 (56:159).

beings," observes Meyer, "that Saint John places Christian perfection."[41] One understands, consequently, why our orator insists so emphatically on "compassionate pity" as "the means of likening ourselves to God,"[42] a pity which expresses itself more in spiritual alms than in the material gift.[43]

However, although the imitation of the divine art of charity[44] may be the most powerful means of our assimilation to God, it could not constitute the essential element of this likeness. Indeed, in "the true life after death,"[45] in heaven after resurrection, the apostolic compassion and charity will no longer exist; immortality, impassibility, and union with God, on the contrary, will become perfect and permanent. Also due to these gifts, the elect will be like this "indestructible and immutable nature," like this "invariable and unshakeable glory," which is God.[46]

262

⚬

In short, although we may not have found any text in his immense work where the patriarch of Constantinople made use of the terminology of divinization, the main elements of this doctrine are found again with him. In spite of numerous points of contact with his predecessors, especially with Basil, Chrysostom clearly distinguishes himself from the Alexandrians and the Cappadocians, as much by his frame of mind as the manner of his exposition. Indeed, he shows himself to be more attached to the concrete language of the Scripture and less open to abstractions of a speculative nature.

This difference between the two schools will become even more noticeable with the most characteristic representative of the school of Antioch.

2. Theodore of Mopsuestia

It is still only in the implicit state that the idea of deification is contained in the vast work of the bishop of Mopsuestia.[47] The one whom, to this day, the Nestorians of Syria consider to be the "Interpreter," i.e., the exegete par excellence,[48] also advocates the traditional ideal of humankind's assimilation to God,

263

---

[41]   Meyer, *Saint Jean Chrysostome*, 210-215.
[42]   *Hom. 2 Tim.* 6.3 (62:633-634): Τοῦτό ἐστιν, ᾧ ἐξισοῦσθαι δυνάμεθα τῷ θεῷ, ἐλεεῖν καὶ οἰκτείρειν.
[43]   *Hom. Gen.* 3.4 (53:37).
[44]   Cf. *Hom. Matt.* 52.4 (58:523).
[45]   *Fr. contin.* (*Consol. mort.* 1.7) (56:299).
[46]   *Hom. Rom.* 3.4 (60:415).
[47]   What remains of the work of Theodore is reproduced in large part in PG 66:124-1020. The commentary on the Epistles of Saint Paul other than those on Romans, Corinthians, and Hebrews, as well as the dogmatic fragments, will be quoted according to H. B. Swete, *Theodori episc. Mopsuesteni in epistolas B. Pauli commentarii* (2 vols.; Cambridge, 1880 and 1882). Since then, M. A. Mingana has published the Syriac translation, accompanied by an English translation, of Theodore's commentaries on: a) the Nicene Creed (in the *Woodbrooke Studies* collection, vol. 5 [Cambridge, 1933]); b) the Lord's Prayer; as well as c) the catecheses on baptism and the Eucharist (*ibid.*, vol. 6 [Cambridge, 1933]). We will cite Mingana, vol. 5 or vol. 6.
[48]   Cf. Bardenhewer, *Geschichte*, 3:313.

through the immortality which Christ has put within our reach. But on the economy of salvation, and on the role of humankind in the universe and that of the two Adams, Theodore has some personal views which were not without influence on his conception of the divine likeness and filiation.

I

All the fathers we have studied so far conceive of divinization according to a divine plan of salvation in three stages. Indeed, they distinguish an original stage, a present stage, and a future stage for humanity. With all of them one encounters, furthermore, the fundamental idea whereby the early stage, which is considered as ideal, has been restored by the redemptive work of Christ. We have just seen that this is clearly the perspective of Saint John Chrysostom.

His friend Theodore, on the contrary, has a very different conception of the economy of salvation. For him, the history of humanity only includes two large phases or, as he says, two "catastases."[49]

> There is only one God in the Old as well as in the New Testament, the Lord and Creator of all things, who, with a view to a unique goal, has arranged the other [catastasis] as well as this one. Having from the very beginning determined to realize the future catastasis—the beginning of which He manifested in the economy according to the Lord Christ[50]—He deemed it nevertheless necessary to put us initially in this one, the present one, I say, in order then to transfer us later to the other by the resurrection from the dead, in order that, by comparison, we may better grasp the greatness of the promised benefits.[51]

Modifying the idea of humankind as a microcosm, our doctor presents the human being as the link and center of the universe.   264

> Wanting to make one cosmos of the universe and to epitomize in one being the whole creation, which is composed of such diverse natures: mortals and immortals, reasoning and deprived of reason, visible and invisible, God constituted humankind as the link of all things. This is why He has brought everything back for their use, in order that the entire creation might be united in them and they might be for it a manifest guarantee of friendship.[52]

It is by that, precisely, that humankind are the image of God:

> The Demiurge of creation made the entire world, adorning it with various works. But, last of all, He introduces to it humankind as His own image, in

---

[49] Καταστάσεις, i.e., states or conditions.

[50] By "economy" Theodore means virtually the entire life of Christ, from birth to passion. Cf. Mingana 5:6:3, 67.

[51] Thdr. Mops. *Fr. Jo.* (66:517c).

[52] According to Thdt. *Qu. 1 in Gen.* (80:109a). The same conception is expressed by Theodore: *Comm. Rom.* 8.9 (80:824c); *Comm. Eph.* 1.10 (S 1:128-129).

order that the entire creation might appear as if constrained to the service of humankind.[53]

If Theodoret is to be believed, our exegete would have rejected as ridiculous the opinion that humankind would be the image of God on account of their power of dominion or intelligence, since these advantages are common to them and many other beings, such as the invisible powers, good or evil. What is certain for Theodore is the fact that humankind are the image of God because they are like the center of the universe to which all the other creatures relate, so that, while being part of the world, they hold there, so to speak, the place of God.[54]

265 However, our first parents were called to a still higher destiny. Indeed, God promised to endow them, after a victoriously sustained test, with stability in the good and incorruptibility. With this aim, He gave them a precept, imposing it upon pain of death.

In actual fact, the promise and threat were only educational processes which God used, on the one hand, to prevent the reproach "of not having granted immortality from the beginning," and, on the other, to provide humankind with the opportunity of experiencing their weakness and the usefulness of their mortality. God knew indeed that the first human beings would not observe His precept. Furthermore, He foresaw that, having been endowed with immortality, "they would have even more easily thought to become gods [εἶναι θεοί] through disobedience" and "to receive the divine dignity [τὸ τῆς θεότητος ἀξίωμα]." He also foresaw that "the firm possession of immortality would have engendered in them a boldness and persistence in sin." For all these reasons, "it was in their interest that, once the body has been dissolved by death, sin might be dissolved at the same time." In anticipation of this, the Creator "prepared humankind for mortal life," the result of which was a differentiation of sexes.[55]

But the subjection to death entails for humankind the submission to change, changeability, which made a fall of Adam possible.[56] This was not a long time in happening. Deceived by the devil,[57] our first parents, "quite recently called to life," being as innocent as they were inexperienced,[58] transgressed the divine

[53] Thdt. *Qu. 1 Gen.* (80:109a-b). Cf. Mingana 6:2:21: "Our Lord God made man from dust in His image and honored him with many other things. He especially honored him by calling him His image, from which man alone became worthy to be called God and Son of God." One could not say with certainty whether, in this text, Theodore alludes to Psa 82:6 or to Christ.

[54] Thdt. *Qu. 1 Gen.* (80:112-113a). Cf. J. A. Dorner, *Theodori Mopsuesteni doctrina de Imagine Dei* (Königsberg, 1844), 11; Henri Kihn, *Theodor von Mopsuestia und Junilius Africanus als Exegeten* (Freiburg im Breisgau, 1880), 171-172.

[55] *Fr. Gen.* 3 (66:640c-641a). Cf. *Comm. Gal.* 2.15-16 (S 1:25-32).

[56] Cf. *Comm. Gal.* 2.15-16 (S 1:26); *Comm. Eph.* 1.10 (S 1:126); *Comm. Rom.* 7.14 (66:813b): "Due to their mortality, human beings have a very strong penchant for sin."

[57] Mingana 5:5:56.

[58] Cf. *Fr. Gen.* 3.7 (66:640a-b). For the Interpreter, the state of innocence only seems to have lasted a few hours. Cf. *Fr. mir.* (*Fr. dogm.*) (66:1006, 1011). See Dorner, *Theodori Mopsuesteni doctrina*, 21.

commandment. Following this sin, and while remaining a simple inevitability for the human nature, death took on a penal character.[59]

Other harmful consequences were added to it. The harmony of the cosmos was broken: 266

> When, after his transgression, humankind became mortal due to disobedience, the soul was, of course, separated from the body and the link with nature constituted by humankind was snapped.[60]

The spiritual natures turned away from sinful humankind,[61] who plunged still more into evil.[62] Thus we "became mortals through sin"[63] and sinners through mortality, which entails mutability.[64]

In short, for the Interpreter, Adam's history is the typical example of the lot common to all mortals. The apostle, he says in specific terms, "makes use of it to describe our common nature."[65] Just as with Adam, the law is given to his descendants for them to learn to distinguish good from evil and to know both their strength and their weaknesses. From this perspective, the original experience appears as a simple episode in the history of humanity; the original state is to be seen within the present condition of humanity, where sin and death hold sway.

Having ceased being the link of the world and holding the place of God there, sinful humankind lost the state of image: "We had lost the honor of this 267 image through our carelessness"[66]; in exchange, we have "accepted and completed the image of the devil."[67]

II

Left to themselves, humankind could not have recovered from their misery nor regained the state of divine image, still less reached immortality. Assuredly, God had given them the law. This made known to them what they should love and what they should hate, but it could not deliver them from sin. Its role was to prepare humanity for the coming of the Savior.[68]

---

[59] See Kihn, *Theodor und Junilius,* 173-177.

[60] *Comm. Rom.* 8.19 (66:825b). Cf. *Comm. Eph.* 1.10 (S 1:129-131); *Comm. Col.* 1.16 (S 1:267-269; Mingana 6:1:21).

[61] *Comm. Rom.* 8.19 (66:825b).

[62] *Comm. Rom.* 7.14, 17-18 (66:813b-c). Cf. *Comm. Eph.* 2.10 (S 1:147).

[63] *Comm. Col.* 1.16 (S 1:268). Cf. *Comm. Rom.* 5.13 (66:797a). For our exegete, death is the penalty for personal sins. See Gaudel, "Péché originel," 12:356; Tixeront, *Histoire des dogmes,* 2:209-210; Kihn, *Theodor und Junilius,* 176-178.

[64] Cf. Mingana, 5:5:56: "Sin entered the world through man, and death entered through sin....If sin were not abolished, we would have by necessity remained in mortality, and we would have sinned in our mutability; and when we sin, we are under punishment, and consequently the power of death will by necessity remain." Cf. *ibid.,* 6:2:21.

[65] *Comm. Rom.* 7.7-8 (66:809b-812b): ὑποδείγματι κέχρηται [ὁ Ἀπόστολος] τοῖς περὶ τὸν Ἀδάμ....Τοῖς τοῦ Ἀδὰμ εἰς ἀπόδειξιν κέχρηται τῶν κοινῶν.

[66] Mingana 6:2:30.

[67] Mingana 6:2:21.

[68] Cf. *Comm. Rom.* 7.14; 5.13; 10.14-15 (66:813b, 776b-797b, 845c-847d); *Comm. Gal.* 2.15; 3.23-24 (S 1:28-29, 51-55).

Only through Christ has salvation come to us:

> In Christ God "restored," or better, "recapitulated" all things, those which are in
> the heavens as much as those which are on the earth, making through Him a kind
> of renewal and universal restoration of all creation. By making His body incor-
> ruptible and impassible by resurrection and by uniting it to the incorruptible be-
> ing of His soul in such a way that it may no longer be parted as corruptible, He
> manifestly made a gift of a bond of friendship to all creation.[69]

This is by virtue of God the Word who dwells in Christ[70] as in a temple[71] and
makes Him both the type and agent of our immortalization.

Being assumed by the Logos from the time of His miraculous conception,
and having remained innocent due to this merely moral but indissoluble
union,[72] the human being Jesus is the visible image of the invisible divinity.[73]

268 He possesses the adoptive filiation in a unique fashion, in a way that, with good
reason, He is called God. "At baptism, He received the indwelling of the Spirit,"
in the strength of which He accomplished all that was necessary for our salvation.[74] Constantly being in His position as a human being, "the Lord ultimately
suffered death as the debt of nature,"[75] but with a view to our redemption.
Seeing that Christ was without sin, Satan had "inflicted an unrighteous death
on Him by the hands of the Jews." He was, moreover, forced to let go of his
prey. The Savior "rose from the dead by the power of the Holy Spirit and became worthy of a new life in which the wishes of the soul are immutable, and
He made the body immortal and incorruptible."[76] With the resurrection, the
present condition came to an end for the human being Jesus. His permanent
union with the Logos brought about for his body incorruptibility and
impassibility, for His soul strengthening in the good, and for his entire nature
ascension to heaven and the sitting at the right hand of the Father. In other
words, the transfer into the future condition.[77]

---

[69] *Comm. Eph.* 1.10 (S 1:130). Cf. *Comm. Col.* 1.16 (S 1:268-271).

[70] *Comm. Eph.* 1.10 (S 1:130).

[71] Cf. Mingana 5:6:66.

[72] See especially *Fr. inc.* 7 (S 2:293-298; Mingana 5:8:87-90). On the christology of Theodore, see
É. Amann, "La doctrine christologique de Théodore de Mopsueste," *RevScRel* 14 (1934): 161-190;
Tixeront, *Histoire des dogmes*, 3 (8th ed.): 14-22; Kihn, *Theodor und Junilius*, 182-197.

[73] Cf. *Comm. Col.* 1.15 (S 1:261-263). Our exegete formally rejects the traditional idea whereby the
Logos as such has right of image in relation to the Father. For Him, it is the human being Jesus who is
the image. On this point, Theodore is of the same opinion as Marcellus of Ancyra. See Euseb. *Marc.* 2.3;
(PG 24:805).

[74] *Comm. 1 Tim.* 3.16 (S 2:136-137). Cf. Mingana 6:4:66-67.

[75] *Fr. dogm.* (66:1010a). Cf. *Comm. Phil.* 2.8 (S 1:221): "Sustinebat enim mortem et nolens,
secundum dudum positum terminum naturae" [He indeed suffered death even unwillingly, in accordance with the formerly ordained boundary of nature]; Mingana 5:5:53, 61; 5:6:66; 6:2:19, and *passim*.

[76] Mingana 5:5:61. Cf. 5:5:68-69. More than once, Theodore alludes to a debate which would have
taken place at the tribunal of God between Jesus, having been put to death, and Satan. Cf. *ibid.* 6:2:22,
29-30; 5:5:60.

[77] On the ascension of the Lord, see Mingana 5:7:76-78. Cf. 6:2:19, where it is said that nothing
mortal enters into heaven.

Therefore, according to Theodore, the union of the Word with the human being Jesus had a continuous intensification, notably at the baptism, at the resurrection, and at the ascension of the Lord. These strengthenings resulted in a radical transformation of the *Assumptus Homo*, a transformation which is a genuine "progressive divinization,"[78] although this expression is not found under the pen of our author.

But he does not cease to proclaim that "the events which took place around Christ were the beginnings of our salvation"; in other words, what happened to the Savior re-occurs for each of His believers.[79] "By His union with our nature," the Son of God has become for us "an earnest of our own participation" in His glory.[80] The human being Jesus, for his part, due to His "close union with the Divine Nature," has become "instrumental for conferring immortality on others."[81] This means that, "with the crucified Christ, all our nature, which is subject to death, has been crucified, so to speak, and all of it is resurrected with Him."[82] The power of the Lord's resurrection "made for us" is such "that we all obtain a similar resurrection,"[83] followed by an ascension.[84]

269

III

However, the likeness of nature with the glorified Jesus is not sufficient to assure us of those blessings "that transcend human nature."[85] As much as possible, we must conform our life to His, which "became our model."[86]

This assimilation is carried out especially through baptism, the "spiritual rebirth" which in an "unutterable way" unites with Christ those who believe in Him and turn away from evil.[87] Indeed, "we die with Him in baptism, and we rise symbolically with Him, and we endeavor to live according to His law in the hope of future good things, which we expect to share with Him at the resurrection."[88]

270

---

[78] The expression is from Kihn, *Theodor und Junilius,* 181.

[79] *Comm. 1 Tim.* 3.16 (S 2:137).

[80] Mingana 6:2:20.

[81] Mingana 6:5:75.

[82] *Comm. Rom.* 6.6 (66:801b). Cf. *Comm. Col.* 2.14 (S 1:289).

[83] *Comm. Phil.* 3.10 (S 1:237).

[84] Mingana 6:2:19-20.

[85] Mingana 5:6:67.

[86] Mingana 5:6:69. In what concerns the present condition, it is well established for Theodore that *gratia data naturam non immutat* [The grace that has been given does not change the nature]. Cf. Kihn, *Theodor und Junilius,* 184.

[87] *Comm. Eph.* 5.32 (S 1:187, combined with Mingana 6:3:35-48). Cf. *Comm. Rom.* 6.17 (66:804c-d); *Comm. 1 Tim.* 3.2 (S 2:107-108). According to this last text, the efficacy of baptism would depend on the faith of the subject.

[88] Mingana 5:6:70. The Interpreter willingly pauses on the baptismal mysticism of Saint Paul. See in particular his catechetics on baptism, Mingana 6:2-4:16-70, as well as *Comm. Rom.* 6.17 (66:804c-d); *Comm. Gal.* 2.15-16 (S 1:30): Baptisma formam habet mortis et resurrectionis Christi [Baptism has the form of the death and resurrection of Christ].

From this life on, we recover the honor of being the image of the Creator, imparted by the grace of God in baptism.[89] Furthermore, we receive the Holy Spirit,[90] who is called the "Spirit of life" because He "is the agent of immortal life" in us.[91] This very Spirit makes us children of God and urges us to give God the name of Father;[92] we are not, of course, children by nature as the Only Begotten, but children "by grace," following in the footsteps of the man Jesus.[93] Basically, adoption is nothing other than the gift of immortality, since to be a child of God for Saint Paul is equivalent to being immortal.[94]

By applying to the baptized verse six of Psa 82, "I say, 'You are gods, and all children of the Most High,'" and identifying, with the holy author, the expressions *to be gods* and *to be children of God*,[95] Theodore shows that the adoption conferred by Christ and the Holy Spirit is infinitely superior to that of the Old Testament, precisely because the Jews remained mortal, whereas the Christians "will be transformed into an immortal and incorruptible nature."[96] However, even in this passage where we would most expect it, our exegete does not speak of divinization.

While expecting that the promised incorruptibility be actually granted to us, "we occupy an intermediate position between the present life and the future life," seeing that we remain mortal, subject to changeability and exposed to sin.[97] This means that our divine filiation is still imperfect.[98] Nonetheless, although the tendency toward sin persists, we can form our life after the fashion of our future existence.[99] And all the more so since, in the eucharistic gifts, we possess, along with a bodily remedy of immortality, a spiritual nourishment adapted to the new life we received in baptism.[100]

For the righteous, death will be only a "long sleep" which will last until the resurrection.[101] Then "that birth by grace" will take place "in which we are all born in resurrection to the future life," namely, to immortality in our bodies and immutability in our souls, to perfect righteousness, even to impeccabil-

271

---

[89]   Cf. Mingana 6:2:30.

[90]   *Comm. 1 Tim.* 3.6 (S 2:112).

[91]   *Comm. Rom.* 8.2 (66:817c).

[92]   *Comm. Rom.* 8.15 (66:821d). Cf. (824b).

[93]   Mingana 5:5:51. Cf. *Fr. inc.* 12 (66:985).

[94]   *Comm. Rom.* 8.19 (66:825c-d): τὴν υἱοθεσίαν τὴν ἀθανασίαν καλῶν, ἐπειδὴ υἱῶν εἶναι νομίζει θεοῦ τὸ ἀθανάτους εἶναι. Cf. *Comm. Gal.* 3.26 (S 1:55-56).

[95]   *Comm. Rom.* 8.19 (66:825c-d).

[96]   Mingana 6:4:66. Cf. Mingana 6:2:21.

[97]   *Comm. Gal.* 2.15-16 (S 1:30-31).

[98]   *Comm. Rom.* 8.15 (66:826a).

[99]   *Comm. Tit.* 2.13-14 (S 2:250). Cf. *Comm. Rom.* 6.12-15 (66:802c-804b).

[100]   Cf. Mingana 6:5 ("Catechesis on the Eucharist and the liturgy"): 71-96. One finds here the conception, already often encountered, that the body of Christ, rendered immortal by the power of the life-giving Spirit, has become able "to confer also immortality on others."

[101]   Mingana 6:4:51.

ity.[102] In other words, our adoption and transfer into the reign of Christ will become perfect.[103]

Being inseparably united with the glorious Christ and, in Him, with God Himself, and being equally united in God with our fellow human beings and with all creation,[104] "we shall truly enjoy perfect freedom and happiness."[105] Thus, "the bond of the universe" will be re-established and rendered forever indissoluble—the harmony [φιλία] of creation, then, will remain indestructible.[106]

On the whole, the theme of deification under the guise of the divine filiation 272 occupies a considerable place in the writings of the bishop of Mopsuestia. But in its outworking according to personal views, which on some fundamental points depart from traditional conceptions, this theme appears completely distorted.

Whereas all the earlier fathers present the divinization of the Christian as a restoration of the original state, our author sees in it the inauguration of an entirely new condition. This is because his literalism and his naturalism did not allow him to see in the Genesis account the raising up of our first parents to a perfection superior to nature, nor, consequently, to measure the entire depth, the whole significance, of their fall.

Concerning the agent of our deification, the gap is no less great. Assuredly, with tradition, Theodore links the blessing of immortality to Christ. But because the two natures of Christ in his eyes are also two persons,[107] he sup-

---

[102] *Comm. Gal.* 4.24 (S 1:77-79). Cf. *Comm. Gal.* 2.15-16 (S 1:28-31); *Comm. Rom.* 9.32-33 (66:844c-d; Mingana 6:5:71-72).

[103] *Comm. Rom.* 8.19 (66:825d). Cf. *Comm. Col.* 1.13 (S 1:259-260; Mingana 5:7:76-78; 6:4:69). The resurrection is called by our author a "second birth," baptism being the first. Furthermore, Theodore also singles out a two-fold natural birth: the first, "of the man in the form of the human seed"; the other, of the woman.

[104] *Comm. Eph.* 1.13-14, 22-23 (S 1:134, 140-142). In this last passage, it is especially the mystical Body of Christ that is mentioned. Cf. *Comm. Col.* 3.14 (S 1:303).

[105] Mingana 5:7:78.

[106] *Comm. Rom.* 8.19 (66:825c). Cf. *Comm. Eph.* 1.10 (S 1:128-131); *Comm. Col.* 1.16 (S 1:267-269).

[107] Theodore was unable to conceive of a complete human nature which was not at the same time a person. On this point, he seems to have undergone the influence of some Aristotelian notions of nature and of person. Though it is difficult to prove this dependence in a direct way, it is unquestionable that our author is sometimes inspired by Aristotle. Thus, as Harnack has already noted (*Dogmengeschichte* [4th ed.; 1909], 2:349), in his catechesis on the Nicene Creed, he makes use of the Aristotelian category of *secundum quid*. The passage in question, according to Swete 2:323, is: "Omnia enim quaecumque secundum aliquid duo sunt et secundum aliquid unum, non interimunt per unitatem utriusque divisionem." [For all things that, in a certain respect, are a duality and, in a certain respect, are also a unity do not, on account of their unity, do away with the separateness of each.] We encounter this text again in Mingana 5:5:90, lines 4-8.

poses a progressive divinization of the human being Jesus, which would render the latter capable of deifying those who unite with Him.

Thus Theodore has caused the traditional theme of divinization to go through a veritable distortion. However, since this alteration, as well as the errors which are its cause, was not apparent when he was alive, it is not surprising that his views could be taken up again, in large part, by the last great representative of the school of Antioch, Theodoret of Cyrrhus.

3. Theodoret of Cyrrhus

273   Not a very original thinker, yet a great scholar and a remarkable compiler, the bishop of Cyrrhus shows himself to be more respectful of tradition than his master Theodore. Consequently, we will not be surprised to encounter in his writings not only the idea but also the terminology of *theopoiesis*.

Most certainly, on the divine likeness of our first parents, and on the loss and restoration of this similitude, he does not hesitate to make the bold statements of Theodore his own, but he softens the naturalism of the latter by accommodating more traditional elements.

Concerning the state of divine image that the Bible recognizes in the first man, our exegete makes a kind of synthesis of all that has been said before him. In substance, he writes that humankind are an image of God because they sum up creation, which is completely at their service; because, in the example of God, they exercise a power of dominion over earthly things; because they also create, although not without matter, instruments and works; because they reign and judge, etc. In humankind, it is the invisible νοῦς in particular, endowed with intelligence and power, which is in the image of the Creator[108] and which is "deiform."[109]

For Theodoret, being designated image of God is equivalent to being called god: "Thus humankind have been called god as well, since they have been called an image of God" by Saint Paul.[110] "But, whereas the God of the universe
274   possesses the divine nature, not the bare designation, humankind, on the contrary, as the image, have merely the name, being deprived of the thing itself."[111]

Nevertheless, in the same work, our author implies that our first parents were favored with a divine likeness superior to the simple state of image granted to nature. Indeed, he writes that humankind, who were formed from

---

[108] See in particular Thdt. *Qu. 20 in Gen.* (80:104-108) and *Inc.* 15 among the works of Saint Cyril of Alexandria (75:1445b). This piece of writing is certainly of Antiochene inspiration. There are good reasons to attribute it to Theodoret. See Albert Ehrhardt, *Die Cyrill von Alexandrien zugeschriebene Schrift* Περὶ τῆς τοῦ Κυρίου ἐνανθρωπήσεως: *ein Werk Theodorets von Cyrus* (Tübingen, 1888). Cf. Bardenhewer, *Geschichte*, 4 (1924): 47, 226-227.

[109] *Qu. 9 in Ex.* (80:232b). The "reasoning nature" is here called τὸ θεοειδές.

[110] Theodoret quotes 1 Cor 11:7: "For a man ought not to have his head veiled, since he is the image and reflection of God."

[111] *Qu. 20 in Gen.* (80:105d-108a).

earth, have been "raised to a much better nature" and that, not having kept the divine commandment, they were returned "to their previous nature."[112]

Theodoret does not specify in what this elevation consisted. Without doubt, elsewhere he affirms that without sin the first human beings "would not have received death in punishment for their sin and that, not being mortals, they would have been exempt from corruption."[113] But does he mean by this that Adam and Eve were already in possession of immortality or simply—following his master Theodore—that they would have received it had they obeyed? The texts do not permit us to settle this question.

"By wanting to become god, Adam lost the state of God's image;"[114] but the incarnated Logos "has restored His own image destroyed by sin."[115]

In order to describe the salvific work of Christ, the bishop of Cyrrhus borrows from his predecessors, without scruple, some expressions in which the terminology of divinization is found. Thus, he quotes the word from Saint Athanasius that humankind would not have been deified, if the Logos had not become flesh.[116] Concerning 1 Tim 2:5, "For there is one God; there is also one Mediator between God and humankind, Christ Jesus, himself human," Theodoret writes, following Gregory of Nazianzus:

> Indeed He intercedes also as a human being and even now, for my salvation. This is because He is with the body which He assumed in order to make me god (ἕως ἂν ἐμὲ ποιήσῃ θεόν) by the power of His incarnation, although He is no longer seen according to the flesh...[117]

Our exegete, moreover, did not fail to note that in the Scripture God Himself honors human beings, the saints in particular, not only with the title of "children of God" but also with that of "gods,"[118] designations which he considers as synonymous.[119]

Along with Theodore, our author presents the deification of the Christian as similar to that of the human being Jesus;[120] he makes it consist essentially in immortality and impassibility, conditions which are indispensable to the "spiritual life" awaiting the righteous after the resurrection.[121]

---

[112] *Qu. 37 in Gen.* (80:137a).
[113] *Comm. Ps.* 50.7 (80:1244c-1245a).
[114] *Inc.* 34 (75:1477a).
[115] *Inc.* 8 (75:1425c).
[116] Cf. *Eran.* 2 (83:177c-d). It goes without saying that our exegete is no more in favor of the physical theory of deification than Theodore. It should be noted that Theodoret commonly makes use of the term θεοποιεῖν in order to denote the act of idolatry. Thus it is that he writes that the Jews "deified" the golden calf (*Qu. 2 in Gen.* [80:80a]; cf. *ibid.* [80:77 a, 160a]).
[117] *Ibid.* (192c-193a).
[118] Cf. *Ep.* 144 (83:1397c-1401b); *Comm. Ps.* 81 (80:1528b-1529c).
[119] Cf. *Comm. Ps.* 81.6 (80:1529a), where the author attributes these words to Yahweh: "I have thus honored you and have made you participate in my own name and have called you my children."
[120] On the Christology of Theodoret, see Tixeront, *Histoire des dogmes*, 3 (8th ed.): 99-103.
[121] *Ep.* 146 (83:1405c).

This patently results from a passage from *De incarnatione Domini*, in which the bishop of Cyrrhus attributes the following language to our Lord:

> Having been assumed, your nature has obtained resurrection, due to the indwelling of the Deity and His union with it, and, after having put down corruptibility and the passions, it has been destined for incorruptibility and immortality. In the same way, you others will be delivered from the harsh servitude of death and, after having put down corruptibility with the passions, you will put on impassibility.[122]

276   The same doctrine is in the *Eranistes*. After having assumed the human nature, the Creator "kept it pure from all sin and rendered it free from the tyranny of the devil." Seeing that the body of the Lord was unjustly seized by death, God "first resurrected what was held contrary to the law; then He promised release also to those who were subjugated with good reason."[123]

It is unnecessary to make our exposition longer. What precedes sufficiently shows that though in language and some views of secondary importance Theodoret is close to tradition, his conception of divinization does not essentially differ from that of his master.

In short, the fundamental theme of divinization was well known at Antioch, but it went through some variations in accordance with local tendencies. That is why the respective conceptions of the Antiochenes have nothing in common with the theory "which, being inspired by an excessive realism, imagines that the simple physical contact of the Word with the human nature, considered as a whole, would be sufficient to explain its redemption."[124] On the contrary, a deification conceived of as the fruit of the Savior's passion was consistent with their thought.

From this viewpoint, we can place Saint John Chrysostom next to Saint Basil. But the other two, Theodore and Theodoret, fit with difficulty into traditional frameworks: they seem like loners whose views on divinization are irreparably compromised by an erroneous Christology.

All things considered, the doctrinal climate of the school of Antioch was not very favorable to *theopoiesis*. On the contrary, at Alexandria in the same period—the first half of the fifth century—this matter experienced a real renaissance in the theological sphere before blossoming at the end of the fifth century, and probably in the very country of the Antiochenes, into a mysticism of divinization.

---

[122]   *Inc.* 28 (75:1468d).
[123]   *Eran.* 3 (83:245c).
[124]   Amann, "La doctrine christologique de Théodore," 171. The author only speaks of Theodore, but what he says is also valid for the other Antiochenes.

CHAPTER ONE

THE THEOLOGY OF DIVINIZATION:
SAINT CYRIL OF ALEXANDRIA

With Cyril the glory and influence of the school of Alexandria as well as the   277
patriarchal see of that city reach their highest point. Its bishop from 412 to
444, he "remains, along with Origen, the most powerful theologian that the
Greek church possessed, and, along with Saint Athanasius, the doctor whose
authority was the most decisive for the definition of Christian doctrine."[1]

A victorious defender against Nestorius of the dogma of the unity of Christ,
Cyril became particularly famous as a doctor of the incarnation. Moreover, as
all the Alexandrians, he explains "the salvific work of Christ on the basis of the
divine Logos."[2] Conceived of as deification, this work assumes, of course, the
divinity of the Savior, and so each new affirmation of this divinity helps to
advance the idea of divinization.

One can make the same observation about the Holy Spirit, whose divinity
was also defended by our doctor.

Under these conditions, and considering the worship of tradition which
he possesses to an eminent degree,[3] we will not be surprised to find in   278
the voluminous literary heritage of Cyril the elements of a theology of
divinization.

The general scope of his doctrine is more or less the same as that of
Athanasius, from whom our author, moreover, prefers to draw inspiration.[4] In
the vast domain of being, Cyril, in his turn, distinguishes "two natures": the
uncreated nature, "incorruptible and indestructible by essence [ἄφθαρτον καὶ
ἀνώλεθρον οὐσιωδῶς],"[5] and the created nature, "necessarily subject to corruption"[6] and to the return to its origin, which is nothingness.[7]

All creation owes its existence to the Logos. This One preserves as well as
sustains it "by mingling, so to speak, with beings who, according to their own

---

[1] Tixeront, *Histoire des dogmes,* 3:2-3.

[2] Édouard Weigl, *Die Heilslehre des hl. Cyrillus von Alexandrien* (Mainz, 1905), 108.

[3] Cf. Weigl, *Die Heilslehre des hl. Cyrillus,* 5-6.

[4] Cf. Bardenhewer, *Geschichte,* 4:31.

[5] Cyr. *Comm. Jo.* 1.14 (73:160b). Cf. *Dial. Trin.* 7 (75:1081d). One would expect to find next to
ἄφθαρτος the adjective ἀγέννητος. Now, in the same work, dialogue 2 (73:713-785), Cyril explains at
length—following the Cappadocians—that this last term could not be suitable for the divine nature as
such, but for the Father uniquely, of whom "unbegottenness" is a personal property. Cf. *Thes. Trin.* 31
(75:44 ff.).

[6] *Hom. pasch.* 15 (77:744a).

[7] *Comm. Jo.* 1.4 (73:88b). Cf. 14.20 (277a).

nature, do not possess eternal duration; He becomes their life in order that what has become may last and live, every being according to the specific essence of nature, according to the word of the evangelist: The one who has been made, in this one was life."[8] Thus humankind, for the sake of whom the universe was created,[9] have a participation in the Logos, not only in His being, but also in His intelligence.[10] One recognizes here the theory, traditional in the school of Alexandria, of the Logos as Creator and Keeper of the cosmos.

It goes without saying that our doctor not only places the goal of humankind in their participation in the blessed incorruptibility of God, but conceives of its realization according to the tripartite plan sanctioned by tradition.

I

279   Regarding the original state, Cyril reproduces, with some modifications of secondary importance, the optimistic views of his environment.

According to him, "God created all things in *aphtharsia*,"[11] thus humankind as well. However, the latter did not have incorruptibility from his own nature, but "from God, incorruptible and indestructible in essence," who had made him "partaker of His own nature. Indeed He breathed upon his face a breath of life, that is to say, the Spirit of the Son. For He is the life, with the Father, holding all things in existence." This divine breath is therefore not the soul, as some have thought, but the Holy Spirit, whom the Creator has imprinted, "as a seal of His own nature," in the man "who has already arrived at the ownership of his perfect nature, composed of his two elements: the soul...and the body."[12]

In other words, the immortality which our first ancestor enjoyed was not a result of this participation in the Word to which he owed his existence and which he shared, to a higher degree, of course, with the other creatures, but it resulted from a communication of the divine Spirit, added on top of the nature already fully constituted.

Having been established in an incorruptible life, Adam led a holy existence in the paradise of delights: "His νοῦς was entirely and continually in the divine vision [ἐν θεοπτίαις]"; his body was in harmony and calm, without any wrong sensual desire, because "the tumult of out-of-place impulses" was not in him.[13]

---

[8] *Comm. Jo.* 1.3-4 (73:85d-88a). Cf. 1.7 (93a). To be noted, in the quotation from the fourth Gospel, is the punctuation, which is different from ours.

[9] *Glaph. Gen.* 1.2 (69:20a).

[10] *Comm. Jo.* 1.7 (73:93c). Cf. Hubert du Manoir, "Le problème de Dieu chez Cyrille d'Alexandrie," *RSR* 27 (1937): 564-567.

[11] *Comm. Jo.* 1.9 (73:145a).

[12] *Comm. Jo.* 14.20 (74:277a-d). *Glaph. Gen.* 1 (69:20b-c); *Dial. Trin.* 4 (75:908).

[13] *Expl. Rom.* 5.18 (74:789a). Cyril seems to have felt that, by attributing to Adam an absolute perfection, one renders his fall inexplicable. Also, he acknowledges the presence, in innocent Adam, of carnal impulses (*Expl. 1 Cor.* 15.44-45 [74:908d-909c]), but ones entirely governed by the νοῦς (*C. Juln.* 3 [76:637c]).

Due to this marvellous endowment, the first man was "a living being, truly beautiful and very much like God [θεοειδέστατον], the imprint of the supreme glory and the image of the divine power on earth."[14] Adam possessed the characteristic of the divine image in different qualifications:[15] "He is said to be made in the image [ἐν εἰκόνι] of God insofar as he was a reasoning animal, inclined to virtue [φιλάρετον] and in charge of terrestrial things."[16] But it is uniquely in the soul that one must look for the divine likeness of humankind and not in the body, as the anthropomorphites do.[17]

"However, the most glorious part of his similitude with the Creator-God consisted in incorruptibility and indestructibility," which the man had received along with the special gift of the Spirit. Indeed, through Him "he has been formed just like the archetypal beauty and perfected to the image of the Creator, sustained with a view to all kinds of virtues, by the strength of the Spirit, who was indwelling him."[18]

Consequently, Cyril distinguishes a twofold divine likeness in Adam: the one given with his reasoning and free nature; the other, due to the presence of the Holy Spirit in him. The latter is far superior to the former because it makes humankind partake of incorruptibility, which is an essential property of the divine nature.

Basically therefore, Cyril takes up again the distinction of Saint Irenaeus, but with the difference that he vigorously affirms the perfect synonymy of the biblical terms εἰκών and ὁμοίωσις.[19]

Adam, whose nature, not yet completely spiritualized,[20] was changeable, let himself be circumvented by the devil, "the inventor of sin."[21] Due to his disobedience, "he was rejected and fell outside of God and the union with the Son brought about by the Spirit."[22] The loss of the Spirit made him lose whatever he did not possess "from his own content" [οἴκοθεν][23] or "in essence."[24] In other words, he was deprived of incorruptibility[25] and, by that, of his superior divine likeness.[26] Immediately the innate corruptibility of the human nature reappeared with its gloomy procession: powerlessness, wretchedness, the

---

[14] *Glaph. Gen.* 1 (69:20b-c).
[15] *Comm. Jo.* 14.20 (74:277a).
[16] *Ep. Calos.* (76:1069-1072). Cf. *Comm. Jo.* 14.20 (74:277d).
[17] *Ep. Calos.* 3 (76:1081d-1084a). Cf. (1068).
[18] *Comm. Jo.* 14.20 (74:277a-d). Cf. *Fr. Mt.* 24.51 (72:445c).
[19] This synonymy, assumed in the texts cited just now, is formally proven by Cyril in *Ep. Calos.*, 5 (76:1085b-1088c).
[20] *Regin.* 2.43 (76:1396b). Cf. *Ex. Heb.* 7.27 (74:975c). See also 220 n. 13 above.
[21] *Ex. Rom.* 5.12 (74:784b). Cf. *Glaph. Gen.* 1 (69:20d-21a).
[22] *Dial. Trin.* 4 (75:908d).
[23] *Dial. Trin.* 4 (75:1016a). Cf. *Comm. Jo.* 7.39 (72:753c).
[24] Cf. *Regin.*, oration 2.43 (76:1396b), where it is said that the "begotten nature" [φύσις γεννητή] does not possess immutability "in essence" [οὐσιωδῶς].
[25] *Ep. Calos.* 8 (76:1092a-b).
[26] *Ep. Calos.* 10 (76:1096).

tyranny of rebellious instincts, that is to say, concupiscence.[27] However, "no damage was brought upon the nature."[28]

II

Issuing from Adam after he had become corruptible, all his descendants are born mortal like him, namely, deprived of the superior divine likeness, of ἀφθαρσία.[29] If abandoned to themselves, they would have been powerless to recover the lost immortality.

> How could [ἔδει] humankind on the earth, subjugated by death, return to incorruptibility? It was necessary to give to the dying flesh the participation in the life-giving power of God. And the life-giving power of God the Father is the only begotten Logos. Therefore this is the One whom He sent to us as Savior and Liberator, and He became flesh. He did not undergo any modification or change into what He was not; He did not cease being Logos any longer. But born according to the flesh of a woman, He appropriated the body [taken] from her in order to establish Himself in us by an indissoluble union and to render us stronger than death and corruption. He put on our flesh in order to resurrect it from death and to thus open up the way of return to incorruptibility for the flesh which had given itself over to death.[30]

282

For Cyril, redemption is therefore essentially the "restoration of the ancient beauty of nature" [τὸ ἀρχαῖον τῆς φύσεως ἀνακομισάμενοι κάλλος], an elevation "because of Christ to the high position above nature" [εἰς τὸ ὑπὲρ φύσιν ἀξίωμα], namely, the adoptive divine filiation, which merits for us the titles *children of God*, even *god*, according to Psa 82.[31] "This deification," Father Mahé observes, "is a dogma so common and universally accepted that Cyril of Alexandria—as all the fathers of the fourth century moreover—starts there in order to prove the divinity of the Holy Spirit;"[32] and, we can add, that also of the incarnated Logos.[33]

---

[27] *Expl. Rom.* 5.3-12, 18-19 (74:781d-789b). Cf. *Expl. 1 Cor.* 15.42 (74:908b); *C. Juln.* 3 (76:641b-c). See Weigl, *Die Heilslehre des hl. Cyrillus*, 37-39.

[28] *Dial. Trin.* 1 (75:676a).

[29] See also *Expl. Rom.* 5.18 (74:788c-789b), where our author makes it clear that all human beings have been constituted sinners, not because "they transgressed with Adam, for they did not yet exist, but because they are of his nature, which has fallen under the law of sin."

[30] *Fr. Lc.* 5.19 (72:908d-909a). Cf. *Comm. Jo.* 14.5-6 (74:192b); *Dial. Trin.* 5 (75:968c-d). Cyril subordinates the necessity of the incarnation to the fact of sin. See Rivière, *Rédemption: étude historique*, 188.

[31] *Comm. Jo.* 1.12 (73:153b). In this text, the term φύσις refers to, first of all, the nature in the original state, then the fallen nature. Elsewhere Cyril writes: "In order to be called gods, we are not raised above our nature, everything remaining in its own nature" (*Dial. Trin.* 4 [75:888a-889b]; cf. [908c-d], *Comm. Jo.* 1.9 [73:128c]). These texts show that with our author, the word φύσις is ambiguous and that it is far from having the technical sense of nature as opposed to super-nature, which it will receive later.

[32] Joseph Mahé, "La sanctification d'après saint Cyrille d'Alexandrie," *RHE* 10 (1909): 38.

[33] Cf., for example, *Thes. Trin.*, ass. 20 (75:284, 333c): "If the Logos of God is a creature, how are we united with God and deified [θεοποιούμεθα] by union with Him?"

We could expect here a priori that Cyril, who is so attached to the doctrine of the "holy fathers," and to that of Athanasius and the great Cappadocians in particular, would take up again the theme of divinization. Therefore all interest is concentrated on the question of how he conceives of the process of the deification of the Christian.

In many passages of his work, the bishop of Alexandria takes up again, for his account, the physical conception dear to his great predecessor.

283

In his *Commentary on Saint Luke,* we have already heard him state in principle that only a participation in the life-giving power of God, which is the Logos, could give back to humankind the lost incorruptibility.[34] It is in the incarnation that this communication of divine life, which deifies human nature, is carried out.

> Being life by nature [ζωὴ κατὰ φύσιν], [the Logos of God] appropriates a body subject to corruption, in order to destroy the power of mortality [which is found] in it and to transform it with a view to incorruptibility. Just as iron, having been put in intimate contact with fire, immediately takes on the color of the latter, likewise the nature of the flesh, after having received into it the divine Logos, incorruptible and life-giving, no longer remained in the same condition, but became exempt from corruption.[35]

The image of iron having been made fiery by the fire clearly shows that in the thought of our author it is a matter of a deification by contact.

What is thus deified is the human nature entirely:

> In order to deliver from corruption and death the one who had been condemned by the ancient curse, He became humankind, fitting Himself, so to speak, to our nature, being life by nature. Thus, the strength of death and the power of corruption received into us have been overcome; and since the divine nature is absolutely exempt from the propensity for sin, He has kept us by His own flesh. Indeed, we were all in Him, insofar as He appeared as a human being, in order to alter the members which are on the earth, namely, the passions of the flesh.[36]

The generic realism of Athanasius and Gregory of Nyssa which reappears here, is affirmed elsewhere with clarity:

> When the Logos became human, He had all nature in Himself, in order to restore it entirely by re-establishing it in the primitive state.[37]

> Although rich, He became poor, providing us with His own riches, and through the flesh with which He is united, having us all in Himself.[38]

284

---

[34] Above, 222.
[35] *Hom. pasch.* 17 (77:785d-788a). With Basil we have already encountered the comparison of iron and fire, but in a different context. See above, 192.
[36] *Comm. Jo.* 16.6-7 (74:432a-b). Cf. *Dial. Trin.* 1 (75:692 f.); *Inc. unigen.* (75:1212d-1213c).
[37] *Comm. Jo.* 7.39 (73:753c).
[38] *C. Nest.* 1 (76:17a). Cf. *Hom. pasch.* 16.2 (77:733d-736a).

Indeed, all of us were in Christ, and the shared nature of humanity comes alive again in Him.[39]

In brief, Cyril with Athanasius and Gregory of Nyssa form the group of the most brilliant representatives of the physical conception of divinization. Therefore it is not rash to think that it is in this conception especially that the great fighter has drawn on the untiring zeal with which he defended the unity of Christ. Indeed, according to him our Savior had to be both perfect God and complete human: God, in order to divinize,[40] and human, in order that in Him the entire human nature might be deified; for "what has not been assumed has not been saved."[41] In this, once again, the interdependence of soteriology and Christology is manifested.

It is not that Cyril forgets the salutary role of the sacrifice of Christ. Assuredly, no more than his predecessors does he link deification directly to the death of the Savior, since he attributes it formally to the incarnation. Rather, he does it in an equivalent way, by very often presenting this death as the cause of our death's destruction[42] and the source of our new life. Here are some particularly expressive texts:

285   If [Christ] had not died for us, we would not have been saved; the dominion of death would not have been broken.[43]

The Logos became flesh and lived among us exclusively in order to suffer the death of the flesh and by that to triumph over the principalities and powers, and to reduce to nothing that very one who held the power of death, that is, Satan, in order to take away corruption and also to drive out with it the sin which tyrannizes us, to thus render ineffectual the ancient curse which the human nature in Adam was subject to, as in the principle [ἀπαρχῇ] of genus and the prime root.[44]

The death of Christ became like the root of life, the destruction of corruption, the removal of sin, and the end of wrath.[45]

---

[39]   *Comm. Jo.* 1.14 (73:161c): Πάντες γὰρ ἦμεν ἐν Χριστῷ, καὶ τὸ κοινὸν τῆς ἀνθρωπότητος εἰς αὐτὸν ἀναβιοῖ πρόσωπον. We translate πρόσωπον by *nature*. Cf. A. Michel, "Hypostase," *DTC* 7:388-389. On Cyrillian realism, see L. Janssens, "Notre filiation divine d'après saint Cyrille d'Alexandrie," *Ephemerides theologicae lovanienses* 15 (1938): 233-278. The author writes on p. 238: "For Cyril, as for the Greek fathers of the fourth century (Athanasius and the Cappadocians), the substance, the numerical unity of which makes human beings consubstantial among themselves and Christ consubstantial with us as humankind, is the flesh. According to them, consubstantiality, just as its origin, i.e., generation, proves, is the numerical unity, not of the secondary substance but of the concrete substance."

[40]   Cf. *Thes. Trin.*, ass. 15 (75:284b).

[41]   *Comm. Jo.* 12.27 (74:89d). Cf. *Inc. unigen.* (75:1213d).

[42]   They are the negative effects, especially, of the redemption which Cyril links to the death of Christ.

[43]   *Glaph. Ex.* 2.2 (69:437b).

[44]   *Expl. Rom.* 5.3 (74:781d).

[45]   *Fr. Heb.*, 2.14 (74:965b).

Death could not have been destroyed any other way if the Savior had not died; it is the same for each of the affections [παθῶν] of the flesh.[46]

In his ardor to magnify the efficacy of the death of Christ, Cyril goes to the point of affirming that without it "the mystery of the economy according to the flesh," namely, the incarnation, would have been "useless to us."[47]

Faced with such assertions, one wonders whether, by writing them, the patriarch of Alexandria had not completely lost sight of his physical theory.

The fact is that, in order to interpret the deifying work of the Savior, Cyril has recourse sometimes to the incarnation as such and sometimes to the passion, according to the needs or the conveniences of the moment, without however asking himself how these two viewpoints are able to be reconciled.

III

Along with the earlier fathers, our doctor teaches that in order to appropri-   286
ate the deification carried out by the incarnated Word, every individual must
be united with Him by faith,[48] by a sincere conversion of the heart,[49] and, in
particular, by baptism.

This last-mentioned rite is indispensable, for "the perfect and genuine gnosis" of Christ and "the full partaking of Him" are only obtained by "the grace of baptism and the illumination of the Spirit."[50] The Christian initiation makes us images of the archetype who is the natural Son of God and thereby adoptive children of God.[51] His action extends both to the soul and to the body.

> Since human beings are formed and not simple by nature, since they are a min-
> gling of two elements, namely, a sensitive body and a spiritual soul, they needed a
> two-fold treatment as well, which would be, as it were, homogeneous with each
> one of the two parts. Now the spirit of the human being is sanctified by the Spirit;
> the body is sanctified by water, which is itself sanctified. For just as water poured
> into containers and exposed to rays of fire appropriates the power of the latter, in
> the same way the water that is perceived by the senses, raised by the power of the

---

[46] *Comm. Jo.* 12.27 (74:92d). Cf. *Comm. Jo.* 20.19-20 (705d), where the destroying of death is attributed to the resurrection of Christ; *Apol. orient.* 12 (76:381c). On the effects of the death of Christ, see Rivière, *Rédemption: étude historique*, 190-201.

[47] *Expl. 1 Cor.* 15.12 (74:897a).

[48] Cf. *Comm. Jo.* 6.47 (73:560a), where faith is called "the door and the way [which lead] to life, the return from corruption to incorruptibility"; *Comm. Jo.* 6.70 (73:629a); *Fr. Lc.* 5.5 (72:832b). See Weigl, *Die Heilslehre des hl. Cyrillus*, 129-136.

[49] Cf. *Comm. Jo.* 7.11 (73:649c); 15.1 (74:344cd); *Fr. Lc.* 19.2 (72:865c).

[50] *Glaph. Ex.* 2 (69:432a).

[51] *Expl. Rom.* 1.3 (74:776a). On our divine filiation according to Saint Cyril, see Janssens, "Notre filiation divine d'après Cyrille."

Spirit to a divine and unutterable power, in its turn sanctifies those to whom it is applied.[52]

Elsewhere our theologian gives us further details on this two-fold "sanctification":

287

[The baptismal water] purifies us from every stain, so that we become a holy temple of God and communicate with His divine nature through a participation in the Holy Spirit.[53]

To the deifying action of baptism is added that of the eucharistic communion:

The purification which is in the Spirit is brought to its completion [τελεῖται] by the sanctification which the body of our Savior, bearing the energy of the Logos who lives in Him, puts into us.[54]

Whereas in baptism it is the soul in particular which is filled with divine life, communion has the special effect of giving life to the body as well.

The flesh of the Savior became life-giving insofar as it was united with life by nature, namely, with the Logos of God. When we taste it we have life in us, and we also are united with it, just as it is united with the Logos who lives in it. This is why we read that in order to resurrect the dead the Savior has not worked by the word alone or by orders worthy of a God, but He preferred to use His holy flesh for this purpose, as a cooperator, in order to show that it became as it were a single being with Him, the body being, in truth, His own body and not that of another.[55]

After putting forward, by way of example, the resurrection of Jairus's daughter (Mark 5:35-37) and the young man of Nain (Luke 7:13-17), Cyril continues:

---

[52] *Comm. Jo.* 3.5 (73:244d-245a). The idea that through the benediction, the baptismal water is filled with the power of the Holy Spirit is clearly manifested with Saint Basil who writes: "If the baptismal water possesses a certain grace in itself, it does not have it from its own nature but from the presence of the Spirit [ἐκ τῆς τοῦ Πνεύματος παρουσίας]," *Liber de Spiritu sancto* 15 (32:132a). In the formula of benediction of baptismal fonts, which the *Euchologion of Serapion* gives, one asks of God "to fill the waters with the Holy Spirit" (Funk, *Didascalia et constitutiones apostolorum* [2 vols.; Paderborn, 1905], 2:180-182). The ancient sacraments, still in use, contain an analogous formula: Descendat in hanc plenitudinem fontis virtus Spiritus tui [or Sancti] [Let the powers of Your (Holy) Spirit descend into this fullness of baptismal waters]. See L. Duchesne, *Origines du culte chrétien* (5th ed.; Paris, 1920), 330.

[53] *Fr. Lc.* 22.8 (72:9040). Cf. *Glaph. Gen.* 1 (69:29c); *Glaph. Num., Vacc. ruf.* (69:625c). Note that according to Cyril it is baptism which imparts the Spirit. The chrismation, which was part of the Christian initiation, is for him only a symbol of the gift of the Spirit which was already obtained. Cf. *Comm. Is.* 25.6-7 (70:651d). In his commentary on Joel, our author mentions in passing, "the use of the oil which is useful for the perfecting [πρὸς τελείωσιν] of those who have been sanctified in Christ through baptism" (*Comm. Joel*, 2.21-24 [71:373b]). Weigl, *Die Heilslehre des hl. Cyrillus*, 169-171, and Tixeront, *Histoire des dogmes*, 3:229, consider that the point there is the sacrament of confirmation. Nothing could be less certain since this vague allusion does not establish any relationship between the anointing and the conferment of the Spirit.

[54] *Fr. Mt.* 8.15 (72:389c).

[55] *Comm. Jo.* 6.54 (73:577b-580a).

If the corrupt one is given life by simple contact [διὰ μονῆς ἁφῆς] with the sacred 288
flesh, how would we not receive, with more fruit, the life-giving blessing,[56] seeing
that we eat of it? For it will transform by its own good, namely, incorruptibility,
those who have partaken of it. And do not be surprised by this, neither search for
the how of it, in the manner of the Jews ['Ιουδαϊκῶς]. Think rather of the water
which, cold by nature when poured into a cooking-pot and put in contact with
fire, nearly forgets its own nature and goes into the energy of a conqueror [εἰς τὴν
τοῦ νενικηκότος ἐνέργειαν ἀποφοιτᾷ]. In the same way we, though corruptible
because of the nature of the flesh, after having been delivered from our own
weakness by the mingling [τῇ μίξει] with the [true] life, are restored to what is
the distinctive feature of this blessing, namely, life. Indeed, it was necessary not
only that the soul be recreated by the Holy Spirit with a view to the newness of life
but also that this cumbersome and earthly body be sanctified by a more tangible
[παχυτέρας...μεταλήψεως] and homogeneous partaking, and thus be called to incorruptibility.[57]

This passage very much accentuates the deifying virtue that our doctor
attributes to the Eucharist with regard to the flesh of the Christian. Furthermore, it has the advantage of showing that Cyril applies to communion the
principle whereby it is the contact with the Word that deifies. The Logos "elevates, sanctifies, glorifies, and divinizes [θεοποιοῦσα] the [human] nature in
Christ first of all [ἐν πρώτῳ Χριστῷ]."[58] Thus deified, the flesh of Christ then
divinizes the flesh of those who, through the eucharistic communion, unite
themselves with it.[59] The relationship which is established between the Savior 289
and the communicant is comparable to the indwelling of the Logos in the
human nature that He assumed.

However, an essential difference exists between these two forms of union. As
ἔνωσις φυσική, the second ends up—according to the expression preferred by
Cyril, which he held from Apollinarius without knowing it—at the μία φύσις
τοῦ θεοῦ Λόγου σεσαρκωμένη,[60] at the single incarnated nature of the Logos
God. From the eucharistic communion, on the contrary, only a ἔνωσις σκετική
results, a union by relationship, an indwelling which, although also "physical,"
but in another sense,[61] leaves intact the two persons united.[62]

---

[56]   The Eucharist is called ἡ ζωοποιὸς εὐλογία. Further along (73:581c), the expression ἡ μυστικὴ
εὐλογία is found, and this recurs frequently. Cf. *Comm. Jo.* 17.3 (74:488a); *Glaph. Num., Vacc. ruf.*
(69:625c); *Ep. Calos.* (76:1073).

[57]   *Comm. Jo.* 6.54 (73:577b-580a). Cf. (581), where it is said that "by His own flesh, our Lord hides
the life in us and puts in us a kind of seed of incorruptibility, which destroys all the corruption which is
in us." See also *Comm. Jo.* 6.35 (520d-521a).

[58]   *Thes. Trin.* 20 (75:333c).

[59]   See also *Comm. Jo.* 6.64 (73:601c-605a); *Ep.* 27.11 (77:121c-d); Weigl, *Die Heilslehre des hl.
Cyrillus*, 203-220.

[60]   For the references, see J. Mahé, "Cyrille d'Alexandrie," DTC 3:2513. Cf. Tixeront, *Histoire des
dogmes*, 3:60-75; A. Gaudel, "La théologie de l' "Assumptus Homo," *RevScRel* 17 (1937): 64-90.

[61]   Physical union, in contrast with moral union.

[62]   Cf. *C. Thdr. Mops.* 3 (76:408c), where "physical" is set against "non-real and schetic," which once
more shows the imprecision of the Cyrillian language.

The conception which the patriarch of Alexandria has of baptism and the Eucharist as the means of our deification so very much resembles Gregory of Nyssa's that it seems difficult to explain this relationship in any other way than by a direct dependence.

IV

Thus the Christian is divinized, body and soul, by the incarnated Logos and His Spirit. Is this to say that God the Father does not share in the work of our sanctification? Not at all. Sometimes Cyril makes it clear that our salvation is carried out jointly by the three persons of the Trinity.

Thus concerning John 15:1, "I am the true vine, and my Father is the vinegrower," he writes:

> For what reason, then, does He call the vinegrower His Father? It is because the Father is neither idle nor inactive with regard to us, while in the Holy Spirit the Son is nourishing us and keeping us in the good. Our restoring is as the work of the entire holy and consubstantial Trinity, and it is through all the divine nature, and in all that is done by it, that the will and the strength pass. For this reason,...our salvation is truly the work of the unique Deity. And although to each person seemingly is attributed something of what is done in our regard or carried out in the creature, we do not believe less that all is from the Father by the Son in the Spirit [πάντα ἐστὶ παρὰ τοῦ Πατρὸς δι᾽ Υἱοῦ ἐν Πνεύματι]. Therefore you will be fully in the truth in thinking that the Father nourishes us in piety by the Son in the Spirit. In the same way He functions as the vinegrower, that is to say, He observes, watches over, and takes care of our restoration by the Son in the Spirit.[63]

290

Here our doctor expresses with vigor the great principle of trinitarian theology, too often forgotten, according to which every divine action *ad extra* is common to all the Trinity. But innumerable texts require us to admit that Cyril has seen in sanctification, in the divinization of the Christian, a work which concerns the Holy Spirit "to a special degree, which is not suitable for the other two persons."[64] Was he thinking of a characteristic or a simple appropriation? Being unaware of this distinction, our theologian could not make use of it for clarifying his thought.

Father Mahé seems to have understood correctly when he explains this doctrine, which is also that of Basil, by "three reasons, all three based on the Greek conception of the Trinity": the Holy Spirit for the Greeks "is the *bond*, the link which joins our souls to the Son and to the Father"; "the image of the Son" who, "by imprinting Himself in our souls, re-forms them to the image of the Son and, therefore, to the image of the Father"; and finally, "the *sanctifying*

---

[63] *Comm. Jo.* 15.1 (74:333d-336b). Cf. 6.45 (73:556b-d).

[64] Mahé, "La sanctification d'après saint Cyrille d'Alexandrie," 480, 475-479. Cf. Petau, *Dogmata theologica*, 3:445-450, 454, 485.

power of Divinity," in the sense that "holiness is as essential to the Holy Spirit as fatherhood is to the Father and filiation to the Son."[65]

Because the Holy Spirit Himself is the "form" of our divinization—an idea already encountered with Saint Basil—any created intermediary is superflu-   291 ous. This is what Cyril applies himself to establish in some expositions which contain something of a synthesis of his doctrine on individual deification.

In his *Thesaurus*, after recalling that the Holy Spirit sanctifies the heavenly spirits, our theologian continues:

> This same sanctifying power, which proceeds physically from the Father and which perfects the imperfect, we call the Holy Spirit. And it is obviously superflu-ous for the creature to be sanctified by some intermediary, since the philanthropy of God does not disdain stooping down to the smallest of beings and sanctifying them by the Holy Spirit, all being His work... If the Holy Spirit does not work in us through Himself [αὐτουργεῖ], if He is not by nature what we understand [of Him], if it is by participation that He is filled with holiness from the divine essence, and if He only helps transmit to us the grace that has been given to Him, it is manifest that the grace of the Holy Spirit is administered to us by a creature, which is not true. For the law is through Moses or the angels; grace and truth, on the contrary, are through our Savior. It is therefore through Himself that the Spirit acts in us, truly sanctifying us, uniting us with Himself by contact with Him [ἑνοῦν ἡμᾶς ἑαυτῷ διὰ τῆς πρὸς αὐτὸ συναφείας], and making us partakers of the divine nature.[66]

In a passage from the seventh dialogue on the Trinity, a text which did not escape Petau,[67] Cyril is even more explicit.[68]

> A. Are we not saying that on earth humankind has been made in the image of God?
> B. Surely.
> A. Is it not the Spirit who gives us the divine image and, like a seal, imprints on us the superterrestrial beauty [τὸ ὑπερκόσμιον κάλλος]?
> B. But not as God, he says, only as a minister of the divine grace.
> A. Is it therefore not Himself, but the grace which, through Him, is imparted to us?
> B. It seems.   292
> A. Then it would be necessary to call humankind the image of grace rather than the image of God....But when they were established in being, they were formed like God, the breath of life having been breathed into them. After losing their holiness...they were not called back to the original and ancient beauty in a way different from the beginning. Indeed, Christ breathed upon the holy apostles saying: "Receive [the] Holy Spirit,"...If the grace given by Him was separate from the essence of the Spirit, why does the blessed Moses not clearly say that, after having made the living being, the Demiurge of the universe breathed grace into

---

[65] Mahé, "La sanctification d'après Cyrille" 480, 475-479.
[66] *Thes. Trin.*, ass. 33 (75:597a-c).
[67] Cf. Petau, *Dogmata theologica*, 3:462-463.
[68] In the quotation which follows, A. indicates the author himself; B. introduces an imaginary interlocutor.

this one by the breath of life? And [why does not] Christ [say] to us: Receive grace by the ministry of the Holy Spirit? Now the first says: breath of life. This means that the nature of the Deity is real life, if it is true that we live, we move, and we exist in it. In its turn, the voice of the Savior says: Holy Spirit. This is the same Spirit whom, in truth, He makes indwell and whom He brings into the souls of the believers, by whom and in whom He changes them into the original form, that is to say, into Himself, into His own likeness by means of sanctification, renewing us in that way to the archetype of the image, namely, the nature of the Father,...[and] the Son. But the complete and physical similitude [ὁμοίωσις] of the Son is the Spirit. Configured to Him by sanctification, we are shaped just like the very form [μορφή] of God. This is what the word of the apostle teaches us: "My children," he exclaims, "whom I beget once again, until Christ be formed in you." Now He is formed by the Spirit, who through Himself restores us according to God. Since then we are formed according to Christ, who is Himself indeed engraved and reproduced in us by the Spirit, as if by someone who is physically like Him [ὡς δι' ὁμοίου φυσικῶς τοῦ Πνεύματος], the Spirit is God—He who makes like God, not as by a ministerial grace, but by giving Himself[69] to the righteous one in the participation of the divine nature.

B. I have nothing to correct in what has just been said.

293   A. We are called, and we are, temples of God, and even gods. Why? Question the adversaries whether we actually partake only of a grace, bare and devoid of hypostasis [εἴπερ ἐσμὲν ἀληθῶς φιλῆς καὶ ἀνυποστάτου χάριτος μέτοχοι]. But it is not so. For we are temples of the Spirit, who exists and subsists; because of Him, we are also called gods insofar as, by our union with Him, we have entered into communion with the divine and ineffable nature. If the Spirit who deifies [θεοποιοῦν] us through Himself is actually foreign and separate, as to essence, from the divine nature, then we have been defrauded of our hope, assuming for ourselves who knows what vain glory. How, indeed, would we then still be gods and temples of God, according to Scripture, by the Spirit who is in us? For how would the one who is deprived of being God confer this capacity on others? But we are in reality temples and gods....The divine Spirit is therefore not of an essence different from that of God [ἐτερούσιον πρὸς θεόν].[70]

What preoccupies our author in this text is the proof of the full divinity of the Holy Spirit. The process of our divinization interests him only insofar as it is able to serve him as an effective weapon against the Pneumatomachi. The latter acknowledged with all the believers that the sanctification which Christianity provides is a deification. Starting from this common conviction, Cyril argues in this way: It is the Holy Spirit who divinizes us through Himself. Of course nothing created could do this. Therefore the Spirit is truly God. In order to give this argument the maximum convincing force, our theologian excludes any intermediary from the deifying action, any grace which would act separately from the person of the Holy Spirit and would thus be "empty and deprived of hypostasis."

---

[69]   The ἑαυτῷ of the text ought, from all evidence, to be changed to ἑαυτό.
[70]   *Dial. Trin.* 7 (75:1088b-1089d). Cf. (905a).

The patriarch of Alexandria does not necessarily rule out by that any possibility of a grace which, while being inseparable from the Third Person of the Trinity, would be distinct from Him, that is to say, a created grace.[71] Several of his explanations even seem to assume its existence.

Indeed, for Cyril the divine Guest of the righteous soul is not inactive there; by His substantial presence He carries out a profound transformation in it. Already the comparisons that our doctor uses in order to describe the intimacy of our union with the Spirit—that of iron made red-hot by fire—and the metaphors with which the Spirit's operation is presented—those of re-formation, of re-creation, for example[72]—are revealing on this point.

294

But these allusions become clearer when Cyril exalts the marvelous effects which the Holy Spirit produces in us. This One "conforms us to Christ, namely, by the quality [which is] in sanctification [διὰ τῆς ἐν ἁγιασμῷ ποιότητος],"[73] in such a way that Christ "is engraved and reproduced in us."[74] The same Spirit, "by sanctification and justice introduces into us a certain divine conformation" [θείαν τινὰ μόρφωσιν],"[75] imprints us with a seal,[76] and "makes us pass to another state" [εἰς ἑτέραν τινὰ μεθίστησιν ἕξιν].[77]

It is impossible to identify all these results of our sanctification with the person of the divine Spirit Himself, who, indeed, could not be a "form," a "quality," a *habitus* of our soul. It does not seem too much, consequently, to conclude that beside the uncreated grace of the Holy Spirit substantially present in the Christian, Cyril aknowledges a created grace, distinct but inseparable from the first.[78] We must recognize, however, that on this question the thought of our theologian is far from being of an absolute clarity and firmness; and it is only with the benefit of this reservation that Cyril merits the title of doctor par excellence of sanctifying grace which has been given to him.[79]

---

[71] It is, we believe, in this sense that we should understand Fr. Mahé when he writes, in relation to the text quoted above: "What Cyril dismisses here is a grace which would be distinct and separate from the Holy Spirit," i.e., both distinct and separate. See Mahé, "La sanctification d'après saint Cyrille d'Alexandrie," 10:485.

[72] Cf. Weigl, *Die Heilslehre des hl. Cyrillus,* 183-184.

[73] *Hom. pasch.,* 10 (77:617d).

[74] *Dial. Trin.* 7, quoted above, .

[75] *Comm. Is.* 44.21-22 (70:936b). Cf. *Dial. Trin.* 4 (75:1013d).

[76] *Regin.* 2 (76:1384d).

[77] *Comm. Jo.* 16.6-7 (74:433c-d), the word ἕξις means *habitus,* manner of being.

[78] *Expl. Rom.* 3.21 (74:780a), Cyril speaks of a "justifying grace" [δικαιοῦσα χάρις]. But this expression appears to point to the divine gifts as a whole which carry out our justification.

[79] E.g., by Cayré, *Précis* 2:33. On the Cyrillian doctrine of grace, see Petau, *Dogmata theologica,* 3:482-483; Weigl, *Die Heilslehre des hl. Cyrillus,* 176-202. The theses of this last author have been taken up again, with a more refined critical and historical sense, by Father Mahé, "La sanctification d'après Cyrille," 467-485.

V

295   Although the Cyrillian conception of deification may be very complex, it is not difficult to distinguish, among the many elements which compose it, those which are essential and, as it were, the source of the others.

Clearly, it is in the substantial presence of the divine Spirit in us and, through Him, of the entire Trinity, that our doctor sees the formal cause of our deification. The indwelling of the Triune God has the effect of transfiguring our nature—without however changing its depths[80]—to the point of rendering it like the uncreated nature. This transformation is a secondary element of our divinization, and one may well recognize in it our sanctifying grace.

Here is the two-fold source from which all our other privileges follow: for the soul, a beauty and dignity "above the creature,"[81] a special conformity with Christ,[82] a cause of brotherhood in relation to Him[83] and of adoptive filiation in relation to the Father;[84] for the body, incorruptibility and impassibility, at least in seed form, due to the presence in it of the eucharistic Christ.

However, throughout this life, our deification remains amissible[85] and perfectible.[86] Thus, it should unceasingly gain in intensity, so that, for Cyril, "the redemption of the individual is an uninterrupted process of divinization."[87] And
296   this will attain its ultimate perfection after the *parousia* and the resurrection,[88] when the union of the elect with the Lord will be indissoluble. Then our understanding [νοῦς] will be filled with "a certain divine and ineffable light"[89] and, in the presence of "the most brilliant gnosis" which will be granted to us, the one from here below will fade just like the stars in front of the sun.[90] Freed from all hindrances, and "having no need of any figure, or riddle, or parable," "we will

---

[80]   Cf. *Dial. Trin.* 1 (75:676b).

[81]   *Dial. Trin.* 4 (75:905a).

[82]   Besides the texts already quoted, see also *Comm. Is.* 64.18-19 (70:1445c).

[83]   *Hom. pasch.* 24 (77:897b). Cf. *Expl. 1 Cor.* 15.20 (74:101c). The deified soul even becomes the wife of Christ, *Fr. Mt.* 12.8 (62:436c); *Ador.* 8 (68:541b-c).

[84]   *Hom. pasch.* 10 (77:620a-b). On the grace which deifies, see Weigl, *Die Heilslehre des hl. Cyrillus,* 221-239. Conformity with Christ as the foundation of our divine filiation is very much accentuated by Janssens, "Notre filiation divine d'après Cyrille," 233-278.

[85]   Cf. *Comm. Jo.* 16.16-17 (74:536a-c).

[86]   Cf. *Expl. 2 Cor.* 3.18 (74:932b-c).

[87]   Weigl, *Die Heilslehre des hl. Cyrillus,* 259.

[88]   *Ep. Calos.* 16 (76:1104c-1105b). Cf. *Comm. Mal.* 4.2-3 (72:360a). According to Cyril, the resurrection certainly extends to all those who belong to Christ. Cf. *Expl. 1 Cor.* 15.12 (74:896c-904c). Concerning the others, he does not clearly express an opinion. Moreover, he considers that before the return "of the Judge of all and the resurrection of the dead," "it is absurd to think that recompense for their evil or good works has already been given to some." *Ep. Calos.* 16 (76:1105a). After having left the bodies, the souls of the righteous "would go into the hands of the Father of the universe" (*Comm. Jo.* 19.30 [74:669a-b]).

[89]   *Comm. Mal.* 4.2-3 (72:360a).

[90]   *Comm. Mal.* 4.2-3 (72:360c).

see our King and God face to face."[91] And this "perfect gnosis of God,"[92] which is a "kind of divine knowledge,"[93] will fill us with delights.

The resurrected body will also have its share of bliss. It will be spiritualized; "that is to say, it will now only be concerned with the things of the spirit"; it will lay down corruptibility along with all its other infirmities.[94] Its members "will participate in the life and glory of Christ, for He will transform the body of our humility by making it conformed to His glorious body."[95] Deified forever in the soul and in the body, the chosen one will share blessed eternity with the glorified Christ.

Among the many honorary titles with which Cyril has been laden through the admiration of posterity, that of *seal of the fathers* [ἡ σφραγὶς τῶν πατέρων] is unquestionably one of the best chosen.[96] Undoubtedly, it was given to him by Anastasius the Sinaite for his trinitarian doctrine, but it suits him no less from the point of view which is occupying us. 297

With Cyril of Alexandria the doctrine of divinization indeed appears as the sum total of all that the previous fathers have written on this theme. It is true that being receptive rather than individualistic and penetrating, our theologian did not attempt to organize the materials prepared by his predecessors into a perfectly coherent and well-balanced synthesis. At least he has the merit of having outlined a theology of individual deification carried out by the incarnated Logos and His Spirit. For the full development of this theme, he lacked no more than a mysticism of divinization.

---

[91] *Comm. Jo.* 16.25 (74:464b), combined with *Glaph. Ex.* 2 (69:432d).
[92] *Comm. Jo.* 14.21 (74:284c).
[93] *Glaph. Ex.* 2 (69:429a).
[94] *Fr. Lc.* 5.27 (72:892c).
[95] *Expl. 1 Cor.* 6.15 (74:872a). Cf. *Hom. pasch.* 10 (77:625c-d). The glorification of the elect appears as the exclusive work of Christ.
[96] Anast. S. *Hod.* 7 (PG 89:113).

CHAPTER TWO

THE MYSTICISM OF DIVINIZATION

1. Pseudo-Dionysius

298   "The names of Theodoret and Saint Cyril," writes Tixeront, "in a way close the list of the great writers of the Greek church: the literary vein is exhausted, and an age of less eloquent, but more discerning theology begins."[1] From the fifth to the eighth century, one is content to live on the treasures accumulated by the "fathers," just as innumerable dogmatic anthologies of them testify,[2] in which the christological controversies that continue to dominate theological thought go on.

    But it is here, at the beginning of the sixth century, that a work appears for the first time in history, and this in monophysite circles, which though not very extensive, is one of unparalleled singularity and boldness.[3] The author, who prefers the calm exposition of the truth over argument,[4] makes himself out to be a direct disciple of Saint Paul[5] and suggests clearly enough that he is identical with Dionysius the Areopagite of Acts 17:34.[6]

299   Rarely has literary fiction known a success as complete and long-lasting. Were it not for the present day consensus over the pseudepigraphical character of the *Corpus Dionysianum,* it would still not be possible to extract from it the secret of its author. Its composition is generally dated from the end of the fifth century or the beginning of the sixth.[7]

    However fascinating these questions of authorship and date may be, they are only secondary for us. This is because the Dionysian writings are of interest to us here insofar as they represent an attempt on a grand scale—one unique in its genre, the view of which is to interpret the Christian message with the help of Neoplatonic philosophy—to establish a mystical theology

---

[1] Tixeront, *Histoire de dogmes,* 3:4.

[2] Cf. Bardenhewer, *Geschichte,* 4:8-9.

[3] Cf. Bardenhewer, *Geschichte,* 4:282-289.

[4] Cf. Dion. Ar. *Ep.* 7.1 (PG 3:1080).

[5] *Div. nom.* 2.11 (3:649d). Cf. 3.2; 7.1 (681a, 865c).

[6] Cf. *Ep.* 7.3 (3:1081).

[7] Cf. Bardenhewer, *Geschichte,* 4:289-296; Joseph Stiglmayr, *Des heiligen Dionysius Areopagita angebliche Schriften über die beiden Hierarchien* (Bibliothek der Kirchenväter; Munich, 1911), 21-25; P. Godet, "Denys l'Aréopagite (le Pseudo-)," *DTC* 4:430-433. In an article on "Denys le Mystique et la θεομαχία," *RSPT* 25 (1936): 1-75, Father Ceslas Pera, basing himself on considerations of a doctrinal nature, endeavors to establish that the *Corpus Dionysianum* was composed in Asia Minor in the second half of the fourth century. On its own, the method employed by this author could not yield a definitive result. This is also G. Bardy's opinion, "Chronique d'histoire des origines chrétiennes," *RAp* 66 (1938): 112-113.

worthy of Christianity and capable of competing with the mysticism of Plotinus and Proclus.[8] We have seen that the latter is a mysticism of deification.[9] It is the same for the mysticism of the pseudo-Areopagite.

But in order to comprehend his mysticism, it is essential to be acquainted with, at least in its main lines, the theological synthesis which served as its framework.

I

The entire theology of our mystic is governed by an idea of God most pure and most sublime. Infinitely beyond anything which can be imagined, the Supreme Being is the source of every good, of all beauty, and of the unity and order in the universe. With equal force—one is tempted to write, with an equal exaggeration—the author affirms both the divine transcendence and the divine immanence.

> God exceeds all speech and all understanding, He surpasses absolutely every intellect [νοῦς] and every essence, because He grasps, embraces, grips, and penetrates all things, while being Himself totally incomprehensible, offering to be grasped neither by the senses, nor by the imagination, nor by the opinion, nor by a name, nor by a description, nor by touching, nor by understanding....The super-essential Deity does not have a name; He is above every name....We could neither express nor imagine what the One [τὸ ἕν] is, the unknowable [τὸ ἄγνωστον], the super-substantial [τὸ ὑπερούσιον], the good in Himself [αὐτὸ τ' ἀγαθόν].[10]

Precisely because He is the good in Himself, that is, the good through kindness, God has created the intelligible world and the perceptible world.

> Just as our sun, without reflection or any deliberation, but by the single fact of its own existence, illuminates whatever is capable of receiving its light, and that in the measure appropriate to each nature, likewise the Good—who outshines the sun as utterly as the original, by what it is alone, outshines a faint image— sheds, in an analogous manner, rays of complete kindness on all beings. To these rays intelligible and intelligent essences, powers, and virtues owe their existence; due to them, they have their existence and an indestructible and unchanging life, being emancipated from all corruption, death, matter, and generation, free also from instability, decay and every other change. Incorporeal and immaterial, they are intelligible; as intellects [νόες], they are superhumanly [ὑπερκοσμίως] intelligent,

300

---

[8]   Cf. *Ep.* 7.2 (1080a-b), where the author defends himself against the reproach of employing ungodly tactics against the Greeks that are from their own wisdom.

[9]   See above, 53-55, 57.

[10]   *Div. nom.* 1.5 (593a-b). In order to establish the translation of the excerpts that we quote, we have drawn on G. Darboy, *Saint Denys l'Aréopagite* (Paris, 1932), whose translation is, nevertheless, somewhat of a paraphrase. That of Fr. Stiglmayr in German, on the contrary, is of exemplary accuracy; but it only gives two hierarchies.

enlightened concerning the specific reasons for things, and they once again transmit their benefits to their kind.[11]

301   After these venerable and holy intelligences, souls and all the benefits of souls exist because of the superabundant kindness.[12]

Again it is to the divine kindness that "the unreasoning souls or the animals," "all the plants," as well as "the natures deprived of soul and life" owe their existence.[13]

Assuredly, the often employed comparison of the sun as well as similar images and expressions does not fail to have a rather pronounced and unpleasant emanatistic odor, a sign of their Neoplatonic origin.[14] But more than once, and with all desirable clarity, Dionysius affirms the dogma of the creation and the absolute transcendence of the Creator. Thus he writes:

> The eternal One is the origin and end of all that exists: the origin insofar as the cause; the end, because the beings are made for Him. He is the conclusion of all things, the infinity of every infinity and the pinnacle, by distinction, of opposites [πέρατος ὑπεροχικῶς τῶν ὡς ἀντικειμένων]. For in His unity,...He thoroughly knows beforehand [προέχει] and has made all beings to live on, present to all and everywhere, and this according to His unity and His perfect identity; He inclines toward the creatures, while remaining in Himself. He is at rest and in motion; without beginning, or middle, or end; not existing in any of the beings and not being any of the beings.[15]

The creative and illuminating action of God, which our mystic loves to call the "going out" of God, is exercised according to a law of gradation. At first it reaches the incorporeal nature, the "invisible and heavenly hierarchy,"[16]
302   arranged in three triads of three orders each. These nine angelic choirs, the classification of which Dionysius is the author, are subordinated among themselves in such a way that "the lower orders of heavenly essences are informed of divine matters by the higher orders, whereas the most elevated of all are illuminated and initiated, as much as possible, by the supreme Divinity Himself."[17]

---

[11]   *Div. nom.* 4.1 (693b-696a). Cf. 4.4 (697c-d), where the sun is called an "echo [ἀπήχημα] of the Good." On the use of the sun as an image of the divine kindness in Greek philosophy, see Koch, *Pseudo-Dionysius*, 236-242. It goes without saying that, as presented by Dionysius in the passage quoted, the comparison of the sun compromises the freedom of the creative act.

[12]   *Div. nom.* 4.2 (696b-c).

[13]   *Div. nom.* 4.2 (696c-d). Cf. *Cael. hier.* 4.1-2 (3:177b-180b).

[14]   See also *Div. nom.* 5.10 (825b); 13.2 (977c-980a); *Cael. hier.* 4.10 (481c-d). Cf. Koch, *Pseudo-Dionysius*, 194-195; H. F. Mueller, *Dionysios, Proklos, Plotinos*, (Münster in Westphalia, 1918), 40-47.

[15]   *Div. nom.* 5.10 (825b). Cf. 2.10-11 (648c-652a); 8.2 (889d); *Cael. hier.* 13.4 (304b-d).

[16]   *Eccl. hier.* 1.2 (3:373a).

[17]   *Cael. hier.* 7.3 (209a). Cf. 13.3 (301c-304b).

The divine light passes through the angelic world to the human or ecclesiastical hierarchy.[18] In its turn, the latter, that is, the church, consists of three hierarchies of three orders: the triad of the consecrators, namely, bishops, called "hierarchs" [ἱεράρχαι], priests [ἱερεῖς], and deacons [λειτουργοί];[19] that of the initiated ones, namely, monks [μοναχοί or θεραπευταί], believers [ἱερὸς λαός], and catechumens, "energumens," and penitents[20]—these last three categories considered as a single group; finally the triad of the sacred rites, namely, baptism, chrismation (confirmation), and the Eucharist or synaxis.[21]

The radiance of the infinite kindness thus extends upon all beings, but with greater or lesser intensity, depending on whether the creature is drawn more or less near to the divine source, and also depending on whether it is more or less receptive. This mysterious current of light and energy which, becoming subdued, passes through the whole creation from the loftiest beings down to the most lowly, goes back again to its source; this is the return to God, with which the famous eternal cycle draws to a close.

> One calls God lovable and beloved because He is fine and good; one also calls Him love, even tender-love, insofar as He is a power which attracts and leads beings to Himself, the only essential beauty and kindness, and who is, so to speak, His own manifestation to Himself, a flow [πρόοδον] of the supreme unity and a tide of love [ἐρωτικὴν κίνησιν], simple, self-moved [αὐτοκίνητον], endowed with His particular activity, preexisting in the Good, and, from the Good, overflowing onto the beings, in order to return again to the Good. In this it excellently appears that the holy love is without end or beginning, like an eternal cycle [ἀΐδιος κύκλος]: because of the Good, [from] the Good [ἐκ τἀγαθοῦ], in the Good and toward the Good, moving in an unshakeable revolution, without going out of Himself, always proceeding, remaining, and returning.[22]

303

So therefore the return of all beings to the Creator,[23] of the many to the One, is the great law which governs the universe. It is particularly the raison d'être of the hierarchies, for "the goal of the hierarchy is assimilation and union with God, as far as possible [ἡ πρὸς θεόν, ὡς ἐφικτόν, ἀφομοίωσίς τε καὶ ἕνωσις]."[24] This assimilation is a genuine divinization.

---

[18] Cf. *Eccl. hier.* 5.1.4 (the second numeral of the three indicates a particular section of the chapter) (504c-505a); *Cael. hier.* 4.2; 13.3-4 (180b, 301b-305c).

[19] *Eccl. hier.* 5.1.5-7 (505a-509a).

[20] *Eccl. hier* 6.1.1-3 (529-533a).

[21] *Eccl. hier.* 2-3 (392a-445c). Cf. 5.1.1 (500d-501a) and 5.3.8 (516a-c).

[22] *Div. nom.* 4.14 (712c-713a). The same conception is expressed a little further on (4.17 [713d]): "There exists one single power which, by itself, establishes a certain unitive harmony from the Good even to the last of beings, and from the latter goes back again by the same route through the beings to the Good, performing of itself, in itself, and on itself its own circular movement [ἀνακυκλοῦσα] and ever withdrawing into itself in the same way." See also *Div. nom.* 4.4 (697b-700c); *Cael. hier.* 1.1 (120b-121a). Note the paradoxical language of which the author is fond, when he speaks of God, the source and end of the world.

[23] We have seen that this idea of a return of all creatures to God already plays a large role in the thought of Origen and Gregory of Nyssa.

[24] *Cael. hier.* 3.2 (165a). Cf. *Eccl. hier.* 2.1 (392a).

This is what Dionysius states, in precise terms, in his *Ecclesiastical Hierarchy:*

> The origin of the hierarchy is the source of life, the essential kindness, the unique cause of the universe, the Trinity who, in His kindness, imparts being and perfection to all things. This supreme Bliss, who is above all [πάντων ἐπέκεινα],[25] the Triple Monad who truly exists, has conceived the plan, incomprehensible to us but known to Himself, of saving the intelligent natures, ours as much as those above us. But this salvation cannot be achieved if those who should be saved are not deified [μὴ θεουμένων τῶν σωζομένων]. Deification [θέωσις], in its turn, is the assimilation and union with God as far as possible.[26]

304

A little further on, our author thus sums up his thought:

> We are saying, then, that in His divine kindness, the supreme Bliss, the Deity by nature [ἡ φύσει θεότης], the origin of deification [ἡ ἀρχὴ τῆς θεώσεως] from whom all those who are deified receive divinization, has established the hierarchy with a view to the salvation and deification of all the reasoning and spiritual essences.[27]

We can see with what skill Dionysius is able to combine the ancient theme of θέωσις with his new theory of the hierarchies. He never ceases repeating that divinization by the assimilative union with God is the final goal of the hierarchies, and even of all creation, as well as of the redemption. This has allowed someone to say, with good reason, that "the intimate union of humankind with God, the deification of humankind, is the mainspring of the theology of pseudo-Dionysius."[28]

Of course, by casting the traditional idea in the mold of his hierarchical conception of the creation, our author has stamped it with the mark of his genius.

II

The supreme agent of divinization, "the origin and essence of every hierarchy, sanctification, and theurgy" is Jesus, the "divine and super-essential νοῦς." He illuminates in a more brilliant and spiritual way the blessed spirits who are superior to us,[29] whereas, conforming to our nature, He instructs us by means of "a host of perceptible symbols, through which we are raised, according to our capacities, toward uniform deification [ἐπὶ τὴν ἐνοειδῆ θέωσιν], toward God and a divine virtue."[30]

305   But, in what concerns humanity, the deifying action of Christ is only a restoration. Through the Savior, the human nature recovers "the divine benefits which it had senselessly lost at the beginning...: the divine and heaven-

---

[25] An expression dear to the Neoplatonists. See above, 51. Cf. Koch, *Pseudo-Dionysius,* 212, 250-251.

[26] *Eccl. hier.* 1.3 (373c-376a). Cf. *Cael. hier.* 3.1-2; 7.2 (164d-165c, 208-209a).

[27] *Eccl. hier.* 1.4 (376b).

[28] Godet, "Denys l'Aréopagite," 434.

[29] *Eccl. hier.* 1.1 (372a).

[30] *Eccl. hier.* 1.2 (373a). Cf. 1.4 (376b-c).

ward-oriented life, from which it had voluntarily fallen" for having "miserably exchanged eternity for mortality."[31]

Without lingering here, on several occasions the *doctor hierarchicus* broaches the problem of the conditions according to which Christ has carried out our divinization. Thus, in his *Ecclesiastical Hierarchy,* on the subject of the incarnation he writes:

> The boundless philanthropy of the supreme kindness...has really taken on all our weaknesses, except for sin, and, being joined together with our lowness while keeping the condition of His own nature without confusion or any alteration, He has favored us, as if relatives, with likeness with Him and has made us partakers of His own benefits."[32]

A little further, in the same treatise, when applying the fundamental thought of his system to the mystery of the incarnation, namely, that of the repose of God in Himself [μονή], of His going out [πρόοδος], and of His return [ἐπιστροφή], Dionysius expresses himself in these terms:

> By becoming man through kindness and philanthropy, the one, single and hidden nature of Jesus, of the divine Logos, advanced [προελήλυθε] without undergoing any modification toward the compound and the visible, and has successfully carried out our unitive communion with itself, marrying in a sublime manner our lowness with its divine excellence, if however we are joined together harmoniously with Him, as members with the body, in the same spotless and divine life and we do not become, after having been killed by the corrupting passions, unfit for dealings with the divine and healthy members, incapable of sharing their life.[33]

In these texts and some similar passages, we think we are hearing an echo, feeble and yet sufficiently distinct, of the physical theory of divinization, an impression which becomes clearer so as to approach certainty when, in the same writing, we read the following:

306

> God, who in His natural and sympathetic kindness to the inhabitants of the earth and in His philanthropy, has deigned to stoop down to us, and through union has assimilated to Himself that which was united in the manner of fire, in the measure of its fitness for deification.[34]

It is true that here, as in many other cases moreover, the solemn and appealing clarity-obscurity, which the author is fond of when expressing his thought, hardly permits coming to a conclusion in an apodictic manner. Nevertheless the whole text and particularly the employment of the metaphor of fire, dear to the

---

[31] *Eccl. hier.* 3.3.11 (440c-441a). Cf. 3.3.7 (436c-d); *Div. nom.* 8.9 (897a-b). With the tradition, the pseudo-Areopagite distinguishes three stages in the history of our salvation.
[32] *Eccl. hier.* 3.3.11 (441a-b).
[33] *Eccl. hier.* 3.3.12 (444a-b). Cf. 3.3.3 (429a); *Ep.* 4 (1072).
[34] *Eccl. hier.* 2.2.1 (393a).

representatives of the physical conception,[35] show clearly enough that Dionysius alludes to that theory.

A recent author did not hesitate to write that with Dionysius "we do not find a trace of the central idea of Pauline theology, namely, the redemption by the blood of Jesus Christ."[36] This is an obvious exaggeration. Several times, in fact, the pseudo-Areopagite implies, and once he clearly affirms, the salvific value of the death of the Savior.

Thus, in his eighth letter addressed to the monk Demophilus and inspired by John 10:11, our doctor writes concerning Christ that He "gives His soul for those who flee from Him."[37] Later, in the same letter, he cites 1 John 2:2: "He Himself [Christ] is the propitiation for our sins."[38] In the famous vision of Carpus, recounted in the same writing, the Lord who appears declares Himself "ready to suffer again for the salvation of men."[39] All these hints become clear, finally, in the light of a passage from *Ecclesiastical Hierarchy*, where our mystic comments on the custom of pouring perfumed oil in baptismal fonts while tracing a cross. Here is his commentary:

> By pouring the myron in cruciform streams into the baptistry which purifies, the hierarch shows to the contemplative eyes that, by the cross, Jesus has descended even into death itself, with a view to our birth from God [ὑπὲρ τῆς ἡμῶν θεογενεσίας] and that, precisely by this divine and victorious descent, through kindness He snatches those who are baptized into His death, according to the mystical word,[40] from that ancient abyss of pernicious death and renews them with a view to an existence that is full of God [ἔνθεος] and eternal.[41]

So then, just like Cyril of Alexandria, the pseudo-Areopagite seems to link θέωσις sometimes to the incarnation as such, and sometimes to the passion of Christ. But whereas the former does it with the clearness which characterizes the champion of orthodoxy, the latter employs undulating formulas which, without offending anyone, can be accepted by all.

III

With the entire tradition, Dionysius teaches that humankind must cooperate in their own divinization. But, concerning the practical details of this cooperation, his thought is hardly more definite than it is on the details of the redemptive work of Christ. His writings contain, in fact, a description of two ways leading to the deifying union with God: one by ecstatic love and the other

---

[35]   We have already come across this metaphor with Saint Cyril of Alexandria. See above, 223.
[36]   Mueller, *Dionysios*, 36.
[37]   *Ep.* 8.1 (1088b).
[38]   *Ep.* 5 (1096c).
[39]   *Ep.* 6 (1100c). On the literary sources of the vision of Carpus, see Koch, *Pseudo-Dionysius*, 18-27.
[40]   The "mystical word" is Rom 6:3.
[41]   *Eccl. hier.* 4.3.10 (484b).

by means of the ecclesiastical hierarchy. There is not a word on the relation-ships that these ways could have between them.

We begin with the way of ecstasy, since it is described in the first two Diony-sian treatises: *On the Divine Names,* which is the most important of all, and *Mys-*   308
tical Theology.[42]

In *On the Divine Names,*[43] after having recalled that the Scripture employs the term love to indicate God, our mystic magnifies the unitive virtue of love in general, and then, more particularly, of this "thing, incomprehensible to the masses, which is the fusion produced by the divine and one love" [τὸ ἑναῖον τοῦ θείου καὶ ἑνὸς ἔρωτος].[44] This means that love unites with God beyond every activity of the senses, indeed even of the intelligence:

> When, by its spiritual energies, our soul turns toward the intelligible things, sen-sations become superfluous; as also the intellectual powers themselves [become useless], when the soul, having become deiform, plunges, in blind rushes and through an incomprehensible union, into the rays of the inaccessible light.[45]

It is an unutterable union, because it takes place in ecstasy:

> The divine love is ecstatic; it does not allow those who love to be to themselves, but to those who are loved....That is why the great Paul, seized by the divine love and its ecstatic power, uttered this divinely inspired word: "I live, or better, it is not by myself, but Christ lives in me,"[46] as a true lover outside of himself and lost in God, according to His own expression,[47] no longer living his own life, but the supremely precious life of the Beloved.[48]

It is also by something in us which is superior even to the νοῦς that the ecstatic union with God is realized:

> We should know that the νοῦς in us has the intellectual faculty [τὴν δύναμιν εἰς τὸ νοεῖν], by means of which it sees the intelligible things; but it also possesses a   309
> union which goes beyond the nature of the νοῦς [τὴν δὲ ἕνωσιν ὑπεραίρουσαν τὴν τοῦ νοῦ φύσιν] and by which it becomes attached to that which is beyond it-self [δι' ἧς συνάπτεται πρὸς τὰ ἐπέκεινα ἑαυτοῦ]. Therefore, we must consider the divine things according to this union, not according to our means [οὐ καθ' ἡμᾶς] but having come wholly out of ourselves and having become [the property]

---

[42] On the chronological order of the Dionysian writings, see Bardenhewer, *Geschichte,* 4:283-284.

[43] *Div. nom.* 4.11-13 (708b-712b).

[44] *Div. nom.* 4.12 (709c).

[45] *Div. nom.* 4.11 (708d). Cf. 1.5 (593).

[46] Gal 2:20, quoted a little freely.

[47] Allusion to 2 Cor 5:13: "If we are outside of ourselves [ἐξέστημεν], it is for God [θεῷ]."

[48] *Div. nom.* 4.13 (712a).

of God [ὅλους θεοῦ γιγνομένους]; for it is better to be to God than to ourselves [κρεῖττον γὰρ εἶναι θεοῦ, καὶ μὴ ἑαυτῶν].[49]

From this incomprehensible union results "the most divine gnosis of God, which is obtained through ignorance" [ἡ θειτάτη τοῦ θεοῦ γνῶσις ἡ δι' ἀγνωσίας γινωσκομένη], when the νοῦς, "after having withdrawn from all things and given itself up, is united with the transluminous rays by which it is enlightened in the unfathomable depth of wisdom."[50]

The paradox of gnosis-ignorance, reached through the ecstatic union, returns within other but still accentuated expressions in *Mystical Theology*.

This small treatise opens with a prayer to the Trinity and an exhortation to Timothy, doubtless the disciple of Saint Paul to whom the piece of writing is supposed to be addressed—literary methods which allow the author to set forth his theme in an original fashion:

> Supra-essential Trinity, most divine, supremely good, guide of Christians into theosophy [θεοσοφίας], lead us toward the sublime summit of mystical words which eludes all knowledge and surpasses all light. There the simple, perfect, and unchanging mysteries of theology are veiled by the very luminous obscurity of a silence full of secret teachings, an obscurity which, while very profound, is radiant with a most vivid brilliance and which, being unable either to be grasped or seen, floods the blind spirits [τοὺς ἀνομμάτους νόας] with its shining beauty. Such was my prayer. You, O beloved Timothy, practice, without respite, the mystical contemplations [περὶ τὰ μυστικὰ θεάματα]; leave behind you sensations and intellectual processes, all perceptible and intelligible things, all that is not[51] and all that is, and beyond all knowledge [ἀγνώστως] strive as much as possible toward the union with the One who is above every essence and every gnosis. For it is by this irresistible, absolute, and clear-cut coming out [ἐκστάσει] from yourself and from all the rest that you will leap, free and clear, toward the super-essential ray of the divine obscurity.[52]

310

Along with Philo and Gregory of Nyssa, our doctor sees in Moses' ascent of Sinai an image of the mystical ascension, and he compares the phases of the latter with the stages of the former.

> It is not without reason that the divine Moses is charged first to be purified himself, then to be separated from impure things; the whole purification having been completed, he hears the polyphonic trumpets, sees the numerous lights emitting pure and innumerable rays; finally, he leaves the multitude and, in the company of the chosen priests, goes up to the summit of the divine mountain. But there,

---

[49]   *Div. nom.* 7.1 (865c-868a). See in Koch, *Pseudo-Dionysius*, 158, an analogous passage of Proclus. Dionysius often speaks of the "union above the νοῦς" (*Div. nom.* 7.3 [872a]) or of "the union which surpasses all that is possible and that our reason and understanding may obtain" (*Div. nom.* 1.1 [585-588a]).

[50]   *Div. nom.* 7.3 (872a-b).

[51]   Cf. Plot. *Enn.* 5.1.2 (ed. Bréhier 5:17, lines 26-27), where inert matter [σῶμα νεκρόν] is called μὴ ὄν.

[52]   *Myst.* 1.1 (3:997a-1000a).

still he is not with God; he does not contemplate God Himself (for He is invisible), but the place where He stands.[53] This signifies, I think, that the most exalted and divine things that we may see and of which we may have intelligence are somewhat symbolic expressions [ὑποθετικούς τινας εἶναι λόγους] of what is fundamentally of the One who is above all. By these manifestations His presence [παρουσία][54] is shown, a presence which surpasses all knowledge and is above the pinnacles blessed with the intelligence of His most holy places.[55] And then [the intellect] frees itself from what is seen and what sees in order to plunge into the truly mystical obscurity of ignorance, and, giving up all scientific investigation, it enters into what is absolutely intangible and invisible, completely in the One who is beyond all [πᾶς ὢν τοῦ πάντων ἐπέκεινα], not belonging to anyone, neither to itself nor to another, united in what it possesses that is more noble [κατὰ τὸ κρεῖττον], with the One who is absolutely unknowable by the cessation of intellection [τῇ πάσης γνώσεως ἀνενεργησίᾳ], but drawing from this ignorance a knowledge which goes beyond the νοῦς.[56]

311

The texts we have just read bring into full light the characteristic features of the union with God advocated in the first two treatises of Dionysius. As both a divine gift and the fruit of human effort, this union is accessible to all Christians. Considered in itself, it is a direct contact between God and the soul, therefore a mystical union in the strict sense.[57] But since it comes about through the most noble part of the soul and since, for that reason, it is even above the νοῦς, the mystical union surpasses all our categories of thought such that the knowledge of God resulting from ecstasy in comparison seems like ignorance, although it is the most sublime gnosis.

It is a curious thing that our mystic only points to prayer[58] and asceticism as the means of acquiring "theosophy." His silence with regard to Christ and the sacraments of the church seems strange, even if one assumes, as is probable, that these first two writings are intended exclusively for Christians.[59]

312

---

[53] An allusion to Exo 24:10. In the Hebrew text we read: "they saw the God of Israel." The Seventy have translated: "they saw the place where the God of Israel was standing." Dionysius obviously is refering to this translation.

[54] Dionysius would have us understand that, in divine manifestations, whether tangible or purely intelligible, we do not grasp God such as He is in Himself, but a presence, a special activity of God. On the role that the concept of παρουσία plays in pagan mysteries and with Proclus, see Koch, *Pseudo-Dionysius,* 174.

[55] By the dwelling-place of God our mystic seems to mean the intelligible world of which the higher angels are like the intelligent pinnacles. Cf. Koch, *Pseudo-Dionysius,* 163.

[56] *Myst.* 1.3 (1000c-1001a). Cf. 2 (1025); 3 (1033b-c); *Ep.* I (1065). It is to be noted that the author discerns in Moses' ascent three stages which correspond to the threefold way of mystical ascension, namely, purification, illumination, and union.

[57] We have already pointed out that very often Dionysius employs the adjective "mystical" in the sense of disclosed, hidden, and mysterious.

[58] Cf. *Div. nom.* 3.1 (680b-c), where the author recognizes in prayer the virtue of immediately uniting the soul with God. On the Dionysian theory of prayer and its Neoplatonic sources, see Koch *Pseudo-Dionysius,* 178-190. On prayer in Platonism in general, cf. Arnou, "Le Platonisme des Pères," 2370-2372.

[59] Dionysius's silence regarding the sacramental rites of the church will be such for almost all of the mystics. This is because with them the Christian milieu is understood.

Would it be that to fill this gap, in the last of his treatises, Dionysius shows a second way which leads to the deifying union by means of the ministers and the sacred rites of the ecclesiastical hierarchy?

IV

One thing which is for certain is the fact that in *Ecclesiastical Hierarchy* a way is outlined which leads man from the Gentiles to Christianity and even to the mystical union with God who deifies. Here are the principle stages of it, and here they are still three in number.

Dionysius sets down in principle that, in order to be united with the most divine life of Jesus Christ and in order to become "partaker of God and of divine things," a person must imitate the Savior.[60] But an imitation of a purely moral nature—as necessary as it may be[61]—would not be able to suffice: recourse to the sacred rites of Christian initiation is obligatory.

A person must first of all "die with Christ," which in mystical language means, "die to sin in baptism"[62] in order to then be born again to "a divine mode of being." This divine birth is indispensable, since it grants "an existence intimately united with God" [τὸ ὑπάρχειν ἐνθέως],[63] without which one cannot know anything or accomplish "divinely revealed things."[64]

313   The distinctive feature of baptism is to purify and to illuminate. Purification consists in eliminating all the obstacles which are opposed to a participation in the One [τὸ ἕν], firstly, the immoderate tendencies which, dividing a person, bring that one into contradiction with the divine unity. "Catharsis" is thus essentially the removal of every foreign element, the reducing of that which is divided in us "to a deiform monad and to a unity which imitates that of God" [εἰς θεοειδῆ μονάδα συναγόμεθα καὶ θεομίμητον ἕνωσιν].[65] Finally, illumination by the rays of the divine Sun, helping us to grasp the spiritual sense hidden beneath the symbolic language of our Holy Books and revealing to us the profound truths which the symbols of our sacred rites cover, reinforces and completes the unity of the soul, for the divine "light is one and unifying."[66]

---

[60] *Eccl. hier.* 3.3.12 (444c-d).

[61] The adherence "to the sacred teachings" as well as a true conversion of the heart are required for admission to baptism. Cf. *Eccl. hier.* 2.2. (393-396). See Joseph Stiglmayr, "Aszese und Mystik des sog. Dionysius Areopagita," *Schol.* 2 (1927): 185-188.

[62] *Eccl. hier.* 2.3.6-7 (404a-b).

[63] *Eccl. hier.* 2.1. (392b): τὸ εἶναι θείως ἐστὶν ἡ θεία γέννησις. A little earlier (392a), baptism is called an ἀναγέννησις; often it is described as θεογενεσία, e.g., 3.3.6; 4.3.10; 5.5 (432c, 484b, 505b). Cf. Rahner, "Die Gottesgeburt," 377.

[64] *Eccl. hier.* 2.1. (392b). Cf. 3.1. (425a-b).

[65] *Div. nom.* 1.4 (589c). Cf. 4.9 (705a-b); *Cael. hier.* 3.3 (165d-168a). The close relationship between the Dionysian κάθαρσις and that of the Neoplatonists is quite obvious. Cf. Stiglmayr, "Aszese und Mystik," 192-193.

[66] *Div. nom.* 4.6 (701a-b). Cf. *Eccl. hier.* 4.3; 6.1.6 (473-485; 505c-508b).

Due to purification and illumination, the "one" [ἕν] of the soul manages to isolate. Now, by and in its ἕν the human intellect, having become "uniform" [ἐνοειδής], that is, unified in itself, and having returned to the purity of its form, is joined with the divine Ἕν in order to be filled with it.[67]

This union is the distinctive effect of the Eucharist. Assuredly, all the rites of initiation contribute toward "bringing our divided life back to a uniform deification [εἰς ἐνοειδῆ θέωσιν] and toward procuring for us, by the deiform unification [θεοειδεῖ συμπτύξει][68] of what is divided in us, the communion and union with the One." But, as the name already suggests, it is above all the synaxis, that "initiation of initiations" [τελετῶν τελετή],[69] which "achieves our communion and union with the Ἕν" [τὴν πρὸς τὸ ἕν ἡμῶν κοινωνίαν καὶ σύναξιν].[70]

To the threefold stage whereby the soul rises to God, which in rough outline   314 is the *via purgativa, illuminativa*, and *unitiva* of later mysticism,[71] corresponds the threefold order of the sacred ministers, "who can be distinguished into an order which purifies, an order which enlightens, and an order which perfects."[72]

This perfecting is nothing other than divinization. Having been "initiated into the divine things and deified" [τελεσθῆναι κατὰ τὰ θεῖα καὶ θεωθῆναι], the hierarch "helps the subordinates participate as well, each according to rank, in the holy deification [ἱερᾶς θεώσεως] which the hierarch has received from God [θεόθεν]."[73] But as soon as duties allow, the hierarch withdraws into the ἕν in order to unite with God:

Free again and not held back by the lower things, without having experienced any decreasing, [the pontiff] returns to the origin which is familiar and, having made the spiritual entry into the personal ἕν [εἰς τὸ ἕν ἑαυτοῦ νοερὰν ποιησάμενος εἴσοδον], clearly sees the unchanging reasons for the performed

---

[67]   *Eccl. hier.* 2.3.5 (401a-c), combined with 4.3.3 (477a-b).

[68]   Following Proclus, our mystic uses the terms θεοειδής and ἐνοειδής as synonyms. Cf. Koch, *Pseudo-Dionysius*, 169.

[69]   Of note is our doctor's partiality for the language of the mysteries, of which no other ecclesiastical writer makes use in as large a measure. Cf. Koch, *Pseudo-Dionysius*, 92-134.

[70]   *Eccl. hier.* 3.1. (424c-425b). To be noticed is the play on words with σύναξις. Cf. 2.3.5 (401a-c). See also 5.1.3 (504b-c), where the author writes that "the synaxis and the consecration of the μύρον perfect one in the knowledge and learning of theurgical acts, a learning whereby the unitive ascension toward the divine origin and the beatifying union with Him are consummated in a saintly way."

[71]   We have seen that Dionysius distinguishes clearly enough these three stages or ways, but he does not make a theory of it. See Stiglmayr, "Aszese und Mystik," 188-205; Koch, *Pseudo-Dionysius*, 174-178.

[72]   *Eccl. hier.* 5.1.3 (504c). In this fifth chapter especially, the artificial nature of the triadic hierarchy is evident. Into it Dionysius stubbornly insists on pressing the organization and the life of the church. One has the impression that he wanted, at any price, to cast Christianity into the triadic mold, made fashionable by certain Neoplatonists. Cf. Koch, *Pseudo-Dionysius*, 178; Zeller, *Die Philosophie der Griechen* (1903), 3:2:847-864.

[73]   *Eccl. hier.* 1.2 (372c-d).

[rites], thus making a more divine return toward the highest things out of the completion of the descent toward the subordinate things.[74]

Union with God, perfection, or divinization—identical expressions for our author—are the completion of the hierarchical way. Since the deifying union appears as a contact without intermediary between the divine One and the "one" of the soul, it deserves the qualifier of mystical. In other words, the two Dionysian ways end at the same goal.

315

V

Although basically traditional, the two Dionysian ways of divinization, especially the hierarchical, give an impression of something new—less perhaps due to their triadic framework than on account of that mysterious ἕν of the soul, found for the first time with Dionysius under an ecclesiastical pen. From whence does this concept come, and what is its exact significance? Here again, one imagines, it is a matter of borrowing from Neoplatonism, and more particularly from Proclus.

Starting from the old principle that "the similar is everywhere known by the similar," Proclus, developing ideas already outlined by Plotinus,[75] states as a matter of principle that the divine One, who is beyond the Noῦς,[76] could not be grasped by human intelligence. Consequently, he acknowledges the existence in the soul of an element which is also "superior to the voῦς which is in the soul," a kind of image or trace of the supreme Ἕν: a human ἕν, which is like the "flower" or "pinnacle" of our essence. It is "according to this ἕν that we are brought into contact [συναπτόμεθα] with the divine."[77] On account of its being above the voῦς, the ἕν eludes all analysis.[78]

316   The identity of the human ἕν of Dionysius with that of Proclus is quite obvious.[79] In adopting this notion, the hierarchical doctor could not but be conscious of innovating, which, as we have seen, did not frighten him. But from

---

[74] *Eccl. hier.* 3.3.3 (429b). In this passage, the author applies to the bishop, in a certain manner, his plan of repose, of going out and of return. See also 6.3.3 (477a-b).

[75] See Plot. *Enn.* 3.8.9; 5.1.1-3; 6.9.4. Cf. Arnou, "Le Platonisme des Pères," 2282, 2381-2383.

[76] I.e., the second of three Neoplatonic hypostases, which are the One, the Intelligence [Noῦς], and the Soul [Ψυχή]. See above, 51-52.

[77] See the texts of Proclus in Koch, *Pseudo-Dionysius*, 154-156, 162 and Zeller, *Die Philosophie der Griechen*, 879-880. We know that the mystics readily speak of the peak or summit of the soul, etc. Cf. Stiglmayr, "Aszese und Mystik," 192; Arnou, "Le Platonisme des Pères," 2380.

[78] For the same reason, the human ἕν could not be "the pure consciousness of one's self" [*das reine Selbstbewusstsein*]—as Koch, *Pseudo-Dionysius*, 154 and Zeller, *Die Philosophie der Griechen*, 879, think— since intellectual consciousness is a function of the intelligence.

[79] The relationship which in general exists between the works of Dionysius and those of Proclus has been observed from antiquity. But we have explained it in terms of the former's dependence on the latter, as Maximus the Confessor does, for example, in *Prol. Dion.* (PG 4:21d).

all evidence, he did not realize the fact that the concept thus borrowed by him was concealing something incompatible with traditional anthropology.[80]

The analysis of the two Dionysian ways thus completed, the problem of their reciprocal relations very naturally arises. At first sight, the way of ecstasy appears to be simply the continuation of the hierarchical way. But in order to dismiss this hypothesis it is sufficient to remember that both end up at the same goal. Instead, it seems that we may be facing two successive views of the author. In any case, nowhere do we see him undertaking the slightest attempt at harmonization. On the contrary, in his *Ecclesiastical Hierarchy*—the writing, moreover, where normally such an attempt should have found a place—he writes that "our assimilation and union with God are obtained only [μόνως], as the divine word teaches, by the love of the very majestic commandments and by holy deeds."[81]

How do we explain this notable difference which separates the two Dionysian conceptions of deification? Perhaps by a difference of viewpoints in which the author appears to be successively placed. In fact, in the first two treatises the impression is especially one of a Christian philosopher speaking, in order to show that Christianity is a "theosophy" and an asceticism of divinization, which yield in nothing to those of the philosophy then in fashion. In the *Ecclesiastical Hierarchy*, on the contrary, we believe we are hearing, above all, a man of the church, anxious to present the church as a divinely established institution for leading people to salvation, namely, to the deifying union with God. The intention is to supplant the theurgy of Proclus.

In the course of our exposition we have pointed out numerous characteristics of the Dionysian doctrine on divinization. There is however, one which has still not held our attention. Unlike the great majority of the fathers, our mystic does not seem to place the principal element of deification in the immortalization of humankind. For him, as we have seen, it is above all the unification of the soul, its reduction to the ἕν that is in it, which renders it like the divine Ἕν and thereby deiform.

But we would be mistaken to conclude from this that Dionysius does not attribute any part to incorruptibility in the process of our divinization. On the contrary, along with the entire tradition he teaches that divinization is consummated only by the gift of blessed immortality in the hereafter.

Assuredly, from this life on the baptized ones lead "a very deiform life in Christ;"[82] but "in this world, the holy souls are always exposed to lapses into

---

[80] Koch, *Pseudo-Dionysius,* 159, endeavors to find in the Dionysian ἕν a sense acceptable from the Christian point of view. To listen to him, Dionysius would have conceived of it "as the sum total of the powers of the soul concentrated in a unique focus, as the quintessence of its powers which would nevertheless become ὑπὲρ νοῦν ἕνωσις." But however concentrated we may suppose it, we do not see how the sum of the soul's faculties could become superior to it.

[81] *Eccl. hier.* 2.1. (392a). It follows the quotation of "the divine word," namely, John 14:23: "Those who love me will keep my word, and my Father will love them, and we will come to them and make our home with them."

[82] *Eccl. hier.* 7.1.2 (553b-c).

evil." It is only after the "holy regeneration" of death[83] that "they will obtain the most deiform strengthening in the immutability" of an entirely divine life,[84] in "the bosom of the patriarchs," that is, in "the most divine and beatifying abodes." Heaven will receive "all those who are deiform with a view to their eternal and blessed consummation" by an "immortality completely free from sorrow and flooded with light."[85]

The bodies of the elect will join in this bliss after the resurrection:

318

The pure bodies of the holy souls who have borne the same yoke and traveled the same paths, who were enlisted[86] and fought together with these souls their divine battles, will receive their own resurrection when the souls are established in the immutability of a divine life.[87]

Then the whole human being will be deified and the salvation of the human being totally carried out.[88]

All things considered, the mysticism of divinization contained in the *Corpus Dionysianum* appears to be an attempt to christianize Neoplatonic mysticism, which had found in Proclus an apostle dangerous to the church. To that end, the author applies himself to cast in the molds prepared by that philosopher the substance of Christian mysticism, worked out by the Alexandrians and, in particular, by Gregory of Nyssa. How difficult and perilous an enterprise! Also, without wishing to cast doubt on the Christianity and good faith of the pseudo-Areopagite and while paying homage to an effort which was not lacking in magnitude, we must recognize that he gave Neoplatonism much more than its due.[89]

The mystical way bears only a distant and very vague relationship with the Christian faith and Christian moral doctrine. Thus, we would search here in vain for any allusion to the necessity of a divine Mediator. More clearly marked with the Christian seal, his hierarchical theory of divinization is compromised by the concept of the human ἕν, which constitutes an essential element of it.

At least his Christian sense safeguarded Dionysius from an even more dangerous pitfall which Neoplatonism was hiding—pantheistic resorption of the ἕν of the soul by the supreme Ἕν. One recalls that, for Plotinus, the soul in ecstasy is now nothing but one with God, to the point that the human being then "becomes God, or rather, he is Him" [ἑαυτὸν...θεὸν γενόμενον, μᾶλλον δὲ

319 ὄντα].[90] Our Christian mystic takes this formula up again, but by exorcizing it,

---

[83] *Eccl. hier.* 7.1.3 (556b). Note that, just like baptism, death is called a "holy regeneration."
[84] *Eccl. hier.* 7.1.1 (553a-b).
[85] *Eccl. hier.* 7.3.5 (560b-c).
[86] I.e., enrolled in the register of the baptized.
[87] *Eccl. hier.* 7.1.1 (553a-b).
[88] Cf. *Eccl. hier.* 7.3.9 (565b-c).
[89] Cf. Fr. Aug. Preuss, *Ad Maximi Confessoris de Deo doctrinam adnotationes* (Schneeberg, 1894), 4-8.
[90] Plot., *Enn.* 6.9.10; (ed. Volkmann, 2:522-523). See above, 55.

so to speak, by means of an ingenious correction. Concerning those who have reached the ecstatic union he indeed writes, not that they have become God, but that "they have wholly become [the property] of God" [ὅλους θεοῦ γιγνομένους].[91]

The pseudo-Areopagite has exerted an influence that is difficult to exaggerate, as much on dogmatic theology—is he not "the author most often cited by Saint Thomas (more than seventeen thousand times)"?[92]—as on Christian mysticism. This fortune "he without doubt owes in large part to the illustrious confessor," Saint Maximus, who "fixed the catholic interpretation" of the Dionysian works,[93] which he regarded as inspired.[94]

2. Saint Maximus the Confessor

Monk of the monastery of Chrysopolis opposite Constantinople, Maximus "ranks among the most penetrating theologians and the most profound mystics that the Greek church has produced."[95] Out of His numerous writings, none of which contains a systematic and complete exposition of his thought, emerges a soteriology which we can call a theology and mysticism of divinization.

I

Having gone out from God by creation, all things must again return to Him. First cause and final end of the creatures, the Logos is not only the agent of their creation but also the worker of their return to God. One might as well say that He is "origin, middle, and end of all time. The time preceding Christ is that of preparation for the incarnation, the time subsequent to Christ is that of the   320 divinization of humankind."[96] The last-mentioned is therefore the end of the creation as well as of the incarnation.[97] As culmination of the work of the Demiurge, it had to have this One as author:

> It was necessary [ἔδει], in truth, that the One who, by nature, was the Demiurge of the essence of things become also the author of the deification of the creatures by grace [τῆς κατὰ χάριν αὐτουργὸν...θεώσεως], in order that the bestower of being might appear also as the giver of well-being [εὖ εἶναι].[98]

---

[91] *Div. nom.* 7.1 (868a); text cited above, 242.

[92] Marcel Viller, *La spiritualité des premiers siècles chrétiens* (Paris, 1930), 132.

[93] Marcel Viller, "Aux sources de la spiritualité de saint Maxime. Les oeuvres d'Évagre le Pontique," *RAM* 11 (1930): 158, and *La spiritualité des premiers siècles chrétiens*, 137. Cf. V. Grumel, "Maxime de Chrysopolis ou Maxime le Confesseur," *DTC* 10:450.

[94] Cf. Max. *Myst.* 24 (91:716b-c).

[95] Bardenhewer, *Geschichte*, 5:30.

[96] K. Juessen, "Maximus Confessor," *LTK* 7:22.

[97] Cf. *Cap.* 1.42 (90:1193); *Or. dom.* (90:873d); *Ep.* 24 (91:609c); *Ep.* 43 (91:640c); *Ambig.* (91:1084c). See Preuss, *Ad Maximi Confessoris*, 21-22.

[98] *Qu. Thal.* 60 (90:624d).

From the time of his formation, Adam was "an image and a likeness of God" because of his "reasoning and spiritual soul, by which, particularly, humankind is and is called humankind."[99] However, humankind did not owe this state of divine image uniquely to the reasoning nature but also to the "gracious gift of incorruptibility [ἀφθαρσία]" and of impassibility [ἀπάθεια], apart from which the ideal of perfection, τὸ εὖ εἶναι, cannot be conceived. Our first father had only to transform the impassibility into "immutability" [ἀτρεψία] in order to "become God by deification...and to possess by grace [κατὰ χάριν] the same perfect knowledge of things as God, because of transformation of the intelligence and of the sense, with a view to divinization [πρὸς θέωσιν]."[100]

But from the first moment of his existence [ἅμα τῷ γενέσθαι], Adam willfully turned away from God. By his disobedience he lost immortality and got involved in passions, distress, and death.[101]

One of the fatal consequences of the transgression of the first human being was fleshly generation, stained by blameworthy concupiscence,[102] a generation which necessarily ended up in a birth in sin and in an existence subject to suffering and to death.[103]

II

Only the Logos was able to set humanity free from all its miseries. This is what Maximus says clearly in a passage of *Quaestiones ad Thalassium*,[104] which Gaudel summarizes as follows: "The only way to snatch us out of the corruption of our entrance into life and departure from it, was for the incarnate Word to purify both, by a conception protected from concupiscence and a death that was not a debt incurred, due to a natural generation stained by concupiscence. Whereas in Adam, by fleshly and concupiscent generation we have met with condemnation to the death of our nature, in Christ, who was born of a virgin, our nature meets with the condemnation of sin."[105]

By his spotless generation, the God-Man "has given to our nature another beginning, that of the second birth of the Holy Spirit,...imparting to our nature, by His own incarnation, the grace which goes beyond our nature, namely,

[99] *Myst.* 4 (91:684d).

[100] *Qu. Thal.* Prolog. (90:257d-260a). Cf. *Opusc. theol.* 1 (91:33b-36a). See M. Th. Disdier, "Les fondements dogmatiques de la spiritualité de saint Maxime le Confesseur," *EO* 34 (1930): 302-307. Sometimes Maximus distinguishes between εἰκών, the divine image given with the human nature, and ὁμοίωσις, the likeness of a moral nature acquired by personal effort; for example *Carit.* 3.25 (90:1024). But he never applies this distinction to Adam, without doubt because the superior divine likeness had been granted to him free of charge.

[101] *Qu. Thal.* 41 (90:405c-409a), combined with 61 (628a).

[102] *Qu. dub.* 3 (90:788ab). With Gregory of Nyssa, our author writes in this passage that "the original intention of God was that we not spring from corruption by fleshly union [διὰ γάμου]." Cf. *Qu. Thal.* 61 (90:632c). The same conception is in Jo. D. *Fid. orth.* 2.30 (94:976b).

[103] *Qu. Thal.* 61 (90:628ff). Cf. *Ascet.* 1 (912). See Gaudel, "Péché originel," 429.

[104] *Qu. Thal.* 61 (90:632-636).

[105] Gaudel, "Péché originel," 429.

deification [διὰ τῆς ἰδίας σαρκώσεως, τὴν ὑπὲρ φύσιν χάριν δωρησάμενος τῇ φύσει, τὴν θέωσιν]."[106] By His suffering and undeserved death, and especially by His resurrection, He has abolished our death and suffering.[107]

Does this text not contain a clear enough allusion to the physical theory of divinization, indeed even an interesting attempt at juxtaposing it to the traditional doctrine of salvation by the death of Christ? Unfortunately, our monk's ingenious synthesis is based on a debatable conception of concupiscence and its role in generation as well as of its relationships with the sin of Adam, a conception which is clearly close to the Augustinian doctrine.[108]

Contrasting, along with Saint Paul, the salutary work of Christ with the harmful work of Adam, Maximus sometimes seems to attribute to the former the same kind of efficacy as to the latter.[109] But in numerous passages of his writings, he expressly teaches that Christian salvation, and consequently deification, presupposes personal effort and the employment of certain rites.

Thus, to have a share in the fruits of the redemption, we must "be born again out of Christ according to the will in the Spirit by the washing of regeneration." Furthermore, it is necessary to "keep intact and pure the grace of the innocence received in baptism [τὴν ἐν τῷ βαπτίσματι χάριν τῆς ἀναμαρτησίας] and the virtue of the mystical adoption in the Spirit by the law of the evangelical commandments."[110] For if in His love God condescended to us, He will deify by His grace only those who, in spirit, rise up to Him.[111] To that end, we must be "exact imitators" of Christ,[112] our "model and example." Just as the human will of the Savior "was fully deified" [διόλου τεθέωτο] because it was perfectly subject to the divine will, so will it be for our own if we imitate His submission to God.[113]

The new life which results from baptism involves degrees. In the first stage, the believer trains himself in the practice of the divine commandments and of virtues in order to gain impassibility [ἀπάθεια]: this is the working life [ἡ πρακτική]. The second degree is that of gnosis [γνῶσις] or of contemplation [θεωρία], itself usually subdivided into two phases.[114] In this way, the monk of

322

323

---

[106] *Qu. Thal.* 61 (90:632a-b). Cf. *Cap.* 1.62 (1204), where the author writes that by being incarnated the Logos has deified the human being with whom He united and that, for this reason, He granted "to the nature of human beings the firm expectation of deification [τῆς πρὸς ἐκθέωσιν ἐλπίδος]."

[107] *Qu. Thal.* 61 (90:632a-b). It is to be noted that, with Maximus, "the idea of atonement for the offence done to God does not appear in the least" (Grumel, "Maxime," 457).

[108] Cf. Gaudel, "Péché originel," 429.

[109] See in particular *Qu. Thal.* 61 (90:632).

[110] *Qu. Thal.* 61 (90:636c). Cf. *Ascet.* 2-3 (90:914a-c).

[111] *Opusc.* Georg. (91:57a-b).

[112] *Ascet.* 34 (90:940b).

[113] *Opusc.* Marin. diacon. (91:80d). Cf. (81d-84). We see the place that Maximus, in his doctrine of divinization, gives to the dogma of the two wills in Christ, of which he was "the most illustrious champion" and martyr. See Tixeront, *Histoire des dogmes,* 3:188. For him, to deny this dogma is to render inexplicable the deification of the Christian. Cf. P. Pourrat, *La spiritualité chrétienne* (4 vols.; Paris, 1928-1935), 1:475-476.

[114] For the breakdown of all these divisions, see Viller, "Aux sources de la spiritualité de saint Maxime," 162-166, where the references in Maximus' writings are to be found.

Chrysopolis arrives at a tripartite division of the spiritual life which he describes in these terms:

> The intellect that succeeds in the practical [life] progresses toward prudence [πρὸς φρόνησιν]; the one that succeeds in contemplation advances toward gnosis. It is up to the first [life] to bring the one that struggles to the distinction between virtue and vice; [it is up to] the second, on the contrary, to lead the one that participates in this distinction to the knowledge of incorporeal and corporeal beings. But one is finally judged worthy [καταξιοῦται] of the grace of the knowledge of God [τῆς θεολογικῆς χάριτος] who, having surpassed by the wings of love all that has just been enumerated and settling down in God [ἐν θεῷ γενόμενος], applies the intellect, as much as possible for the human νοῦς, to the study of the knowledge which has God as the object.[115]

In order to see God and the treasures which He contains, we must then "be purified by love and continence"; the more we are purified, the better we will see God.[116] This means that only the intellect detached from earthly things is capable of devoting itself in a continuous way [ἀπερισπάστως] to prayer,[117] which, in turn, "separates the νοῦς from every thought, places it bare before God Himself, and unites it with Him."[118] Having arrived at this "summit of prayer," high above the flesh and the world, the νοῦς becomes "entirely immaterial and without form [ἄϋλον πάντη καὶ ἀνείδεον];[119] "contemplating what is simple, it also becomes simple and perfectly like the light [φωτοειδής];"[120] conversing with God, the νοῦς becomes bare, and finally "deiform."[121] In the impulse of prayer, it "is seized [ἁρπαγῆναι] by the divine and infinite light; it no longer has the perception either of itself or of any being in general, except exclusively of the One who by love brings about such an illumination in it."[122]

In short, "the prayer of the theologian [θεολογικός]" is "a mysterious silence" [ἀπόρρητος σιγή] ending up in the "union which surpasses thought and gnosis."[123] And those who "have been mystically rendered worthy" of this unitive contemplation reproduce the "image which perfectly and unfailingly

324

---

[115] *Carit.* 2.26 (90:992). Cf. *Qu. Thal.* 10, 25 (288b, 333d-335a).

[116] *Carit.* 4.72 (90:1065).

[117] *Carit.* 2.1, 3, 5 (90:984-986).

[118] *Ascet.* 19 (90:925-928). Cf. *Ascet.* 24 (929), where it is said that the "grace of prayer unites [συνάπτει] the νοῦς with God."

[119] *Carit.* 2.61 (90:1004).

[120] *Carit.* 3.97 (90:1045).

[121] *Ascet.* 24 (90:929).

[122] *Carit.* 2.6 (90:985b). Cf. *Dion. Ar. Myst.* 1.3 (3:1000c-1001a) cited above, 243.

[123] *Qu. Thal.* 25, schol. 14 (90:340bc). Although the scholia which accompany the *Qu. Thal.* may be "of an unknown author of the eleventh century" (see Grumel, "Maxime," 450), we think we can cite them here because they are manifestly in accordance with the thought of Maximus.

imitates the divine beauty,"[124] namely, the Logos. This means that "they receive from God to be gods" [ἐκ θεοῦ τὸ θεοὶ εἶναι λαβόντες].[125]

From all evidence, the higher prayer advocated by Maximus is an ascension of the soul toward the ecstatic union with God, modeled on the mystical way of Dionysius. But the disciple shows himself to be more sober and prudent than the master. Assuredly with Maximus too, the ecstatic encounter with God takes place outside of the normal activity of the νοῦς, the latter then being as though flooded by torrents of divine light. However, with his sharper Christian sensitivity, our monk seems to have detected the danger of pantheism implied by the Neoplatonic concept of the human ἕν, emanating from the divine Ἕν and reverting to Him. In any case, he creates the impression of wishing to guard against this danger.

III

In the scholia which our author has devoted to the works of the "divine Dionysius,"[126] his constant preoccupation to eliminate from them everything offensive to orthodoxy shows itself even more clearly. To be convinced of this, it is sufficient to glance at the scholia relating to the Areopagitic passages where the ἕν of the soul appears.

We have seen that Maximus, without hesitation, adopts the Dionysian expression "to become one" [ἓν γίγνεσθαι], in order to indicate this simplification of the soul, which is both a condition and an effect of the union with God: "By striving toward God, we become, by means of this unity, a single ἕν,...a uniform ἕν [ἓν ἀμερὲς,...ἓν ἑνοειδές]."[127] But where the hierarchical doctor speaks of the human "one" as of the noblest part of the soul, superior even to the νοῦς and seat of the mystical contact with God, our confessor either passes over this notion in silence or discreetly sets it aside under the pretext of explaining it.

Thus the passage from the *Ecclesiastical Hierarchy* quoted above,[128] where Dionysius speaks of the hierarchs' spiritual entry "into the personal ἕν," is simply set aside by his commentator.[129]

In the same writing, the pseudo-Areopagite says that hymns and sacred readings "fill up, in blessed and spiritual contemplations, the ἑνοειδές of those perfected by the divine Ἕν by uniting it to Him."[130] Under the pen of Maximus,

---

[124] *Qu. Thal.* 10 (90:288d).

[125] *Carit.* 1.28 (90:1189)[?]. In numbers 27 and 28, the deifying union with God is presented as an effect of love. But basically, perfect love for Maximus merges with higher prayer.

[126] *Prol. Dion.* (4:20a, 20d). Dionysius is also called μέγας (4:16a), πάμμεγας (4:17b), ἅγιος (4:17c), μακάριος (4:21d). Saint John of Damascus, moreover, hardly shows himself to be less enthusiastic for our mystic, in describing him as θεῖος ἀνήρ (*Imag.* 1.11 [94:1241a]) and as θεοφόρος καὶ τὰ θεῖα πολὺς Διονύσιος (*Fid. orth.* 3.6 [94:1005a]).

[127] *Schol. div. nom.* 1.3 (4:196a).

[128] Above, 246.

[129] *Schol. eccl. hier.* 3.3.3 (4:140a-b).

[130] *Schol. eccl. hier.* 4.3.3 (3:477a-b).

this ἐνοειδές becomes "that which [is directed] toward the [divine] Ἕν, namely, the νοῦς itself which sees the divine, and of which Dionysius also says that it is united with the Ἕν Itself, and fulfilled by the union with It."[131]

Another example of this process is supplied by the text of *On the Divine Names* where the ecstatic union is described as a "union which surpasses the nature of the νοῦς and by which the latter is united with the one who is beyond it."[132] The paraphrase of Maximus explains it as a matter of "the union of the νοῦς [ἔνωσιν τοῦ νοῦ]...by which it is raised toward the One who is beyond itself, that is to say, tends toward the contemplation of God."[133]

By thus identifying, and not without skillfulness, the ἕν of the soul with the νοῦς, our author clears this concept of its specifically Neoplatonic meaning. As a result, he renders it easily assimilable by Christian thought. But he also deserves that we apply to him, mutatis mutandis, the famous aphorism: *Traduttore, traditore!*

Nevertheless, it is a fact that by interpreting the Dionysian mysticism in an orthodox way and attaching it more closely to the body of the doctrine of the church,[134] Maximus not only assured its success but rendered the most outstanding service to Christian mysticism.

In the final analysis, despite numerous differences of detail, Dionysius and Maximus agree in seeing deification through the mystical union with God as the goal of creation and of the incarnation, as well as of the moral activity of humankind. If it is true—as we commonly accept[135]—that the *Corpus Dionysianum* was composed in Syria, it would be necessary to conclude from this that in the fifth century the ideal of divinization made amazing progress in the homeland of the great Antiochenes. In any case, the writings of the pseudo-Areopagite and of the monk of Chrysopolis prove that the doctrine and, perhaps even more, the mysticism of *theopoiesis* were indeed playing a

---

[131]   *Schol. eccl. hier.* 4.3.3 (4:156a): Τὸ ἐνοειδές φησὶ τὸ πρὸς τὸ ἕν, ἤγουν τὸν τὸ θεῖον ὁρῶντα αὐτὸν νοῦν, ὃν καὶ ἐνοῦσθαι λέγει πρὸς αὐτὸ τὸ ἕν, καὶ τῆς τούτου ἀποπληροῦσθαι ἑνώσεως.

[132]   *Div. nom.* 7.1 (3:865c). See above, 242.

[133]   *Schol. div.nom.* 7.1 (4:344a). Cf. 7.3 (4:353a); *Schol. myst.* 1.3 (4:421a).

[134]   This improvement seems due, in large part at least, to the preponderant influence of Evagrius Ponticus, from whom Maximus derived "the framework of his spirituality." Cf. Viller, "Aux sources de la spiritualité de saint Maxime," 260. In what remains to us of the writings of Evagrius, we find some traces of the theme of divinization. Like Origen and Gregory of Nyssa, Evagrius sees gnosis, which he conceives of as a direct, mystical union with God, as the completion of the Christian life. Cf. J. Moisescu, Εὐάγριος ὁ Ποντικός, (Athens, 1937), 142-144. Now, among those who have achieved this contemplative union, there are no longer either teachers or disciples, "but all are gods" [ἀλλὰ πάντες θεοί εἰσιν] (*Cent.* 4.51 [ed. W. Frankenberg, *Euagrius Ponticus*; Berlin, 1912, 293]). Elsewhere he specifies that the gnostic does not become god by nature, but by grace: the νοῦς favored by the contemplation of the Trinity "is even called god by grace having become the perfect image of its Creator" (*Cent.* 5.81 [ed. Frankenberg, 355]). Cf. *Sp. sent.* 24 (PG 40:1269): ψυχὴ καθαρὰ μετὰ θεὸν, θεός.

[135]   Cf. Bardenhewer, *Geschichte*, 4:294.

role of the first order in the theological thought and piety of the Greek church of the sixth and seventh centuries.[136]

---

[136] With Leontius of Byzantium, "the most remarkable theologian" of the first half of the sixth century (cf. Bardenhewer *Geschichte,* 5:12), we do not find the terminology of θέωσις. He presents salvation as the recovery of the divine likeness and of the divine filiation; but he does not speak of divinization, not even concerning the humanity assumed by the Word. Perhaps this was in order not to furnish weapons to his adversaries, the Aphthartodocetae, for whom "the flesh of the Savior, by virtue of his union with the Word, was impassible and incorruptible" (V. Grumel, "Léonce de Byzance," *DTC* 9:420; cf. V. Grumel, "La sotériologie de Léonce de Byzance," *EO* 40 [1937]: 385-397).

CHAPTER THREE

THE CONCLUSION OF GREEK PATRISTICS:
SAINT JOHN OF DAMASCUS

328   In the eighth century, iconoclasm comes to be associated with monotheism and arouses impassioned controversies in the church of the East. In the fervor of the conflict, defenders of the catholic dogma of the time too often neglect to rise to the level of its governing principles. Fortunately, Greek theology is to find a first-rate compiler in Saint John of Damascus, who will endeavor to summarize the doctrinal tradition of his church into a more or less systematic and complete whole, and pass it on, not merely to the East—where the *Source of Knowledge* has remained the classical handbook of dogmatic theology[1]—but also to the West.

It is enough to glance through the Damascene's masterpiece, *On the Orthodox Faith*, in order to notice that the teaching on God, cosmology, and Christology take up by far the greatest space. In contrast, the author did not even consider it necessary to devote a special chapter to soteriology. By collecting the allusions which he makes to it, here and there, we nevertheless manage to reconstruct his conception of the redemption, which, moreover, has nothing original. In this matter John has fully realized his intention of being only an echo of the earlier, "better teachers."[2] But as a faithful echo, he reserved an important place for the traditional theme of divinization.

I

329   As we might expect, the doctor from Damascus presents the deification of the Christian as a return to original perfection. Along with the representatives of the school of Alexandria, he has a very high view of the original state, and this clearly emerges in the details—especially those contained in the second book of *On the Orthodox Faith*—which he devotes to paradise. One recognizes there a veritable mosaic of citations, as many scriptural as patristic, the latter taken for the most part from the Cappadocians, especially from Gregory of Nazianzus, the favorite teacher of John.

The Damascene distinguishes in Adam the divine image and the divine likeness: "τὸ κατ᾽ εἰκών," he writes, "signifies the intelligence and the free will [αὐτεξούσιον]; τὸ δὲ καθ᾽ ὁμοίωσιν, the likeness of virtue, as much as is possi-

---

[1]   Cf. Bardenhewer, *Geschichte*, 5:52.
[2]   Jo. D. *Dialect.* Prooem. (PG 94:524c-525).

ble."[3] The divine likeness was a gift of God for our first parent, the result of a "divine participation" which consisted in the contemplation of the Creator.

Such is the profound significance that John sees in the paradisiacal account. After recalling that, among the fathers, some had conceived of paradise as perceptible, others, on the contrary, as purely spiritual [νοητόν], and desirous of reconciling the two points of view, he offers the following opinion:

> Humankind having been created both sensitive and spiritual, their place of sojourn was made very holy, being also both sensitive and spiritual, thus presenting a two-fold aspect. In their bodies, they were living in the very divine and very beautiful land, as we just recounted; in their soul, on the contrary, they were sojourning in the higher place of an incomparable beauty, having God who was living in them [Θεὸν ἔχων οἶκον τὸν ἔνοικον] as a dwelling-place[4] and was acting as their splendid garment, clothed as they were in His grace [χάριν], enjoying and feeding, as if angels, uniquely on the very sweet fruit of their contemplation [θεωρία], which has been called, with good reason, the tree of life. Indeed, the sweetness of the divine partaking imparts a life uninterrupted by death to those who receive it.[5]

330

Thus, due to their "communion with God,"[6] or—as John expresses himself again following Gregory of Nazianzus[7]—"by their propensity toward God, humankind have been deified [θεούμενον]; deified, however, by a participation in the divine splendor and not by a transformation into the divine essence."[8] According to the preceding quotation, this participation in the glory of God consisted in incorruptibility or blessed immortality.[9]

Not content with his partaken-of divinity, Adam allowed himself to be seduced "by the hope of a divinity" of nature.[10] He had cause to regret it:

> Deceived by the devil, the author of sin, the man did not observe the precept of the Creator; he was stripped of grace, deprived of the reassuring confidence in God [ἡ πρὸς θεὸν παρρησία], and encircled by the harshness of a painful life; this is what the leaves of the fig tree signify. Furthermore, he was surrounded with dead things, namely, with mortality and with the weight of the flesh; which the garment of skin signifies.[11] He was driven out of paradise according to the just sentence of God, condemned to death and given over to corruption. But the

---

[3] *Fid. orth.* 2.12 (94:920b). Cf. 4.14 (1108a-b). We will see that the Damascene does not always remain faithful to this distinction.

[4] According to *Fid. orth.* 4.13 (1137b), Adam had received the gift of the Holy Spirit who was living in him.

[5] *Fid. orth.* 2.11 (916b-c). Cf. 2.30 (976c-977a).

[6] *Fid. orth.* 4.4 (1108b).

[7] Cf. Gr. Naz. *Or.* 38.11 (36:324a). See above, 194. Note that the Damascene immediately adds an explanation concerning the nature of Adam's deification.

[8] *Fid. orth.* 2.12 (924a).

[9] Cf. *Fid. orth.* 2.11 (917c-d); 2.30 (977b-c); 4.4 (1108b).

[10] Cf. Gr. Naz. *Or.* 39.13 (36:349a-b).

[11] Cf. Gr. Naz. *Or.* 38.12 (36:349a-b).

merciful [God], who had given being to him and favored him with well-being [τὸ εὖ εἶναι],[12] did not give him up.[13]

331   On the contrary, by the most diverse means God reopened to humankind "the return to well-being."[14] But all these means proved to be insufficient.

II

This means that in order to destroy the tyranny of death, the consequence of sin, a Redeemer, who was without sin and thus not subject to death, was necessary [ἔδει] to restore the human nature and to teach by His example "the way of virtue which removes from corruption and leads to eternal life."[15] In short, a God-Man was necessary. This is why the divine Logos Himself was incarnated:

> In the depths of His mercy, the Creator and Demiurge of our kind became like us, being made human in everything except sin and uniting with our nature. Since He had imparted to us His own image and His own Spirit and since we had not kept them,[16] He took on Himself our poor and feeble nature, in order to purify us, to make us again incorruptible and participants of His own divinity....
>
> By His birth or incarnation, by His baptism, His passion, and His resurrection, He thus delivered our nature from the sin of our first parent, from death, and from corruption; He became the origin of resurrection and offered Himself as the way, the example, and the model, in order that, following in His footsteps, we might become by adoption [θέσει] what He Himself is by nature [φύσει]: children and heirs of God and His coheirs. He also gave us, as He said, a second birth, in order that, just as being born of Adam we have been likened to him, having in-herited the curse and corruption, in the same way also, born of Christ, we might become like Him and heirs of His incorruptibility, His blessing, and His glory.[17]

332

This fine text is like an abridgement of the Damascene's soteriology, indeed even of the soteriology of the Greek church. Actually, it more or less sums up the traditional views on the salvific work of Christ.[18] Salvation here is presented,

---

[12]   An expression already encountered with Maximus the Confessor. See above, 249.

[13]   *Fid. orth.* 3.1 (981), where John summarizes Gr. Naz. *Or.* 38.13 (36:325). Cf. *C. Man.* 31 (1437d), where the Damascene speaks of the great sin which the creature, who claims to be able "to go beyond his own nature" and to become god, commits—an impossible thing for anyone who has a be-ginning [ἀδύνατον γὰρ τὸν μὴ ἄναρχον εἶναι θεόν].

[14]   *Fid. orth.* 3.1 (981).

[15]   *Fid. orth.* 3.1 (981).

[16]   The Damascene seems here to forget the distinction between divine "image" and divine "like-ness," about which there was some question above (256-257). In any case, what humankind did not keep was the higher divine likeness. Perhaps it is a matter of a simple oversight of our author who, once more, seems to follow Saint Gregory of Nazianzus. Cf. *Or.* 38.13 and 45.9 (36:325 and 636a). The latter did not make the distinction in question. See above, 193-196.

[17]   *Fid. orth.* 4.13 (1137a-c). Cf. 4.4 (1108).

[18]   Lacking in our text is the theme of the devil's defeat, which the author nevertheless develops else-where. Following the bishop of Nazianzus, he rejects the theory of the rights of the devil in order to re-tain only the theory of the abuse of power. Cf. *Fid. orth.* 3.1, 27 (981c-984a, 1096-1097).

negatively, as a deliverance from sin and corruptibility, and positively, as the divine adoption, a participation in the glorious immortality of God, in short, a deification. The whole is connected with the life and entire activity of the Savior, the different stages of which are nevertheless placed on the same plane. But elsewhere John attributes a special redemptive efficacy, sometimes to the incarnation considered separately and sometimes to the death of Christ.

More often than not, our doctor only mentions the expiatory sacrifice of the cross as the cause of our redemption. This means that traditional realism governs his soteriology. Here, as an example, is a particularly significant passage:

> All the actions and miracles of Christ are great, divine, and worthy of admiration; but the most admirable of all these things is the precious cross. Indeed, by nothing else has death been destroyed, has the sin of our first parent been erased, has hell been despoiled, has resurrection been granted,...has the return to original bliss been prepared, have the doors of paradise been opened again, has our nature been placed at the right hand of God; by nothing else have we become children and heirs of God, if it is not by the cross of our Lord Jesus Christ.[19]

John does not use the terminology of *theopoiesis* any more than his predecessors when he exalts the redemptive value of the passion and of the resurrection of our Lord. On the other hand, this terminology reappears whenever he begins to describe the benefits of the incarnation as such. At the same time, the generic realism at the root of the physical theory of divinization reappears.

333

In the christological part of his *Orthodox Faith,* where he appears preoccupied with defending dyophysism, the Damascene repeats more than once this axiom of Gregory of Nazianzus: "That which has not been assumed has not been healed."[20] From this he comes to a conclusion about the perfect identity of the human nature in Christ and in us. What he considered an absolute, numerical identity is that which comes out again conspicuously from chapters three and six of the third part of the same treatise.

After recalling that the error of the monophysites consisted in identifying nature [φύσιν] and hypostasis [ὑπόστασιν], our author develops the catholic conception. He starts by stating in principle that in the many and different hypostases there is only one and the same nature or essence, like the unique human nature in all people.[21] Not that the essence subsists in itself [ἡ οὐσία δὲ καθ᾽ ἑαυτὴν οὐχ ὑφίσταται]; it only exists in the hypostasis, which is defined as "an essence with accidents" [οὐσία μετὰ συμβεβηκότων].[22] But "every

---

[19] *Fid. orth.* 4.11 (1128d-1129a). Cf. 3.25, 27 (1093, 1096b-c); 4.4, 9 (1108c-1109b, 1120c-1121a). See Rivière, *Rédemption: étude historique,* 206-209; M. Jugie, "Jean Damascène," *DTC* 8:737.

[20] See above, 196.

[21] *Fid. orth.* 3.3 (992): μίαν τῶν ἀνθρώπων φύσιν φαμέν...τῶν πλείστων καὶ διαφόρων ὑποστάσεων μίαν φύσιν φαμέν.

[22] *Fid. orth.* 3.6 (1001c-1004a).

essence is common to the hypostases which it contains, and one does not find any nature or essence to be special and individual; otherwise, it would be necessary to say that the same hypostases are both consubstantial and of different essence, and that the holy Trinity is both consubstantial and of different essence according to divinity. It is consequently the same nature that one sees in each of the hypostases."[23] As a result, if a hypostasis suffers, every respective essence is said to suffer in one of its hypostases; "however it is not necessary that all the hypostases of the same kind suffer with the one which suffers."[24]

334

Now, "by the contact with divinity" [τῇ συναφείᾳ τῆς θεότητος],[25] due to "the hypostatic union" and also "to the mutual penetration [περιχώρησις] of natures" comparable to the ignition of iron, the human nature has been deified in Christ.[26] This enabled John to exclaim in the first of his *Orations on the Sacred Images:*

> We were really sanctified when [ἀφ' οὗ] the Logos-God became flesh, having been likened to us in everything except sin, when He was mingled with our nature without confusion, and when, without changing it [ἀμεταβλήτως], He deified [ἐθέωσε] the flesh by the mutual penetration [περιχώρησις], without fusion, of His divinity and His flesh.[27]

No more than this is necessary to justifiably conclude that the last of the fathers knew and sometimes made use of the physical theory of divinization.

III

335

The doctor from Damascus does not think that a real deification of all individuals is due to the very fact of the incarnation, any more than the other repre-

---

[23] *Fid. orth.* 3.6 (1008a-b): Πᾶσα γὰρ οὐσία κοινή ἐστι τῶν ὑπ' αὐτῆς περιεχομένων ὑποστάσεων, καὶ οὐκ ἔστιν εὑρεῖν μερικὴν καὶ ἰδιάζουσαν φύσιν, ἤτοι οὐσίαν ἐπεὶ ἀνάγκη τὰς αὐτὰς ὑποστάσεις καὶ ὁμοουσίους καὶ ἑτεροουσίους λέγειν, καὶ τὴν ἁγίαν Τριάδα καὶ ὁμοούσιον καὶ ἑτερούσιον κατὰ τὴν θεότητα λέγειν. Ἡ αὐτὴ τοίνυν φύσις ἐν ἑκάστῃ τῶν ὑποστάσεων θεωρεῖται.

[24] *Fid. orth.* 3.6 (1004a).

[25] *Fid. orth.* 3.18 (1072c).

[26] *Fid. orth.* 3.17 (1068b-1069b). The chapter is entitled: "Concerning the deification [τεθεῶσθαι] of the nature of the flesh of the Lord and of His will." John does not hesitate to write: ἡ σάρξ τοῦ κυρίου τεθεῶσθαι λέγεται, καὶ ὁμόθεος, καὶ θεὸς γενέσθαι; and this is following Gr. Naz. *Or.* 39.16 and 45.9 (36:353b and 633d). In *Fid. orth.* 4.9 (1125a), our author says of the body of Christ: τῇ θεώσει θεός. He conceives of this deification as a communication of the divine energies, which, without exempting the flesh of the Lord from suffering and from death—the simple φθορά — kept it from permanent dissolution, called διαφθορά (*Fid. orth.* 3.28 [1097-1100]).

With regard to the word περιχώρησις, the bishop of Nazianzus first employed it in order to express the compenetration of the two natures in Christ (*Ep.* 101.6 [37:181]). The relationships between the natures not being identical for the two sides, the choice of the term does not seem felicitous. Cf. G. L. Prestige, *God in Patristic Thought* (London, 1936), 297-299.

[27] *Imag.* 1.21 (94:1253ab). The reading παραχωρήσεως (relinquishment) from the text of Migne is clearly incorrect, as it comes from *Fid. orth.* 3.17 (just quoted) and from *Volunt.* 28, 44 (95:161, 184).

sentatives of this conception. Applying to the incarnation the distinction between nature and person, he formally declares that, in order to join the human nature, the Logos "has not assumed all hypostases."[28] The divinization of the human nature which results from the incarnation is thus by no means a deification of persons. The latter, on the contrary, depends on the imitation of Christ, whose θεώσις is the model of our own,[29] an assimilation which presupposes moral effort and the common practice of the rites of the church.

First of all, it is necessary to be born again to the Christian life by faith, which involves a total conversion of the heart, and by baptism.[30] Being clearly inspired by Saint Cyril of Alexandria,[31] John distinguishes a twofold effect of the "second birth":

> Since human beings are twofold, [made up] of a soul and a body, God has granted us a twofold purification as well, namely, by the water and the Spirit. By that of the Spirit, He renews in us what is according to image and likeness;[32] by that of the water, He purifies the body of sin by the grace of the Spirit and delivers it from corruptibility [φθορά],[33] the water being the image of death and the Spirit giving the guarantee of life.[34]

336

By virtue of baptism, the divine Spirit dwells in the saints from their earthly life onwards;[35] He restores the divine likeness to them; in short, He "deifies them without being deified" [θεοῦν οὐ θεούμενον][36] Himself, since He is true God.

---

[28] *Fid. orth.* 3.11 (1021-1024a). In this curious passage, John distinguishes three meanings of the word φύσις. This term can mean: a) "the nature considered ψιλῇ θεωρίᾳ, which does not subsist in itself"; b) the "nature considered in the species and which is common to all hypostases of the same species and is composed of them [συνάπτουσα]"; c) the "nature considered in an individual [ἐν ἀτόμῳ θεωρουμένη φύσις] and which is identical to the nature considered in the species." Now the Logos has not assumed either the first of these three natures—an assumption which would only have been a pretence of incarnation—or the second—"for He did not assume all hypostases" [οὐ γὰρ πάσας τὰς ὑποστάσεις ἀνέλαβεν]—"but the nature in the individual which is identical to that in the species." "The nature considered in the species" and "the nature considered in the individual" are manifestly conceived of by our author as concrete. Basically identical, they nonetheless differ since the first "is composed of all hypostases of the same species," whereas the second is in a single hypostasis. We see to what expedients the negation of the concrete individual nature drove our author.

[29] *Fid. orth.* 4.13 (1137a-c). Text cited above, 258.

[30] Cf. *Fid. orth.* 4.9 (1117-1125).

[31] See above, 225-226.

[32] Note the synonymy of εἰκών and ὁμοίωσις which reveals the influence here of Cyril. See above, 221.

[33] The body here seems like the seat of sin!

[34] *Fid. orth.* 4.9 (1121a). With many fathers, the Damascene acknowledges that "through prayer and the invocation, the Holy Spirit comes upon the water." On the twofold birth, see also *Fid. orth.* 4.13 (1137d).

[35] Cf. *Imag.* 1.19 (1249c-d). After the death of the saints, writes John, "the grace of the Holy Spirit remains indissolubly united both with their souls and with their bodies in the graves, as well as with their figures and holy images; this is not according to essence, however, but by grace and virtue [χάριτι καὶ ἐνεργείᾳ]."

[36] *Fid. orth.* 1.8 (821c).

By uniting us with the Holy Spirit, the baptismal rite unites us, at the same time, with the entire Trinity, which is inseparable [ἀχώριστος][37]: He makes us adoptive children and heirs of God by making us "partakers of His own divinity,"[38] of His own nature.[39]

For the new life given in baptism, an appropriate food is necessary which enables it to "attain to the measure of perfection."[40] This food is none other than "the bread of the altar, as well as the wine and the water, which, by the invocation and presence [ἐπιφοίτησις] of the Holy Spirit,[41] are marvelously [ὑπερφυῶς] changed into the body of Christ and His blood, to the point of being no longer two things but one and the same thing."[42]

337   The fruits of the eucharistic communion extend to the body and to the soul of those who "receive it with faith and justly." These are the remission of sins, the safeguard for the soul and the body, "incorruptibility with a view to the enjoyment of eternal bliss,"[43] indeed, even the participation in the divinity of Jesus.[44] This means that the body of the Lord possesses "a divine and life-giving virtue."[45] We may compare it to a burning coal which sets on fire and thus assimilates everything that makes contact with it:

> We draw near to it with a fervent desire and, after crossing our hands, we receive the body of the crucified One. After applying our eyes, lips, and forehead to it, we take the divine coal in order that the fire of our desire, increased by the heat of the coal, may consume our sins and enlighten our hearts, in order that by participation in the divine fire we may be set ablaze and deified [θεωθῶμεν].[46]

Thus each of the two great mysteries of Christian initiation deifies man, but more particularly the Eucharist.

Fragile and unfinished during this life, our deification becomes permanent after death due to our union, indissoluble by that time, with God.[47] Incorruptibility will be fully realized after the resurrection.[48] But ἀφθαρσία as such is not the supreme good. Common to the chosen and the reprobates, it is merely

---

[37] *Fid. orth.* 4.9 (1124a).

[38] *Fid. orth.* 4.13 (1137b-c). Cf. 4.15 (1164a).

[39] *Imag.* 1.4 (1236b).

[40] *Fid. orth.* 4.13 (1137b).

[41] An allusion to the epiclesis.

[42] *Fid. orth.* 4.13 (1144-1145). In *Fid. orth.* 4.13 (1141a) the eucharistic transformation carried out by the Spirit is compared to His action in the incarnation.

[43] *Fid. orth.* 4.13 (1148).

[44] *Fid. orth.* 4.13 (1153a). Cf. (1152b), where it is said that the communicants "become bodies of Christ."

[45] *Fid. orth.* 4.13 (1152b-c).

[46] *Fid. orth.* 4.13 (1149a-b). To be noted are the details given in this text on the way of receiving the Eucharist.

[47] Cf. *Rect. sent.* 1 (94:1421a); *C. Man.* 75 (94:1573b); *Spir. neq.* (95:93d); *Fid. orth.* 4.15, 27 (94:1164c, 1221b).

[48] *Fid. orth.* 4.27 (1220a).

their condition. Supreme joy consists in the eternal and glorious life with God, a life which will only be granted to the saints.[49]

Admitted at last to the vision [θέα] which causes them "to partake spiritually...of the divinity of Christ"[50] and having become completed images of God, "the chosen will even be gods [θεοὶ οἱ ἅγιοι]." The Scripture says, in fact, "God holds judgment in the midst of the gods"—as "the divine [θεῖος] Gregory explains "—to distribute rewards.[51]

338

⊗

In short, along with the majority of the Greek fathers, Saint John of Damascus sees divinization as the pinnacle of salvation. His conception of *theopoiesis* hardly reveals any personal characteristics. On one point, however, he surpasses his teachers. Much more clearly than they, indeed, he distinguishes between the deification of the nature and that of human persons, without, however, saying it formally.

The φύσις common to all individuals is deified once and for all in the incarnation due to contact with divinity. Persons, on the contrary, must gain their deification by the imitation of Christ. This assimilation presupposes a moral effort guided and sustained by the doctrine, example, and grace of the Savior; it is dependent on the common practice of the sacred rites of the church, by means of which the Spirit applies to the individual the fruits of Christ's work, particularly of His death and of His resurrection.

Is there not here, at least in the early stages, the first synthesis which harmonizes the physical theory of divinization with the traditional doctrine of the redeeming death of Christ?

In any case, the work of the last of the fathers testifies clearly to the vitality of the Christian ideal of θέωσις in the Greek church of the eighth century.

---

[49] *Fid. orth.* 4.27 (1228).
[50] *Fid. orth.* 4.13 (1153c).
[51] *Imag.* 1.19 (1249c). The author refers to Gr. Naz. *Or.* 30.4 (36:108c). See also *Fid. orth.* 4.15 (1164a-b), where the saints are called "gods, lords, and kings," not, however, by nature but by grace.

CONCLUSION

339   It remains for us to condense the main results of this long investigation into a final synthesis.

I

Since antiquity a certain divinization appears as the ideal to which the best among the Greeks aspire. Quite naturally, they conceive of this ideal according to their notion of divinity. Thus the ancient poets, such as Homer and Hesiod, for whom the gods are like immortal human beings, dream of a happy existence, free from suffering and death, an almost divine life, which they reserve, however, for an exceptional and privileged few.

In order to assure themselves of a similar afterlife, the followers of the mystery religions endeavor to gain the favor of a savior-god by imitating the trials and tribulations of that one's existence through the rites of initiation.

Inasmuch as the idea of divinity is spiritualized, due to the mystics and the philosophers, the conception of the future life is refined as well. In the end, one settles on the ideal of an assimilation, indeed, even of an identification with God of the soul's most noble part, the spiritual or divine element in a human being.

All the way through this advancement, the sought-after aim remains basically identical: it is always the participation in the blessed immortality of divinity. What changes is the way of visualizing the divine life and, consequently, the divinized life in which one desires to participate.

340   Very different is the essentially religious ideal advocated in the sacred books of the Israelite people. Their strict monotheism and their very intense feeling of the divine transcendence absolutely forbids the Israelites to envisage a deification of humankind, in whom, at the very most, they recognize a likeness to the Creator.

Having become, by covenant, the chosen people, Israel considers itself as the "son" of God, that is, as united with God by a special bond of belonging and by a commonness of interests. The prophets vigorously fight against the tendency of the people to see in their divine filiation only an external relationship and one merely based on descent from Abraham. They do not cease proclaiming that only the true servants of Yahweh, the righteous, will have a share in the divine promises, that is, in the national restoration, which will inaugurate a union, a new theocracy, in which a great material prosperity, eternal justice, and eternal peace will prevail.

This tendency toward the personalization of religious expectation is strongly increased by the ordeal of the exile. In Hellenic Judaism, it ends up in the idea of a divine filiation resulting from a moral assimilation, from a person's participation in the wisdom of God. It follows that the collective conception of recompense, without disappearing completely, gives precedence little by little to the personal conception of prospects undreamed of until then. The divine filiation exalted by the author of Wisdom will indeed blossom for the righteous after death into a blissful and eternal life with God.

Thus, in the last book of the Old Testament, the Jewish ideal of the divine filiation finds its purest and loftiest expression. While recalling it in some respects, it leaves the ideal of divinization proposed by Greek philosophy far behind.

With Philo, the reconciliation of Jewish and Greek conceptions of salvation increases to the point of becoming almost an identification. In fact, the whole of his theosophy is a large-scale attempt with a view to transforming the Jewish religion into a "mystery" of deification comparable to the Hermetic mysteries. He is also the first Jew who speaks clearly of a divinization of humankind.

With Christianity there appears a higher conception of divine filiation.   341

In the Synoptics, Jesus infuses into the traditional metaphor a new soul filled with trusting love for God or even intimacy with Him. In order to become a child of the heavenly Father, one must carry out His will, imitate His perfection, especially His love, and enter into the kingdom founded by His Messenger. Doing this, one is assured of eternal life in the age to come.

The seeds contained in the synoptic Gospels develop in the Epistles of Saint Paul to become the first Christian soteriology. Christ, the incarnated Son of God, by His death and resurrection has atoned for Adam's work of sin and death, and has brought in a new life. In order to be born again with this life, which is none other than the very life of Christ and of His Spirit, it is necessary to be assimilated into, to be blended with, the Savior by mystically imitating His death and resurrection, with the aid of the rites of Christian initiation. Such an assimilation transforms a human being into an adoptive child of God, into a temple of the Holy Spirit, and into an heir of heaven. The heavenly inheritance is eternal life for the whole person, body and soul, the company of the glorified Jesus, the vision of God face to face, and thus a participation in the life and in the glory of God.

The same ideal is affirmed in the Johannine writings under the cover of different analogies. By uniting with Jesus Christ, the Logos of life made human, the believer escapes the darkness of sin and death to enter into communion with the indestructible light and life. But the divine life and filiation which the believer possesses from this life onwards will display all their splendor only in the kingdom of God, that is, in heaven.

It is precisely this heavenly bliss that the author of the Second Epistle of Saint Peter calls partaking of the divine nature. Only the word *deification* is lacking.

II

Making the most of the biblical facts, along with the resources of their environment, the fathers work out a doctrine of divinization.

In actual fact, in the writings of the apostolic fathers, this theme only appears in a potential state. Saint Ignatius is the only one who, following the example of Saint Paul and Saint John, presents salvation clearly enough as a participation in the divine life. Yet he does not speak of divinization. But from the second and third centuries onward, the struggle against Gnosticism brings substantial progress to the idea of θέωσις.

Against the gnostics, who limit the redemption to a simple redivinization of the divine seed hidden in the pneumatics, who are the only true Christians, the apologists defend the traditional hope of an incorruptibility extending to the whole human composition and which is within the reach of all. But they take care to specify that this is only a question of a shared immortality, of a gift from God, who is the only One incorruptible by nature. If, therefore, the immortalized human being can be called a god, this one is nevertheless, to speak with Theophilus, only an "assumed God."

On this principally eschatological conception of divinization, that of Saint Irenaeus is of notable progress. Drawing his inspiration from Saint Paul and Saint John, the bishop of Lyons sees blessed immortality as a simple continuation of the divine life which we possess from this world on, due to our union with Christ and the Holy Spirit. It is to the indwelling of the Logos and of His Spirit in us that we owe our likeness with God and not to that inamissible divine seed which, according to the Gnostics, would constitute the essence of the pneumatic.

When he touches on the cause of our redemption, Irenaeus presents it sometimes as the result of the incarnation as such and sometimes of the death of the Savior. In the first perspective, the Logos, having become human, sums up in Himself the whole of humanity and gives it immortality and the divine likeness by uniting it with His divinity; this is, without the term, the first hint of the physical theory of divinization. Elsewhere, by linking salvation with the passion, the bishop of Lyons echoes the biblical and traditional doctrine. Almost all subsequent development will follow the paths shown by him.

The originators of the school of Alexandria, however, have a personal way of dealing with the theme of deification. More speculative and bold than Saint Irenaeus, and continuing the method of the apologists, they do not hesitate to

342

forge from this theme a weapon against the heretical gnosis with its magical redivinization by contrasting with it a Christian gnosis of divinization.

For this purpose, Clement and Origen christianize the Greek ideal of an assimilation of humankind to God by means of knowledge and of asceticism. The true gnosis is the perfect understanding of the heavenly doctrine revealed by the incarnate Logos. It is both a fruit of human effort and a divine favor. By imparting to Christians impassibility, wisdom, love, or even the contemplation of the Supreme Being, gnosis assimilates them to God, who possesses all these perfections by nature. This makes Clement—who is the first to apply this term to the Christian—say that gnosis "deifies" a person.   **343**

Here below, this deification reaches its culmination in the gnostic's ecstatic union with God. Thus gnosis is coupled with a mysticism of divinization. But unlike the Neoplatonic mystics, our Christian mystics are very careful to conceive of the deifying union of human beings with God—and this might be the perfect union in the hereafter—as an identification.

By being employed more and more, the terminology of *theopoiesis* will become standard.

This will not be the case with the over-intellectualist theory of the first Alexandrians. The theory will be adopted by no one just as it is; but the later fathers, under the influence of Origen especially, will grant the intellectual element a choice place in their doctrine of divinization. Nevertheless, with them it is the idea of incorruptibility, somewhat neglected by the Alexandrians, which again occupies the foreground.

This different viewpoint is already very perceptible with Saint Hippolytus and Saint Methodius of Olympus, who try to harmonize the complex facts supplied by tradition concerning divinization. Although modest in themselves, their attempts at synthesis prepare for the blossoming that this theme will experience in the great patristic age, which will be the golden age of the doctrine of deification.

III

It is not that one expects to find treatises specially devoted to divinization with the fathers of the fourth and fifth centuries: no ecclesiastical writer has studied it for its own sake. But one would make a big mistake if one concluded, for this reason, that the theme of deification is only an hors d'oeuvre to them.   **344** Quite to the contrary, with almost all the Greeks this theme makes up, as it were, the framework of their soteriology.

This is because they see divinization as the completion of salvation, the supreme destiny of humankind. The account of Adam's formation and of paradise seems definite to them on this point. Being made in the image of God, that is, of the divine Logos, in whom he participates through the νοῦς, favored by friendship, indeed even by divine contemplation, and assimilated to God due to the gifts of impassibility and incorruptibility, our first ancestor was actually a deified human being. Adam is the perfect type of humanity. Therefore the latter was called to divinization.

But deiformity was only granted to Adam on a fragile and revocable basis. By his obedience, he ought to have made it permanent. In actual fact, by his rebellion, he lost it for himself and for all his descendants.

Perhaps fallen humankind would have been able to recover the divine favor by penitence, but they were certainly powerless to free themselves, by themselves, from corruption and from mortality, which are the penalties for sin. Nevertheless, God was bound to Himself not to abandon His masterpiece and not to let the devil triumph.

This is why the Logos was incarnated. By transmitting divine strength to humanity, He superabundantly gives back to it the deiform life and immortality which were lost. A person will only have to unite with Christ and with His Spirit in order to appropriate these blessings.

That the Christian may live a divinized life is a truth universally acknowledged from the fourth century onwards; it is not, however, a purely speculative and abstract truth, but a profound conviction, a key idea which was perhaps the most powerful motivating force of Christian piety of the time. And the proof of this is that, in the christological and trinitarian struggles, the fathers start from this commonly received fact in order to defend dogma.

And this is the way, in order to confound the Arians, that Saint Athanasius sets against these deniers of the divinity of the Logos the fact of the deification of the Christian. For, he says, if the Savior was not God, He would not be able to divinize us.

345   Against the Apollinarists, who deny a human soul to Christ, the Cappadocians, Gregory of Nazianzus in the lead, resort to an analagous argument. The Christian, they argue, is divinized entirely. But this divinization presupposes, besides the divinity of the Savior, His perfect humanity, including a body and a soul, by virtue of the soteriological principle, that only what is assumed by the Word is healed.

This argumentation receives its most rigorous form among the promoters of the physical theory of divinization, especially in the writings of Athanasius and Gregory of Nyssa, who apply their generic realism to the incarnation.

These doctors conceive of every nature or concrete essence as numerically one and common to all hypostases of the same kind. So the concrete human nature is unique and common to all persons. The Platonic origin of this realism is hardly questionable. In the concrete generic nature one recognizes without any difficulty the typical idea of Platonism—but transposed from the ontological domain into the physical domain. It is a strange thing that our authors seem to have been led to such a transposition by trinitarian dogma, for it is by starting from the unity of nature in the trinity of persons in God that they come to a conclusion, generally speaking, about the uniqueness of the concrete nature in which all hypostases of the same kind would participate. Needless to say, while the starting point is right, the conclusion is manifestly wrong.

Applied to humankind, the generic realism perfectly explains our joint responsibility with sinful Adam: in him we all have a share in the fallen nature.

The same realism sheds light especially on the physical theory of deification, of which it constitutes a kind of philosophical base: by being incarnated, the Logos joins *the* human nature and brings it in contact with His divinity. As a result, He fills with divine strength, immortalizes, in short, divinizes this nature and, consequently, in a certain sense, the whole of humanity—all of us. This is to attribute a kind of physical efficacy to the incarnation.

Nevertheless, none of the fathers concluded from the physical theory an automatic deification of individuals. When it is a question of the divinized nature, they instinctively rule out the automatism that they make use of, all the same, in the case of the fallen nature.

But it is necessary to wait for Saint John of Damascus in order to meet with an attempt at the rational justification of this difference in attitude. Utilizing the distinction between nature and hypostasis, the last of the fathers does indeed make it clear that by joining the human nature the Logos has not assumed and consequently has not deified all hypostases. 346

Without stopping for an analysis of the Damascene, we accept the fact that, while acknowledging the divinization of the human nature as such by the simple contact with the divinity of the Word, realized in the incarnation, no advocate of the physical theory teaches the magical deification of individuals that Harnack ascribes to them. On the contrary, all such advocates subordinate individual divinization both to the moral effort of the subject and to the common practice of Christian rites.

IV

According to the Christian faith, salvation in general and the return to the divine likeness and to immortality in particular are effects of Christ's death. One might as well say that our divinization is the fruit of the passion, although it may never be formally linked with it, just as it is with the incarnation in the physical theory. The reason for this is that the advocates of the physical conception are thinking of a deification by contact with the human nature such as they understand it, whereas others have an individual divinization in view, realized directly by the sacred rites with which the Holy Spirit applies grace, as the fruit of the passion, to us.

This role of the Spirit in the work of individual deification is given more and more prominence from the second half of the fourth century, in opposition to the Pneumatomachi.

Against these deniers of the divinity of the Holy Spirit, the fathers again appeal to the fact of our divinization. Since the Pneumatomachi themselves also recognize in the Spirit an active part in divinization, our doctors deduce the absolute divinity of the Spirit from this common idea, because, they say, in order to be able to divinize, He must be God by nature. Consequently, we may understand their concern to bring to full light the deifying action of the Third Person of the Trinity.

347   This action appears first of all in baptism. Made present in the baptismal water by the benediction, the Spirit purifies the body of the baptized one and spreads to the soul, to make it partake of His own nature and transform it into a temple of God. Saint Irenaeus already taught—and was followed in this from the fourth century by all the Greeks—that the Holy Spirit is present in the Christian not only by His virtue, but by His essence. Basil and Cyril of Alexandria are particularly definite on this point.

Moreover, the latter two doctors imply clearly enough that the divine Dweller, not content to dwell in the righteous soul substantially, becomes, as it were, its "form" and produces in it a "quality" which assimilates it to Christ. In this "divine conformation," which seems like a created grace, distinct but inseparable from the Holy Spirit, we may well recognize our habitual or sanctifying grace.

The operation of the divine Spirit extends to the Eucharist, by virtue of which individual divinization reaches completion. Indeed, in accordance with the liturgy, the fathers usually attribute to this operation the changing of the bread and the wine to the body and the blood of Christ.

This mysterious conversion allows the Savior to insert into us His own flesh as a ferment of incorruptibility, destined to destroy all corruption in us. Thus, by its union with the divinized flesh of Christ, our own flesh is deified. This is to apply to the Eucharist the principle of deification by contact.

In the final analysis, all the Greeks conceive of individual divinization according to the realistic doctrine of salvation, which stresses the salvific death of Christ and is only an organic—and therefore legitimate—development of biblical facts.

The physical theory, on the contrary, inasmuch as it attributes to the incarnation, considered separately, the deification of the human nature, conceived of as concrete and common to all persons, seems as debatable a speculation as the principle which is its base.

V

348   For all the Greek doctors, the deification obtained through Christian initiation should normally be the starting point of a continuous ascent toward a more and more perfect divinization. Some among them put the ecstatic union with God at the end of this ascent. And so Christian mysticism is born. Pre-

pared for by the Pauline and Johannine writings, and sketched out by Origen and Gregory of Nyssa, it reaches its full blossoming with Dionysius the mystic.

In the writings of the pseudo-Areopagite, the Neoplatonic influence already very perceptible with his two predecessors is manifest. In the second half of the fifth century, Neoplatonic mysticism, revived by Proclus, seems to have enjoyed a real success. Convinced that one may only dismiss what one replaces, Dionysius does not shrink from the task, as difficult as it is delicate, of Christianizing it.

According to Proclus, the goal to reach is deification, in other words, union, indeed identification, with God the supreme One. Now, if it is true that the like is only known by the like, it must be admitted that, in order to be able to enter into communion with God, the soul must contain a divine element. Being superior to the νοῦς, this trace of the divine One, this ἕν of the soul, is like the "flower" of our essence, the point by which we can enter into contact with the supreme One. However, this is on condition of freeing the ἕν which is in us from every connection with matter and the senses, and of even setting it apart from the νοῦς, in order to bring it back to its native purity and to its native "uniformity."

Without hesitation, Dionysius adopts this theory. But he parts with Proclus when it is a question of pointing out the paths leading to the setting apart of the ἕν and to the ecstatic union.

The first way is that of ecstatic love, the unitive power par excellence. After freeing itself from every fetter, the "one" of the soul rushes into the divine obscurity by an irresistible impulse of love in order to unite with the One who is above all.

Less direct but easier is the way of Christian sacraments. Conceived of according to the triadic plan of Proclus, it leads to deification in three stages—purification, illumination, and union—with the help of three orders of ministers and three orders of sacred rites, which the ecclesiastical hierarchy has at its disposal. 349

But however intimate the deifying union, thus realized, can be, Dionysius never identifies it with the merging or absorption of which the Neoplatonists speak; on the contrary, the union remains a simple assimilation which shows respect for the infinite distance between Creator and creature.

Thanks to Maximus the Confessor, who interprets the Areopagitic work in accordance with the demands of a more refined orthodoxy, Dionysius has become the father of Christian mysticism.

VI

The clear result of our investigation is that from the fourth century the doctrine of divinization is fundamental for the majority of the Greek fathers. It forms a kind of center for their soteriology. The whole redemptive work of

Christ, from the incarnation to the resurrection, as well as the action of the Holy Spirit and of the church which continues this work, converge on deification as the completion of our salvation.

But what exactly do they mean by deification? Is it a question of an exaggeration, as bold as it is devoid of meaning, or does the expression include a reality?

Actually, none of the Greeks who employ the term θέωσις or its equivalents give a definition of it. But this vagueness itself allows them to accommodate, under the terminology to which they have recourse, a host of things which are neither on the same level nor of the same nature.

Nevertheless, on one point there is complete agreement: the divinization of the Christian is not an identification with God; it is only an assimilation, a very eminent restoration of the original divine likeness.

This assimilation certainly involves a conformity of a moral nature. The Christian participates by grace in the perfections that God possesses by nature, such as wisdom, impassibility, and love.

350   There is more. Beyond the moral likeness, the fathers discern something else much closer, due to the presence and activity of the Holy Spirit in the righteous. The Spirit transforms the soul to the image of the Logos, the natural Son of God, thus making the Christian an adoptive child of God. Affecting, it seems, the very essence of the soul, this mysterious conformation is not of a moral nature only but of a physical nature; it is a veritable partaking of the divine nature and of the divine life.

Of the essential perfections of divinity, namely, unbegottenness and incorruptibility, only the latter is communicable to creatures. To partake of the divine nature is thus, above all, to partake of incorruptibility. We see, consequently, how all the Greek doctors strongly stress this aspect of divinization, to the point of often identifying the terms *deify* and *immortalize*.

Without doubt, real immortality will be granted to us only in the hereafter. But from this world onwards Christians possess, in their assimilation to Christ and in the dwelling of the Holy Spirit in them, a kind of seed of divine life, which will blossom in heaven into a blessed and eternal life with the glorious Lord and with God. Spreading at last, after the resurrection, to the whole human composition, deification will become complete and inamissible.

We can thus conclude without exaggeration that the Greek fathers' doctrine concerning the divinization of the Christian —so varied and so rich—contains, at least virtually and under the covering of a not very technical terminology, the basic points of our treatises on sanctifying grace. But clearly their concrete and colorful manner of conceiving of and describing this mysterious reality has a great advantage since it enables us to grasp its richness more easily and live in it more directly. To be convinced of this, it is sufficient to read the following passage taken from Saint Gregory of Nyssa:

Human beings, who count for nothing among beings, and who are dust, grass, vanity, once adopted as children by the God of the universe, become the intimate friends of this Being, who is of an excellence and greatness such that one can nei- 351 ther see Him nor hear Him nor comprehend Him. What thanksgivings worthy of such a favor can one find? By what word, by what thought, by what impulse of spirit can one exalt the superabundance of this grace? Humankind transcend their own nature: from mortal they becomes immortal; from perishable, imperishable; from fleeting, eternal; in a word, from human beings they become gods. Indeed, made worthy of becoming children of God, they will have in themselves the dignity of the Father, enriched with all the paternal benefits. O munificence of the Lord most rich!...How great are the gifts of unutterable treasures![1]

---

[1] Gr. Nyss. *Beat.* 7 (PG 44:1280b-c).

BIBLIOGRAPHY

1. Sources

Unless otherwise indicated, the Holy Scripture is quoted, for the Old Testament, from F. Vigouroux, *La Sainte Bible polyglotte* (Paris, 1900-1909); for the New Testament, from E. Nestle, *Novum Testamentum graece et latine* (Stuttgart, 1921). For translation, we have made use of Crampon, *La Sainte Bible* (Paris, 1923).

As a general rule, the fathers are quoted from J.-P. Migne, *Patrologiae cursus completus*, the Greek series of which was edited from 1857-1866. For several fathers we have had to resort to the following collections:

Die Griechischen christlichen Schriftsteller der ersten [drei] Jahrhunderte. Edited by the Academy of Berlin (Corpus of Berlin). Leipzig, 1897–.

Graffin, R. and F. Nau. *Patrologia Orientalis.* Paris, 1903–.

Hemmer, H. and P. Lejay. *Textes et documents pour l'étude historique du christianisme.* Paris, 1904–.

The editions taken from these collections are indicated in the text of our work.

For the secular authors, especially for Plato and Aristotle, we have by preference made use of the "Collection des Universités de France" (Coll. Budé) and, in its absence, the editions of Teubner.

Here are the other principle sources:

Arnim, H. von. *Stoicorum veterum fragmenta.* Leipzig, 1903-1905.

[Cohn, Wendland, and Reiter. Philo. *editio minor.* Berlin, 1896-1915.]

Conybeare, F. C. *Philostratus.* London, 1912.

Diels, H. *Doxographi Graeci.* Berlin, 1879.

Frankenberg, W. *Euagrius Ponticus.* In vol. 13, no. 2 of Abhandlung der königl. Gesellsch. der Wissenschaften zu Göttingen, Philologisch-Historische Klasse. Neue Folge. Berlin, 1912.

Funk, F.-X. *Didascalia et constitutiones apostolorum.* 2 vols. Paderborn, 1905.

———. *Patres apostolici.* 2 vols. Tübingen, 1901.

Funk, F.-X., and K. Bihlmeyer. *Die apostolischen Väter.* Tübingen, 1924.

Kautzch, E. *Die Apokryphen und Pseudepigraphen des Alten Testaments.* 2 vols. Tübingen, 1900.

[Mansi, J. D. *Sacrorum conciliorum nova et amplissima collectio.* Florence, 1759-1798.]

Mingana, M. A. *Commentary of Theodore of Mopsuestia on the Nicene Creed.* Vol. 5 of Woodbrooke Studies. Cambridge, 1932.

————. *Commentary of Theodore of Mopsuestia on the Lord's Prayer and on the Sacraments of Baptism and the Eucharist.* Vol. 6 of Woodbrooke Studies. Cambridge, 1933.

Nauck, A. *Porphyrii philosophi platonici opuscula.* Leipzig, 1886.

Otto, Th. von. *Corpus apologetarum christianorum saeculi secundi.* 9 vols. Jena, 1851-1881.

Parthey, G. *Jamblichi De mysteriis liber.* Berlin, 1857.

Scott, Walter. *Hermetica.* 4 vols. Oxford, 1924-1936.

Swete, H. B. *The Old Testament in Greek according to the Septuagint.* Cambridge, 1901-1903.

————. *Theodori episc. Mopsuesteni in epistolas B. Pauli commentarii.* 2 vols. Cambridge, 1880 and 1882.

Usener, H. *Epicuren.* Leipzig, 1887.

Vliet, J. van der. *Apuleii metamorphoses.* Leipzig, 1897.

[Volkmann, R. *Plotini Enneades.* Leipzig, 1884.]

2. Works

Achelis, H. "Hippolytstudien." In vol. 16, fascicle 4 of *Texte und Untersuchungen.* Leipzig, 1897.

Alès, A. d'. *La théologie de saint Hippolyte.* Paris, 1906.

Amann, É. *Le dogme catholique dans les Pères de l'Église.* Paris, 1922.

————. "Hippolyte." In vol. 6 of *Dictionnaire de théologie catholique.* Edited by A. Vacant, et al. Paris, 1903-1950.

————. "La doctrine christologique de Théodore de Mopsueste." *Revue des sciences religieuses* 14 (1934): 161-190.

Arnou, R. *Le désir de Dieu dans la philosophie de Plotin.* Paris, 1921.

————. "Platonisme des Pères." In vol. 12 of *Dictionnaire de théologie catholique.* Edited by A. Vacant, et al. Paris, 1903-1950.

Aufhauser, J.-B. *Die Heilslehre des hl. Gregor von Nyssa.* Munich, 1910.

Bachelet, X. Le. "Dieu." In vol. 4 of *Dictionnaire de théologie catholique.* Edited by A. Vacant, et al. Paris, 1903-1950.

Bardenhewer, O. *Geschichte der altkirchlichen Literatur,* 5 vols. Freiburg im Breisgau, 1912.

Bardy, Gustave. *Didyme l'Aveugle.* Paris, 1910.

————. "Aux origines de l'école d'Alexandrie." *Recherches de science religieuse* 27 (1937): 65-90.

————. "Jean Chrysostome." In vol. 8 of *Dictionnaire de théologie catholique.* Edited by A. Vacant, et al. Paris, 1903-1950.

————. "L'église et l'enseignement au IVe siècle." *Revue des sciences religieuses* 14 (1934): 525-549; 15 (1935): 1-27.

————. "Millénarisme." In vol. 10 of *Dictionnaire de théologie catholique.* Edited by A. Vacant, et al. Paris, 1903-1950.

————. "Origène." In vol. 11 of *Dictionnaire de théologie catholique.* Edited by A. Vacant, et al. Paris, 1903-1950.

————. "Philon le Juif." In vol. 12 of *Dictionnaire de théologie catholique.* Edited by A. Vacant, et al. Paris, 1903-1950.

[————. "Chronique d'histoire des origines chrétiennes." *Revue Apologétique* 66 (1938).]

Bareille, G. "Gnosticisme." In vol. 6 of *Dictionnaire de théologie catholique*. Edited by A. Vacant, et al. Paris, 1903-1950.

Barion, Jacques. *Plotin und Augustinus*. Berlin, 1935.

Barre, A. de La. "Clément d'Alexandrie." In vol. 3 of *Dictionnaire de théologie catholique*. Edited by A. Vacant, et al. Paris, 1903-1950.

[Bartmann, Bernard. *Dogma und Religionsgeschichte*. Translated by M. Gautier. Paderborn, 1922.]

———. *Précis de théologie dogmatique*. Translated by M. Gautier. 8th ed. Mulhouse, 1935.

[Batiffol, P. *L'Église naissante et le catholicisme*. 9th ed. Paris, 1927.]

Baur, Louis. "Untersuchungen über die Vergöttlichungslehre in der Theologie der griech. Väter." *Theologische Quartalschrift* 98 (1916) – 101 (1920).

Bayer, J. *Gregors von Nyssa Gottesbegriff*. Giessen, 1935.

Berve, Helmut. *Griechische Geschichte*. Vol. 4 of *Geschichte der führenden Völker*. Freiburg im Breisgau, 1931.

Boehm, Alfred. *Die Gottesidee bei Aristoteles auf ihren religiösen Charakter untersucht*. Strasbourg, 1914.

Bonsirven, J. *Le Judaïsme palestinien au temps de Jésus-Christ: La Théologie*. 2 vols. Paris, 1934-1935.

Bornhäuser, Karl. *Die Vergottungslehre des Athanasius und Johannes Damascenus*. Gütersloh, 1903.

Bousset, W. *Kyrios Christos*. 2d ed. Göttingen, 1921.

Bréhier, Émile. *Histoire de la philosophie*. Paris, 1927-1932.

———. *Les idées philosophiques et religieuses de Philon d'Alexandrie*. Paris, 1908.

———. *La philosophie de Plotin*. Paris, 1928.

Bremond, André. *La piété grecque*. Paris, 1914.

———. "Rationalisme et religion." *Archives de Philosophie* 11 (1935): cahier 4.

Capitaine, W. *Die Moral des Clemens von Alexandrien*. Paderborn, 1903.

[Casel, O. In *Jahrbuch für Liturgiewissenschaft* 5 (1925).]

Cayré, F. *Précis de patrologie*. 2 vols. Paris, 1927.

Cerfaux, L. "Gnose préchrétienne et biblique." In vol. 3 of *Dictionnaire de la Bible: Supplement*. Edited by L. Pirot and A. Robert. Paris 1928–.

Colon, J.-B. "Paul." In vol. 11 of *Dictionnaire de théologie catholique*. Edited by A. Vacant, et al. Paris, 1903-1950.

———. "A propos de la 'mystique' de Saint Paul." *Revue des sciences religieuses*, 15 (1935): 157-183, 325-353.

Condamin, A. "Prophétisme israélite." In vol. 4 of *Dictionnaire apologétique de la foi catholique*.

Congar, M.-J. "La déification dans la tradition spirituelle de l'Orient." *Vie spirituelle* 43 (1935): [91]-[107].

Corte, Marcel de. *La doctrine d'intelligence chez Aristote*. Paris, 1934.

———. "Anthropologie platonicienne et aristotélicienne." *Études carmélitaines*. Fascicle entitled, "L'Esprit et la vie." Year 23. April 1938: 64-98.

Cumont, Franz. *Textes et monuments figurés relatifs aux mystères de Mithra*. Brussels, 1899.

———. *Les religions orientales dans le paganisme romain*. 3d ed. Paris, 1929.

Darboy, G. *Saint Denys l'Aréopagite*. Paris, 1932.

Dennefeld, Louis. "Judaïsme." In vol. 8 of *Dictionnaire de théologie catholique.* Edited by A. Vacant, et al. Paris, 1903-1950.

———. *Le judaïsme.* Paris, 1925.

[———. "Chronique biblique (Ancien Testament)." *Revue des sciences religieuse* 17 (1937): 316-335.]

Diekamp, F. *Die Gotteslehre des heiligen Gregor von Nyssa.* Münster in Westphalia, 1896.

Diès, Auguste. *Le cycle mystique.* Paris, 1909.

———. *Autour de Platon.* 2 vols. Paris, 1927.

Dieterich, Albrecht. *Eine Mithrasliturgie.* Leipzig, 1910.

Disdier, M. Th. "Les fondements dogmatiques de la spiritualité de saint Maxime le Confesseur." *Échos d'Orient* 34 (1930): 296-313.

Dorner, J. A. *Theodori Mopsuesteni doctrina de Imagine Dei.* Königsberg, 1844.

[Duchesne, L. *Origines du culte chrétien.* 5th ed. Paris, 1920.]

[Duhm, B. *Die Psalmen.* Vol. 14 of *Kurzer Hand-commentar zum Alten Testament.* Edited by D. Karl Marti. Freiburg im Breisgau, 1899.]

Ehrhardt, Albert. *Die Cyrill von Alexandrien zugeschriebene Schrift Περὶ τῆς τοῦ κυρίου ἐνανθρωπήσεως: ein Werk Theodorets von Cyrus.* Tübingen, 1888.

———. *Die Kirche der Märtyrer.* Munich, 1932.

Eibl, Hans. *Die Grundlegung der abendländischen Philosophie.* Bonn, 1934.

Ermoni, V. "La déification de l'homme chez les Pères de l'Église." *Revue du clergé français.* Year 3 (1897). 11:509-519.

Faller, O. "Griechische Vergottung und christliche Vergöttlichung." *Gregorianum* 6 (1925): 405-435.

Farges, J. *Les idées morales et religieuses de Méthode d'Olympe.* Paris, 1929.

Faye, E. de. *Clément d'Alexandrie.* 2d ed. Paris, 1906.

———. *Gnostiques et gnosticisme.* Paris, 1913.

———. *Origène.* 3 vols. Paris, 1923-28.

Feldmann, F. *Das Buch der Weisheit.* Bonn, 1926.

Festugière, A. –J. *L'idéal religieux des Grecs et l'Évangile.* Paris, 1932.

———. *Contemplation et vie contemplative selon Platon.* Paris, 1936.

———. "Les mystères de Dionysos." *Revue biblique* new series 44 (1935): 192-211, 366-396.

Festugière, A. J., and Pierre Fabre. *Le monde gréco-romain au temps de Notre-Seigneur.* Paris, 1935.

Fonck, A. "Mystique." In vol. 10 of *Dictionnaire de théologie catholique.* Edited by A. Vacant, et al. Paris, 1903-1950.

Fonsegrive, George. *Le catholicisme et la vie de l'esprit.* 2d ed. Paris, 1906.

———. *Le catholicisme et la religion de l'esprit.* Paris, 1913.

Frey, J.-B. "Apocryphes de l'Ancien Testament." In vol. 1 of *Dictionnaire de la Bible: Supplement.* Edited by L. Pirot and A. Robert. Paris 1928–.

———. "Le concept de vie dans l'évangile de Saint Jean." *Biblica* 1 (1920): 37-58, 211-239.

[Fritz, G. *RevScRel* 17 (1937): 336-343.]

Fruhstorfer, Karl. *Die Paradiesessünde.* Linz, 1929.

Gaudel, A. "La doctrine du Λόγος chez saint Athanase." *Revue des sciences religieuses* 11 (1931): 4-14.

———. "Péché originel." In vol. 12 of *Dictionnaire de théologie catholique*. Edited by A. Vacant, et al. Paris, 1903-1950.

———. "La théologie de l' 'Assumptus Homo.'" *Revue des sciences religieuses* 17 (1937): 64-90, 214-234; 18 (1938): 45-71, 201-217.

Geffken, J. *Zwei griechische Apologeten*. Leipzig, 1907.

Gernet, Louis, and André Boulanger. *Le génie grec dans la religion*. Vol. 11 of *L'évolution de l'humanité*. Paris, 1932.

Godet, P. "Grégoire de Nysse." In vol. 6 of *Dictionnaire de théologie catholique*. Edited by A. Vacant, et al. Paris, 1903-1950.

———. "Denys l'Aréopagite (le Pseudo-)." In vol. 4 of *Dictionnaire de théologie catholique*. Edited by A. Vacant, et al. Paris, 1903-1950.

Gomperz, Th. *Griechische Denker*. 3 vols. 2d ed. Leipzig, 1903.

Grumel, V. "Léonce de Byzance." In vol. 9 of *Dictionnaire de théologie catholique*. Edited by A. Vacant, et al. Paris, 1903-1950.

———. "La sotériologie de Léonce de Byzance." *Échos d'Orient* 40 (1937): 385-397.

———. "Maxime de Chrysopolis ou Maxime le Confesseur." In vol. 10 of *Dictionnaire de théologie catholique*. Edited by A. Vacant, et al. Paris, 1903-1950.

Harnack, Adolf von. *Das Wesen des Christentums*. 2d ed. Leipzig, 1900.

———. *Lehrbuch der Dogmengeschichte*. 3 vols. 4th ed. Tübingen, 1909.

Heigl, B. *Antike Mysterienreligionen und Urchristentum*. Münster in Westphalia, 1932.

Heinisch, P. *Das Buch der Genesis*. Bonn, 1930.

[Hemmer, H. *Les Pères apostoliques*. 4 vols. Paris, 1907.]

Hempel, Jean. *Gott und Mensch im Alten Testament*. Stuttgart, 1936.

Hering, Jean. *Étude sur la doctrine de la chute et de la préexistence des âmes chez Clément d'Alexandrie*. Paris, 1923.

Herkenne, H. *Das Buch der Psalmen*. Bonn, 1936.

Herrmann. *Gregorii Nysseni sententiae de salute adipiscenda*. Halle, 1875.

[Heschel, Abraham. *Die Prophetie*. Krakow, 1936.]

Hilt, F. *Des hl. Gregor von Nyssa Lehre vom Menschen*. Cologne, 1890.

Holl, K. *Amphilochius von Ikonium*. Leipzig, 1904.

Imschoot, P. van. "Sagesse et Esprit dans l'A. T." *Revue biblique* 47 (1938): 23-49.

Isaye, Gaston. "L'unité de l'opération divine dans les écrits trinitaires de saint Grégoire de Nysse." *Recherches de science religieuse* 27 (1937): 422-439.

Ithurriague, Jean. *La croyance de Platon a l'immortalité et la survie de l'âme humaine*. Paris, 1931.

Ivanka, E. v. "Vom Platonismus zur Theorie der Mystik." *Scholastik* 11 (1936): 163-195.

Jacquier, E. "Mystères païens (les) et Saint Paul." In vol. 3 of *Dictionnaire apologétique de la foi catholique*.

Janssens, L. "Notre filiation divine d'après saint Cyrille d'Alexandrie." *Ephemerides theologicae lovanienses* 15 (1938): 233-278.

Jolivet, R. *Essai sur les rapports entre la pensée grecque et la pensée chrétienne*. Paris, 1931.

Juessen, K. "Maximus Confessor." In vol. 7 of *Lexikon für Theologie und Kirche*.

Jugie, M. "Jean Damascène." In vol. 8 of *Dictionnaire de théologie catholique*. Edited by A. Vacant, et al. Paris, 1903-1950.

Junker, Hubert. *Die Biblische Urgeschichte*. Bonn, 1932.

[———. *Das Buch Deuteronomium*. Bonn, 1933.]

Kammer, Édouard. *Ein ästhetischer Kommentar zu Homers Ilias*. Paderborn, 1906.

Kiefer, Othon. Plotin. *Enneaden.* 2 vols. Leipzig, 1905.

Kihn, Henri. *Theodor von Mopsuestia und Junilius Africanus als Exegeten.* Freiburg im Breisgau, 1880.

Klebba, E. *Die Anthropologie des hl. Irenäus.* Münster in Westphalia, 1894.

Kleinknecht, H. "θεός." In vol. 3 of *Theologisches Wörterbuch zum Neuen Testament.* Edited by Gerhard Kittel and G. Friedrich. Stuttgart, 1932-1979.

Koch, H. *Pseudo-Dionysius Areopagita in seinem Beziehungen zum Neoplatonismus und Mysterienwesen.* Mayence, 1900.

———. "Das mystische Schauen beim hl. Gregor von Nyssa." *Theologische Quartalschrift* 80 (1898): 397-420.

[Koenig, Éduard. *Die Genesis.* Gütersloh, 1919.]

Krafta, G., and H. Eibl. *Der Ausklang der antiken Philosophie.* Munich, 1928.

Krakowski, Éd. *Plotin et le paganisme religieux.* Paris, 1933.

Labriolle, Pierre de. *La réaction païenne.* Paris, 1934.

Lagrange, M.-J. "La paternité de Dieu dans l'Ancien Testament." *Revue biblique* 5 (1908): 481-499.

———. "Les mystères d'Éleusis et le christianisme." *Revue biblique* new series 16 (1919): 157-217.

———. "Attis et le christianisme." *Revue biblique* new series 16 (1919): 419-480.

———. "L'hermétisme." *Revue biblique* new series 33 (1924) – 35 (1926).

———. "La génération et la filiation divine dans les mystères d'Éleusis." *Revue biblique* new series 37 (1929): 63-81, 201-214.

———. *L'orphisme.* Paris, 1937.

Lange, Herm. *De gratia.* Freiburg im Breisgau, 1929.

Lavedan, Pierre. *Dictionnaire illustré de la mythologie et des antiquités greques et romaines.* Paris, 1931.

Lebreton, J. "Le désaccord de la foi populaire et de la théologie savante dans l'Église du IIIᵉ siècle." *Revue d'histoire ecclésiastique* 19 (1923): 481-506; 20 (1924): 5-37.

———. *Histoire du dogme de la Trinité.* 2 vols. 7th ed. Paris, 1927-1928.

Leipoldt, J. *Didymus der Blinde.* Vol. 14, Facs. 3 in Texte und Untersuchungen zur Geschichte der altchristlichen Literatur. New series. 1905.

———. *Sterbende und auferstehende Götter.* Leipzig, 1923.

Leisegang. "Gnosis." In vol. 2 of *Die Religion in Geschichte und Gegenwart.* 2d ed. Tübingen, 1928.

[Lelong, A. *Le pasteur d' Hermas.* Paris, 1912.]

[———. *Ignace d'Antioch.* Paris, 1910]

Lods, Adolphe. *Israël.* Paris, 1930.

Loisy, A. *Les mystères païens et le mystère chrétien.* Paris, 1930.

[———. *Remarques sur la littérature épistolaire du Nouveau Testament.* Paris, 1935.]

[———. *Les origines du Nouveau Testament.* Paris, 1936.]

Loofs, F. *Leitfaden zum Studium der Dogmengeschichte.* 4th ed. Halle, 1906.

Lot-Borodine, M. "La doctrine de la 'déification' dans l'Église grecque jusqu'au XIe siècle." *Revue de l'histoire des religions* 105 (1932): 1-43; 106 (1932): 525-574; 107 (1933): 8-55.

Louis, M. *Doctrines religieuses des philosophes grecs.* Paris, 1909.

Mahé, Joseph. "Cyrille d'Alexandrie." In vol. 3 of *Dictionnaire de théologie catholique.* Edited by A. Vacant, et al. Paris, 1903-1950.

————. "La sanctification d'après saint Cyrille d'Alexandrie." *Revue d'histoire ecclésiastique* 10 (1909): 30-40, 469-492.

Mangenot, E. "Éphésiens (Épitre aux)." In vol. 5 of *Dictionnaire de théologie catholique*. Edited by A. Vacant, et al. Paris, 1903-1950.

Manoir, Hubert du. "Le problème de Dieu chez Cyrille d'Alexandrie." *Recherches de science religieuse* 27 (1937): 385-407, 549-596.

[Mazon, Paul. Introduction to *Hesiod*. Collection des Universités de France. Paris, 1928.]

[Méridier, L. *Grégoire de Nysse: discours catéchétique* (Paris, 1908) in Textes et documents pour l'étude historique du christianisme. Edited by H. Hemmer and P. Lejay. Paris, 1904–.]

Mersch, Émile. *Le corps mystique du Christ*. 2 vols. 2d ed. Paris, 1936.

Meunier, Mario. *Apollonius de Tyane ou le séjour d'un dieu parmi les hommes*. Paris, 1936.

Meyer, Louis. *Saint Jean Chrysostome, maître de perfection chrétienne*. Paris, 1934.

[Michel, A. "Hypostase." In vol. 7 of *Dictionnaire de théologie catholique*. Edited by A. Vacant, et al. Paris, 1903-1950.]

Moisescu, J. Εὐάγριος ὁ Ποντικός. Athens, 1937.

Morice, Henri. *La vie mystique de Saint Paul*. Paris, 1932.

Moulard, A. *Saint Jean Chrysostome, le défenseur du mariage et l'apôtre de la virginité*. Paris, 1923.

Mueller, H. F. *Dionysios, Proklos, Plotinos*. Münster in Westphalia, 1918.

Naegele, A. *Die Eucharistielehre des hl. Johannes Chrysostomus*. Freiburg im Breisgau, 1900.

Noetscher, Fr. *Altorientalischer und alttestamentlicher Auferstehungsglauben*. Würzbourg, 1926.

[Nourry, N. Le. *Dissertationes in Clem. Alex.* In vol. 9 of Patrologiae cursus completus: Series graeca. Edited by J.-P. Minge. 612 vols. Paris, 1857-1886.]

Otto, Walter F. *Die Manen oder von den Urformen des Totenglaubens*. Berlin, 1923.

Pascher, Joseph. Ἡ βασιλικὴ ὁδός. *Der Königsweg zu Wiedergeburt und Vergottung bei Philon von Alexandria*. Paderborn, 1931.

Pell, G. A. *Die Lehre des hl. Athanasius von der Sünde und Erlösung*. Passau, 1888.

Pera, Ceslas. "Denys le Mystique et la θεομαχία." *Revue des sciences philosophiques et théologiques* 25 (1936): 1-75.

Petau. *Dogmata theologica*. Edited by Fournials. 8 vols. Paris, 1865-1867.

Pourrat, P. *La spiritualité chrétienne*. 4 vols. Paris, 1928-1935.

————. *La théologie sacramentaire*. Paris, 1910.

Prat, F. *La théologie de Saint Paul*. 2 vols. 7th ed. Paris, 1923.

Prestige, G. L. *God in Patristic Thought*. London, 1936.

Preuss, Fr. Aug. *Ad Maximi Confessoris de Deo doctrinam adnotationes*. Schneeberg, 1894.

Pruemm, Karl. *Der christliche Glaube und die altheidnische Welt*. 2 vols. Leipzig, 1935.

Puech, Aimé. *Recherches sur le discours aux Grecs de Tatien*. Paris, 1903.

————. *Les apologistes grecs du IIᵉ siècle*. Paris, 1912.

————. *Histoire de la littérature greque chrétienne*. 3 vols. Paris, 1928.

Rahner, Hugo. "Die Gottesgeburt." *Zeitschrift für kath. Theologie* 59 (1935): 333-418.

Randenborgh, G. van. *Vergottung und Erlösung*. Berlin, n.d.

Régnon, Th. de. *Études de théologie positive sur la sainte Trinité*. 4 vols. Paris, 1892.

Reitzenstein, R. *Poimandres.* Leipzig, 1904.

———. *Die hellenistischen Mysterienreligionen.* Leipzig, 1910.

Richard, L. *Le dogme de la rédemption.* Paris, 1932.

Ritschl, A. *Die christliche Lehre von der Rechtfertigung und Versöhnung.* 2d ed. Bonn, 1882.

Rivière, Jean. *Le dogme de la rédemption: essai d'étude historique.* Paris, 1905.

———. *Saint Justin et les apologistes du second siècle.* Paris, 1907.

———. *Le dogme de la rédemption: étude théologique.* 3d ed. Paris, 1931.

———. *Le dogme de la rédemption: études critiques et documents.* Louvain, 1931.

Rohde, Erwin. *Psyché: Le culte de l'âme chez les Grecs et leur croyance à l'immortalité.* French edition. Paris: Auguste Reymond, 1928.

Ross, W. D. *Aristotle.* Paris, 1930.

Rousselot, Pierre. "La grâce d'après saint Jean et d'après saint Paul." *Recherches de science religieuse* 18 (1928): 87-104.

[Sanday, William. *Inspiration: Eight Lectures on the Early History and Origin of the Doctrine of Biblical Inspiration.* Being the Bampton Lectures for 1893.]

Scheck, Ad. *De fontibus Clementis Alexandrini.* Augsbourg, 1889.

Schermann, Th. *Die Gottheit des Heiligen Geistes.* Freiburg im Breisgau, 1901.

Schmidt, W. *Origene et évolution de la religion.* Translated by Lemonnyer. Paris, 1931.

Schuetz, Rodolphe. *Les idées eschatologiques du livre de la Sagesse.* Strasbourg, 1935.

[Schwarz, H. *Der Gottgedanke in der Geschichte der Philosophie.* Cited in H. Kleinknecht, "Θεός." *Theologisches Wörterbuch zum Neuen Testament.* Edited by Gerhard Kittel and G. Friedrich. Stuttgart, 1932-1979.]

Seeberg, R. *Lehrbuch der Dogmengeschichte.* 4 vols. 2d ed. Leipzig, 1910.

Siouville, A. *Philosophoumena,* 2 vols. Paris, 1928.

Slomkowski, A. *L'état primitif de l'homme dans la tradition de l'Église avant saint Augustin.* Paris, 1928.

Sprinzel, J. *Die Theologie der apostolischen Väter.* Vienna, 1880.

Staffelbach, G. *Die Vereinigung mit Christus als Prinzip der Moral bei Paulus.* Freiburg im Breisgau, 1932.

Steffes, J. P. *Das Wesen des Gnostizismus und sein Verhältnis zum katholischen Dogma.* Paderborn, 1922.

Stiglmayr, Joseph. *Des heiligen Dionysius Areopagita angebliche Schriften über die beiden Hierarchien.* Bibliothek der Kirchenväter. Munich, 1911.

———. "Die Schrift des hl. Gregor von Nyssa 'Über die Unsterblichkeit,'" *Zeitschrift für Aszese und Mystik* 2 (1927): 334-359.

———. "Aszese und Mystik des sog. Dionysius Areopagita." *Scholastik* 2 (1927): 161-207.

Stolz, Anselme. *Theologie der Mystik.* Ratisbon, 1936.

Straeter, H. *Die Erlösungslehre des hl. Athanasius.* Freiburg im Breisgau, 1894.

Struker, A. *Die Gottebenbildlichkeit des Menschen.* Münster in Westphalia, 1913.

Tixeront, J. *Histoire des dogmes.* 3 vols. 11th ed. Paris, 1928-1931.

Tobac, E. *Les cinq livres de Solomon.* Brussels, 1926.

———. "Grâce." In vol. 2 of *Dictionnaire apologétique de la foi catholique.*

[Turmel, J. (H. Delafosse, pseud.) *Les écrits de Saint Paul.* 4 vols. 1926-1928.]

[———. *Histoire des dogmes.* Paris, 1935.]

Ueberweg, Friedrich, and F. Heinze, *Grundriss der Geschichte der Philosophie*. 4 vols. Berlin, 1903-1916.

Vaganay, Léon. "Porphyre." In vol. 12 of *Dictionnaire de théologie catholique*. Edited by A. Vacant, et al. Paris, 1903-1950.

———. *Le problème eschatologique dans le IVᵉ livre d'Esdras*. Paris, 1906.

Verfaillie, C. *La doctrine de la justification dans Origène d'après son commentaire de Épitre aux Romains*. Strasbourg, 1926.

Vernet, F. "Irénée." In vol. 7 of *Dictionnaire de théologie catholique*. Edited by A. Vacant, et al. Paris, 1903-1950.

Verrièle, A. "Le plan du salut d'après saint Irénée." *Revue des sciences religieuses* 14 (1934): 493-524.

Viller, Marcel. *La spiritualité des premiers siècles chrétiens*. Paris, 1930.

———. "Aux sources de la spiritualité de saint Maxime. Les oeuvres d'Évagre le Pontique." *Revue d'ascétique et de mystique* 11 (1930): 156-184, 239-268.

Virey, Philippe. *La religion de l'ancienne Égypte*. Paris, 1910.

Weber, S. *Irenäus*. Kempten-Munich, 1912.

Weigl, Édouard. *Die Heilslehre des hl. Cyrillus von Alexandrien*. Mainz, 1905.

Wickenhauser, A. *Die Christusmystik des hl. Paulus*. Münster in Westphalia, 1928.

Willmann, M. *Die Ethik des Aristoteles*. Ratisbon, 1920.

Willms, H. *Philo von Alexandreia*. Part One of Εἰκών: *Eine begriffsgeschichtliche Untersuchung zum Platonismus*. Münster in Westphalia, 1935.

Windelband, W., and E. Rothacker. *Lehrbuch der Geschichte der Philosophie*. Tübingen, 1921.

[Wittman, M. *Die Ethik des Aristoteles*. Ratisbon, 1920.]

Zeller, Édouard. *Die Philosophie der Griechen*. 6 vols. Various editions. Leipzig, 1919.

[Zorell, Fr. *Psalterium*. Rome, 1928.]

INDEX OF EDITORS AND AUTHORS OF SECONDARY WORKS

INDEX OF PRINCIPAL GREEK WORDS

INDEX OF BIBLICAL AND APOCRYPHAL WORKS

SUBJECT INDEX

Ablabius, 183
Abraham, 67, 113
absorption by God, 34
accidents [συμβεβηκότον] and
    divinization, 13, 131, 259
Acherousian lake, 42
Adam
    carnal impulses of, 220 (n. 13)
    changeability of, 221
    and Christ, 82, 120
    deification of, 180, 257
    divine likeness of, 61–62, 100–101,
        117, 129, 164, 200–202, 221, 257
    fall of, 82, 113, 118, 143, 166, 181,
        191, 208–9, 220–22, 250, 257-58
    fall of, resulting in concupiscence, 155
    flesh of, becoming body of Logos, 168
    free of passions, 201
    as gnostic, 164, 195
    as image of God, cf. of incarnate
        Logos, 154
    immortality of, 133, 143, 215, 220
    impassibility of, 180
    indwelt by the Spirit, 221
    original state of, 150, 154, 194, 250,
        256
    transgression of, 133
    two-fold divine likeness of, 221
    wisdom and prophecy of, 201
adoption, of the children of God, 124,
    129, 203, 222
    by baptism, 225
    as deification, 259
    as distinct from the act of creation,
        164
    as the gift of immortality, 212-13
    identified with deification, 198
    by the indwelling of the Logos, 165

    perfected in resurrection, 212-13
adoption, of the Son of God, 106–107,
    210, 260 (n. 26)
aeons, in Gnosticism, 108–109
Areopagus, Saint Paul's message on, 87
afterlife, 17, 68
Agatha, the virgin, 155
Alexander of Aphrodisias, 46
Alexander the Great, 19 (n. 47)
Alexandria, school of, 175, 190, 197,
    219, 256. *See also* Alexandrian
    theology; Antiochenes and
    Alexandrians compared
Alexandrian theology. *See* Athanasius,
    Basil, Clement of Alexandria, Cyril,
    Gregory of Nazianzus, Gregory of
    Nyssa, Origen, physical theory of
    deification
Anastasius Sinaita, 233
Anaxagoras, 37
ancestor worship, 15
angels, as intermediaries, 75
anthropomorphites, 221
Antioch, school of, 200–216, 254. *See
    also* Chrysostom, Theodore of
    Mopsuestia, Theodoret of Cyrrhus
Antiochenes and Alexandrians compared,
    206, 213
apatheia. See impassibility
Aphthartodocetae, 255 (n. 136)
aphtharsia. See incorruptibility
apocatastasis (the restoration), 148
Apocrypha, Hellenistic, 71–73
Apocrypha, Palestinian, 70–71
Apollinarists, 196, 268
Apollinarius, 227
Apollonius of Tyana, 50